Problem Solving in Microeconomics

A Study Guide for Microeconomics by Eaton, Eaton, & Allen

Fifth Edition

Rose Anne Devlin
University of Ottawa

Nancy T. Gallini
University of Toronto

Prentice Hall
Toronto

0-13-033015-9

Acquisitions Editor: Dave Ward

Developmental Editor: Madhu Ranadive

Production Editor: Gillian Scobie

Production Coordinator: Janette Lush

3 4 5 06 05 04 03

Printed and bound in Canada.

Contents

Preface.....v

Part I An Introduction to Microeconomics

Chapter 1 Microeconomics: A Working Methodology.....1

Part II Individual Choice

Chapter 2 A Theory of Preferences.....11
Chapter 3 Demand Theory.....23
Chapter 4 More Demand Theory.....41
Chapter 5 Intertemporal Decision Making and Capital Values.....59

Part III Production and Cost

Chapter 6 Production and Cost: One Variable Input.....69
Chapter 7 Production and Cost: Many Variable Inputs.....79

Part IV Markets for Goods

Chapter 8 The Theory of Perfect Competition.....91
Chapter 9 Applications of the Competitive Model.....105
Chapter 10 Monopoly.....119

Part V Resource Markets and General Equilibrium

Chapter 11 Input Markets and the Allocation of Resources.....133
Chapter 12 The Distribution of Income.....149
Chapter 13 Competitive General Equilibrium.....161

Part VI Imperfect Competition

Chapter 14 Price Discrimination and Monopoly Practices.....173
Chapter 15 Game Theory and Oligopoly.....183
Chapter 16 Product Differentiation.....199

Part VII Uncertainty and Asymmetric Information

Chapter 17 Choice Making Under Uncertainty.....209
Chapter 18 Asymmetric Information, the Rules of the Game, and Externalities.....219
Chapter 19 The Theory of the Firm.....231
Chapter 20 Asymmetric Information and Market Behaviour.....239

Preface

Problem Solving in Microeconomics offers a comprehensive review of the concepts taught in intermediate microeconomics courses. The study guide is designed to complement the fifth edition of *Microeconomics* by B. Curtis Eaton, Diane F. Eaton and Douglas W. Allen. Both books teach students how to think as economists do; hence, the emphasis is on economic applications. *Problem Solving in Microeconomics* uses real-world applications to help students understand economics. Students learn basic economic principles, not through rote memorization but through problem solving, which will enable them to develop an intuition for economic theory.

To make economics accessible to all students of intermediate microeconomics, each chapter includes several problems of varying length and difficulty. In addition, a chapter summary, case studies, key words, multiple-choice questions, and true-false questions prepare the student for the applied problems by reviewing and testing the student's basic understanding of the economic theory developed in the chapter. This Study Guide offers a variety of problems and case studies. It also makes good use of calculus in the solving of problems; those requiring this tool are marked with an asterisk.

Detailed answers to all the problems are included at the end of each chapter. These answers show students how to approach economic problems and gives them an opportunity to check their understanding of the material.

Problem Solving in Microeconomics offers five ways for students to review and test their understanding of economics:

A chapter summary outlines the important concepts. Students should read the summary carefully and return to their textbook when they do not recall a particular concept, before working through the problems.

Key words, listed after the summary, enable students to check and review the main concepts in the chapter quickly.

Case studies present students with interesting real-world applications of one or more fundamental economic concepts covered in the chapter.

Multiple-choice and true-false questions test students' knowledge and understanding of economic theory, the primary tool required for economic applications.

Short and long problems enable students to apply economic knowledge to a variety of everyday situations. Those who work through these problems can feel very confident that they understand the material in the chapters.

We are grateful to the many people who helped contribute to the evolution of this study guide over the years, especially the many instructors at the University of Toronto who have contributed problems over the past several years, which have been revised and are now part of this book. In particular, we wish to thank Al Berry, Don Campbell, John Ham, Sue Horton, Mike Krashinsky, Ron Saunders, Aloysius Siow, George Slasor, Dan Trefler, Roger Ware, and Ralph Winter.

Several other people have contributed to this and other versions of the workbook: Scott Amerman, Jerry Butters, Gary Carlson, Stephen Dietrich, Jim Dodd, Maurice Esses, Nancy Harbin, Ed Lazear, Beverley Limketkai, Edgar Olson, Diana Siemens, Dane Rowlands, Jackie Wood and Marjorie Walker. Finally, we are indebted to Diane and Curtis Eaton and Doug Allen for writing their wonderful textbook and for giving us the opportunity to contribute to the project.

Rose Anne Devlin
Nancy T. Gallini

CHAPTER 1

Microeconomics: A Working Methodology

Chapter Summary

The Study of Economics

Our exciting and fascinating study of economics — a systematic attempt to make sense of the world — begins by posing several questions about the world in which we live. Why are houses in Ottawa often kept warmer inside in January than houses in Victoria? Why are some markets monopolized while others are competitive? What can be done to ensure the survival of the northern cod stock off the coast of Newfoundland? Insights to these and many other questions can be gained from economic analysis.

For certain types of resources, private incentives result in their overuse. The fisheries off the coast of Newfoundland fall into this category. Water, oil and minerals may all be categorized as common property resources. Consider the case of oil. Individuals own surface rights to land but do not have a property right over any minerals that lie beneath the surface until they are brought to the surface. This situation is known as the **rule of capture**. Because oil and other minerals typically lie beneath the land of more than one surface owner, each owner has the incentive to capture the resource as quickly as possible, much faster than is socially desirable. These resources suffer from what is called the **common property problem**. For oil fields, a policy known as **unitization**, in which the entire oil field is managed as one unit, solves the common property problem. Fishing quotas help the common property fish problem.

The prices of agricultural goods are subject to wide market fluctuations, largely because of weather conditions. As a result of successful lobbying, several agricultural support programs have been created. Economic analysis can contribute greatly to understanding the costs and benefits of such programs. Using the model of **perfectly competitive markets** — which assumes, among other things, the existence of many buyers and sellers who take prices as given, we can look at the **market demand curve** for a given commodity as well as its **market supply curve** to determine the **competitive equilibrium price** and **competitive equilibrium quantity** in this market. With this information, we can then analyze the impact on buyers and sellers of various price support programs.

Economic analysis provides a powerful tool for analyzing how individuals and firms interact in an economy. First, let's turn to a description of what we mean by an economy.

Building Blocks of an Economy

Economic activity transforms **resources**, both physical and human, into goods and services — or **goods** for short. **Economics** is the study of the allocation of scarce resources to the production of alternative goods. An **economy** is composed of at least four essential features. First, a **resource endowment** describes all the scarce resources available in the economy. In the real world, most resources are scarce, and many competing uses of resources can be defined; a central aim of economics is to study the allocation of scarce resources to the production of alternative goods. Second, the economy must have a **technology** that produces goods from these resources. Together, the resource endowment and the technology describe all combinations of goods that the economy can produce.

The third building block of **individual preferences** tells us what people would like to buy. Given an individual's ordering of all bundles of goods and services from the most to the least preferred, we can predict the consumer's behaviour under the **theory of self-interest**: Individuals choose actions that yield the *most preferred* bundle in their **preference ordering**.

Finally, an economy is made up of **institutions** that provide the "rules of the game" followed by all individuals in the economy. Institutions can be anything from competition laws for corporations to the informal practice of leaving a rental deposit on a pair of cross-country skis. The common feature of all institutions is that they regulate economic activity. Unlike the first three building blocks, which are relatively immutable, institutions change whenever there are changes in underlying policies and laws, particularly those that govern property rights in society.

Economic Models and the Concept of Equilibrium

In economics, we are interested in how goods are distributed among individuals in the economy; that is, we are interested in the **social state** actually attained in the economy. Given the institutional setting of common property, private property, or some alternative arrangement, our goal is to predict the social state achieved in the economy using the **method of equilibrium.** We can achieve this by constructing a model of the economy that captures the four essential building blocks. From the model an **equilibrium** can be found, which is a set of individual choices and a corresponding social state such that no individual can improve himself or herself by making another choice.

An important component of the method of equilibrium is known as a **comparative statics analysis** in which we change one or more conditions to determine the effect of that change on the equilibrium. Here are two simple examples of comparative statics exercises: An increase in the price of cream cheese (a complementary good) will shift the **demand curve** for bagels downward, resulting in a lower equilibrium price and quantity. An increase in the price of wheat, an input in the production of the good, will shift the **supply curve** to the left, resulting in a higher equilibrium price and lower quantity.

The benchmark model used throughout this text is that of the **pure market economy** with its institutions of private property and its minor role for government. A market economy can be described with a circular-flow diagram. Individuals own resources and supply their labour and other resources to firms, the demanders of these resources. The firms produce goods from these resources and supply the goods to individuals, the demanders of the goods. In equilibrium, a price and quantity can be determined in every resource and goods market.

Positive and Normative Economics

When we look for an equilibrium we are engaged in an exercise in **positive economics.** We asked an "if, then" question: *If* consumers are taxed on every empty pop can *then* what will happen to the price and consumption of soda pop? To answer this question, we make reference to objective facts. Suppose instead that we want to ask whether a particular market solution is desirable by some criteria. In this case, we ask a "should" question: Where *should* firms locate? Questions such as these lie in the domain of **normative economics** because they involve ethical or value judgements. We often attempt to rank the desirability of different social states by appealing to the underlying value judgement: the well-being of the individual members of society is of primary importance.

In contrast to positive economics, normative economics compares the alternative economic states to determine the most preferred state from a social point of view. On discovery of this social state, we may want to return to positive economic tools to determine the institution that will direct the economy to this most preferred state.

Pareto Criterion and Cost-Benefit Analysis

To answer normative questions, we often implement the **Pareto criterion** for comparing economic states. Under the Pareto criterion, state 1 is said to be better than state 2 if everyone is as well off and at least one person is better off in state 1. **Pareto optimality**, or **efficiency**, occurs when no other social state is Pareto-preferred to it. Unfortunately, the Pareto criterion may be too restrictive for making some policy decisions because it is unable to rank social states under some circumstances. An alternative approach for ranking states is the **cost-benefit criterion**. Under this rule, all social states are ranked according to their **net social benefits**, that is, the **gross social benefit** realized by all individuals less the **gross social cost** incurred by society. State 1 is said to be better than state 2 according to cost-benefit analysis if the net social benefits are larger in state 1.

Model Building

To construct an **economic model**, we abstract from the real world; that is, we reduce the multitude of real-world complexities of the problem to a set of essential elements that approximate reality. This is exactly what the **assumptions** of the model do. For example, suppose we want to build a model that explains the clustering (or **minimum differentiation**) of computer stores (this was the motivation for Hotelling's model). We might begin by assuming that consumers live uniformly along a line and will buy their computer from the store nearest to them. This assumption leads to the **deduction** or **prediction** that computer stores will locate in order to be closest to the largest number of consumers. If we examine the location decision of two firms, the method of equilibrium will lead us to predict that both firms will locate back-to-back in the middle of the line. However, this model is not very robust insofar as changing the assumption of two firms to, say, three firms will lead to a completely different equilibrium outcome.

Many economic questions can be answered with a well-defined body of economic theory or models. This body of economic theory is the essence of the following chapters. Throughout this book, you will learn how to use this economic theory to answer a wealth of fascinating economic puzzles. We now begin the intriguing study of **microeconomics.**

KEY WORDS

Assumptions
Common property problem
Comparative statics analysis
Competitive equilibrium price
Competitive equilibrium quantity
Cost-benefit criterion
Deduction
Demand curve
Economics
Economic model
Economy
Efficiency
Equilibrium
Goods
Gross social benefit
Gross social cost
Individual preferences
Institutions
Market demand curve
Market supply curve
Method of equilibrium
Microeconomics
Minimum differentiation
Net social benefit
Normative economics
Pareto criterion
Pareto optimality (efficiency)
Perfectly competitive markets
Positive economics
Prediction
Preference ordering
Pure market economy
Resources
Resource endowment
Rule of capture
Social state
Supply curve
Technology
Theory of self-interest
Unitization

CASE STUDY: PROPERTY RIGHTS IN THE FISHERIES

Many fisheries can be described as common-property resources because no one "owns" a fish until it is captured. Left to their own devices, individuals would have the incentive to over-fish the oceans, compromising the integrity of the fish stock. The fisheries are an important resource to Canada, employing some 165 000 people and generating an annual catch worth about $3 billion.[1] For some years now, Canada has been experiencing various crises in its fisheries. Two cases have been particularly notable: the salmon fishery in British Columbia and the cod fishery in Newfoundland. In both cases, problems have been compounded by the fact that fish migrate, swimming in and out of Canada's territorial waters. In the Pacific salmon case, there has been an ongoing dispute between Canada and the United States regarding the capture of salmon that are on their way to Canadian rivers to spawn. Despite numerous attempts to solve this problem by, for instance, allocating quotas on both sides of the border, this dispute continues to jeopardize the viability of the BC salmon fishery.

One problem in the cod fishery arises because of fishing outside of Canada's 200 nautical mile territorial waters. It so happens that the nose and tail of the continental shelf known as the Grand Banks, which is a particularly attractive area for fish, fall outside of this limit. Fishers from around the world, especially Europe, fish in this lucrative area. Over-fishing occurs elsewhere as well; the so-called inshore fisheries just off the coast of Newfoundland provide a livelihood to thousands of people. Because of the sheer quantity of fishing that occurs, the off-shore fishery has had a tremendous impact on the in-shore fishery. Since the early 1990s the Canadian government has banned cod fishing in an attempt to restore the cod stocks, which had reached critically low levels. Among other things, this moratorium has cost the federal government some $2.5 billion in support for the workers who have lost their livelihood as a result of the crisis.

A Describe the property right problem in the fisheries. Is this an interesting economic problem? How does the international component of the problem compound the difficulties?

B Several policies have been implemented in different fisheries: a quota system which allows the holder of the quota to fish a given quantity of fish; a quota system which is also transferable (i.e., can be bought and sold); limiting the size of vessels; limiting the length of the fishing season. Discuss how each of these may apply to the Pacific salmon and Atlantic cod cases and whether they will lead to a Pareto-efficient allocation of resources.

C Discuss the likely short-run and long-run consequences of a program which compensates fishers for not fishing.

[1] These estimates as well as an interesting discussion of the Canadian fisheries are contained in R. Q. Grafton and D. E. Lane, "Canadian Fisheries Policy: Challenges and Choices," *Canadian Public Policy/Analyse de Politiques*, 24, no.2, June 1998: 133–147.

EXERCISES

Multiple-Choice

Choose the correct answer to each of the following questions. There is only one correct answer to each question.

1 Which of the following is *not* an important feature of an economy?
- **a** Institutions.
- **b** Individual preferences.
- **c** The technology that produces goods from resources.
- **d** Resource endowments.
- **e** All the above are important features of an economy.

2 A resource allocation problem is interesting from an economics point of view if
- **a** There is an unlimited amount of the resource available.
- **b** The resource is limited in supply.
- **c** There are many alternative uses for the resource.
- **d** Both **a** and **c**.
- **e** Both **b** and **c**.

3 A social state describes
- **a** The allocation of resources to the production of goods.
- **b** The profits made by all firms in the society.

c The allocation of goods to individuals.
d The quantities of resources supplied by individuals.
e None of the above.

4 Which of the following could result in a decrease in the equilibrium price of cereal products?
a An increase in the price of eggs.
b Good weather for agricultural products.
c A decrease in the price of milk.
d An increase in income.
e None of the above.

5 Which represents a positive economic statement?
a An increase in a sales tax on automobiles leads to a decrease in the number of new-car purchases.
b All countries should engage in free trade because it is efficient.
c If a minimum wage is increased, some individuals will become unemployed.
d All the above.
e Only **a** and **c**.

6 Which is the normative statement?
a We should redistribute income from the rich to the poor.
b Since the market is efficient, we should allow it to work without government intervention.
c Since all society is against discrimination, policies should be imposed to combat it.
d All the above.
e Only **a** and **c**.

7 An economic model is a good one if, among other characteristics, it
a Is based on assumptions that accurately describe all the complexities of the economic world.
b Makes different predictions when assumptions of the model are changed.
c Yields predictions that are supported by empirical testing.
d Can be applied to a narrow set of economic observations.
e None of the above.

8 An allocation of resources is Pareto-efficient if
a The distribution of income is equitable.
b There is no reallocation of resources that will make some people better off without making some people worse off.
c Total profits in the economy are maximized.
d Only **b** and **c**.
e None of the above.

9 An allocation of resources A is Pareto-improving to an allocation B if
a Some people are better off, and no one is worse off, under allocation A compared with allocation B.
b The net social benefit of moving to state A is positive.
c The distribution of income is equitable.
d The sum of the gains of those made better off exceeds the sum of the losses of those made worse off in moving to allocation A.
e None of the above.

10 Using cost-benefit analysis, in which of the following cases would allocation A be chosen over allocation B?
a Some people are better off, and no one is worse off, under allocation A compared with allocation B.
b Net social benefits under allocation A are larger than net social benefits under allocation B.
c The sum of the gains of those made better off exceeds the sum of the losses of those made worse off in moving to allocation A.
d All the above.
e None of the above.

True-False

11 Determination of the social state that is "best" for society is a problem in positive economics.

12 The equilibrium price in a market is determined by the intersection of demand and supply.

13 A tax placed on firms for every unit product in the market for X will shift the supply to the left, resulting in a higher equilibrium price and lower quantity.

14 The assumption of self-interested behaviour rules out charitable actions.

15 Comparative static analysis is the method of analyzing the impact of a change in a model by comparing the equilibria that result before and after the change.

16 Models built on a set of assumptions that do not explicitly describe details of reality cannot be very useful.

17 All Pareto-efficient allocations of resources are Pareto improvements over Pareto-inefficient allocations.

18 For every Pareto-inefficient allocation of resources, there exists a reallocation for which some people could be made better off and no one made worse off.

19 A metered scheme in which a price must be paid for every unit of water consumed gives consumers less incentive to conserve water compared to a non-metered scheme in which everyone agrees to use a fixed amount of water.

20 A set of locations of two firms along a line is an equilibrium if and only if each firm gets one-half of the industry profits, regardless of the distribution of consumers along that line.

Short Problems

21 Give an example of how institutions can affect the economic state achieved by the economy. Show how positive economics can be useful in directing the economy towards a desirable social state through institutional change.

22 A student in a microeconomics course enjoys leisure activities — playing squash, reading and skiing. She wants to determine how much of the two goods, leisure (measured in hours) and economic knowledge (measured in pages of economics books), she can produce in one day by using the two resources of time and economics books. If she reads 50 pages of economics material in one hour, what will her daily production possibilities set look like?

23 The assumption of self-interest is not relevant to planned economies where prices are not determined by market forces. Discuss.

24 Since positive economics does not provide answers to normative questions, positive economic theory is of little use in resolving important real-world policy issues. Comment.

25 Two stores locate along a street between a residential area and the downtown area of some city. Every day, people from the residential area pass both stores on their way to work and on their way home from work. How does this behaviour of the potential customers affect the results of the Hotelling model?

26 Show that the Hotelling model is not robust to the number of firms, by showing that an equilibrium does not exist when there are three firms.

Long Problems

27 Assume that the market for carrots is perfectly competitive. Using diagrams, determine the impact on the short-run equilibrium price and quantity in the carrot market for each of the following:

- **a** The bean crop is a bumper crop.
- **b** A price ceiling is set below the equilibrium price of carrots.
- **c** A per-unit subsidy is given to carrot producers.
- **d** The price of fertilizer increases.

28 The following data are the market supply and demand schedules for shoelaces, which are products in a competitive market.

Price($)	Quantity Demanded	Quantity Supplied
1	500 000	100 000
2	400 000	200 000
3	300 000	300 000
4	200 000	400 000
5	100 000	500 000

- **a** Graphically construct the supply and demand schedules and determine the equilibrium price and quantity.
- **b** Suppose that a tax of $1 per shoelace is imposed on the producers. What will be the new equilibrium price paid by consumers and the quantity of shoelaces demanded after the tax has been imposed? What will be the price the producers *receive* after the tax has been imposed? Would your answers change if the tax were imposed on the consumers instead of the producers? Explain.
- **c** Derive the algebraic equations of the demand and supply schedules and check the answer you reached in **a** using these equations.

ANSWERS TO CHAPTER 1

Case Study

A No one owns a fish until it is taken out of the water. This rule of capture means that individuals do not have the incentive to fish in a sustainable way. Clearly the issue of property rights in the fisheries is an interesting economic problem because it entails the problem of how to manage a scarce resource. One interesting complication to this type of problem is the fact that optimal management must take account of the benefits that accrue not only to the current generation but to future generations as well.

The incentive to over-fish is heightened by the fact that the fish may be captured not only by the coastal population in Canada, but also by those who live elsewhere. Trying to come up with a solution to this problem is complicated by the fact that there are several governments involved in the process — which adds tremendously to the interests that must be taken into account when looking at solutions. In addition, don't forget that it is extremely costly to monitor and enforce policy solutions especially given the physical size of the fishing areas to be controlled.

B Not surprisingly, there are advantages and disadvantages associated with practically all policies. Policymakers and economists, therefore, are left to find the solution that generates the most benefit for the least cost. Quota systems allow every fisher to fish a certain quantity. Problems with such systems include the difficulties associated with determining the correct quota (or total amount of fish to be caught), the fact that fishers have the incentive to discard or waste any quantities above the quota, monitoring this system may be very costly, and finally, a quota system that does not allow fishers to transfer their rights encourages inefficient fishers to remain in the market. This latter problem is solved with a transferable quota system, rendering such a system more likely to result in an efficient fishing effort and a Pareto optimal allocation of resources. Limiting the size of vessels often leads fishers to change the size of other, non-regulated, equipment, like fishing gear. The biggest problem with limiting the fishing season is that fishers then have the incentive to use bigger equipment and fish more intensively within the allowable time frame. Often this regulation needs to be coupled with another policy, like quotas, in order to be effective. Because of the stated problems, and others, it is unlikely that most of these policies would lead to a Pareto optimal outcome. Transferable quotas may come the closest, if the amount of quota is determined correctly, and sufficient monitoring takes place. All of these problems pertain to both the salmon and cod fisheries. The cod fisheries may be slightly more complicated because of the sheer size of the area to be monitored (although salmon, too, swim in open seas).

C In the short run, compensating fishers for not fishing provides them with the means of survival while, at least in principle, looking for alternative sources of employment. One of the problems in the long run, however, is that such policies may encourage fishers to remain in this line of work rather than, say, retraining and taking up other employment. (Of course, this answer is very simplistic and ignores many of the real-world problems associated with finding alternative employment. In Newfoundland, for instance, finding other employment often necessitates moving out of the province and completely changing one's way of life.)

Multiple-Choice

1 e **2** e **3** c **4** b **5** e
6 d **7** c **8** b **9** a **10** d

True-False

11 F **12** T **13** T **14** F **15** T
16 F **17** F **18** T **19** F **20** F

Short Problems

21 An institution of common property in which anyone could have access to another individual's invention would result in a social state in which there would be little incentive to invest in research and development. Suppose that a social state in which more innovation takes place were desirable. Then positive economics could determine whether institutions such as patent policy, intended to protect inventors' rights, would direct resources toward the desirable social state. For example, the following questions could be answered: What effect would patent protection have on the rate of technological advance? What effect would patent protection have on the prices and quantities of goods produced from an innovation?

22 As shown in Figure A1.1, the student can "produce" 24 hours of leisure and zero economic knowledge or 1 200 pages of economic knowledge and zero leisure hours or any combination of leisure and economic knowledge in the shaded region. Since the cost (in terms of leisure hours) of producing another unit of economic knowledge is constant, the production possibilities curve is a straight line.

FIGURE A1.1

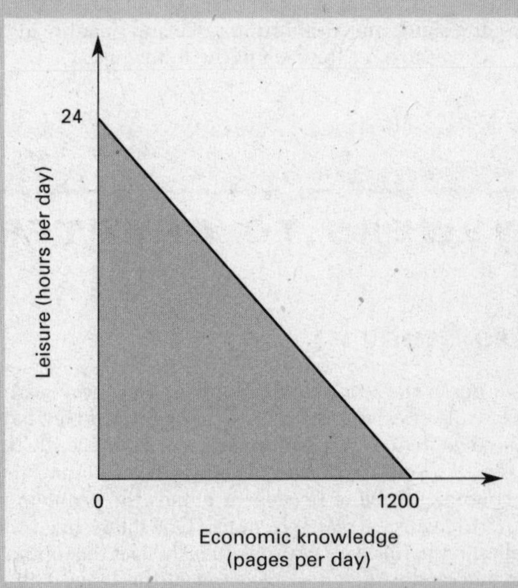

23 Even in planned economies in which prices are determined by some centralized authority, the notion of self-interest is relevant. In setting the prices at which goods are traded, the central authority must recognize that individuals will act on those prices in a way that best achieves some objective; that is, they will act out of self-interest.

24 Although answers to normative questions lie within a set of values and are not the result of a logical economic model, economists can analyze policies by using positive economic theory to predict whether normative goals will be achieved with the policies. For example, to say "We should get rid of discrimination" is a normative statement. The economist's expertise is not to argue the validity of the statement; since the statement is based on value judgements and a set of moral ethics, it is neither true nor false. However, given that a value judgment is accepted (through a democratic vote or successful lobbying), economists can analyze policies such as "equal pay for work of equal value" and quotas to determine whether, as a result of implementing those policies, the goal of reducing discrimination will be achieved.

25 If all individuals pass by both stores on their way to and from work, then the travel costs of buying from the two stores are equal for everyone. Then if the stores are identical, individuals randomly choose one of the stores, so each store will get half the customers as in the Hotelling model; however, there will be no incentive for the stores to locate next to each other.

26 Place the three firms A, B, and C anywhere along a line of unit length and show that each firm will always have the incentive to relocate, given its rivals' locations. For example, initially give the firms equal market shares; that is, place firm A at 1/6, firm B at 1/2, and firm C at 5/6. Clearly, each firm will have the incentive to move right next to its closest rival. For example, firm A will move first to the left of 1/2. But then firm B will want to "jump" over firm A and relocate just to the left of it. This will continue until it pays the next mover to relocate just to the left of firm C. But then firm C will want to move, and so on.

Long Problems

27 a The supply curve for beans shifts to the right, decreasing the equilibrium price and increasing the equilibrium quantity. Since beans and carrots are substitutes, the demand for carrots will fall, decreasing equilibrium price and quantity as shown in Figure A1.2a.

b At the price ceiling p_1, the quantity demanded y_d exceeds the quantity supplied y_s, as shown in Figure A1.2b. The excess demand that results at price p_1 implies that not all consumers will be satisfied. The situation may result in the introduction of a rationing scheme.

c A per-unit subsidy causes a parallel shift in the supply curve of carrots to the right, resulting in a lower equilibrium price and a higher quantity of carrots, as shown in Figure A1.2c.

d An increase in the price of fertilizer shifts the supply curve to the *left*, resulting in the *opposite* effect on equilibrium price and quantity than that shown in Figure A1.2c.

28 a The demand and supply curves are illustrated in Figure A1.3. The equilibrium price of shoelaces is \$3; the equilibrium quantity is 300 000.

b As illustrated in Figure A1.3, a \$1 tax will shift the supply curve upward by \$1 at every quantity. The new price paid by consumers will be \$3.50; the equilibrium quantity will be 250 000. The producers receive \$2.50. If the tax were imposed on consumers, the demand curve would shift down by \$1 at every quantity, resulting in the same answers.

FIGURE A1.2

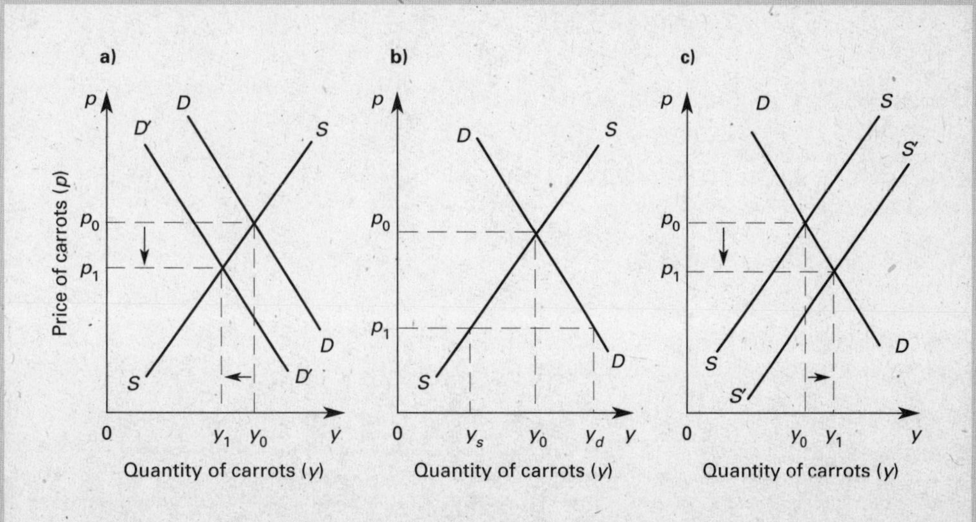

FIGURE A1.3

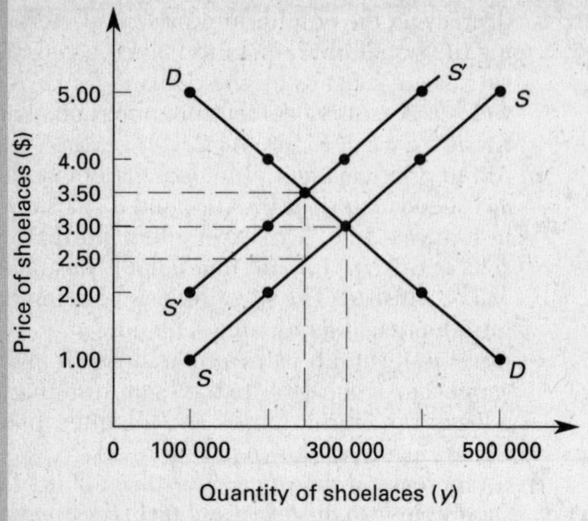

c The demand curve is found by the point–point formula. Using the points (y, p) of (500 000,1) and (100 000,5), the equation for y_d is found as follows.

$$\frac{y_d - 500\,000}{0-1} = \frac{500\,000 - 100\,000}{1-5}$$

$$y_d - 500\,000 = -100\,000(p-1)$$

$$y_d = 600\,000 - 100\,000p$$

Similarly, the supply curve is given by

$$y_s = 100\,000p$$

Quantities demanded and supplied are equated to get

$$600\,000 - 100\,000p = 100\,000p$$

$$p = 3$$

Substituting $p = 3$ into either the demand or supply curve gives

$$y = 600\,000 - 100\,000(3)$$

$$= 300\,000$$

CHAPTER 2

A Theory of Preferences

Chapter Summary

Economic Models

In this chapter, we begin our study of the consumer. The most fundamental assumption about the consumer in economic models is that consumers are motivated by self-interest. Individuals have **preferences** about goods whether the goods are hamburgers and french fries, charitable donations, or Jaguar XK-Es. We assume that the choices consumers make regarding goods, subject to their budget constraints, result from self-interested behaviour. As economists, our task is to figure out how to analyze consumers' choices, given this assumption.

For the notion of self-interest to make any sense, it must be the case that individuals can order bundles of goods that range from most preferred to least preferred so they can choose their favourite **consumption bundle** within the limits of their budget constraints. In order to choose one bundle over another, a consumer must be able to make **preference statements** like, "I am indifferent between eating onion rings and French fries with my hamburger, but prefer to eat salad with my burger." Hence, to analyze consumer choices, we need to define a **preference ordering**. That is, given all possible consumption bundles of all goods, we need to be able to rank those bundles from most preferred to least preferred. This ranking is possible only if the consumer has well-defined preferences. For example, if a consumer chooses consumption bundles in an erratic fashion, then the economist can say very little about that person's choices. So, our first task is to identify a set of assumptions about individual preferences that allows us to construct a ranking. Next, we want to describe that preference ordering by a mathematical function, a utility function, so that we can use the techniques of constrained maximization to analyze the consumer problem.

Consumer Assumptions

The first assumption of consumer choice is the **completeness assumption**: An individual must be able to compare *any and all* consumption bundles. If the individual cannot compare two bundles, the economist will certainly have difficulty predicting the individual's choice. The second assumption is that the consumer is allowed to make only one of the following three statements when comparing two bundles B_1 and B_2: B_1 is preferred to B_2 (B_1 **P** B_2), B_2 is preferred to B_1 (B_2 **P** B_1), or the individual is indifferent between the two bundles (B_1 **I** B_2). This is the **two-term consistency** assumption. Third, if an individual prefers bundle B_1 to B_2 (or is indifferent between them) and prefers B_2 to a third bundle B_3 (or is indifferent between them), then it must be the case that the consumer prefers B_1 to B_3 (or is indifferent between them); that is, preferences must satisfy the **transitivity** assumption. These three assumptions ensure that preferences are consistent and that a preference order exists.

Utility Functions and Indifference Curves

To be able to analyze consumer choice by using constrained maximization techniques, we need to define a **utility function** over this preference ordering; that is, we assign a number to each bundle, reflecting the most preferred to the least preferred, and assign the same number to bundles for which an individual is indifferent. All bundles for which the individual is indifferent can be illustrated by an **indifference curve**. To ensure that these indifference curves are true curves and not single points, we need the **continuity of preferences assumption**. This is a necessary condition for representing a preference ordering by a utility function; it says that a continuous indifference curve can be drawn through every consumption bundle. Another assumption that is useful but not necessary is **nonsatiation**. This assumption simply says "More is preferred to less" and makes the indifference curves non-positively sloped.

A further assumption made by economists is that individuals want to maximize their satisfaction by **maximizing** their preference ordering, i.e., by choosing the bundle of goods they most prefer. This means that individuals will choose the bundle that is assigned the largest utility number. Notice that the assumptions of nonsatiation and maximization imply **scarcity**; in the absence of scarcity, we would never have enough of any one good. Given these assumptions, a utility function exists. A utility function assigns a **utility number** to every consumption bundle in an individual's preference ordering. The higher the number the higher the level of satisfaction; if the number is the same for two bundles then the individual is indifferent between the two bundles. An individual's preference ordering can be represented by many different utility functions. To see this, imagine multiplying all the utility numbers of a particular utility function by 2. The preference ordering would be preserved. This implies that the actual number assigned is of *no significance*. Utility numbers measure **ordinal utility**, not **cardinal utility**, and therefore *cannot* be interpreted as a measure of "happiness" or "satisfaction." Furthermore, comparisons of individuals cannot be made by looking at utility numbers.

Marginal Rate of Substitution

By using indifference curves, we can identity the *rate* at which a consumer is willing to trade one good, good 2, for another, good 1, without changing the level of utility. We can call this rate the **marginal rate of substitution** $MRS(x_1, x_2)$, and it is equal to the rate of substitution associated with a **marginal change** — a very small change — in the quantity of good 1. Technically, this equals the slope of the indifference curve multiplied by –1. If we make an "assumption of convenience" that indifference curves are **strictly convex**, then the $MRS(x_1, x_2)$ declines as one moves down the indifference curve. In other words, the indifference curves are bowed into the origin which means that given any two points on the curve, an individual would strictly prefer any linear combination of these two points to either point itself. This assumption of **diminishing marginal rate of substitution** is a common, but not necessary, assumption of consumer theory. Indifference curves that are bowed-out from the origin are **nonconvex**. In this case, the combination of any two points on the curve is not preferred to either extreme. Indifference curves may be **weakly convex** — i.e., have flat segments where the slope is constant — implying that the individual is indifferent between combinations of two bundles and the bundles themselves.

When economists talk about the **value** of a good they mean the largest amount that someone would be willing to pay for the good. If the individual is buying a very small quantity, we can determine the **marginal value** of the good. Notice that the amount that an individual would be willing to pay for an additional, infinitesimally small, quantity of a good also reflects his or her MRS.

Applications

The theory of preferences is a powerful tool for analyzing a wide range of problems. For example, overtime pay provided in labour markets can be understood if workers have strictly-convex indifference curves over income and leisure: To encourage workers to give up additional hours of leisure, a higher-than-usual wage is required. The theory can also be used to measure the costs to consumers from an increase in "bads" such as "pollution." Finally, incentive schemes to induce students to work hard can be analyzed in this framework.

KEY WORDS

- Cardinal utility
- Completeness assumption
- Consumption bundle
- Continuity of preferences assumption
- Diminishing marginal rate of substitution
- Indifference curve
- Marginal change
- Marginal rate of substitution
- Marginal value
- Maximizing
- Nonconvex
- Nonsatiation
- Ordinal utility
- Preference ordering
- Preferences
- Preference statements
- Scarcity
- Self-interest
- Strictly convex
- Transitivity
- Two-term consistency
- Utility function
- Utility number
- Value
- Weakly convex

CASE STUDY: INTRANSITIVITIES OF YOUTH

In an interesting paper by Arnold A. Weinstein (1968),[1] the results of the following were reported. Individuals were asked to make pairwise comparisons among 10 bundles, each being valued at approximately $3 (1968 dollars). Among the bundles were $3 in cash, a print of El Greco's *View of Toledo*, a pair of white tennis shoes, two glasses of vanilla malted milk per day for 10 days, the three most recent Beatles records, and so on.

The purpose of the experiment was to test whether the individuals had transitive preferences. The percentage of transitive responses for children (9–12 years), teenagers (14–18 years), and adults were, respectively, 79%, 86%, and 93.5%.

A How would you explain the result that younger people have more intransitivities than adults? Do you agree with the author's conclusions that this result "lends some support to the political and economic restrictions placed upon the youth of our society" (p. 311)?

B Given the results from this study, do you think that transitivity is a restrictive assumption of consumer behaviour? Why or why not?

C Discuss the restrictiveness of the assumptions of completeness, nonsatiety, and convexity.

EXERCISES

Multiple-Choice

Choose the correct answer to each of the following questions. There is only one correct answer to each question.

1 Which of the following is *not* a necessary assumption for the existence of a utility function?

- **a** Consumers are able to rank all conceivable bundles of goods.
- **b** If a consumer prefers bundle B_1 to bundle B_2 and bundle B_2 to bundle B_3, he must prefer bundle B_1 to bundle B_3.
- **c** Consumers prefer more to less.
- **d** Preferences must be continuous.
- **e** All of the above assumptions are necessary for a utility function to exist.

2 Consider the following sets of indifference curves in Figure 2.1 for two individuals, Mary and Max. Although both individuals prefer more of each good to less of the good, Mary prefers jelly beans to peanuts considerably more than Max does. Which of the following is true?

- **a** Mary is more likely to have the indifference curves in Figure 2.1a, whereas Max's indifference curves are more likely to be those in Figure 2.1b.
- **b** Max is more likely to have indifference curves given in Figure 2.1a, whereas Mary's indifference curves are more likely to be those in Figure 2.1b.
- **c** Max will have neither set of indifference curves, his indifference curves will be positively sloped.
- **d** Mary will have neither set of indifference curves, her indifference curves will be positively sloped.
- **e** None of the above.

3 A certain individual claims that she likes to eat a peanut butter sandwich only with a glass of milk, and she likes to drink a glass of milk only if she has a peanut butter sandwich to eat. If she is given more than one peanut butter sandwich per glass of milk, she throws it away, and vice versa.

- **a** Her indifference curves between peanut butter and milk are straight lines.
- **b** Her preferences violate the assumption of transitivity.
- **c** Her indifference curves are right angles.
- **d** Her indifference curves violate the assumptions of consumer choice because they intersect.
- **e** None of the above.

4 The absolute value of the indifference curve at any point represents

- **a** The amount of one good the individual is willing to give up to get some of the other good for some increase in utility.
- **b** The total amount of money spent on the bundle.
- **c** The ratio of prices of the two goods.
- **d** The rate at which the individual will trade off one good for another, holding utility constant.
- **e** None of the above.

[1] Arnold A. Weinstein (1968). "Transitivity of Preference: A Comparison Among Age Groups," *Journal of Political Economy*, **76**: 307–311.

FIGURE 2.1

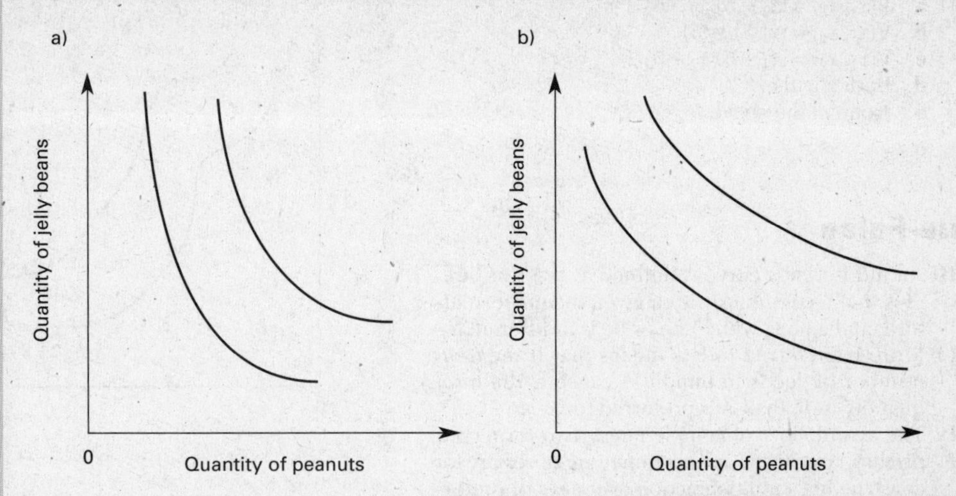

5 For the indifference curves in Figure 2.2,
   a $MRS(x_1, x_2)$ is diminishing.
   b Good 1 but not good 2 is a desirable good.
   c Good 2 but not good 1 is a desirable good.
   d Neither good 1 nor good 2 is desirable.
   e None of the above.

FIGURE 2.2

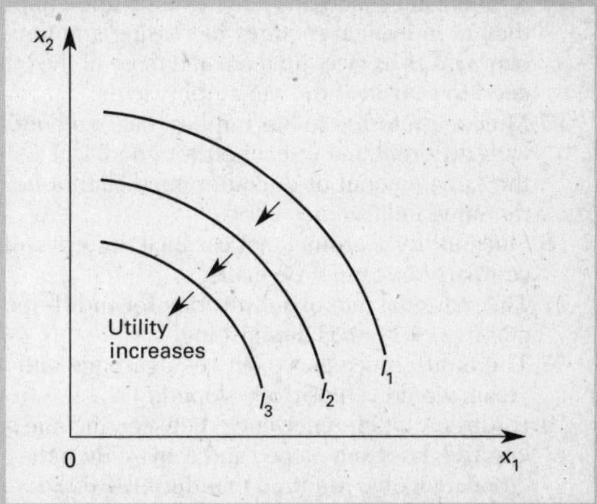

6 Three community bundles, each consisting of two commodities, good 1 and good 2, are listed in the accompanying table.

Bundle	Amount of Good 1	Amount of Good 2
A	2	3
B	1	3
C	2	2

Suppose that an individual ranks the bundles as follows: *A* is preferred to *B*, *C* is preferred to *A*, *B* and *C* are indifferent. Then the individual's preference ordering
   a Violates the assumption of nonsatiety.
   b Violates the assumption of transitivity.
   c Violates the assumption of completeness.
   d Is consistent with all the assumptions of consumer behaviour.
   e Both **a** and **b**.

7 Which of the following statements about indifference curves is *incorrect*?
   a Each point on the indifference curve represents a different combination of quantities of the two goods.
   b All points on the indifference curve are equally preferred by the customer.
   c Some bundles of goods on an indifference curve may not be affordable.
   d An infinite number of indifference curves go through every point in goods space.
   e All the above statements are correct.

8 For the utility function $U = (x_1 + x_2)/5$, the indifference curves
   a Are given by straight lines.
   b Exhibit diminishing $MRS(x_1, x_2)$.
   c Are positively sloped.
   d Violate the assumption that more is preferred to less.
   e None of the above.

9 Which of the following utility functions describes the same preference ordering over goods 1 and 2 as $U(x_1, x_2) = x_1x_2$?

a $V(x_1, x_2) = (x_1 - 5)(x_2 - 5)$
b $V(x_1, x_2) = (x_1/5)(x_2/5)$
c $V(x_1, x_2) = (x_1 + 5)(x_2 + 5)$
d Both **a** and **c**.
e None of the above.

True-False

10 An indifference curve is defined as a set of bundles that a consumer with a given income can afford, and among which she or he is indifferent.
11 More is preferred to less means that if the *total* number of goods in bundle *A* exceeds the *total* quantity in *B*, than *A* is preferred to *B*.
12 The assumptions of completeness, two-term consistency, transitivity, and continuity are necessary for constructing a utility function over a set of preferences.
13 The utility function $V(x_1, x_2) = 5[U(x_1, x_2)]/2 + 7$ represents the same preference ordering as the utility function $U(x_1, x_2)$.
14 A diminishing marginal rate of substitution implies that an individual requires increasing amounts of one good as he gives up more and more of the other good to remain at the same utility level.
15 More is preferred to less implies that two bundles with different amounts of either good 1 or 2 and the same amount of the other good cannot be on the same indifference curve.
16 Since utility is ordinal, not cardinal, interpersonal comparisons cannot be made.
17 The marginal rate of substitution for indifference curves $x_1 + x_2 = c$ is diminishing.
18 The indifference curve between garbage and ice cream would be positively sloped.
19 If Alfred's indifference curve between income and leisure is positively sloped and convex, then the additional income required to induce Alfred to work additional hours is constant and equal to his current wage.

Short Problems

20 Suppose the consumer has the indifference curves illustrated in Figure 2.3. Which of the assumptions about indifference curves do the curves violate?

FIGURE 2.3

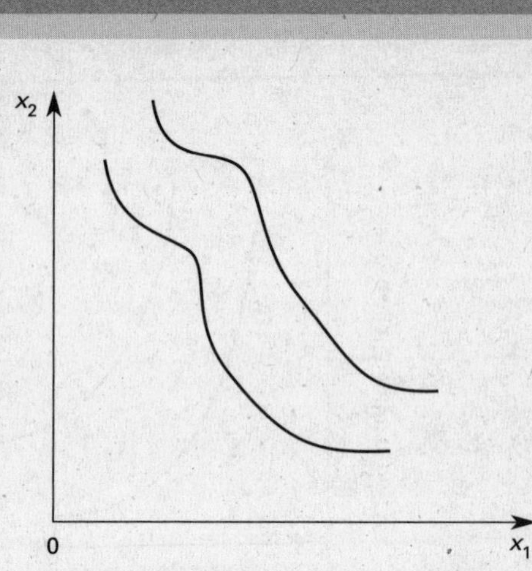

21 Suppose Eleanor consumes two goods: economics books and food. Although Eleanor enjoys economics, she gets satiated beyond 100 books per month. Eleanor can give away any extra books that she acquires over 100 to her friends. (Assume that she doesn't get additional utility from giving the books away.) What do Eleanor's indifference curves look like?
22 Show that the assumption of nonsatiety implies that indifference curves have a nonpositive slope.
23 What is the relationship between utility functions and indifference curves?
24 Jack and Mary go on vacation in Australia. They want to eat at a seafood restaurant and are trying to decide between two restaurants. Restaurant *A* is almost full but restaurant *B* is empty. Which restaurant should they choose? After dinner they decide to see a play. Again, there are two possibilities, but they are not familiar with either play. Play *A* has a long line of interested viewers, whereas play *B* has no line. Which play should they choose?
25 Consider the following preference ordering: An individual consumes two goods, good 1 and good 2. Bundle $A = (x_1^A, x_1^B)$ is preferred to bundle $B = (x_1^B, x_1^B)$ if $x_1^A > x_1^B$ regardless of the amount of good 2 in each bundle. If $x_1^A = x_1^B$, then bundle *A* is preferred to bundle *B* if $x_2^A > x_2^B$. These preferences are called *lexicographic*. Give an intuitive explanation of why a utility function cannot be defined over preferences that are lexicographic. (*Hint*: Recall that the construction of a utility function requires every bundle to be assigned a number with higher numbers given to "more preferred" bundles and the same number given to all "indifferent" bundles.)
***26** For the utility function $U(x_1, x_2, x_3) = x_1^2 x_2 x_3$ determine the MRS_{12} and the MRS_{13} (note that the MRS_{ij} refers to the rate of substitution between good i and j when good i experiences a very small decrease). Is the MRS constant between these pairs of goods? What if the utility function becomes $V(x_1, x_2, x_3) = 100\, x_1^2 x_2 x_3$, how will your answers above change?

Long Problems

27 Consider the following bundles of bottles of beer (b) and bags of peanuts (p).
A: (7, 3) B: (5, 4) C: (12, 1)
D: (1, 9) E: (6, 6)
Suppose an individual has the following preference ordering:
E **P** D **P** C **P** A **P** B
Find a utility function that describes the individual's preferences. Can you find more than one utility function? Explain.

28 Four university students have been asked to assign utility numbers to five bundles of good 1 and good 2, with more-preferred bundles getting higher numbers (see accompanying table). These utility numbers will help us find a representation for each student's utility function, U_1 to U_4. Unfortunately, only one of the university students, who has taken a course in microeconomics, has a utility function that is consistent with all the assumptions of consumer theory. Which is it? Can you explain why the other functions are inconsistent? *Hint:* Plot the bundles in the x_1–x_2 space.

	Amount of		Utility			
Bundle	Good 1	Good 2	U_1	U_2	U_3	U4
A	2	2	2	2	1	6
B	2	5	4	5	3	10
C	4	6	6	6	5	10
D	5	4	6	5	3	6
E	6	1	4	5	5	3

29 Measure bottles of beer on the horizontal axis and bags of popcorn on the vertical axis. Draw indifference curves for the following preferences, and then explain whether these indifference curves satisfy the assumptions of consumer choice. For those indifference curves that do not, explain why.

a Tom likes to drink beer or eat popcorn equally well.

b Rema likes a bottle of beer only with a bag of popcorn.

c The more beer the better, no matter how much popcorn Alejandro has, but if he can't have more beer, he prefers to have more popcorn.

d Let a bundle (b, p) represent the quantities of beer and popcorn, respectively. Beth is indifferent between (2, 3) and (3, 1). She is also indifferent between (2, 3) and (4, 2), but she would rather have (4, 2) than (3, 1).

e Motozo likes beer and popcorn, but three beers knock him out for the night, and he gets sick on four bags of popcorn.

30 Show that a utility function can be constructed using the assumptions of completeness, two-term consistency, transitivity, continuity, and nonsatiety.

31 An individual's preferences can be represented by indifference curves $x_1x_2 = c$, where c is some nonnegative constant. Bundles on an indifference curve identified by a particular c are preferred to those bundles on indifference curves identified by a lower c. (For example, all bundles on $x_1x_2 = 10$ are preferred to all bundles on $x_1x_2 = 2$.) Given the method for constructing a utility function outlined in the previous exercise, construct a utility function that represents these preferences.

*32 **a** Suppose the utility function $U(x_1, x_2) = x_1x_2$ describes Mary's preference ordering. Derive the indifference curves for this preference ordering and show that the indifference curves have the property of diminishing marginal rate of substitution.

b Suppose that Fred has a utility function given by $V(x_1, x_2) = x_1x_2 + 25$. Derive and illustrate the indifference curves for this preference ordering.

c The fact the Mary's utility function assigns a lower number to every bundle than Fred's utility function implies that Fred must enjoy consuming all bundles of goods more than Mary does. True, false, uncertain? Explain.

ANSWERS TO CHAPTER 2

Case Study

A Older people may have more experience with the products or with making decisions.

B If the results of this study are accurate, then transitivity is a restrictive assumption. A theory of consumer behavior, based on transitivity, risks being incorrect a fairly high percentage of the time for individuals without experience. However, as individuals become more familiar with consumption bundles, they would be expected to behave according to this assumption.

C Completeness is not restrictive; it simply requires that people can compare bundles. Nonsatiety is more restrictive because individuals are likely to become satiated with most goods. Locally, however, it is not restrictive. For example, there may be some point at which one gets no additional utility from more money; however, at present she is nowhere near that point. Convexity is a restrictive assumption. It says that individuals prefer a mixture of good 1 and good 2 to bundles that have only good 1 or only good 2 in them. There is no psychological reason why this should be so. However, if commodities are defined broadly, convexity makes more sense; for example, most individuals would prefer a combination of food and clothes to only food or clothing.

Multiple-Choice

1 c 2 b 3 c 4 d 5 d
6 e 7 d 8 a *9 b

True-False

10 F 11 F 12 T 13 T 14 T
15 T 16 T 17 F 18 T 19 F

Short Problems

20 Strict convexity.

21 The indifference curves are shown in Figure A2.1. Eleanor's indifference curves are flat beyond 100 books because she gets neither more nor less utility from more than 100 economics books.

22 Consider point A in Figure A2.2. Given nonsatiety, all points to the northeast of A are preferred bundles because they have more of *both* goods in them; all points to the southwest of A are less-preferred bundles because they have less of *both* goods in them; hence, the indifference curve must pass through the shaded regions.

23 Given a utility function $U(x_1, x_2)$, an indifference curve is defined by $u^0 = U(x_1, x_2)$; that is, an indifference curve is all combinations of good 1 and good 2 that yield the same utility u_0.

24 Jack and Mary should choose restaurant *A* since consumers with similar preferences for seafood have revealed that restaurant *A* is the better one. However, they shouldn't infer much from the long line-ups for play *A*. Among other considerations, the individuals at show *A* may have very different tastes from those of Mary and Jack.

25 Suppose that preferences are lexicographic. Then the set of bundles that is preferred to A in Figure A2.3 consists of all bundles to the right of A, including the solid line above A. Let the utility number for A be x_2^A and assign the number x_2 to each of the preferred bundles (x_1^A, x_2), $x_2 > x_2^A$. After these utility numbers are assigned, all the real numbers larger than x_2^A are used up. All bundles with more x_1 than x_1^A are preferred to all the bundles on the solid line and, therefore, must be assigned larger numbers. However, there are no numbers left to

FIGURE A2.1

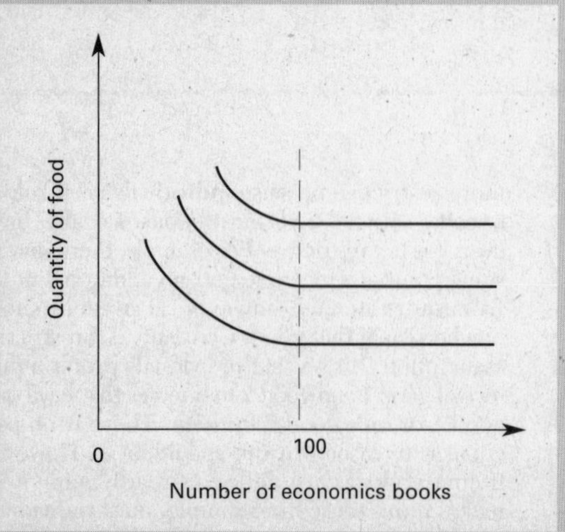

FIGURE A2.2

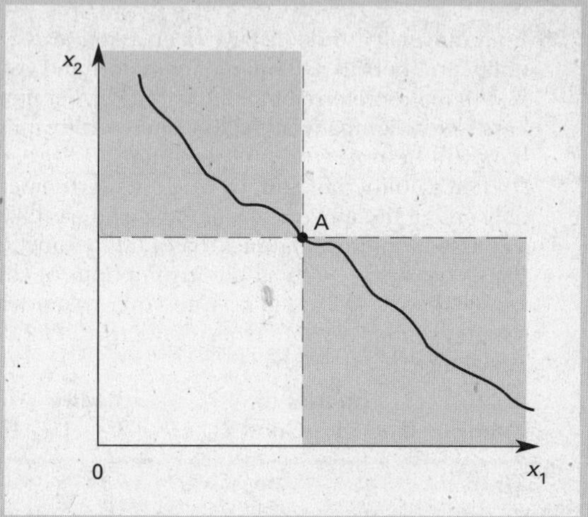

FIGURE A2.3

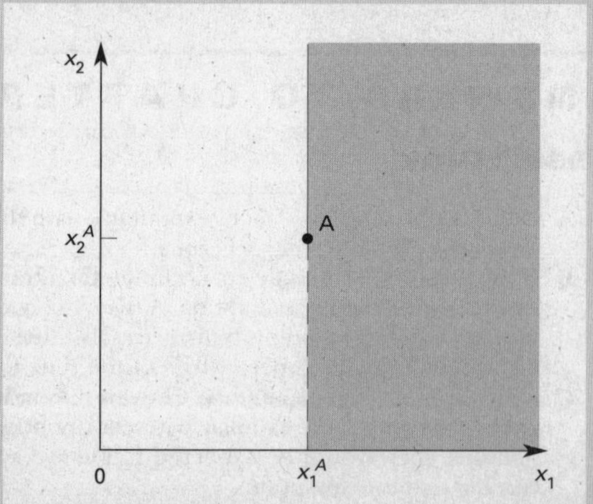

assign to these bundles, hence, a utility function cannot be constructed.

*26 $MRS_{12} = U_1/U_2 = -2x_2/x_1$, and $MRS_{13} = U_1/U_3 = -2x_3/x_1$. Obviously, the MRS is not constant, it depends upon the values of the x_i's. If the utility function becomes $V(x_1, x_2, x_3) = 100\, x_1^2 x_2 x_3$ it will NOT change the value of the MRSs because V is simply a positive transformation of U.

Long Problems

27 $U = 2b + 3p$. To see that this utility function describes the preference ordering, show that

$$U_E > U_D > U_C > U_A > U_B$$
$$U_E = (2)(6) + (3)(6) = 30$$
$$U_D = (2)(1) + (3)(9) = 29$$
$$U_C = (2)(12) + (3)(1) = 27$$
$$U_A = (2)(7) + (3)(3) = 23$$
$$U_B = (2)(5) + (3)(4) = 22$$

Any increasing monotonic transformation also represents the preference ordering. For example, any utility function $V(b, p)$ given by $v(b, p) = c[U(b, p)] + d$, where c and d are parameters, describes the same preference ordering.

28 Student 1's utility function U_1 is consistent with all the assumptions, as shown in Figure A2.4a. Student 2 has concave rather than convex preferences, as shown in Figure A2.4b. Student 3's indifference curves (in Figure A2.4c) intersect and therefore violate transitivity. Student 4 (see Figure A2.4d) violates the assumption of nonsatiation (that is, that more is preferred to less) and so has positively sloped indifference curves.

29 The indifference curves are illustrated in Figure A2.5 for each case. The indifference curves in Figure A2.5a are for perfect substitutes. The preferences represented by these indifference curves can be ordered and represented by a utility function; however, they do not satisfy the assumption of strict convexity.

The indifference curves in Figure A2.5b represent two complements. These preferences can be represented by a utility function; however, they do not satisfy nonsatiety or strict convexity.

In Figure A2.5c are lexicographic preferences that violate the assumption of continuity. Preferences can be ordered, but no utility function can be constructed to represent these preferences.

In Figure A2.5d, transitivity is violated, and no well-behaved preference ordering can be constructed. In Figure A2.5e, "more is preferred to less" is violated; these preferences can be represented by a utility function.

30 If preferences are complete, reflexive, transitive, continuous, and nonsatiety holds, then a continuous utility function that represents those preferences can be constructed. Define a utility function $U(\,) = U(x_1, \ldots, x_n)$ such that

a It assigns a number to all bundles.

b If B_1 **P** B_2, then $U(B_1) > U(B_2)$, and if B_1 **I** B_2, then $U(B_1) = U(B_2)$.

By completeness, the individual is able to make comparisons of all bundles. Consider first those bundles on the 45° line in Figure A2.6. Assign a utility number equal to the amount of x_1 in the bundle; that is, $U(B) = x_1$, where $B = (x_1, x_2)$. By nonsatiety, higher bundles on the 45° line are preferred to lower bundles; for example, B_2 **P** B_1, and by our rule for assigning utility numbers, the more-preferred bundles are assigned higher numbers. This satisfies part **b** of the definition of a utility function for these bundles. Do all bundles get assigned a number (part **a** of the definition)? Consider a bundle B_3 not on the 45° line. By continuity, indifference curves are smooth, and by the rule that more is preferred to less, they are negatively sloped. Then, the indifference curve through B_3 intersects the 45° line at a point, call it B_1. Since B_3 is indifferent to B_1, B_3 is assigned the utility number x_1^1, where the superscript refers to the bundle.

Last, we must show that all bundles off the 45° line will be assigned a number that correctly describes the individual's preferences; that is, part **b** of the definition of a utility function is satisfied for all bundles. Consider two bundles B_3 and B_4. By our earlier argument, there is a bundle on the 45° line that is indifferent to B_3, which we called B_1, and one that is indifferent to B_4, call it B_2. Both B_2 and B_4 are assigned the utility number x_1^2; both B_1 and B_3 are assigned x_1^1. Recall that $x_1^2 > x_1^1$. This assignment of utility numbers will be correct if B_4 **P** B_3. Since B_4 **I** B_2, B_2 **P** B_1, and B_1 **I** B_3, then, by transitivity, B_4 **P** B_3.

31 Indifference curves are given by $x_1x_2 = c$. Consider the intersection of $x_1x_2 = c$ and the ray $x_2 = x_1$. (Note that the indifference curves are symmetric around the ray $x_2 = x_1$.) The intersection occurs at $(\sqrt{c}, \sqrt{c})$. Assign the utility number $x_1 = \sqrt{c}$ to points on the curve $x_1x_2 = c$. Examples of the utility number assignment to bundles on various indifference curves are given in the table.

Utility Number	Bundles on
$\sqrt{1}$	$x_1x_2 = 1$
$\sqrt{2}$	$x_1x_2 = 2$
$\sqrt{3}$	$x_1x_2 = 3$
$\sqrt{c}$	$x_1x_2 = c$

*32 **a** The indifference curves associated with Mary's preference ordering are $u^0 = x_1x_2$. The slope of

FIGURE A2.4

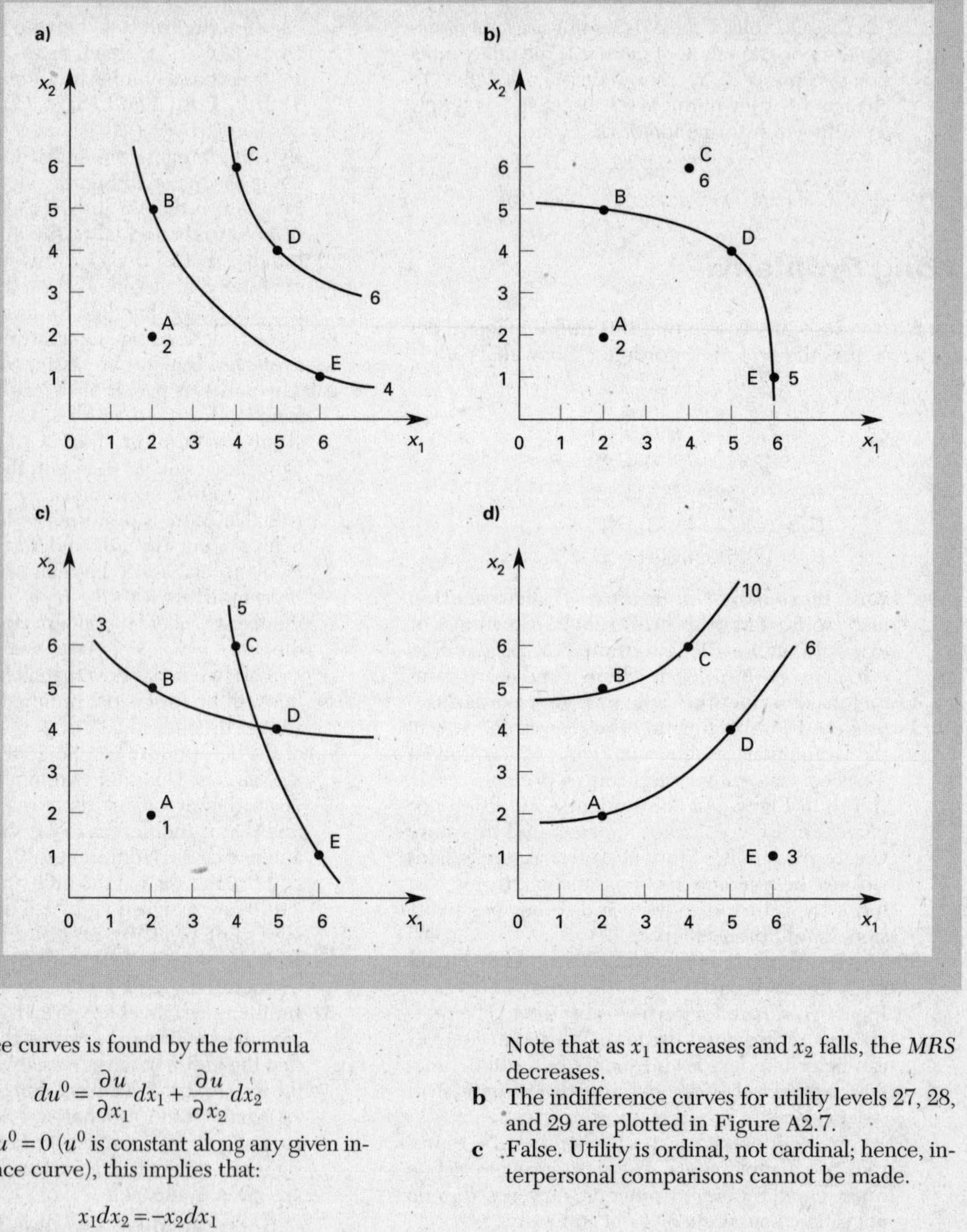

indifference curves is found by the formula

$$du^0 = \frac{\partial u}{\partial x_1}dx_1 + \frac{\partial u}{\partial x_2}dx_2$$

Since $du^0 = 0$ (u^0 is constant along any given indifference curve), this implies that:

$$x_1 dx_2 = -x_2 dx_1$$

$$\frac{dx_2}{dx_1} = \frac{-x_2}{x_1} \quad \text{and} \quad MRS = \frac{x_2}{x_1}$$

Note that as x_1 increases and x_2 falls, the *MRS* decreases.

b The indifference curves for utility levels 27, 28, and 29 are plotted in Figure A2.7.

c False. Utility is ordinal, not cardinal; hence, interpersonal comparisons cannot be made.

FIGURE A2.5

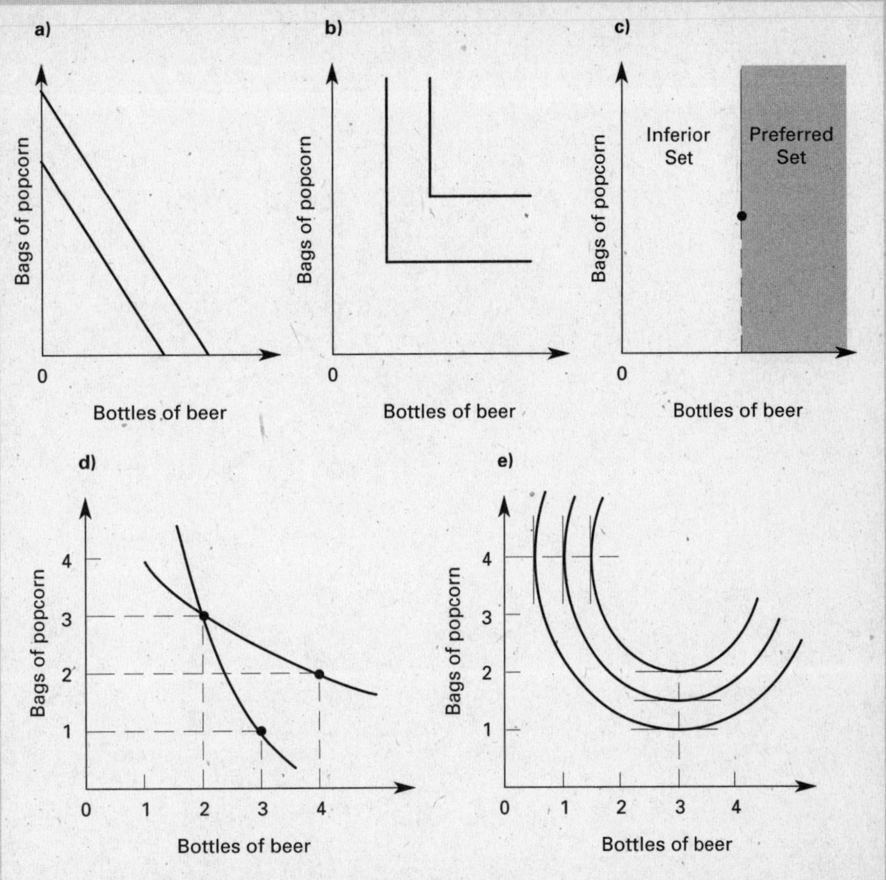

FIGURE A2.6

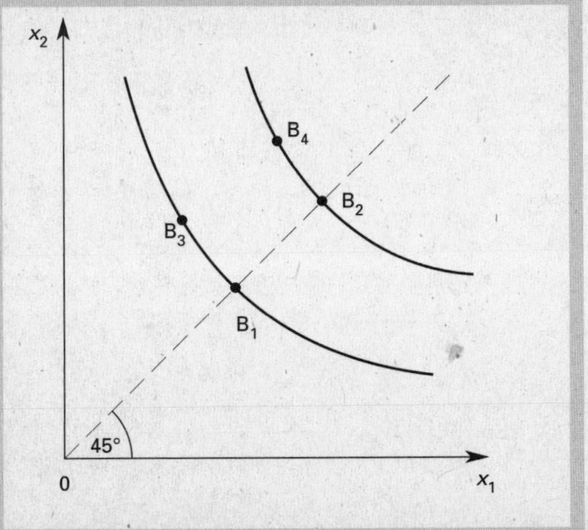

FIGURE A2.7

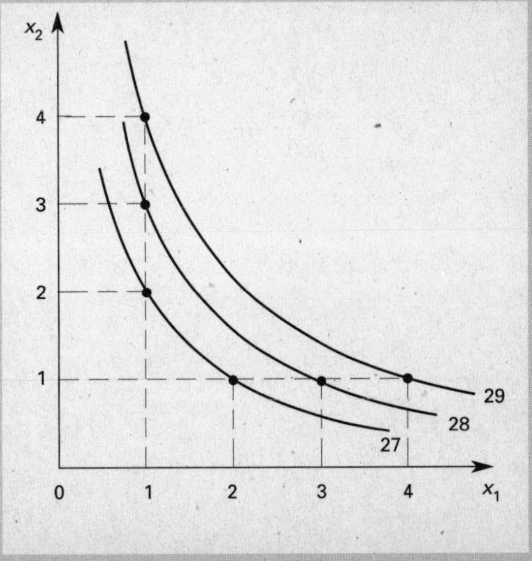

CHAPTER 3

Demand Theory

Chapter Summary

Consumer's Choice Problem

As consumers, we are all involved in the complex task of making choices among competing goods, given constraints on our time, income, and human resources. To study an individual's static consumption decision in any given period of time, we must make several assumptions. First, we assume that the consumer has perfect knowledge of all prices in the economy. Next, we assume that the consumer has an income of M dollars to spend on the n consumption goods. Finally, we assume that the consumer has preferences that satisfy the assumptions of consumer theory laid out in the previous chapter. Given these assumptions, the consumer's choice problem becomes one of choosing quantities of the n consumption goods in such a way that utility is maximized subject to the individual's **budget constraint**. The **budget constraint** identifies the consumer's **attainable consumption bundles**, while the **budget line** indicates all the bundles that exactly satisfy the constraint. While the utility function describes the consumption bundles that the consumer *prefers* to purchase, the budget constraint gives the set of attainable bundles that the consumer *can* purchase.

The budget constraint can also be written in terms of **real income** and **relative prices** by dividing it by the price of one of the goods. Expressing the constraint in this way makes it clear that the individual has **no money illusion** — i.e., it reflects the fact that only real income and real prices matter. The main difference between real and nominal values is **inflation**. **Pure inflation**, where all prices and incomes rise by the same percentage, has no real impact on the consumer's optimal bundle. Relative prices also provide a measure of the **opportunity cost** of purchasing one good instead of another. Budget constraints can be expressed in terms of an individual's endowment of goods and services (usually labour services) rather than in money terms. In economic analysis, we often assume a **representative consumer** whose choices reflect those that would be made by similar individuals in society.

The solution to the consumer's constrained maximization problem, the utility-maximizing consumption bundle, forms a **system of demand functions**. These functions tell us the quantities demanded of the consumption goods (the **endogenous variables**) as a function of the **exogenous variables** of prices and income. The **law of demand** dictates that quantity demanded will fall as price rises, *ceteris paribus*.

Graphical Analysis of Utility Maximization

The solution to the utility-maximization problem can be characterized by one of two possibilities. If indifference curves are smooth, then an **interior solution** (one in which positive quantities of both goods are consumed) occurs where the marginal rate of substitution of good 2 for good 1 equals the ratio of the price of good 1 to the price of good 2, and all the consumer's budget is spent. Alternatively, an interior solution can be characterized as the point of tangency, where the slope of the indifference curve equals the slope of the budget constraint. This solution implies that the amount of good 2 that the individual is *willing* to trade for a unit of good 1 is equal to the amount of good 2 that the consumer can get if she gives up one unit of good 1 (the opportunity cost of good 1). A **corner solution** occurs when the consumer buys all of one good and none of the other. In such a case, the ratio of marginal utilities (i.e., the MRS) does not equal the ratio of prices. This latter good is referred to as an **inessential good**. When goods are **perfect substitutes** an individual will purchase only the good which is cheapest and none of the other goods. A good for which a positive quantity is demanded irrespective of price is called an **essential good**.

To provide a graphical analysis of the consumer's problem, it is useful to define a **composite commodity** good 2, which is simply the expenditure on all other goods. Using Hick's composite commodity theorem, we can reduce the complicated choice problem to one of a choice involving the quantity of some good, say good 1, and the quantity of good 2.

Comparative Statics Exercises

Now that we've solved the consumer's choice problem, we want to examine the effect of changes in the exogenous variables on the quantity demanded; that is, we want to do a **comparative statics analysis**.

Income Changes — Consider a change in income, holding constant all other variables (prices). This simple exercise yields our first taxonomy: If consumption increases with increases in income, then the good is a **normal good**; if consumption falls with increases in income, it is an **inferior good**. If we were to draw a line through the various utility-maximizing bundles as income increases, it would form the **income-consumption path**. An **Engel curve** can also be drawn to show the relationship between income and quantity demanded.

Changes in Own Price — The effect of a change in the price of one good on the utility-maximizing consumption bundle can be represented by a **price-consumption path**. This path can be used to map out the relationship between the price of good 1 (for example) and the quantity demanded, known as the **ordinary demand curve**. Usually, a demand curve is negatively sloped. Notice that an **excise tax**, which adds a surcharge to the price of a good, would have the same effect as an increase in the price of that good. A **lump-sum tax**, by contrast, would reduce the individual's income, leaving prices unchanged.

Changes in the Price of Another Good — When the price of another good, good 2, changes, the response in the consumption of good 1 depends on the relationship between the two goods. The second taxonomy: If an increase in the price of good 2 elicits an increase in the consumption of good 1, then good 1 is a **substitute** for good

2. If the quantity demanded of good 1 falls in response to the increase in the price of good 2, then the good 1 is a **complement** of good 2.

Elasticities

To measure these various effects of price and income changes on the quantity demanded of good 1, we need a unitless measure — one that doesn't change if we measure prices in dollars or British pounds, or quantities in kilograms or tonnes. The economic measure of responsiveness is called **elasticity**, which is the percentage change in quantity demanded with the percentage change in some economic variable (for example, income, price of good 2, or price of good 1).

The **price elasticity of demand**, which measures the demand response to changes in the good's own price, is usually negative. To make things easier, we talk about the absolute value of this elasticity. When the price elasticity of demand is greater than 1, the good is said to be **elastic**; when it is less than 1, it is an **inelastic** good. As the names suggest, an elastic good is relatively more responsive to price changes than an inelastic good. Moreover, when the good is price-inelastic (elastic), the **price consumption path** is positively (negatively) sloped, and total expenditures decrease (increase) for decreases in the price of the good.

The responsiveness of demand to changes in the price of other goods can be measured by the **cross-price elasticity**. Cross-price elasticity is positive when the goods are substitutes and negative when the goods are complementary. Similarly, **income elasticity** measures how demand changes with income. Normal goods have positive income elasticities while inferior goods have negative income elasticities. The magnitude of the income elasticity also provides useful information: a value greater than one indicates that the good is a **luxury** good, while a value between zero and one reflects a **necessity** good.

When the change in the **exogenous** variable (e.g., price or income) is very small, then the appropriate method of calculating elasticity uses the **marginal** or **point elasticity** measure. With large changes in prices or income, the **arc elasticity** measure is used. Unless otherwise stated, elasticity refers to marginal or point elasticity.

KEY WORDS

Arc elasticity

Attainable consumption bundles

Budget constraint

Budget line

Comparative statics analysis

Complement

Composite commodity

Corner solution

Cross-price elasticity

Demand functions

Elastic

Elasticity

Endogenous variables

Engel curve

Essential good

Excise tax

Exogenous variables
Income-consumption path
Income elasticity
Inelastic
Inessential good
Inferior good
Inflation
Interior solution
Lump-sum tax
Law of demand
Luxury
Marginal or point elasticity
Necessity
No money illusion
Normal good
Ordinary demand curve
Opportunity cost
Perfect substitutes
Price-consumption path
Price elasticity of demand
Pure inflation
Real income
Relative prices
Representative consumer
Substitute
System of demand functions

CASE STUDY: GREENHOUSE GASES AND RATIONING GASOLINE IN CANADA[1]

The issue of climate change is on the global policy agenda. In December 1997, representatives from 160 countries, including Canada, met in Kyoto, Japan for the *United Nations Framework Convention on Climate Change*. Canada, as a signatory to the *Kyoto Protocol*, has agreed to reduce its greenhouse gas emissions to 6% lower than 1990 levels by the years 2008–2012. The burning of fossil fuels accounts for at least 80% of greenhouse gas emissions in Canada. One of the major sources of fossil fuel emissions is gasoline use in automobiles — indeed, Canada has one of the highest per capita consumption of gasoline in the world. Various conservation policies have been suggested to encourage Canadians to reduce their consumption of gasoline — including additional taxes on gasoline and/or on automobiles. Another type of policy would impose more direct restrictions on gasoline consumption, similar to the policies that were discussed during the oil crisis of the early 1970s.

Suppose that the following rationing policy were imposed. Each individual is given a certain number of tickets, say 100, every month. Each ticket would allow the purchase of one litre of gasoline at $0.75 (1980 prices). If an individual wanted to purchase more than 100 litres of gasoline per month, he or she would have to pay $2 per litre. Tickets could not be transferred between individuals nor between months. The price of gasoline at the time that this policy was discussed was $1.25 per litre.

A What would an individual's budget constraint for gasoline and all other goods under the two-tier price system look like, given a monthly income of $M = \$500$?

B On an indifference curve diagram, show an individual who consumes less gasoline under this policy than if the price were uniform at $1.25 per litre. Is it possible for an individual (with a $500 income) to consume more gasoline under this two-tier scheme? Illustrate this situation.

Consider an alternative rationing scheme. Instead of charging two prices for gasoline, suppose that, as before, 100 nontransferable ration tickets are given to each driver per month. However, under this scheme, the individual must pay one ration ticket and $1.25 (the current price) for each litre of gasoline. No more than 100 litres of gasoline can be purchased per month.

[1] This case study is challenging. The student is advised to work thorugh the practice problems and chapter exercises before trying it.

C Using an indifference curve diagram, show an individual with a monthly income of $500 who is unaffected by this second rationing scheme relative to the nonrationing situation. On another diagram, show the case of an individual (with a $500 income) who experiences a decline in utility from this scheme relative to the initial situation.

D Given your analyses in **A** to **C**, which policy do you think is the more effective in conserving gasoline? Explain.

EXERCISES

Multiple-Choice

Choose the correct answer to each question. There is only one correct answer to each question.

1 An individual with an *MRS* of milkshakes for hamburgers equal to 1/3 is maximizing utility if

- **a** The price of a hamburger is three times that of a milkshake.
- **b** The price of a hamburger equals that of a milkshake.
- **c** The price of a hamburger is 1/3 the price of a milkshake.
- **d** She trades three milkshakes for a hamburger.
- **e** None of the above.

2 An individual is currently maximizing his utility subject to his monthly budget constraint at point A in Figure 3.1. The government wants to ration goods 1 and 2 and to achieve this by giving each consumer 10 ration tickets per month. In addition to money, the individual must pay one ration ticket per unit of good 1 and $2\frac{1}{2}$ ration tickets per unit of good 2. The individual must now consume

- **a** Less of good 1 than given by bundle *A*.
- **b** Less of good 2 than at bundle *A*.
- **c** More of both goods.
- **d** The same as bundle *A*.
- **e** Cannot say without more information.

3 In Figure 3.2, which of the following is true?

- **a** The price of Brie per kilogram is two-thirds the price of baguettes per dozen.
- **b** The price of Brie per kilogram is 1.5 times the price of baguettes per dozen.
- **c** The individual will consume 1.5 times more baguettes than Brie.
- **d** The individual will consume 1.5 times more Brie than baguettes.
- **e** None of the above.

4 A consumer consumes only two goods, good 1 and good 2. The marginal rate of substitution of good 2 for good 1 at any point (x_1, x_2) is x_2/x_1. Suppose that income M = $260, p_1 = $2, p_2 = $3, and the consumer is consuming 40 units of good 1 and 60 units of good 2. Which of the following is true?

- **a** The consumer is maximizing utility subject to her income.

FIGURE 3.1

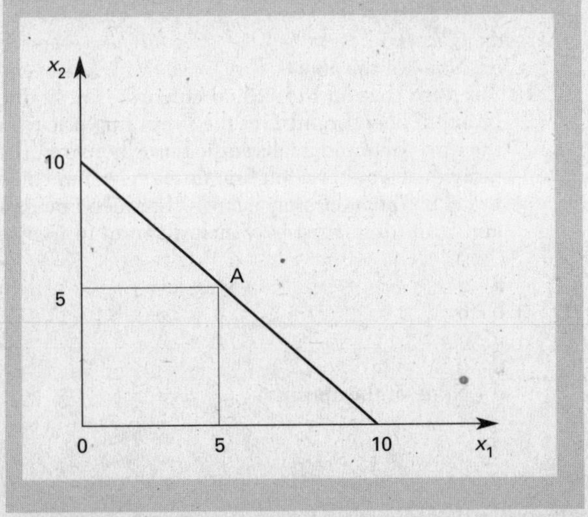

FIGURE 3.2

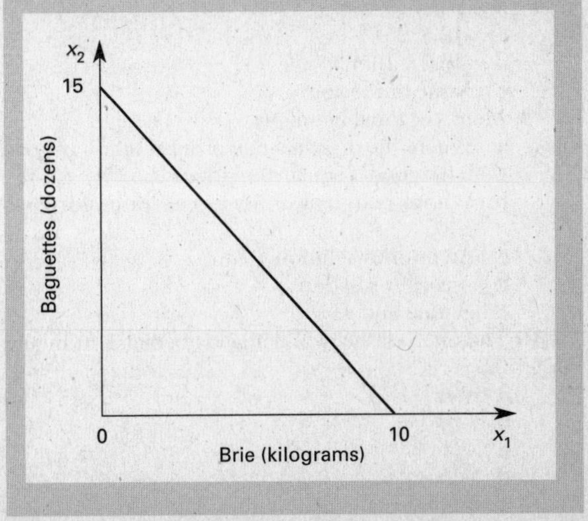

b The consumer could increase utility by increasing her consumption of good 1 and decreasing her consumption of good 2.
c The consumer could increase her utility by increasing her consumption of good 2 and decreasing her consumption of good 1.
d The consumer should increase her consumption of both goods because she is not spending all the income.
e None of the above.

5 An increase in income results in
a An upward shift in the demand curve for an inferior good.
b An upward shift in the demand curve for a normal good.
c No change in demand because price will rise and offset any possible increase in the quantity demanded brought about by the income increase.
d A movement along the demand curve.
e Both **a** and **b.**

6 A movement along the demand curve for a good must occur
a When the buyer's income increases.
b When the prices of other goods change.
c When the buyer's tastes change.
d When the price of the good decreases.
e None of the above.

Answer questions **7–9** with reference to the following information: Suppose an individual, Marc, buys two goods, $p_1 = \$2$ and $p_2 = \$1$, his income is \$50 and his preferences are described by the utility function $U(x_1, x_2) = 3x_1 + x_2$.

7 Marc considers these two goods to be
a Perfect complements.
b Perfect substitutes.
c Luxury goods.
d Necessity goods.
e Both **b** and **d.**

8 Marc's optimal consumption bundle is:
a (0, 50).
b (25, 0).
c (12.5, 25).
d (16.67, 16.67).
e None of the above.

9 Marc's optimal bundle is
a Where the marginal rate of substitution of good 2 for good 1 equals the price ratio.
b Where marginal utility equals price for each good.
c An interior solution.
d A corner solution.
e Both **a** and **c.**

10 The price elasticity of demand at point A in Figure 3.3 is
a $-1/3$
b $-2/5$
c $-2/3$
d $-3/2$
e There is not enough information to tell.

FIGURE 3.3

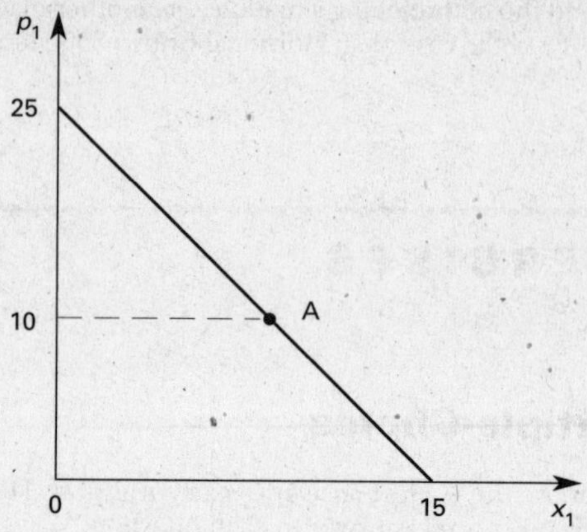

11 An individual's demand curve for peaches is

$$x_1 = 10 - 3p + 0.5M$$

where x_1 is the quantity of peaches measured in 10-kilogram units, p is the price per bushel in dollars, and M is the consumer's income in thousands of dollars. An individual consumes 20 kilograms when the price is \$5 per kilogram and his income is \$10 000. At these values, the price elasticity of demand equals
a -3
b $-(5/2)/3$
c $-(5/2) \times 3$
d $-(5/20) \times 3$
e None of the above.

12 For the demand curve in Exercise 11, the income elasticity at the given values is
a 0.5
b $(10/2) \times 0.5$
c $(10\,000/20) \times 0.5$
d $(10/2)/0.5$
e None of the above.

13 Suppose that an individual consumes only one brand of beer, brand 1, at the prevailing prices. If the price of brand 2 falls sufficiently, however, the individual would switch brands and consume only brand 2. The indifference curves between brands 1 and 2 are described by which diagram in Figure 3.4?
a a
b b
c c
d d
e None of the above.

FIGURE 3.4

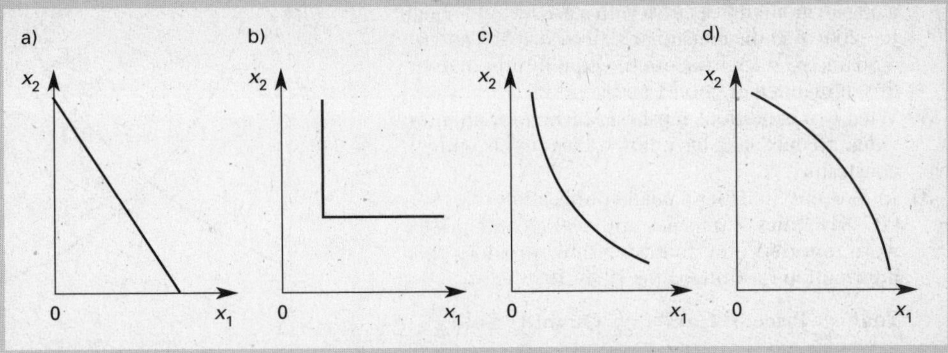

True-False

14 Since the real price of automobiles has increased but the quantity demanded has also increased over recent years, the demand curve for automobiles must be positively sloped.

15 There is no money illusion for the demand curve $x_1 = 5M(p_2/p_1)^{1/2}$.

16 If a consumer's income rises because of inflation then she will be able to afford a different bundle of goods that will make her better off.

17 A consumer with endowments of two goods x_1 and x_2 loses 50% of x_1 and doubles her endowment of x_2. We can then say that her budget constraint will become steeper.

18 If the income elasticity of a good is negative, the demand curve of that good must be negatively sloped.

19 If, at the utility-maximizing bundle of good 1 and good 2, the *MRS* of good 2 for good 1 is greater than p_1/p_2, then good 1 is an inessential good.

20 Suppose that an individual consumes only two goods, good 1 and good 2. If the price of good 1 rises, with all else constant, and the price elasticity of demand for good 1 is -0.7, then the quantity of good 2 will increase.

21 If an individual's income is the same before and after an excise tax is imposed on good 1 and the demand for good 1 is elastic, the excise tax will lead to an increase in spending on other consumer goods.

22 Since a decrease in the price of one unit along a linear demand curve will result in an increase in the quantity demanded by a constant amount, the price elasticity is constant for all quantities along a linear demand curve.

23 If the cross-price elasticity between goods 1 and 2 is positive, then the indifference curves must be those given in Figure 3.5.

FIGURE 3.5

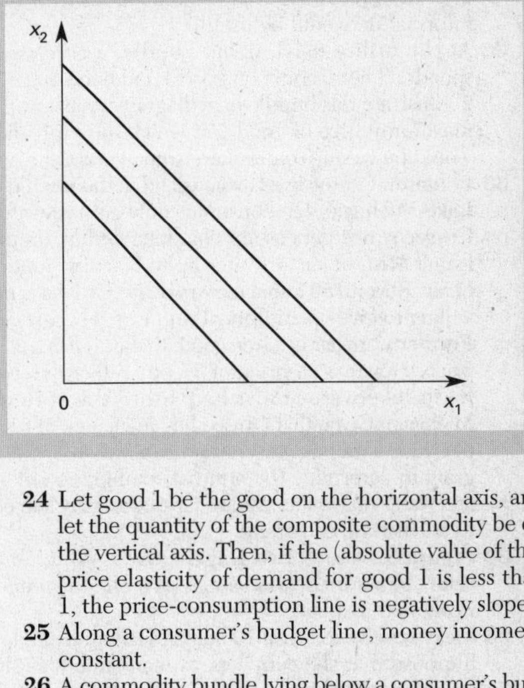

24 Let good 1 be the good on the horizontal axis, and let the quantity of the composite commodity be on the vertical axis. Then, if the (absolute value of the) price elasticity of demand for good 1 is less than 1, the price-consumption line is negatively sloped.

25 Along a consumer's budget line, money income is constant.

26 A commodity bundle lying below a consumer's budget line must be inferior to all bundles lying on the budget line.

27 Assume that a certain individual consumes only goods 1 and 2. If the prices of good 1 and good 2 double and his income doubles, then the quantities demanded for goods 1 and 2 will not change.

28 If a decline in the prices of agricultural products results in a reduction in the *consumption* of these goods by many farmers, then these products must be inferior goods.

Short Problems

29 Suppose the consumer equilibrium is achieved along an indifference curve with a $MRS(x_1, x_2)$ equal to $-200/x_1^2$. If the consumer's income is \$60 and p_1 = \$6 and p_2 = \$3, what are the equilibrium quantities demanded of good 1 and good 2?

30 What two conditions must be satisfied for an individual to maximize his utility subject to his budget constraint?

31 In a recent Statistics Canada publication (No. 63-007-XIB), new cars sales and average car prices were reported. The following table provides this information for Canada for 1996–1998.

Year	Price of Cars	Quantity Sold
1996	\$21 066	807 535
1997	21 937	943 684
1998	21 901	977 834

Looking at the 1996 and 1997 data, can we conclude that the demand for new cars is upward sloping? In order to analyze these data, what further information would be useful?

32 At the utility-maximizing bundle, a consumer spends all her income on good 1 and none on good 2. Illustrate this bundle on a diagram and show the maximum price of good 2 at which the individual would be willing to purchase some good 2.

33 Robinson Crusoe lives on an island in the middle of Lake Michigan. He consumes only air and water. Crusoe's preferences are characterized by diminishing *MRS* of air for water up to 50 cubic meters of air. Beyond 50 cubic meters of air, Crusoe is not willing to give up additional water to get more air. Furthermore, air is a free good; that is, it has a zero price. However, a price of \$1 per cubic meter of fresh lake water must be paid to the state of Michigan. Given that Crusoe has an income of \$100 per year from social security benefits, use a diagram to determine the optimal combination of air and water that will maximize Crusoe's utility subject to his income constraint.

34 Figure 3.6 shows two Engel curves. Which one refers to a normal good and which one to an inferior good? Explain.

35 Vicky is endowed with 10 hours of labour each day. Suppose that she can work as many hours as she likes (up to 10 hours) at an hourly wage of \$15. If she works, however, she has to pay a babysitter \$5 per hour. Vicky's utility is defined over two goods — x_1 and x_2 — with good 2 being a composite commodity. Write out Vicky's utility-maximization problem. In this case, how many hours per day will she work? Suppose, now, that Vicky's utility function is defined over these two goods and one "bad" which represents how much labour she supplies to the market. How would this affect Vicky's utility-maximization problem?

FIGURE 3.6

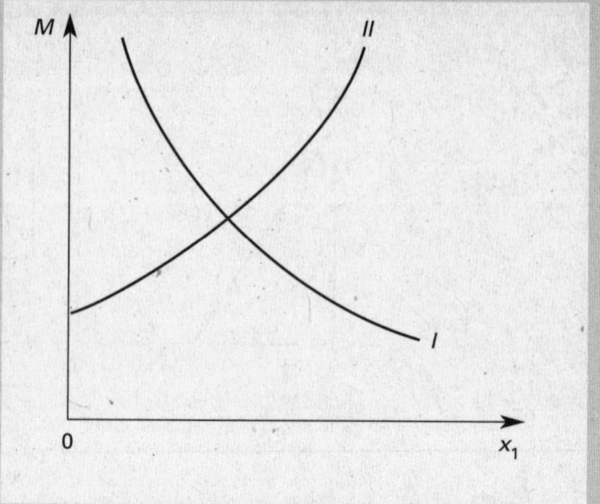

36 Giuseppi owns a vineyard in northern Italy. He provides food and shelter for the grape growers, who make the wine and pay Giuseppi a fixed amount of wine. The workers' rent is Giuseppi's only source of income. Giuseppi consumes some of the wine and sells the rest for income to purchase a second good, good 2, the composite commodity. Suppose that the price of wine p_w rises. Will Giuseppi consume less wine? Explain, using diagrams.

37 Assume that a family consumes the combination of salt and "all other goods" described by point A in Figure 3.7. Show an example of the new utility-maximizing bundle if the price of salt decreases and salt is a price-inelastic good.

38 Compare the price elasticities of demand at *every price* for the two demand curves

FIGURE 3.7

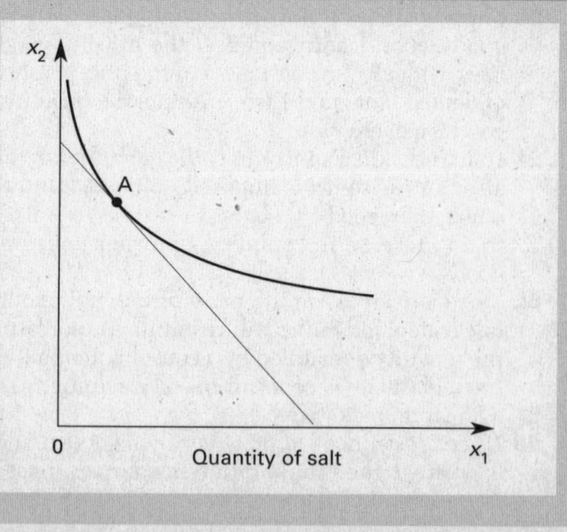

$$x_1 = 450 - p_1$$

$$x_1 = 150 - \frac{p_1}{3}$$

Explain your answer by illustrating the two demand curves.

39 The income (point) elasticity of demand for bread is 1.0 and the own price (point) elasticity is −0.4. The price of bread is \$2, and income is \$100. If price rises to \$3, what level of income would leave the quantity demanded approximately unchanged?

Long Problems

40 The Smith family had a total income of \$30 000 in 2001. Of this amount, its expenditures for certain foods were

Fish	\$5 000
Bread	1 600
Cereal	1 000
Milk	1 400

In 2002, the family's income increased to \$40 000 and its expenditures on the above items were

Fish	\$7 000
Bread	1 000
Cereal	1 400
Milk	1 900

a What assumptions must be made to calculate the income elasticity of demand for any of the food products using the given information?

b Having made these assumptions, calculate the Smith's income elasticity of demand for each of the items listed.

c Is the income elasticity you calculated necessarily the same for all income levels? Why or why not?

41 Suppose that the demand for pencils by a representative consumer is given by

$$x = 19.4 + 0.4M - 8p + 2p_f$$

where x is quantity demanded of pencils, M is income in thousands of dollars, p is price of pencils in dollars, and p_f is price of fountain pens in dollars. Suppose that the values of these variables for the consumer are

$$x = 25$$
$$M = 20$$
$$p = \$0.80$$
$$p_f = \$2$$

a Calculate the own-price elasticity, cross-price elasticity, and income elasticity of demand for pencils, given this information.

b Suppose that an increase in the price of ink refills results in a 20% increase in the price of a fountain pen. What will be the percentage increase in the quantity demanded of pencils?

***42** Suppose that an individual's utility function is given by

$$U = x_1 x_2$$

where x_1 is his own consumption (in dollars) and x_2 is his charitable contributions (in dollars). Assume that the individual's income is \$45 000 per year.

a Solve for the optimal choice of the individual's own consumption and charitable contributions, using the method of Lagrange multipliers.

b Suppose that the government puts a tax of 50% on own consumption but charitable contributions are tax-free. Calculate the new optimum in this case.

***43** Suppose an individual's preferences are defined over two goods: baguettes and Brie cheese. Her utility function is $U(x_1, x_2) = 2\,x_1\,x_2$ where x_1 represents baguettes and x_2 represents each 100 gram piece of Brie cheese.

a Write out the utility maximization problem and solve for the demand functions for baguettes and Brie using the method of Lagrange multipliers.

b What are the two conditions which characterize an interior solution to this problem?

c Suppose that the price of a baguette is \$1, the price of 100 grams of Brie is \$4, and income is \$100 per month. Determine this individual's optimal monthly consumption bundle.

d The government has decided to tax Brie cheese at a rate of \$1 per 100 grams. How much money will it collect?

e Suppose now that the government decides to levy a lump sum tax rather than the excise tax described in part **d**. The lump sum tax will collect as much revenue as did the excise tax. What is the new optimal consumption bundle for this consumer?

f Which tax is preferable from the point of view of the government? The individual?

g Suppose that, rather than as a means to generate revenue, the government wants the tax to discourage the consumption of Brie because of the health effects associated with eating too much rich foods. Would this change your answer to part **f**? Explain.

44 Suppose that James loves coffee (x_1) and doughnuts (x_2). In fact, James must have 2 doughnuts with every cup of coffee (any other combination is simply unacceptable).

a Write out a utility function that describes James's preferences.

b Calculate James's demand functions for coffee and doughnuts.

c Suppose that a cup of coffee costs \$1.50 and a doughnut costs \$1 and monthly income is \$70. How many coffees and doughnuts would James consume in one month?

d Suppose the government imposes an excise tax

FIGURE 3.8

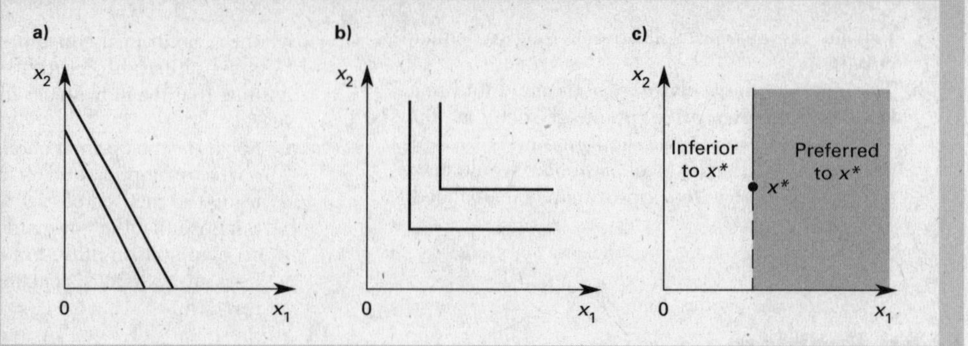

on doughnuts of \$0.75 — how would this affect James's optimal consumption bundle?

e Given a choice between an excise tax and a lump sum tax thatcollects the same revenue, which would James prefer and why?

45 We offer three explanations for the decline in the average family size in Canada. Illustrate the explanations with an indifference curve diagram for "children" and the composite commodity good 2.

a Children have become more expensive.
b People's tastes for large families have changed.
c Children are an inferior good.

46 An individual's income is \$1 000 per week. Her preferences over goods 1 and 2 can be described by convex indifference curves. The price of good 2 is \$1. Using an indifference curve diagram, derive the individual's demand curve for good 1. To derive the demand curve, find three points on the demand curve at which the price p_1 of good 1 is \$2.50, \$5, and \$10. Make the following assumptions: The demand curve is linear, the point of unitary elasticity is at a price of \$5, and the individual maximizes her utility subject to her budget constraint. Make sure your diagram reflects the information given.

47 Figure 3.8 shows sets of "indifference curves" representing preferences that violate one (or more) of the assumptions of consumer choice. In Exercise **28** of Chapter 2, you identified the assumption(s) violated in each case. In this exercise, you are to determine the effect that these nonstandard indifference curves have on the demand curves. For each set of preferences, superimpose a budget constraint on the indifference curve map and find the utility-maximizing bundle of good 1 and good 2. Then let the price of good 1 change to generate points on the demand curve for good 1. Do the preferences represented in the figure imply downward-sloping demand curves? Explain.

48 Suppose that a consumer has the indifference curves illustrated in Figure 3.9.

a Draw a budget constraint and find the consumer's utility-maximizing bundle of goods.
b Is there any portion of the indifference curve that the consumer will never be on? Explain.
c If the indifference curves were made convex (for example, if a line segment were to join points A and B on indifference curve I_1), then what would be the individual's utility-maximizing bundle of goods? When might this lead to incorrect predictions?

FIGURE 3.9

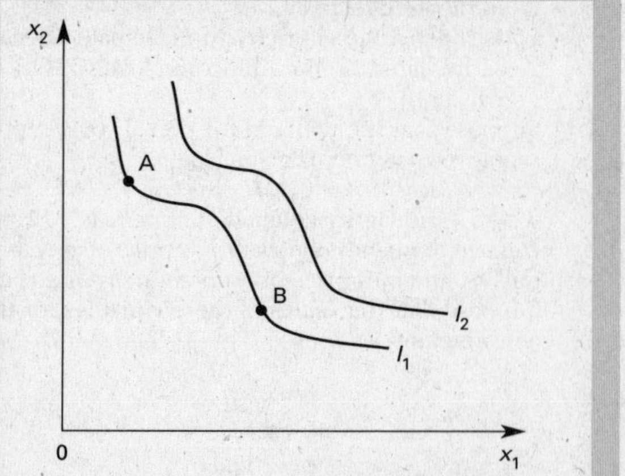

ANSWERS TO CHAPTER 3

Case Study

A The budget constraint under the rationing scheme is shown in Figure A3.1. The intercept on the good 2 axis is \$500, which is the maximum expenditure on good 2 (if gasoline consumption equals zero). On the g axis, the intercept is 312.5, which is the maximum number of litres that could be purchased if $x_2 = 0$. To show this, consider the number of litres above 100 affordable at a price of \$2. The amount of money spent on the first 100 litres with the ration tickets is (\$0.75)(100) = \$75. The additional litres that can be afforded at (\$500 – \$75)/2 = 212.5; hence, 100 + 212.5 = 312.5. At $l = 100$, the budget constraint is kinked; the slope is flatter for $l \leq 100$ than for $l > 100$ to reflect the lower price of gasoline (\$0.75 versus \$2). At $l = 100$, \$425 remains to be spent on good 2.

B The prerationing budgetline is given by AB in Figure A3.2. The individual who consumes less is shown in Figure A3.2a. The individual reduces gasoline consumption from l_0 to l_1. The individual who consumes more is shown in Figure A3.2b. This individual increases gasoline consumption from l_0 to l_1 as a result of the scheme.

C An individual who is unaffected by the second rationing scheme is shown in Figure A3.3a. The utility of the individual who is worse off under the second rationing scheme is shown in Figure A3.3b. Point C is not available because the consumer is not allowed to purchase more than 100 litres.

D The strict rationing regime (the second scheme) will be more *effective* in conserving gasoline. No one will ever be induced to consume more gasoline as a result of it. However, this rationing scheme is not necessarily more efficient in that it may result in a larger loss in utility.

FIGURE A3.1

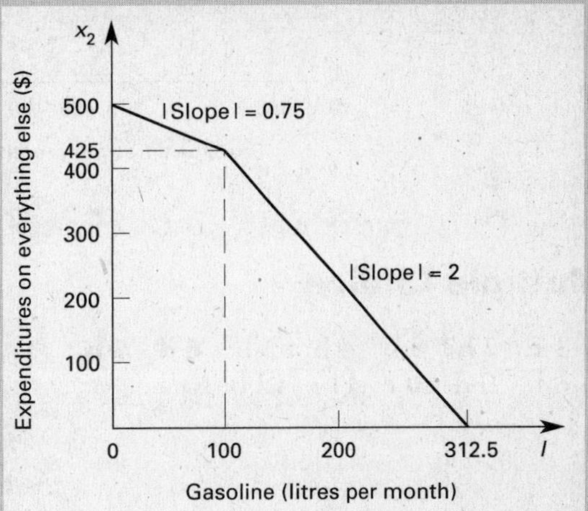

FIGURE A3.2

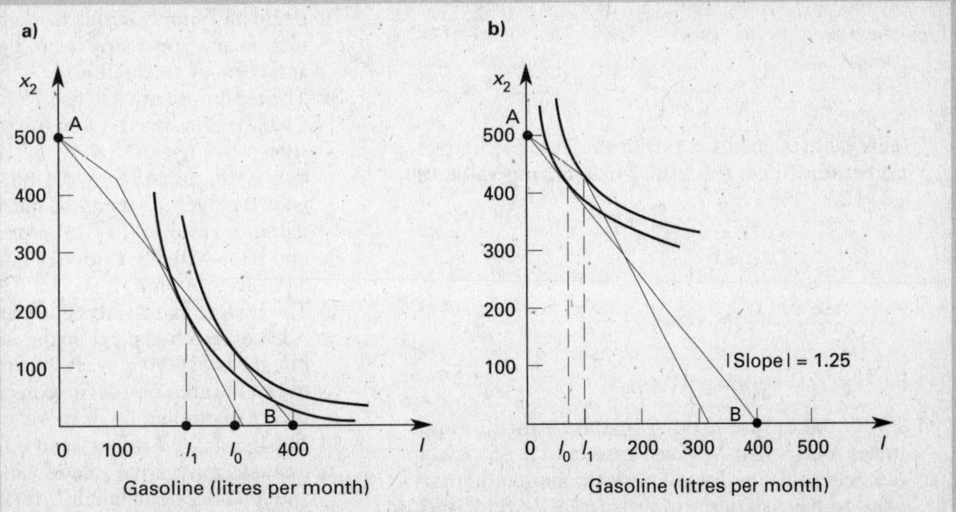

FIGURE A3.3

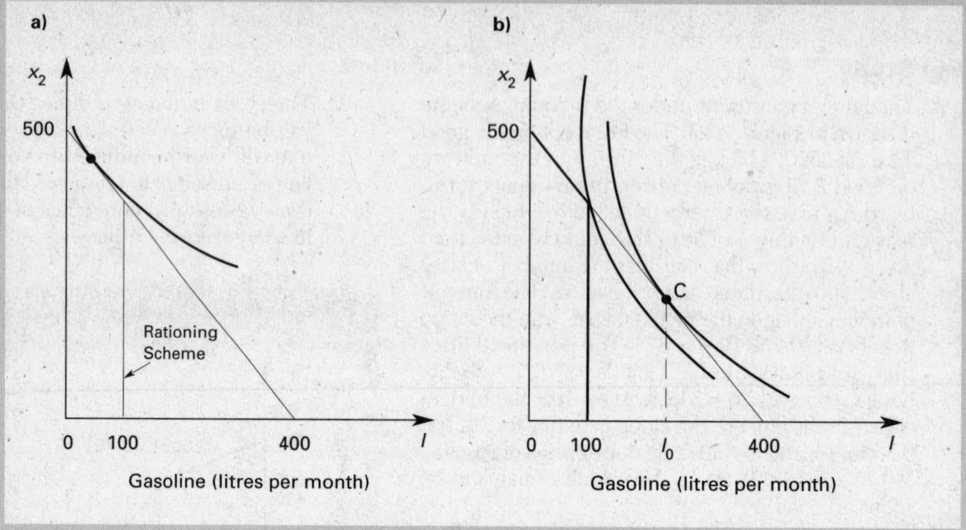

Multiple Choice

1 c 2 b 3 b 4 b 5 b 6 d 7 b
8 b 9 d 10 c 11 c 12 b 13 a

True-False

14 F 15 F 16 F 17 F 18 F
19 F 20 F 21 T 22 F 23 F
24 F 25 T 26 F 27 T 28 F

Short Problems

29 The ratio of the price of good 1 to the price of good 2 is \$6/\$3 = 2. Setting the ratio of prices equal to the *MRS* gives

$$\frac{200}{(x_1)^2} = 2$$

and so

$$x_1 = 10$$

This value of good 1 is substituted into the budget constraint to get the utility-maximizing value of good 2.

$$60 = (6)(10) + 3x_2$$
$$x_2 = 0$$

30 a

$$MRS(x_1^*, x_2^*) = \frac{p_1}{p_2}$$

b

$$M = p_1 x_1^* + p_2 x_2^*$$

31 These data present equilibrium quantities and prices each period — which arise from the forces of demand and supply. Suppose the demand curve were to have shifted upwards from 1996 to 1997 (because of, say, an increase in consumer income), this would account for the increase in price and quantity purchased over this period. To analyze these data and provide reasons for the fluctuations in price and quantity purchased, we would need information on all of the factors underlying demand and supply in this market (e.g., income, population size, prices of related goods like gasoline, and costs of production).

32 The maximum price of good 2 for which some good 2 will be purchased (given the price of good 1) is p_2' shown in Figure A3.4. At p_2', $MRS(\bar{x}_1, 0) = p_1/p_2'$; that is, the price of good 1 relative to the price of good 2 equals the marginal rate of substitution evaluated at $x_1 = \bar{x}$ and $x_2 = 0$. For any higher price of good 2, $x_2 = 0$; for a price of good 2 lower than p_2', a positive amount of good 2 will be demanded.

33 The budget line is a straight line as shown in Figure A3.5. Air is a free good, so the maximum that can be bought is \$100/0 = ∞. Robinson is indifferent between bundles on AB; he consumes 100 cubic meters of water and 50 or more cubic meters of air.

34 In Figure 3.6, *I* refers to an inferior good because it shows a negative relationship between income and quantity demanded; *II* refers to a normal good because it shows a positive relationship between income and good 1.

FIGURE A3.4

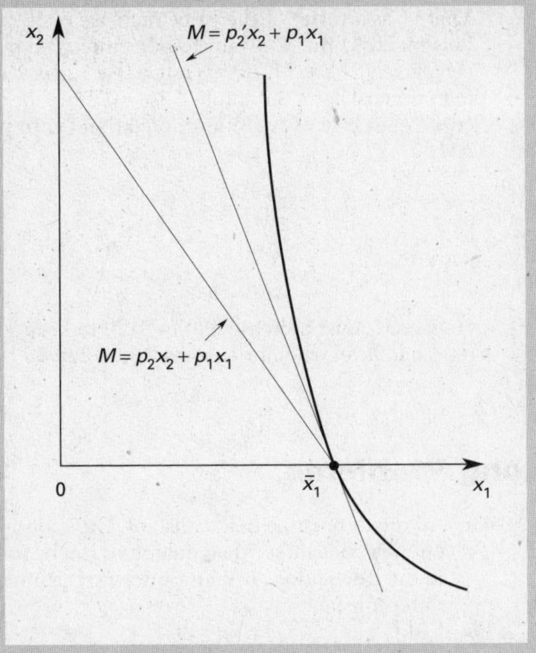

35 Vicky's utility-maximization problem is: Max $U(x_1, x_2)$ subject to: $(p_1/p_2)\,x_1 + x_2 = (15 - 5)L/p_2$. Since there is no disutility associated with working in this problem, and utility is gained from the income earned, she will work 10 hours per day. If her utility falls with hours worked, then her utility function will contain an argument that reflects this "bad": her problem becomes Max $U(x_1, x_2, L)$ subject to: $(p_1/p_2)x_1 + x_2 = (15 - 5)L/p_2$. The treatment of labour in the utility function can be handled in a few ways. In the version presented, you have to remember that L is a "bad" and hence U_L (the partial derivative of the utility function with respect to L) is negative. Alternatively, you could put $-L$ in the Utility function, noting that U_{-L} is positive. Finally, labour economists who look at the labour-leisure choice of individuals would define another "good" — leisure — which is put into the utility function and is clearly a function of the amount of labour worked. This latter approach is detailed in Chapter 14. When explicit account is taken of the disutility associated with labour, then hours worked depends upon balancing the marginal benefits associated with working the last hour (money) with the marginal costs (disutility). We can no longer say without further information whether Vicky will work the entire 10 hours each day.

36 Not necessarily. Wine is a source of income. When the price of wine increases, the maximum amount of wine that Giuseppi can consume remains at $\bar{w}$ (because he is paid in *quantity* of food by the workers). However, Giuseppi can sell all the food and earn $p_w{}'\bar{w}$ to spend on everything else. Giuseppi is shown in Figure A3.6 to consume more wine as a result of this increase in income.

37 Salt is shown to have a price-inelastic demand curve in Figure A3.7 by the upward-sloping price consumption curve.

38 Rewriting the demand curves with price as the dependent variable gives

$$p_1 = 450 - x_1 \quad \text{and} \quad p_1 = 450 - 3x_1$$

Note that the second demand curve is an "isoelastic shift" of the first demand curve; both demand curves have the same price intercept but different slopes. The price elasticities for the two demand curves are the same at every price. The demand curves are illustrated in Figure A3.8.

FIGURE A3.5

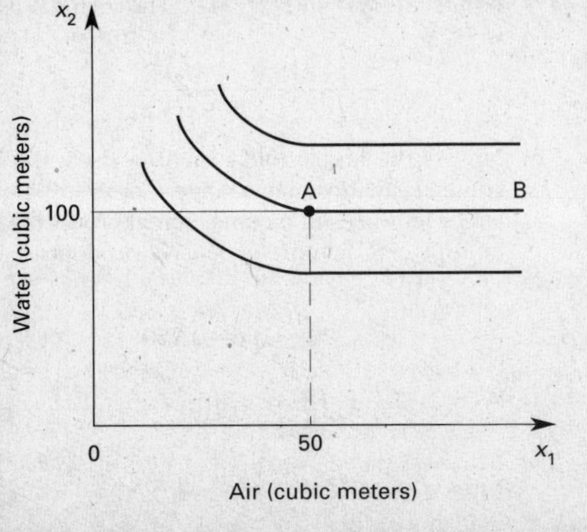

FIGURE A3.6

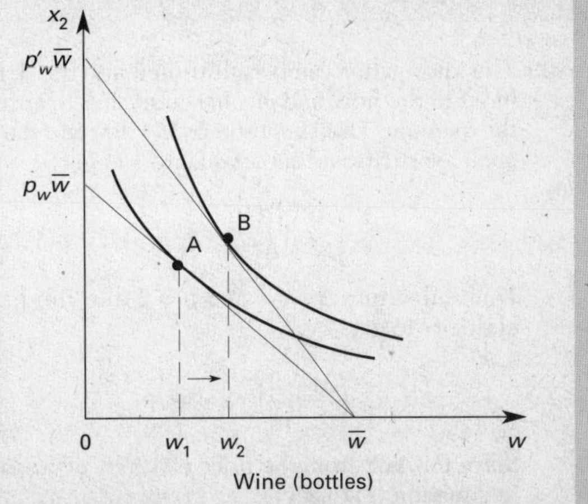

FIGURE A3.7

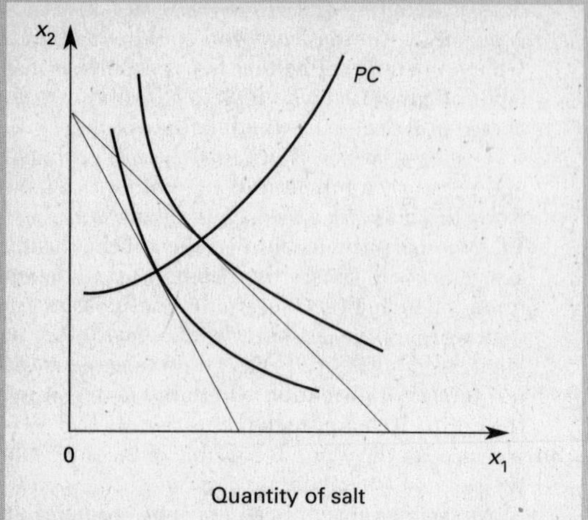

FIGURE A3.8

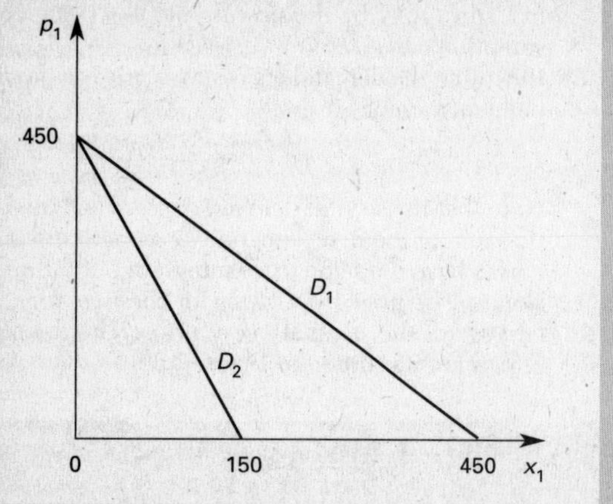

39 The information can be substituted into the definitions of the price and income elasticities to answer the question. That is, substitute $M = 100$ into the income elasticity and set it equal to 1 to get

$$\left(\frac{\Delta x}{x}\right)\left(\frac{100}{\Delta M}\right) = 1 \quad (1)$$

Now substitute $\Delta p = 1$ and $p = 2$ into the price elasticity to get

$$\left(\frac{\Delta x}{x}\right)\left(\frac{2}{1}\right) = -0.4 \quad (2)$$

Solve for $\Delta x/x$ from the price elasticity expression in equation (2) to get

$$\frac{\Delta x}{x} = -0.2$$

That is, as a result of the price increase of 50%, x falls by 20%. But we want to determine the percentage change in M ($\Delta M/M$) such that x goes back to its original level. Substitute $\Delta x/x = 0.2$ into the income elasticity expression in equation (1) to get ΔM:

$$\frac{0.2 \times 100}{\Delta M} = 1$$

and so

$$\Delta M = 20$$

Hence, M must increase \$20 to \$120 to keep x at the same level when price rises from \$2 to \$3.

Long Problems

40 a All prices must be held constant. Expenditures on the goods rather than quantities can be used in the calculations because prices are assumed to be constant.

b Fish

$$\frac{(7000 - 5000)35\,000}{(40\,000 - 30\,000)6000} = 1.17$$

Bread

$$\frac{(1000 - 1600)35\,000}{10\,000 \times 1300} = -1.62$$

Cereal

$$\frac{(1400 - 1000)35\,000}{10\,000 \times 12\,000} = 1.17$$

Milk

$$\frac{(1900 - 1400)35\,000}{10\,000 \times 1650} = 1.06$$

Note that the elasticities are the "arc elasticities"; that is, they are calculated between two points (x_1^1, M_1) and (x_1^2, M_2). The formula used is

$$\frac{(x_1^2 - x_1^1)(M_1 + M_2)/2}{(M_2 - M_1)(x_1^1 + x_1^2)/2}$$

c No. As the household's income rises, the income elasticities may change. For example, for larger increases in income, cereal products may be replaced by more expensive products.

41 a

$$e_p = -8\left(\frac{0.8}{25}\right) = -0.256$$

$$e_f = 2\left(\frac{2}{25}\right) = 0.16$$

$$e_M = 0.4\left(\frac{20}{25}\right) = 0.32$$

b Since $\%\Delta x/\%\Delta p_f = 0.16$, then for $\%\Delta p_f = 20$, $\%\Delta x = 0.16 \times 20 = 3.2$. That is, a 20% increase in the cost of using a fountain pen increases pencil use by 3.2%.

*42 **a** Using the method of Lagrange, we have the Lagrange function $L(x_1, x_2, \lambda) = x_1x_2 - \lambda(45\,000 - x_1 - x_2)$ which is to be maximized with respect to x_1, x_2, and λ. Note that the price of own consumption and charitable giving is one dollar. Setting all the partial derivatives to zero we have the following three equation systems: (1) $x_2 + \lambda = 0$, (2) $x_1 + \lambda = 0$, and (3) $45\,000 - x_1 - x_2 = 0$. From (1) and (2) we have that $x_1 = x_2$, substituting this into (3) gives us $x_1 = x_2 = 22\,500$.

b A 50% tax on own consumption effectively raised the price of good 1 to 1.5. Plugging this into the Lagrange function of part **a** and setting the resulting three partial derivatives equal to zero gives us $x_1 = 15\,000$ and $x_2 = 22\,500$.

*43 **a** $$\text{Max } U(x_1, x_2) = 2x_1 x_2$$

subject to: $p_1 x_1 + p_2 x_2 = M$

Set up the Lagrange multiplier problem by defining the function $L(x_1, x_2) = U(x_1, x_2) - \lambda(M - p_1x_1 - p_2 x_2)$ and maximize this function with respect to x_1, x_2, and λ (i.e., take the first derivative of L with respect to each of the three variables and set it equal to zero). This results in the following three first order conditions which must be solved simultaneously:

(1) $U_1(x_1, x_2) - \lambda p_1 = 0 \Rightarrow 2x_2 - \lambda p_1 = 0$
(2) $U_2(x_1, x_2) - \lambda p_2 = 0 \Rightarrow 2x_1 - \lambda p_2 = 0$
(3) $M - p_1 x_1 - p_2 x_2 = 0$

Where U_i refers to the partial differential of U with respect to x_i for $i = 1, 2$. Combining (1) and (2) we obtain the condition that $U_1/U_2 = p_1/p_2$ (or $x_2/x_1 = p_1/p_2$) — i.e., the ratio of the marginal utilities (the marginal rate of substitution between goods 1 and 2) is equal to the ratio of prices in equilibrium. This condition implies that $x_2 = (p_1/p_2)x_1$ and substituting this expression into (3) above and rearranging gives us that $x_1 = M/2p_1$ — the demand for good 1 — and substituting this into our expression for x_2 gives us the demand for good 2 which is: $x_2 = M/2p_2$.

b The two conditions are that the MRS equals the ratio of prices which we have demonstrated to be true and that the budget constraint is just satisfied which follows from the fact that we had to fulfill equation (3) above.

c From the demand functions we see that the optimal consumption bundle is 50 baguettes and 1.25 kilograms of cheese.

d You have to determine the new bundle of goods when the price of Brie becomes $5 per 100 grams — which is (50, 10). Thus the consumer will purchase ten 100 gram units of cheese and the government will collect $10.

e Now the price of Brie is back to $4 per 100 grams and this individual is taxed a lump sum of $10, meaning that her income becomes $90 — the new consumption bundle is (45, 11.25).

f The government is indifferent between the two taxes as it collects the same revenue (assuming that the costs of collecting the two taxes are the same). Individuals prefer the lump sum tax — to see this look at the $U(50,10) = 1000$ and compare it to $U(45, 11.25) = 1012.5$.

g Clearly if the government wants to discourage the consumption of Brie, an excise tax would be more successful than a lump-sum tax. One of the arguments put forth for taxing goods like cigarettes is that it serves to discourage the consumption of such goods as well as generating revenue for the government. Taxing individual goods leads to distortions in the market price mechanism, which may have other repercussions.

44 **a** $U(x_1, x_2) = \min\{x_1, 0.5x_2\}$ (or any monotonic transformation of this function like $\min\{2x_1, x_2\}$). Note that these goods are perfect complements for James.

b To calculate demand functions we cannot use the Lagrange multiplier method because the utility function is not differentiable. We know that the optimal bundle will be such that $x_1 = 0.5x_2$, i.e., no wastage, and that the budget constraint must be satisfied. Thus, we have two equations and two unknowns. Solving this two-equation system yields the following demand functions: $x_1 = M/(p_1 + 2p_2)$ and $x_2 = 2M/(p_1 + 2p_2)$.

c $x_1 = 20$ and $x_2 = 40$.

d $x_1 = 14$ and $x_2 = 28$ — yielding revenue of $28 \times \$0.75 = \$21$ for the government.

e If a lump sum tax of $28 were levied — James would choose $x_1 = 14$ and $x_2 = 28$, i.e., the same as in part **d**. This result should not surprise you. James considers these goods as perfect complements — hence a tax on one good will affect the consumption of both goods in the same way. There is no substituting between the "taxed" good and the other good (as you saw in question **43** above).

45 **a** If children are more expensive, the "price" of children is higher, pivoting the budget line inward as shown in Figure A3.9a.

b If tastes changed away from large families, then the indifference curves become flatter (indifference curve I_2 in Figure A3.9b) because households are less willing to give up large amounts of good 2 for large families.

c If children are an inferior good, then an increase in real income will reduce the number of children in families as shown in Figure A3.9c.

46 The maximum values of good 1 that can be consumed at prices $2.50, $5, and $10 are 400, 200, and 100, respectively. The utility-maximizing bundle of good 1 and good 2, constrained by the individual's income, are denoted by A, B, and C, respectively. The demand curve for good 1 is shown

FIGURE A3.9

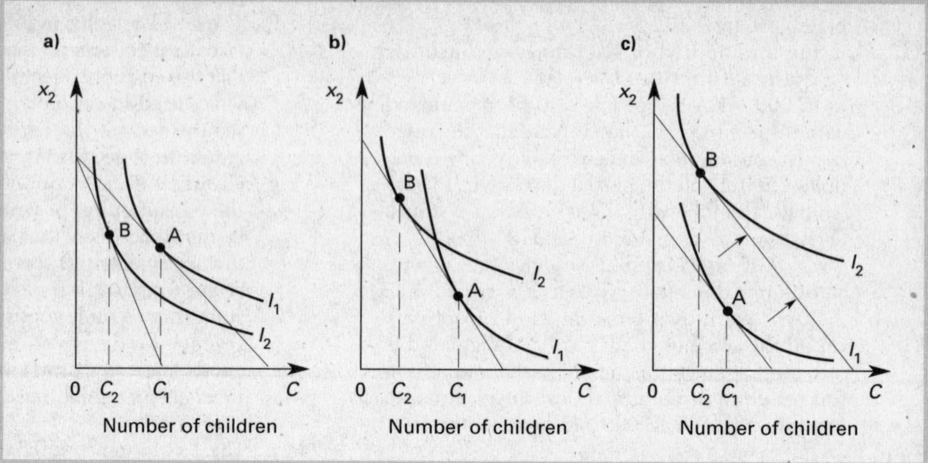

to be linear in Figure A3.10. For high prices, the demand is price-elastic, as indicated by the negatively sloped price-consumption curve (*PC*); for low prices, the demand is price-inelastic, as indicated by the positively sloped *PC*; the point of unitary elasticity is at $p_1 = \$5$. Since the point of unitary elasticity is at the midpoint of a linear demand, the intercept of the demand curve must be at $p_1 = \$10$.

47 The indifference curves in Figures 3.8a, b, and c represent perfect substitutes, perfect complements, and lexicographic preferences, respectively. To find the demand curves in each case, denote income by *M*, let the price of good 2 be \$1, and let the price of good $1(p_1)$ be p_1^1, p_1^2, and p_1^3, where $p_1^1 > p_1^2 > p_1^3$. The three budget lines corresponding to these prices are denoted in Figure A3.11 and A3.12 by *MC*, *MD*, and *ME*, respectively.

Consider the case of *perfect substitutes* in Figure A3.12. For a price of good 1 equal to p_1^1, utility is maximized where $x_1 = 0$. For a lower price p_1^2, the consumer switches from good 2 to good 1 and consumes M/p_1^2. For lower prices, $x_2 = 0$ and $x_1 = M/p_1$. The consumer switches from good 2 to good 1 at $\hat{p}_1$. For prices higher than $\hat{p}_1$, $x_1 = 0$; for lower prices, x_1 increases with decreases in p_1.

Next consider the case of perfect complements in Figure A3.12a. The utility-maximizing bundle is given by the corners of the indifference curves at *F*, *G*, and *H*; that is, since goods 1 and 2 are perfect complements, the two goods are always consumed in the same ratio. The demand curve for good 1 is negatively sloped as shown.

Finally, consider the case of lexicographic preferences. In this case, the consumer prefers any bundle with more good 1; hence, given an income

FIGURE A3.10

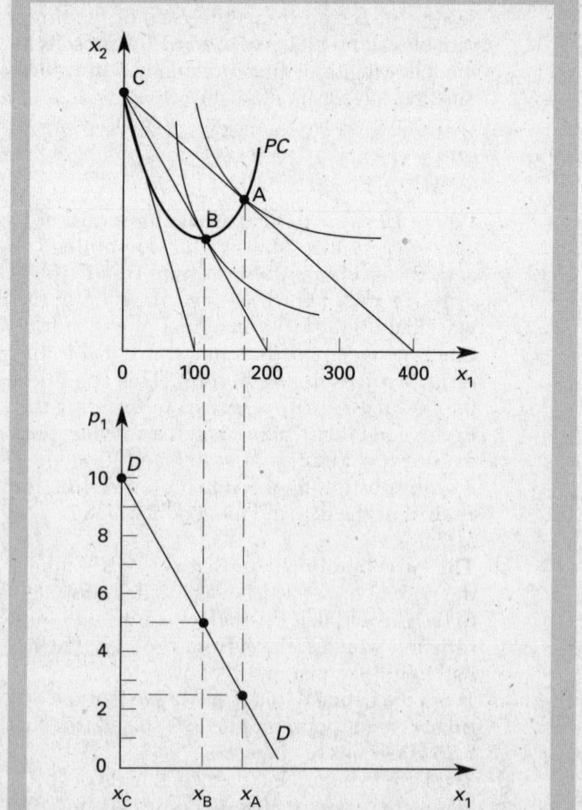

FIGURE A3.11

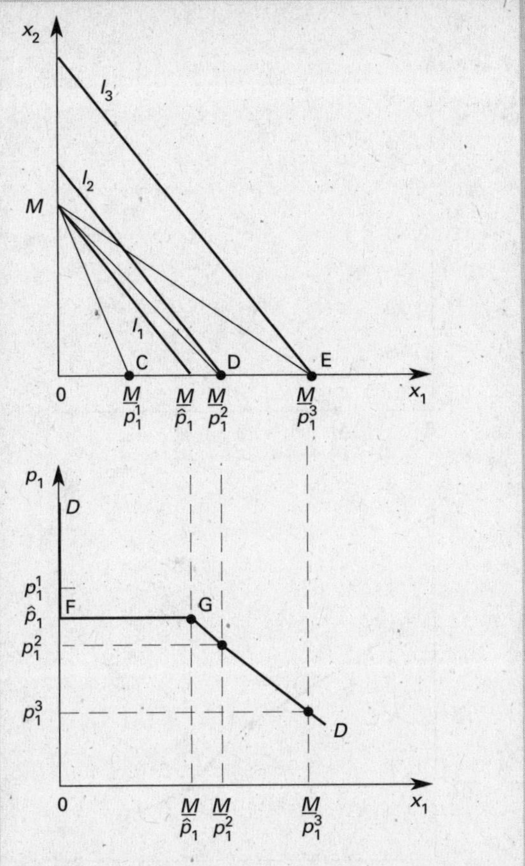

M, utility is maximized by consuming $x_2 = 0$ and $x_1 = M/p_1$ at points C, D, and E in Figure A3.12b. Again, the demand curve for good 1 is negatively sloped.

48 a Given the budget line MM', the individual maximizes utility by choosing point A in Figure A3.13a.

b The consumer will never choose a bundle on the nonconvex portion of the indifference curve; for example, from A to B in Figure A3.13a. If she did, the consumer would be *minimizing* utility subject to the budget constraint.

c If the indifference curves are made convex by drawing a line from point A to B in the diagram in Figure A3.13a, the utility-maximizing bundle will not change. This can lead to problems when the budget line is coincident with the line joining points A and B, as shown in Figure A3.13b. In this case, the prediction of the theory would be that the individual is indifferent among all points between A and B when, in fact, she would choose only A or B.

FIGURE A3.12

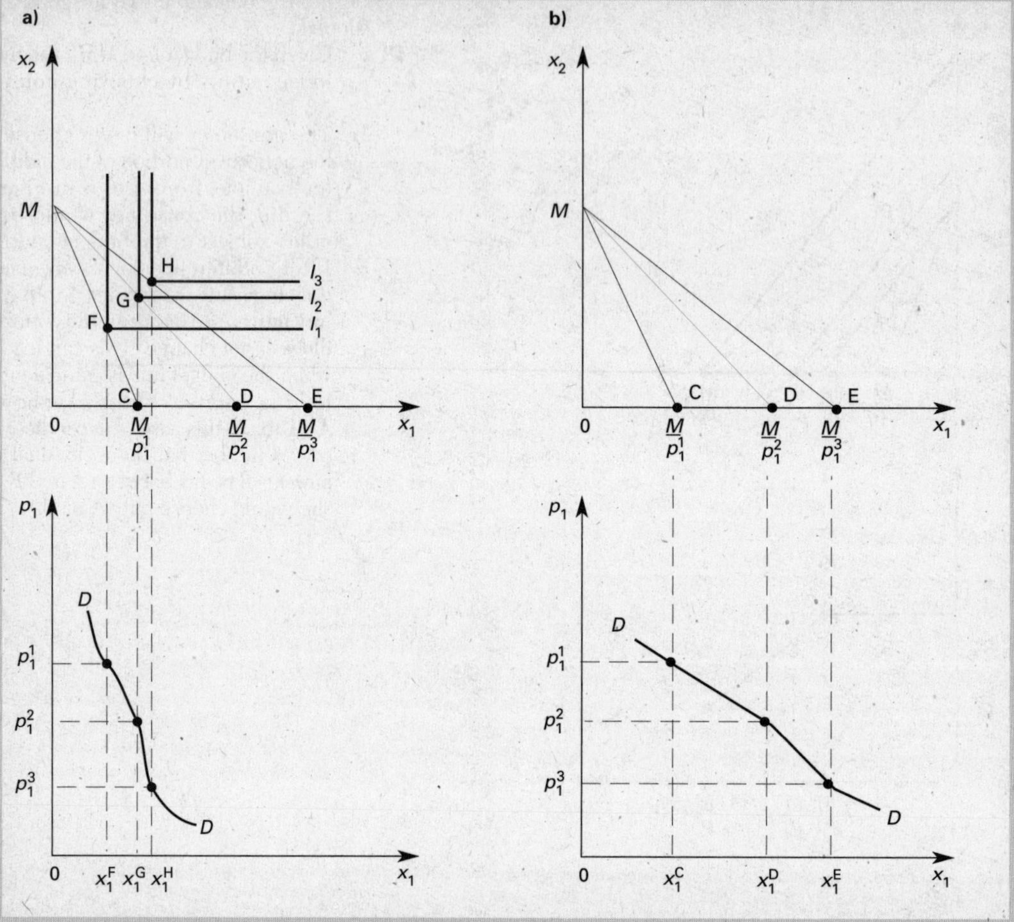

FIGURE A3.13

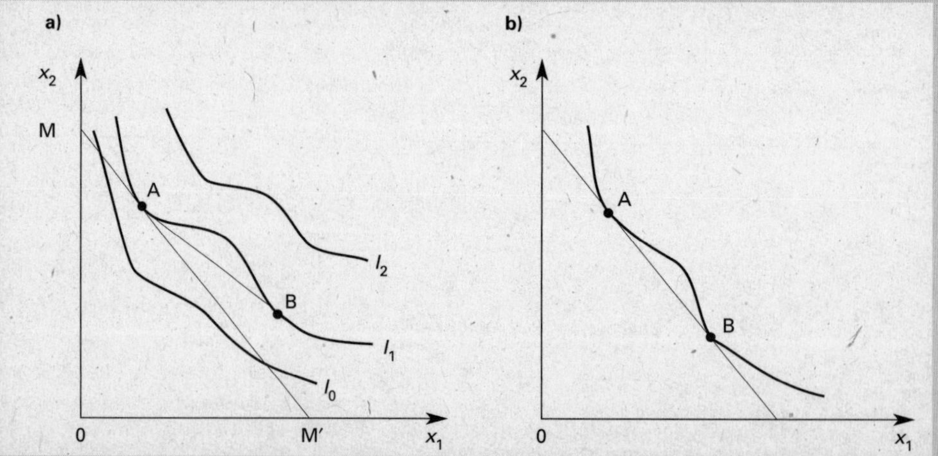

CHAPTER 4

More Demand Theory

Chapter Summary

Law of Demand

Generally speaking, the quantity demanded of a particular good rises as its price falls — this is known as the **law of demand**. Several examples illustrate this law. For instance, as the price of long-distance telephone calls falls, the quantity of calls made increases; as university tuition increases for foreign students, fewer foreign students choose to study at Canadian universities.

Income and Substitution Effects

Quantity demanded is negatively related to price, although some exceptions do apply. Goods whose demand curve is positively sloped are called **Giffen goods**. To understand how this may arise, we turn to an examination of **substitution effects** and **income effects**. Any price change can be decomposed into these two effects. Suppose the price of good 1 changes relative to the price of good 2 — this price change has two effects. The substitution effect arises because the consumer purchases more of the good that has become relatively cheaper (thus, if the price of good 1 falls, then consumers would want to purchase more of that good relative to good 2). However, a second effect — the income effect — takes place because a price change effects real purchasing power or real income. A price fall, for instance, implies an increase in real income. This income effect will result in the individual purchasing more of both goods if both goods are normal, or more of one good and less of the other if this latter good is inferior. Thus, an increase (decrease) in the price of good 1 usually leads to an increase (decrease) in its consumption as a result of the substitution effect and an increase (decrease) in its consumption due to the income effect if the good is normal, while the reverse holds true if the good is inferior. The substitution effect can be zero but can never be negative, whereas the income effect can be positive, zero, or negative. In the case of an inferior good where the income and substitution effects work in opposing directions, a Giffen good arises whenever the income effect dominates the substitution effect.

To calculate income and substitution effects, the following hypothetical exercise is undertaken. Suppose the price of good 1 increases, then we need to determine how much money the individual (Mary) would have to receive in order that she could still afford to buy a bundle on her *original* indifference curve. We then, hypothetically speaking, "give" her this amount of money — resulting in a new **compensated budget line**, which we use to determine the new bundle that she would choose, having received this **compensatory income**. The difference between the original consumption bundle and this hypothetical one (which lies on the original indifference curve) is the substitution effect. The difference between the final bundle — once the compensatory income is removed — and the hypothetical bundle is the income effect. The above exercise can be undertaken in the event of a price decrease. Note, in the case of a price decrease, money would have to be hypothetically taken from Mary so that she could remain on her original indifference curve.

Compensated Demand Curve

The **compensated demand curve** looks at the amount demanded of a given good (in the above example, good 1) whenever its price has changed but the consumer's income has been adjusted so that he or she can remain on the original indifference curve. This demand curve can be determined as the solution to a problem that minimizes the costs of buying any bundle of goods subject to the constraint that this bundle yields some fixed amount of utility.

Time and Money Prices

The **full price** of a good is often not reflected by its monetary price alone. Often, time is an important component in the full price of a good. For instance, consider the price of some particular brand-name jeans. They could be purchased at a jeans boutique with well-informed sales people, a large stock of sizes, and no line-up at the cash register; or, they could be purchased at a bargain department store with virtually no in-store service and long line-ups at the cash register. The same pair of jeans, therefore, would have a monetary price that is much higher in the boutique relative to the bargain store, but a time price that is lower. Thus, people with high time costs (typically those with high market wages) would buy their jeans at the boutique, *ceteris paribus*, while others would go to the department store. Everyone faces a **time constraint**; however, the market value of time differs across individuals. **Full income** is defined as the monetary value of non-market and market time plus any non-market income. In fact, it is the monetary value of the individual's time endowment (which takes account of his or her market wages) plus any non-market income that the individual may receive.

Measuring Benefits and Costs

Government and other kinds of policies may result in individuals changing their consumption patterns, hence affecting their utility. Two methods allow us to put a dollar value on this change in utility: equivalent variation and compensating variation. Before looking at these concepts, define the initial equilibrium as the bundle of goods consumed before the policy change (e.g., price decrease) and the subsequent equilibrium as the bundle of goods consumed after the change. **Equivalent variation** takes as the point of reference the subsequent equilibrium and asks how much money an individual would accept in order to be indifferent between the new prices and the old prices. By contrast, the **compensating variation** asks how much the individual would pay to render him or her indifferent between the initial equilibrium and the new prices.

One basic problem with the equivalent and compensating variation approaches is that they require that we know an individual's preferences. Another measure, known as **consumer surplus**, can be estimated directly from an individual's demand behaviour. Consumer surplus measures the area under the demand curve bounded by the price of the good and the quantity demanded. Simply put, consumer surplus is the difference between what an individual is willing to pay for each unit of output (given by the point on the demand curve for each unit) and how much he or she has to pay.

The marginal rate of substitution (MRS) of a good also measures an individual's **marginal value**. Basically, the marginal value indicates how much an individual is willing to pay for an additional unit of a good. The **total value** of a good is the sum of all of the marginal values. Thus, if the price of a good is low then an individual will buy that good until the point where his or her marginal value equals price, which means that marginal value of this good is also low. Note, however, that this says nothing about the total value of the good, which may be very high. The **water-diamond paradox** refers to this difference between total and marginal values. Water, which is essential for human life, is typically priced very low — thus having a low marginal value — while diamonds, which are not at all essential for life, have a very high marginal value.

Until now, we have assumed that all goods have "one" price. However, we know that this is not the case. Consider, for instance, telephone service. We often have to pay a monthly fee for the right to the service, plus a per-unit charge for each telephone call (especially for long-distance calls). Hydro service is the same — a monthly fixed charge for the service, plus a per-kilowatt charge for usage. This sort of pricing strategy — with a fixed fee and a per-unit fee — is known as a **two-part tariff** and can be a profit maximizing strategy under certain circumstances.

Index Numbers

Creating an index number is a way of comparing two numbers that differ over one characteristic — often time. So, for instance, a statement about how much individuals are earning today in comparison to last year would be based on a **quantity index number**, which compares earnings last year with earnings this year. One could have easily made the comparison at the same point in time but across, say, provinces. A statement that says that people in Newfoundland earn, say, 80% of the earnings of Ontarians, is also based on an index number. A **price index number** says something about the price of a good (or bundle of goods) in one period (or location) in comparison to another.

Index numbers are often used by economists to compare how individuals are doing across time. Several methods exist for calculating index numbers, here we focus on the two most common ones: the **Paasche quantity index** and the **Laspeyres quantity index**. To understand the difference between these two approaches, let's consider the following situation. Suppose an individual, Sherry, consumed bundle B^1 last year and consumes bundle B^2 now. These two bundles consist of different quantities of, say, two goods (x_1^i and x_2^i) and prices for each good which differ across the two periods ($i = 1, 2$). Notice that the value of these two bundles changes for two reasons — because prices *and* quantities are different over the two years. In order to create an index which allows us to compare the bundles over time, we need to eliminate the variation in one of these two factors. For quantity indices, we suppose that the prices of the goods remain the same over the two periods. The Paasche quantity index assumes that the prices of the goods are the second period prices (i.e., today's prices rather than last year's prices) and then compares the value of the bundle chosen today ($p_1^2 x_1^2 + p_2^2 x_2^2$) evaluated at today's prices with the bundle chosen last year evaluated at today's prices (i.e., $p_1^2 x_1^1 + p_2^2 x_2^1$). If $P = p_1^2 x_1^2 + p_2^2 x_2^2 / p_1^2 x_1^1 + p_2^2 x_2^1$ is greater than 1, then B^2 is preferred to B^1. If the index is less than 1, then we cannot say with certainty whether Sherry is better off or worse off now in comparison with last year. The Laspeyres quantity index undertakes the same exercise but is based on first period prices rather than second period prices. The index is thus $L = p_1^1 x_1^2 + p_2^1 x_2^2 / p_1^1 x_1^1 + p_2^1 x_2^1$. If this is less than 1 then Sherry is better off last year in comparison to this year.

A price index fixes quantities purchased over the periods in question and focuses on price changes. The **Paasche price index** is based on second period quantities and is defined as $P' = p_1^2 x_2^1 + p_2^2 x_2^2 / p_1^1 x_1^2 + p_2^1 x_2^2$; the **Laspeyres price index** is based on first period quantities and is defined as $L' = p_1^2 x_1^1 + p_2^2 x_2^1 / p_1^1 x_1^1 + p_2^1 x_2^1$. A value of less than one for either price index indicates that the individual is better off in period 2 while a value of greater than one indicates that the individual is better off in period 1.

KEY WORDS

- Compensated budget line
- Compensated demand curve
- Compensating variation
- Compensatory income
- Consumer surplus
- Equivalent variation
- Full income
- Full price
- Giffen good
- Income effect
- Laspeyres price index
- Laspeyres quantity index
- Law of demand
- Marginal value
- Paasche price index
- Paasche quantity index
- Price index number
- Quantity index
- Substitution effect
- Time constraint
- Total value
- Two-part tariff
- Water-diamond paradox

CASE STUDY: THE LAW OF DEMAND AND THE LONG-DISTANCE TELEPHONE MARKET IN CANADA

Competition in long-distance telephone services has been permitted in Canada since 1992. Since then, several companies have entered into this market, subjecting the hitherto incumbent monopolist to competition. The big entrants into this market have come from the United States where competition in long-distance telephone calls has been permitted since 1984.

Prior to deregulation, the Canadian market was divided into nine different regions, each served by one monopoly company (e.g., Bell Canada in Ontario and Quebec, Newfoundland Tel, B.C. Tel, Saskatchewan Tel and so on), which provided both local and long-distance phone services to customers. A similar pricing scheme was in place across the country: a fixed fee was charged for local telephone calls, with a zero user price, and a price per unit of time was levied for all long-distance calls. It was well established that the long-distance charges cross-subsidized local telephone calls — which were priced below the costs of providing them. Once the long-distance market was subject to competition, this cross-subsidization could no longer take place.

Much innovation has taken place in the pricing of telephone services — particularly in the long- distance market. Now, a menu of different pricing schemes are offered by each telephone carrier to try to encourage customers to buy their services. By offering a range of schemes, customers can "self-select" into the package which best serves their needs. Of course, once entrants began offering interesting deals to new clients, the incumbent firms, watching their market share decline, began to do likewise.

A number of interesting pricing schemes have been offered to customers. The "traditional" pricing regime essentially split the day into three zones: business hours, evening hours, and overnight. Telephone calls were priced differently in each zone — with discounts that increased dramatically outside of business hours. One of the reasons for such a pricing strategy was that, with previous technology, lines could be easily congested. By pricing lower in off-peak times (i.e., after business hours) those who could switch their calls to these times were encouraged to do so. Another reason was simply that the monopoly carrier was price discriminating by charging business clients a higher price than residential clients.

In this case, you are asked to examine the impact of several pricing schemes on the number of long-distance telephone calls. For the ease of analysis, many of the schemes are greatly simplified, leaving only the salient features of the scheme in place. In all cases, you should consider long-distance calls as good 1 with good 2 being a composite commodity.

***A** Let's begin with the traditional pricing scheme. Let's suppose that a representative consumer, Karen, is flexible in terms of when she can make her telephone calls so she will do so when the calls are the cheapest (although calls during the cheap period are less convenient). Suppose that calls cost \$0.55 per minute during business hours and after-hour calls cost \$0.25 per minute. Her preferences are represented by $U(x_1x_2) = x_1^{1/2}\, x_2^4$ where x_1 represents calls and x_2 is other recreational activities; her monthly disposable income for these goods is \$300. Calculate how many minutes of long-distance calls that Karen will make per month.

B A new company comes into the market and eliminates the price distinction between business and after-hour calls. The inconvenience associated with switching telephone companies has a one-shot monetary value of, say, \$10. This company charges \$0.15 per minute for calls. Which company will Karen choose to use? How many calls will she make?

C Another company decides to employ a different pricing scheme to attract customers. In this scheme, a flat monthly fee is charged and the per-unit cost of all long-distance calls is zero. Suppose this monthly charge were \$100 — would Karen use this carrier? Again, determine the number of minutes of long-distance telephone calls that Karen would make. What is the maximum value of the fixed fee F that would render Karen indifferent between this scheme and the two schemes previously outlined?

D In July 1998, Sprint Canada — one of the largest firms to enter into the Canadian long-distance market — launched a long-distance "savings" plan that essentially charged users a flat rate fee (of \$20 per month) in which they could call anywhere in Canada, evenings and weekends, for no additional charge. How would Karen react to such a plan? Do you think that Karen's reaction would be typical of most Canadians' reaction? Would you be surprised to learn that Sprint Canada withdrew this scheme from the market a few months later? What could Sprint Canada learn from the law of demand?

EXERCISES

Multiple-Choice

Choose the correct answer to each question. There is only one correct answer to each question.

1 In Figure 4.1, the consumer chooses bundle A when the budget line is *CC* and bundle B when the budget line is *DD*. If the consumer's preferences have not changed, then which of the following is correct?

a Points in area *F* are preferred to bundle A.
b Points in area *COC* are inferior to bundle A.
c Points in the shaded region are inferior to bundle B.
d All the above are true.
e Only **b** and **c** are true.

2 Suppose that a certain bundle of goods costs \$200 in year 0 and \$250 in year 1. Then, if an individual actually spends \$250 in year 1, and his preferences have not changed, which of the following is true?

a He is no worse off in year 1
b He must be better off in year 0.
c He cannot be better off in year 1.

FIGURE 4.1

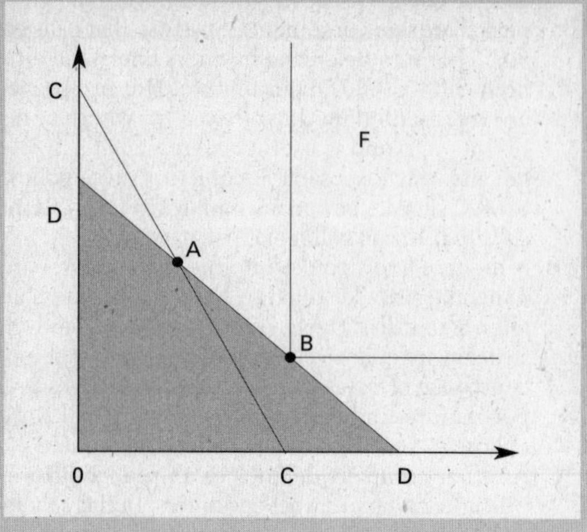

FIGURE 4.2

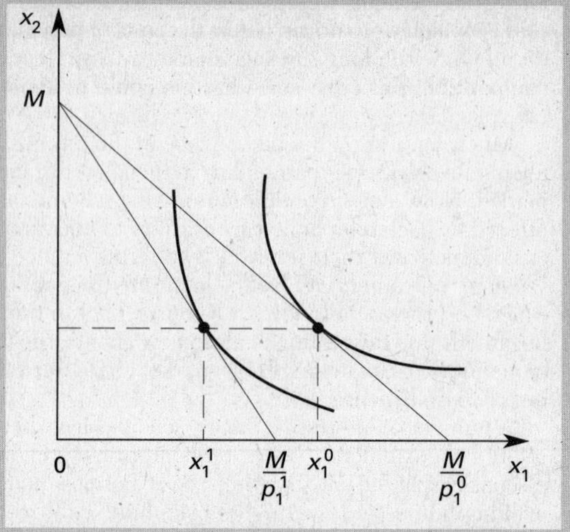

d He is equally well off in the two years.
e None of the above.

Refer to Figure 4.2 when answering the following question:

3 When the price of squash balls is p_1^0 Larry purchases x_1^0 squash balls as shown in figure 4.1. When the price rises to p_1^1, he purchases x_1^1 balls. Which of the following is true?
a Squash balls are an inferior good but not a Giffen good.
b Squash balls are a normal good.
c Squash balls are a Giffen good.
d The income elasticity of demand for squash balls equals 1 because consumption of good 2 stayed the same.
e We cannot tell if it is a normal, inferior, or Giffen good because a price change, not a change in income, brought about a change in the purchase of squash balls.

4 For a reduction in the price of a normal good,
a Consumer surplus overestimates consumers' true willingness to pay for the price reduction.
b Consumer surplus underestimates consumers' true willingness to pay for the price reduction.
c The quantity demanded of the good at the lower price along the compensated demand curve is larger than that quantity along the ordinary demand curve.
d The quantity demanded of the good will fall.
e None of the above is true.

For the following 4 questions, refer to Figure 4.3

FIGURE 4.3

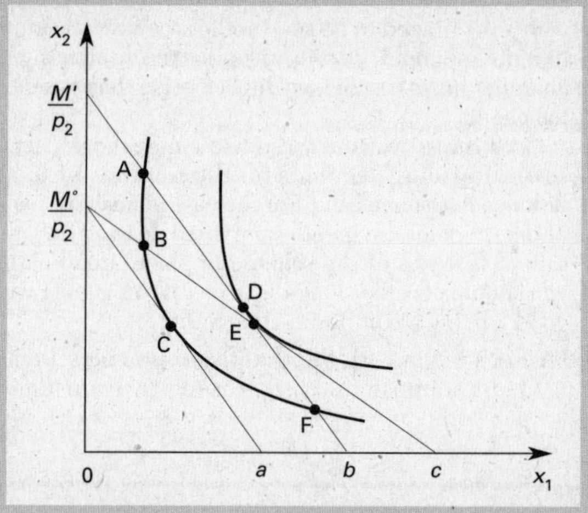

5 Noting that period 0 comes before period 1, Figure 4.3 refers to a situation where
a The price of good 1 increases.
b The price of good 1 decreases.
c The price of good 1 increases while the price of good 2 falls.
d The price of good 1 decreases while the price of good 2 rises.
e The price of good 2 rises.

6 The income effect is:
a B-C.
b D-C.
c E-C.
d E-D.
e None of the above.

7 The substitution effect is
a E-D.
b E-C.
c E-B.
d E-A.
e None of the above.

8 From Figure 4.3 we see that
- a Good 1 is normal while good 2 is inferior.
- b Good 1 is inferior while good 2 is normal.
- c Goods 1 and 2 are normal.
- d Goods 1 and 2 are inferior.
- e We cannot say because this figure refers to a price change, not an income change.

In Figure 4.4, Doug has $1000 in monthly income and faces market prices. Answer the following two questions

9 Suppose that point A is the initial equilibrium and point B is the final equilibrium, then the equivalent variation associated with this price change is:
- a $50.
- b $100.
- c $136.
- d $68.
- e None of the above.

10 In this situation, the compensating variation is
- a $50.
- b $100.
- c $136.
- d $68.
- e None of the above.

Suppose that in 2001 Martine consumed 20 pizzas and drank 10 cases of beer. Her income devoted to pizzas and beer in 2001 was $500. In 2002, Martine was observed buying 18 pizzas and 12 cases of beer. Answer the following three questions using this information.

11 Compared to 2001, Martine is now
- a Better off.
- b Worse off.
- c No better no worse off.
- d Better off as long as her income increased.
- e Cannot say without further information.

FIGURE 4.4

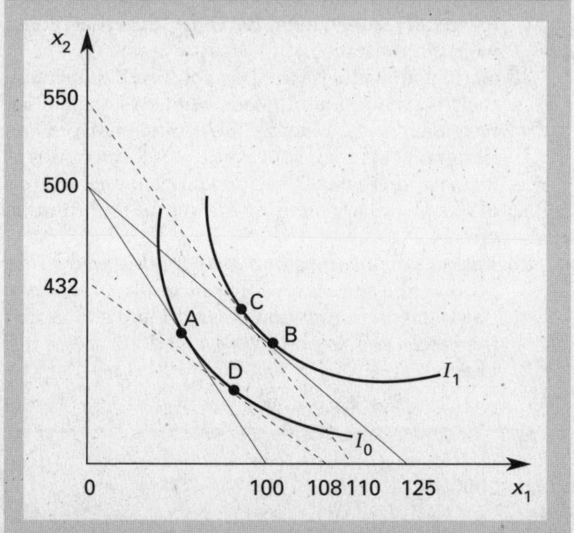

Suppose that in 2001 each pizza cost $15 and each case of beer cost $20. In 1999, pizza cost $17.49 and because of free trade with the United States, the price of a case of beer fell to $15.43.

12 Based on price indices, we can say that
- a Martine is better off in 2002 compared to 2001.
- b Martine is worse off in 2002 compared to 2001.
- c Martine is indifferent between the two years.
- d Cannot determine in which year she is better off.
- e Better off in 2002 according to Laspeyres and worse off according to Paasche.

13 According to the Paasche and Laspeyres quantity indices, Martine is
- a Unambiguously better off today according to both indices.
- b Unambiguously worse off today according to both indices.
- c Better off according to the Paasche index, uncertain according to the Laspeyres index.
- d Better off according to the Laspeyres index, uncertain according to the Paasche index.
- e Uncertain according to both indices.

True-False

14 An exact measure of an individual's willingness to pay for the opportunity to purchase an automobile at some price is consumer surplus.

15 The higher the price of a good, the larger the consumer surplus associated with that good will be.

16 If the Laspeyres price index indicates your cost of living has increased but there has been no change in your disposable income, then you must be worse off than before the cost-of-living increase.

17 If the Paasche price index indicates your cost of living has increased but there has been no change in your disposable income, then you must be worse off than before the cost-of-living increase.

18 If an individual only consumes two goods, both cannot be inferior.

19 Normal goods refer to products which form the regular part of a consumer's consumption bundle.

20 All inferior goods are Giffen goods.

21 All Giffen goods are inferior goods.

22 For goods which are perfect complements, the substitution effect is zero.

23 For goods which are perfect substitutes, the income effect is zero.

24 The compensated demand curve allows income and prices to vary but leaves utility unchanged.

25 People who are not employed in the paid labour force do not face a time constraint.

26 The fact that air is free implies that society places a low value on this commodity.

27 If a company charges a two-part tariff, then the average price of its product falls as consumption rises.

28 If your current consumption bundle could have been bought 10 years ago for one-half of its current costs but your income 10 years ago was one-half of your current income and your tastes have not changed, then you must be equally well off compared with 10 years ago.

Short Problems

29 Figure 4.5 shows the budget constraints faced by an individual in 2001 and 2002. Points *A* and *B* are the respective bundles of goods chosen in the two years. Can you say if the individual is better or worse off in 2001 compared with 2002? Explain.

30 An individual can purchase housing either in the private housing market, in which she can buy any amount of housing she pleases at the market price, or in the public housing market, in which she is offered a particular amount of housing at a price lower than the private market price. Will she necessarily choose the public housing? If she does, will she consume more housing than she would have purchased on the private market? Explain.

31 At the University of Toronto, squash courts are allocated on a first-come, first-served basis. Starting at 7:30 A.M., avid squash players can begin their attempts at reserving a squash court for the following day. A new squash plan has been recently introduced. For $100, a squash membership can be purchased, allowing the holder to book a court one week in advance. Only 300 of these memberships are available. Analyze the pricing scheme. Why was this membership offered? Why were only a limited number of memberships available?

32 On an indifference curve diagram, illustrate the compensating variation and consumer surplus from a reduction in the price of a good with a zero income effect.

FIGURE 4.5

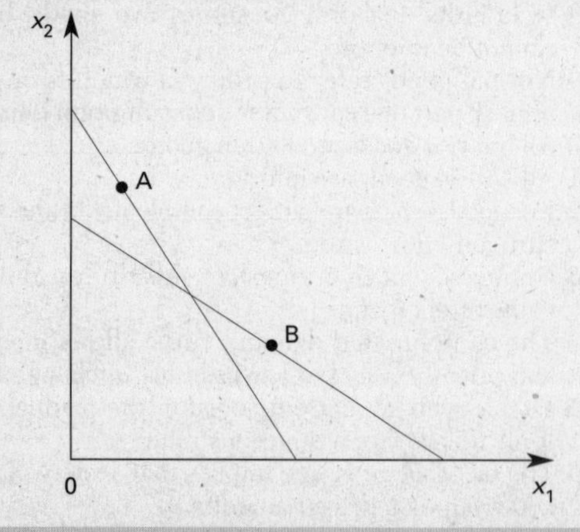

33 A recent Queen's graduate buys only three commodities — good 1, good 2, and good 3 — with his income. In his initial job location in Edmonton, he purchased the following quantities each month at the prices indicated.

Edmonton

	Quantity	Price ($)
Good 1	100	10
Good 2	200	16
Good 3	50	8

He is offered a new job in Vancouver at a substantially higher salary, $6 400 per month. The prices of goods 1, 2, and 3 in the new city are as follows.

Vancouver

	Price ($)
Good 1	12
Good 2	20
Good 3	16

Is he worse off if he takes the job because of the higher prices, or do you need more information to tell? Explain.

34 The government wants to encourage pharmaceutical companies to conduct more research and development in Canada. It is considering a few options including giving a tax credit of $0.50 for every dollar spent on R&D in Canada, and giving the companies a general tax break equivalent to the savings gained from the R&D tax credit, which would result in these firms having more money to spend on R&D or something else. With the aid of income and substitution effects, analyze which policy would result in more R&D in Canada and under what circumstances.

35 Certain individuals have been observed to increase their consumption of goods whenever their price increases. So, for instance, the consumption of Dom Perignon champagne by some people increases as its price increases. Provide an economic analysis of this phenomenon using income and substitution effects.

36 Kathleen consumes only two goods, good 1 and good 2. She spends all of her income on these two goods. Her consumption of good 1 and good 2 and the prices she faced in 2001 and 2002 are as follows:

	P_1	P_2	x_1	x_2
2001	10	15	20	10
2002	8	20	30	9

a In which period is she better off and why?

b If you knew the indifference curves, show how you would calculate the income necessary so that Kathleen is indifferent between her 1998 bundle at 1998 prices and the 1998 bundle at 1999 prices.

Long Problems

37 A consumer spends his income on compact discs (CDs) and all other goods, good 2. CDs cost \$20 per unit and the consumer's income is \$300.

a Draw the consumer's budget constraint and show the optimum for a consumer who buys a positive amount of good 2 and CDs. Let the quantities of CDs and good 2 be x_1 and x_2, respectively.

b Now assume that a CD company offers him the following deal. For a membership fee of \$100, he can buy all the CDs he wants for \$10 each. Draw the new budget constraint under this offer.

c Under the offer, show that anyone buying more than 10 CDs before the plan is introduced will join the plan, but anyone buying fewer than 10 CDs may or may not join the plan.

d Draw an indifference curve diagram showing that if an individual is indifferent between joining and not joining the plan, then she would spend more money on CDs and purchase more CDs under the plan.

38 The Smiths, a family of four, spend \$1 000 out of their \$6 000 annual income on food. After conducting a thorough study, a government agency decides that \$3 000 is the minimum money required to provide proper nutrition for a family of four. Deciding that the Smiths cannot afford to pay more than \$1 000 for food out of their current income, the agency decides to make a gift to them each year of \$2 000 worth of food stamps, which may be used *only* on food.

a On a diagram, draw the Smith's budget constraints before and after the gift of food stamps. Assuming convex indifference curves, show the optimum before and after the gift. *Hint:* Measure food and all other goods in dollars. According to your diagram, has the government succeeded in its objective of ensuring that the Smiths get proper nutrition, that is, \$3 000 worth of food? Explain.

b Suppose that, instead of the food stamp program, the government gives the Smith family a cash subsidy of \$2 000 that can be spent on anything they wish. On the diagram you drew in part **a**, show the new budget constraint and the optimum. Is the government any closer to achieving its objective? Explain.

39 Laura earns \$10 000 per year. She spends her income on education and composite commodity good 2. A unit of education costs \$500 (think of a unit of education as one class). A unit of good 2 costs \$1. Assume education is a normal good.

a Suppose that Laura maximizes utility subject to her budget constraint by consuming eight units of education and spending \$6 000 on everything else. Indicate Laura's optimum on an indifference curve–budget constraint diagram.

Now suppose that the government wants to subsidize Laura's education. It has three policies to choose among:

(1) Pay some portion of the price of each unit of education purchased.
(2) Give an equivalent cash subsidy.
(3) Give an equivalent subsidy-in-kind (that is, give Laura a voucher, or units of education).

b Suppose that the government decides to follow policy (1) by paying \$250 per unit of education purchased by Laura. Redraw your diagram for part **a**, and show the new bundle of education and the composite commodity that Laura will choose under this government program. Indicate on the diagram the amount of money that the government is spending under this program. Will this program result in a shift in or a movement along the demand curve? Explain.

c Now suppose that instead of the per-unit subsidy, the government follows policy (2) and gives Laura a cash subsidy equal to the money spent under the program in part **b**. Redraw the diagram from part **b** and show the effect of this new policy on Laura's choice of education and good 2. Will Laura be better or worse off under this program than under program (1) analyzed in **b**? Explain. Will this program result in a shift in or a movement along the demand curve? Explain.

d Finally, suppose that instead of the per-unit subsidy in part **b** or the cash subsidy in part **c**, the government gives an education voucher as in policy (3). That is, the government spends the same amount of money as it did in **b** and **c** but "pays" Laura in units of education. Show on a diagram Laura's choice of education and good 2, and compare it to her choice under the cash-subsidy program in **c**. Is Laura better or worse off under this voucher program than under the cash subsidy program discussed in **c**? Explain. Will this program result in a shift in or a movement along the demand curve? Explain.

e What have you learned from this exercise?

40 Figure 4.6 is the ordinary demand curve of a representative consumer for bread. Assume that bread is a normal good and that the individual is currently consuming at a rate of 3 loaves per week at a per-unit price of \$1. Because of a new computer-operated dough kneader, the cost of producing bread falls, and the equilibrium price drops to \$0.50 per loaf. The government wants to determine the impact of the machine on consumer welfare and con-

FIGURE 4.6

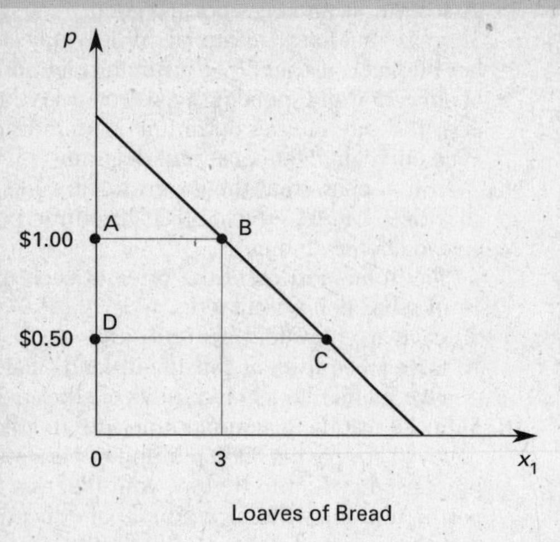

cludes that each individual has experienced an increase in welfare of *ABCD*.

a Would you agree that *ABCD* is the accurate measure of welfare? Why or why not?

b Draw the compensated-demand curve and indicate the compensating variation due to the change in the price of bread.

41 In Canada, there has been a long debate about the merits of various forms of child daycare. Currently, a number of daycare spots are earmarked for poor families who fall below some income cutoff. These families are then eligible for heavily subsidized daycare. Everyone else has to pay the full cost of daycare spaces. To ease the analysis, let's suppose that each full-time daycare spot has a market value of $10 000 and that the government pays the entire $10 000 for families whose income falls below $20 000. However, not all families eligible for subsidized daycare can actually find a spot. In fact, only about one-half of all eligible families can place their children in subsidized daycare. The government is now thinking about changing its daycare policy — and is considering the following policies: a) remove all subsidies and give all low-income families a lump-sum transfer of $10 000; b) subsidize enough daycare spots for all eligible families but by only $5 000 each (i.e., each individual would have to pay $5 000 per child); c) provide free daycare to everyone which would be paid for out of general tax revenue. Discuss each of these policies for a representative family with one child whose income is $15 000, $30 000 and $60 000.

***42** Suppose that Gilles' preferences can be represented by the utility function $U(x, y) = 32x^{1/2} + y$, where x represents litres of ice cream and y represents all other goods (i.e., y is the composite commodity) consumed in a month.

a Determine Gilles' demand functions for x and y.

b Suppose the price of ice cream is $8 per litre (this is very special ice cream) and Gilles' income is $1 000, how many litres of ice cream would be consumed and how much money would be devoted to all other goods?

c Suppose, now, that the price of ice cream doubles to $16 per litre. Calculate the income and substitution effects associated with this price change.

d Is ice cream a normal or inferior good? What about the composite commodity?

e Calculate the equivalent variation, compensating variation and change in consumer surplus associated with this price change.

***43** David's preferences over books and movies may be represented by $U(x, y) = 2ln\ x + ln\ y$.

a Calculate David's demand functions for books and movies.

b Suppose the price of a book is $10, the price of a movie is $8 and his income is $120, what is David's optimal consumption bundle?

c Calculate David's compensated demand functions for books and movies.

d Suppose, now, that the price of books doubles to $20. How much compensatory income would he have to receive in order that this price increase does not affect his utility level?

44 Analyze the following situations:

a Individuals are willing to pay $45 per year in order to have the right to shop at the Price Club, while they could be shopping at Zellers or other low-priced department stores for free.

b Travelling by car from Vancouver to Kelowna individuals choose to take the Coquihalla highway — a toll road that costs $10 each way — which runs directly across the mountains rather than take the highway which takes a longer route.

c People still take the ferry to Prince Edward Island rather than taking the fixed-link bridge.

d In the Rideau Centre in Ottawa, two drugstores are located facing each other, are owned by different companies, and often have different prices for the same goods.

ANSWERS TO CHAPTER 4

Case Study

*A The most efficient way of answering this question starts by determining Karen's demand function for long-distance calls and all other goods. To do this, employ the Lagrangean multiplier technique: Maximize $L = x_1^{1/2} x_2^4 - \lambda(m - p_1x_1 - p_2x_2)$ which leads to the following three first-order conditions: (1) $0.5\, x_1^{-1/2} x_2^4 + \lambda p_1 = 0$, (2) $4x_1^{1/2} x_2^3 + \lambda p_2 = 0$, (3) $m - p_1x_1 - p_2x_2 = 0$. From (1) and (2) we can eliminate λ; and then using (3) we can determine the demand functions for $x_1 = m/9p_1$ and $x_2 = 8m/9p_2$. She will thus make 133.33 minutes of calls per month.

B If Karen were to continue making 133.33 minutes of calls, she would save $13.33 if she switched to the $0.15 a minute scheme. At this price, she would make even more calls (222.22 minutes worth) and would do so during the day.

C For 222.22 minutes of calls, she pays $33.33. Karen would be willing to pay $30 a month for unlimited calls. In this case, since utility increases with calls, Karen would be on the phone all the time. (Technically, her demand for calls goes to infinity. Of course, we know that this is not very realistic. We would predict that Karen would talk on the phone as much as physically possible).

D Karen would be on the phone all the time. Her reaction is probably not far off many Canadians. Indeed, the television news reported some amusing tales of long-distance couples spending the entire evening and night on the phone to each other simply breathing and passing an occasional comment. As a result, phone lines became congested and Sprint withdrew the offer; when $p = 0$ people are going to demand the product until their marginal utility from consuming it is zero! (They have now introduced a slightly different plan where the first 800 minutes a month are "free" with a fixed-monthly fee.)

Multiple-Choice

1 d 2 c 3 b 4 a 5 b 6 b 7 a
8 c 9 b 10 c 11 e 12d 13e

True-False

14 F 15 F 16 F 17 T 18 T 19 F 20 F 21 T
22 T 23 T 24 T 25 F 26 F 27 T 28 T

Short Problems

29 We cannot say because bundle A is not affordable in 2002 and bundle B is not affordable in 2001. Two possible sets of preferences are illustrated in Figure A4.1. In Figure A4.1a, the individual is better off in 2001; in Figure A4.1b, the individual is better off in 2002.

30 Assume that if the individual buys housing in the private market her budget line is *AB*, and it is *AC* if the individual buys in the public market as shown in Figure A4.2. If she buys public housing, *only* point *D* on budget line *AC* is attainable. Figure A4.2a shows the case in which public housing is not preferred. The utility-maximizing bundle in the private market is *E*, which is on a higher indifference curve than the one through *D*. If public housing is chosen, the individual will not neccessarily consume more housing. Figure A4.2b shows a case in which public housing is preferred but less housing is consumed than if housing were purchased in the private market.

31 Without the membership policy, the demand for squash courts would exceed the capacity. The rationing mechanism of first-come, first-served was inefficient because valuable time was wasted. The membership was a way for the university to recover some of the cost savings of an individual's time. Only a limited number were offered for distributional reasons. Realizing that many students may not be able to afford the membership, the university allowed a limited number of memberships (probably purchased by the wealthier faculty members) so individuals with a lower opportunity cost of time (probably students) could still "purchase" squash reservations with their time.

32 Let the price of good 1 fall from p_1^0 to p_1^1 as shown in Figure A4.3. The substitution effect is x_1^0 to x_1^1. The income effect is zero; hence, the substitution effect equals the total effect. In this case, the consumer surplus equals the compensating variation. Both measures give the maximum amount of money the individual is willing to give up to experience the price reduction. This amount of money, when it is given up, will leave the individual on the

FIGURE A4.1

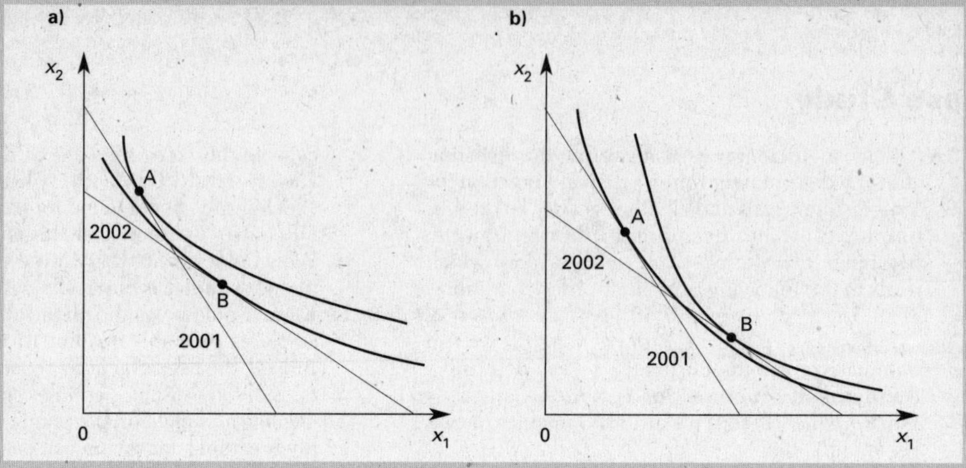

original indifference curve I_1. The compensating variation and consumer surplus in this case, are given by $M - M'$.

33 The Laspeyres price index can be used to determine if he is better off in Vancouver than in Edmonton. If the Laspeyres price index (based on the Edmonton bundle of goods) is less than the expenditure index (Vancouver income divided by Edmonton income), then he is definitely better off in Vancouver:

$$L = \frac{12 \times 100 + 20 \times 200 + 16 \times 50}{10 \times 100 + 16 \times 200 + 8 \times 50} = \frac{6000}{4600} = 1.3$$

$$E = \frac{6400}{4600} = 1.39$$

Since $E > L$, he is better off in Vancouver.

FIGURE A4.2

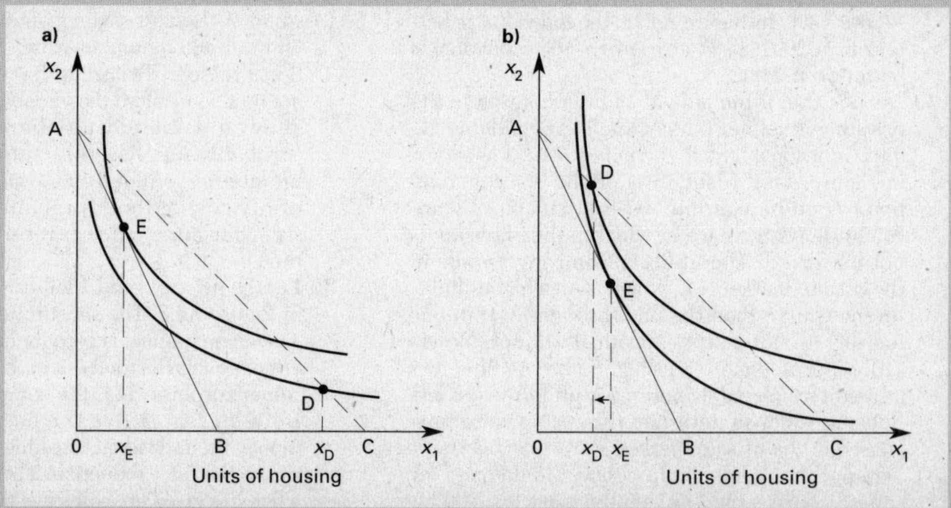

FIGURE A4.3

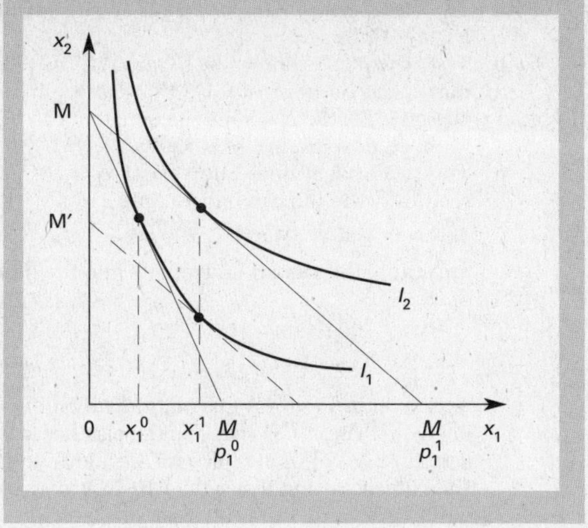

FIGURE A4.4

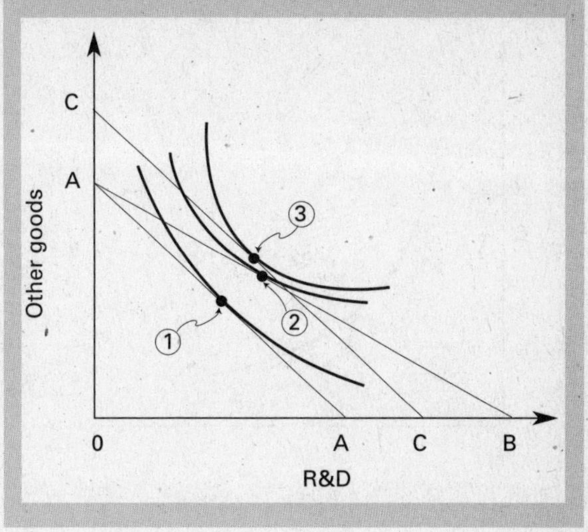

34 The original equilibrium can be depicted diagrammatically as in Figure A4.4. Point 1 is the original point, on the "budget line" *AA*, which shows all the possible combinations of expenditures on R&D and "other goods" possible for the firm. Notice that this budget line has a slope of –1. If the government gives a \$0.50 tax credit on R&D this is tantamount to changing the "price" of a dollar of R&D from \$1 to \$0.50, resulting in the new budget constraint *AB*. In this case, as long as R&D is not a Giffen good, the new equilibrium quantity of R&D will be to the right of point 1, like point 2. If the government decided to give the firm a general tax break equal to the savings gained from the R&D credit, this would mean that the new budget line would be parallel to the original *AA* line but would pass through the point 2. This new line is market as line *CC*. With the *CC* budget constraint, the firm would choose a point like point 3, which gives them a higher level of utility (profits) but would lie to the left of point 2. Point 3 would continue to be to the right of the original point 1. Thus, R&D expenditure would fall relative to the R&D subsidy policy, but firms would be better off with the general tax savings policy.

35 Believe it or not, the fact that champagne consumption increases as its price increases means that it is actually an inferior good. Indeed, it is so inferior that the income effect completely wipes out the substitution effect, resulting in a positively sloped demand curve. Figure A4.5 provides a diagrammatic exposition of what is happening here. Point *A* is the initial equilibrium. The price of champagne increases, and the final equilibrium is point *C* to the right of point *A*. Decomposing this price increase into income and substitution effects we see right away that the move from *A* to *B* represents the substitution effect (less champagne is demanded as its price increases). The move from *B* to *C* is as a result of the income effect — as income falls, the demand for champagne rises. Thus, champagne is a Giffen good for some individuals.

36 a In 2001 Kathleen's income was \$350 and in 2002 it was \$420. The 2002 bundle was not affordable in 2001, but the 2001 bundle was affordable in 2002. Thus, Kathleen is unambiguously better off in 2002.

b In Figure A4.6 the 2001 and 2002 bundles are represented. To calculate the income necessary in 2001 so that Kathleen is as well off as in 2001 at 2002 prices, take the 2002 budget line (*BB*)

FIGURE A4.5

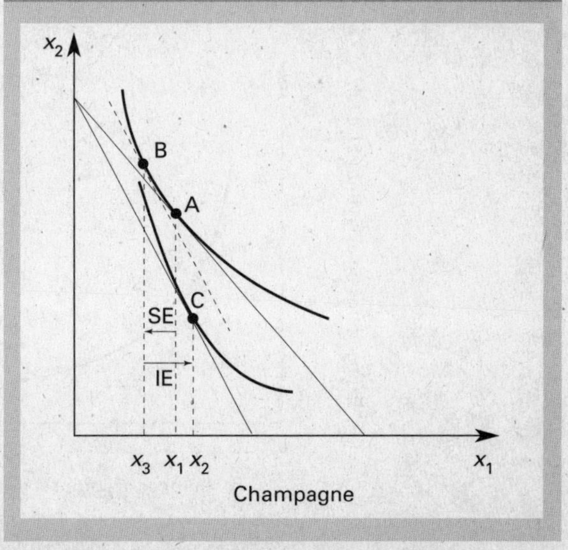

FIGURE A4.6

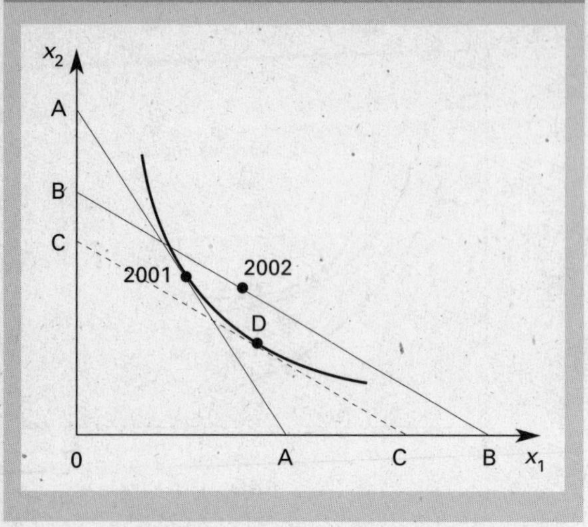

and shift it down in a parallel fashion until it is tangent to her 2001 indifferent curve. This occurs at point *D*. You can then determine the relevant income by multiplying the bundle at point *D* by the 2002 prices. This is Kathleen's compensating variation.

Long Problems

37 a The utility-maximizing bundle is given by *A* in Figure A4.7a.

b The new plan is shown in Figure A4.7b. The maximum number of CDs that can be purchased is 20; the maximum income that can be spent on everything else is $200.

c The two budget lines intersect at $x_1 = 10$. To see this, write the two budget lines:

$$300 = x_2 + 20x_1 \quad \text{and} \quad 200 = x_2 + 10\,x_1$$

Substitute the second budget line into the first one:

$$300 = 200 - 10x_1 + 20x_1$$
$$x_1 = 10$$

As shown in Figure A4.8a, an individual buying more than 10 CDs will join the plan because a higher level of utility can be achieved. Individuals buying fewer than 10 CDs may or may not benefit from the plan. An individual who benefits from the plan is shown in Figure A4.8b.

d Figure A4.9 shows the individual to be indifferent between joining and not joining the plan. Comparison of point *B*, the utility-maximizing bundle under the plan, with point *A* indicates that the individual would purchase more CDs under the plan and have less money to spend on everything else.

38 a The original budget line is *AB* in Figure A4.10. The budget line with the $2 000 food voucher is *BCD*. Before the voucher, they consume the bundle given by point *E*; suppose, after the

FIGURE A4.7

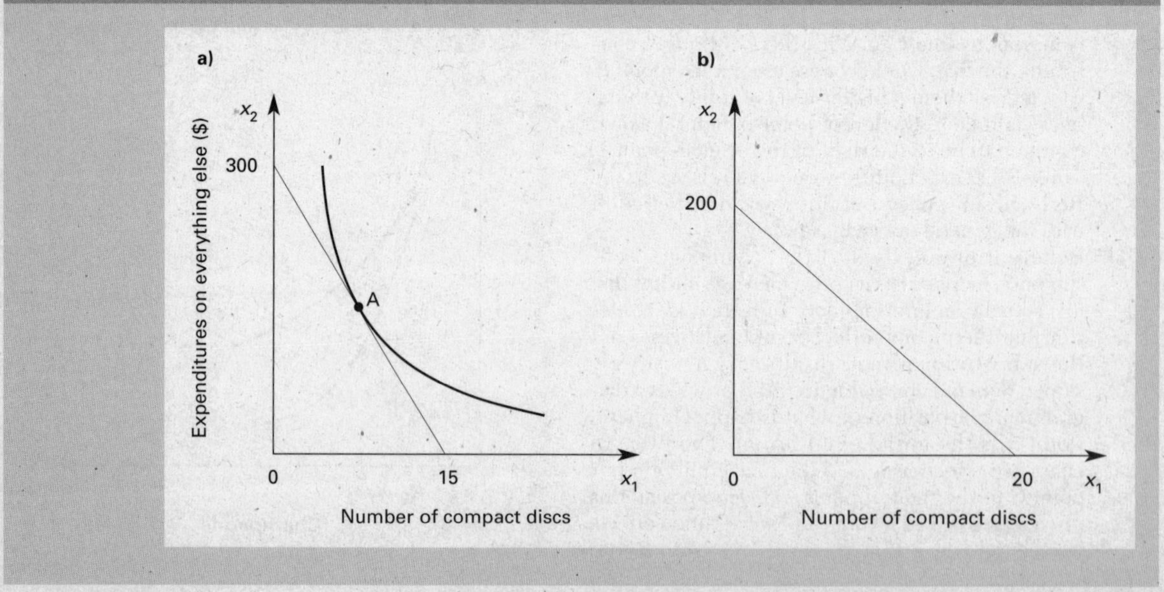

FIGURE A4.8

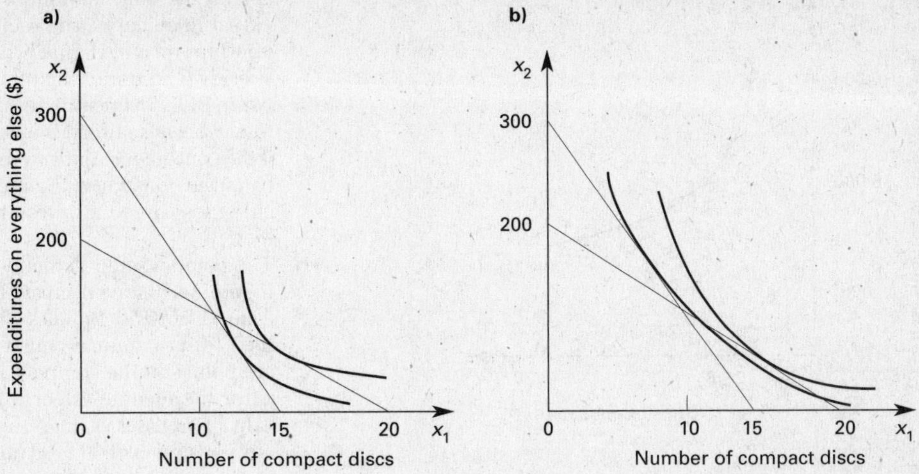

voucher, they consume the bundle given by point C. In this particular case, the Smiths spend only $2000 on food under the voucher. (Note: The optimal bundle could include more food, for example if the optimal bundle were on CD.)

b If the government gives a cash subsidy of $2000, the Smiths may choose to spend some of it on other goods. As shown in the figure, the budget line under the cash subsidy is *FD*. The Smiths may choose point *G* on the budget line. In this case, the government is not closer to achieving its objectives; however, the Smiths are certainly better off.

39 a Laura's utility-maximizing bundles is given by point *A* in Figure A4.11.

b Under the per-unit subsidy, the budget line pivots outward as shown in Figure A4.12a. The government spends *BN*, the difference between the two budget lines at the utility-maximizing bundle *B*. This program will shift the demand curve for education to the right; at every price, more units of education will be demanded.

c If the government gives a lump-sum subsidy equal to the amount spent on the program in **b**, then the budget line will be a parallel increase in the original budget line with slope .

FIGURE A4.9

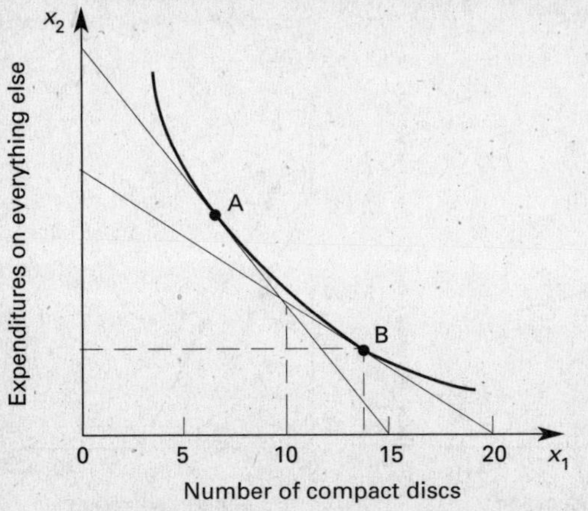

FIGURE A4.10

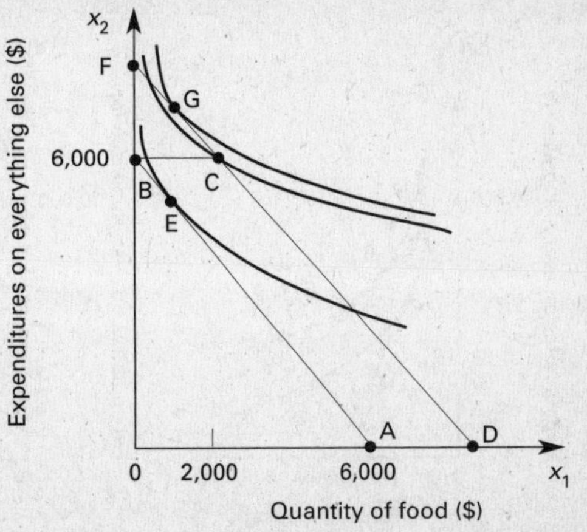

FIGURE A4.11

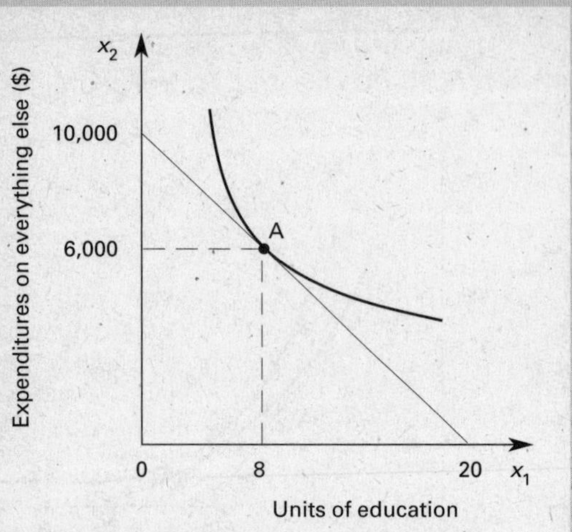

$p_1/p_2 = 500$ through point B. Laura chooses bundle C on a higher indifference curve, as shown in Figure A4.12b. The program will shift the demand curve for education to the right.

d Under the voucher scheme, the budget line will be the same as in **c** except that bundles with more than 10 000 units of good 2 are not attainable. The new budget line is FDG in Figure 4.12c. If Laura's bundle C were to the northwest of point D on the budget line, then she would be worse off under the voucher scheme than under the cash subsidy, since the best she could do would be to consume bundle D. Since C is on the DG portion of the budget line, she is no worse off under the voucher scheme.

e A lump-sum payment (cash subsidy) is at least as efficient as either a per-unit subsidy or a voucher. That is, given that the government spends the same amount of money on the individual in all cases, the recipient can be made no worse off and is usually better off with a cash subsidy than under the other two schemes.

40 a No. ABCD overestimates the true willingness to pay because bread is a normal good. That is, if the consumer surplus were actually taken away from the consumer, the individual would purchase less bread as a result of this income effect.

b The compensated demand curve is derived in Figure A4.13 for a decrease in the price of bread from $1 to $0.50. Bundles C and D are points on the ordinary demand curve; bundles C and E are points on the compensated demand curve. After the income effect is removed, the individual purchases x_1^E units of bread rather than x_1^D units at a price of $0.50. The compensating variation is given by the vertical distance AB in the figure.

41 The problem of the appropriate child care policy is a very complicated one. Here, we can only touch on a few of the relevant issues. Families with very low incomes are often lone-parent families. One problem associated with heavily subsidized daycare that has an eligibility cut-off income is that it forces certain individuals to maintain a low family income, even if other options become available. Suppose this is a single-parent family with an income of $15 000. This individual cannot afford to take a job earning $20 000 because he or she would lose the subsidized daycare spot. Thus, this system works to encourage certain families to maintain a low income. A lump-sum transfer would solve this problem, but depending upon how it is administered (do families above a certain income lose all of it,

FIGURE A4.12

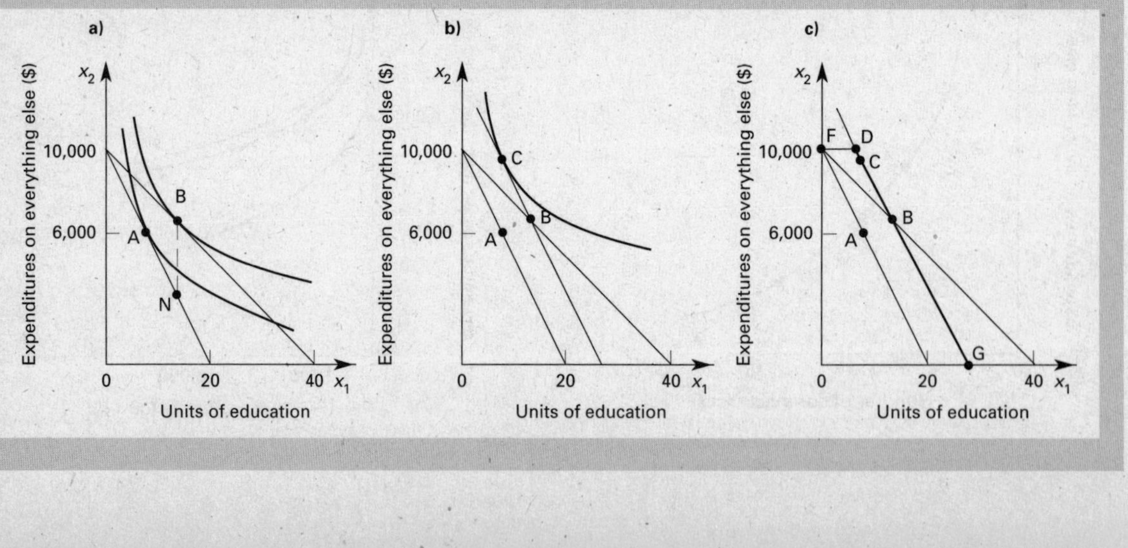

FIGURE A4.13

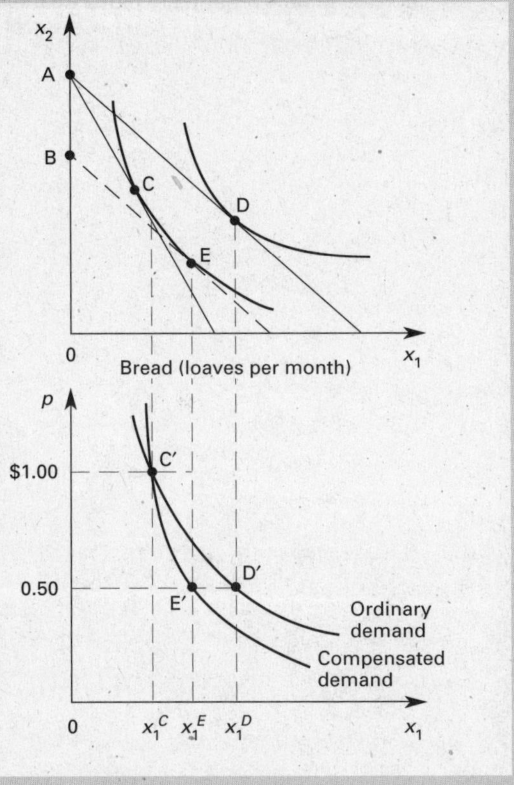

or part of it?) may be very expensive for the government and may also keep people at a low income to be eligible for the transfer. A subsidy of $5 000 would render all groups worse off because of the $20 000 cut-off level. If this were increased, then higher-income groups (who still cannot afford the full cost of daycare) would be better off. Free day care is a tricky issue. On the one hand, we want to encourage everyone who wants to work and increase their future earning possibilities to do so, on the other hand, how sensible is it to pay the equivalent of $10 000 for a daycare spot to someone earning, say, $12 000 per year?

*42 a Set up the Lagrange multiplier:

$$\underset{x,\,y,\,\lambda}{\text{Max}}\ L = 32x^{1/2} + y + \lambda(m - px - y)$$

(note that $p_2 = 1$) from which we obtain three first-order conditions: 1) $16x^{-1/2} - \lambda p_1 = 0$, 2) $1 - \lambda = 0$, 3) $m - p_1x - p_2y = 0$. Solving these three equations simultaneously yields: $x = (16/p)^2$, and $y = m - 16^2/p$.

b If $p = 9$ then $x = 4$ and $y = 968$.

c If $p = 16$ then $x = 1$ and $y = 984$. Notice from the demand function for ice cream that it is not dependent upon income, thus ice cream has a zero income effect for Gilles. The substitution effect of the price change is the entire effect, i.e., 3 litres of ice cream.

*43 a Using the Lagrange multiplier we have:

$$\underset{x,y,\lambda}{\text{Max}}\ L = 2ln\ x + ln\ y + \lambda(m - p_1x - p_2y)$$

which leads to three first-order conditions: 1) $2/x - \lambda p_1 = 0$, 2) $1/y - \lambda p_2 = 0$, 3) $m - p_1x - p_2y = 0$. Solving for x and y we obtain $x = (2m/3p_1)$, $y = m/3p_2$ as demand functions.

b $x = 8, y = 5$

c The compensated demand function comes from minimizing the costs associated with buying some bundle subject to the constraint that utility is fixed (at, say, $\hat{U}$). Formally, we may use the Lagrange multiplier: Max $-p_1x - p_2y + \lambda(\hat{U} - x^2y)$ (note that x^2y is the same utility function as $2ln\ x + ln\ y$; we can use this transformation to make the algebra slightly easier); again we now have three first-order conditions to solve to obtain the compensated demand functions: $x = (\hat{U}_2p_2/p_1)^{1/3}$, $y = p_1/2p_2{}^*(\hat{U}_2p_2/p_1)^{1/3}$. (Note that you can verify that you have the right answer by plugging in $\hat{U}=320$, $p_1 = 10$, $p_2 = 8$ and ensuring that you obtain $x = 8$ and $y = 5$).

d Plug into the compensated demand functions $\hat{U} = 320$, $p_1 = 20$, $p_2 = 8$ to get $x = 6.35$, $y = 7.94$, and hence the income necessary for this bundle is $190.48 which implies a compensating variation of $70.48. He would thus be indifferent between having $120 with prices $10 and $8, or $190.48 with prices $20 and $8.

44 a In order to become a Price Club (or Costco) member certain requirements must be met; certain types of employment, for instance, qualifies individuals for membership. In this way, membership in this club is a type of sorting in the market. People who want reasonably high-quality goods for low unit prices, and who are prepared to buy in bulk, would buy a membership. It thus caters to a much more homogeneous buyer than would a general-type store. It also caters to people with high opportunity costs of time because different sorts of goods can be purchased under the same roof (with one long line up to pay rather than several). Zeller's would cater to the lower-end of the market; people with lower opportunity costs of time relative to PC, for instance, because less choice is offered.

b Time costs can explain much of this decision. The Coquihalla takes about 30 minutes off of the trip to Kelowna.

c A couple of factors may be in place. First, the location of the bridge is not convenient for everyone, so it may be faster to take the ferry. Second, people who want the experience of going to an island may prefer the ferry.

d We often observe shops that sell essentially the same products located very close to each other.

One plausible explanation relies on time costs. A shopper wanting a bundle of goods will go to the store where he or she is most likely to find this bundle at the best price. If one or more of the items could be purchased at a lower price elsewhere this would not compensate for the increase in time required to purchase them.

CHAPTER 5

Intertemporal Decision Making and Capital Values

Chapter Summary

Intertemporal Problems

In this chapter our economic problems take on a dynamic or **intertemporal** dimension. Many of the important decisions you make are intertemporal in nature: Should you embark on a career path that involves a long training period but with promise of a high expected income, or follow a relatively easy-going path with a moderate expected income? Should you spend your earnings on a party this weekend or save it for the trip to Europe that you've been planning? These and similar problems involve trading off consumption today with consumption in the future.

The key market price in this and other intertemporal problems is the **interest rate**, the rate at which individuals can borrow or lend money in the **market for loanable funds**. This price determines how future dollars are translated into **present value** terms for making intertemporal decisions. The present value of $\$x$ to be received t periods from today is that sum of money, $\$y$, such that if we were to invest $\$y$ today at the interest rate, it would be worth $\$x$ t periods from today. Alternatively, the **future value** of $\$y$, t periods from today, is $\$x$.

Intertemporal Value Comparisons

The rate at which individuals lend or supply their money (for example, when they deposit their money in a savings account), must be less than the rate at which individuals are willing to pay to borrow or demand money (for example, when they take out a loan), in order for a transaction to take place. The first rate is the **deposit rate;** the second is the **borrowing rate**. Sometimes we assume that these rates are equal in order to ease the analysis, in which case, we say that the market for loanable funds is perfect.

When the borrowing and deposit rates are different, the decision of which income stream to choose may depend on how you want to consume it. In particular, if you prefer to spend the money today (tomorrow), then you will want to choose the income stream with the highest present (future) value. If both rates are identical, then the present and future value rules yield identical answers. This implies that we can conveniently "separate" the income maximization problem from the choice of consumption expenditures. This **separation theorem** allows intertemporal problems to be solved in two steps: First, choose the income stream with the largest present value; second, choose consumption expenditures to maximize utility, given the income constraint.

An investment that yields an income stream with equal payments each period is called an **annuity**; if these payments last forever, it is called a **perpetuity** or **consol**. The **rate of return** of an asset is equal to its value in period t minus its value in the previous period divided by this latter value. The price of an asset depends upon its expected future return. In the case of capital equipment, its price will reflect its expected productivity over time. Suppose, for instance, that a firm is trying to decide between two types of machines. One machine uses the very latest in technology and promises to be much more efficient in comparison to the other machine which employs an older technology. We expect that the first machine will have a higher price than the second one because the expected return from this machine will be **capitalized** in its price. In this way, the rates of return of both machines are equalized.

When we talk of **capital** we are actually referring to anything that provides services over time: computers and physical buildings are thus capital goods. **Consumer capital** is used to refer to goods which provide individuals (as opposed to firms) with a stream of services — like refrigerators or CD players. We do not "consume" these goods per se, rather we enjoy the benefits that arise from the good. The maximum price that an individual is willing to pay for a good is his or her **reservation price**. If a consumer capital good requires a complementary good, such as a CD player and CDs or cameras and film, then a profit-maximizing firm selling these products will charge the marginal cost of producing the complementary good (e.g., film) and will charge the reservation price for the consumer capital good (e.g., camera).

The Life-Cycle Model

Typically, individuals incur debt when they are young, repay the debt and accumulate savings when middle aged, and consume the savings when they are old. We call this an individual's **life cycle**. We can focus on the important role played by interest rates in these intertemporal consumption and savings decisions by using a simple two-period model. The intertemporal budget constraint takes account of the fact that money can be used for current consumption, or saved, earning a return equal to the rate of interest, and consumed next period. The **budget line** can be thus expressed as: $C_0 + C_1 = I_0 (1 + i) + I_1$ — where C refers to consumption and I refers to investment (or savings) in periods 0 and 1, and i is the interest rate on savings. Notice that if we graph this line with period 0 consumption on the horizontal axis and period 1 consumption on the vertical axis, we see that the slope of the budget line is $-(1 + i)$ — reflecting the fact that the opportunity cost of a dollar consumed today is equal to the future value of that dollar next period.

An individual will maximize his utility — defined over C_0 and C_1 — subject to the intertemporal budget constraint. Given well-behaved indifference curves, the individual will choose a bundle where his or her indifference curve is tangent to the budget line — i.e., where the marginal rate of substitution of consumption in period 1 for consumption in period 0 is equal to $(1 + i)$. For an interest rate greater than zero, this implies that the marginal value of current consumption must be greater than one. Typically, individuals prefer current consumption to future consumption — implying that their **marginal rate of time preference** is positive. If we observe that an individual's consumption in period 0 is the same as her consumption in period 1, and her marginal rate of time preference is less than 1, then she is a **patient** person. However, if her marginal rate of time preference is greater than 1, she is an **impatient** person. People are normally assumed impatient.

Nonrenewable Resources

Like physical and human capital, problems in nonrenewable resources require an intertemporal framework for analysis. The owner of a **nonrenewable resource** (for example, oil) that is fixed in supply faces the following two-stage problem: First, he must allocate his resource over time so as to maximize the present value of his oil income. Second, the owner maximizes his utility subject to this wealth constraint. For this problem, the separation theorem enables us to analyze the first part of the two-stage problem — supply behaviour — without reference to preferences.

In the nonrenewable-resource problem, resource owners will maximize the present value of their asset by supplying the resource on the market in the period with the highest present value income (assuming zero production cost). This implies that as long as the present value income is equal in all periods, or the "price rises at the rate of interest" — **Hotelling's law** — the resource owner will be willing to supply some of his resource in all periods. Indeed, the competitive equilibrium satisfies this law.

KEY WORDS

Annuity
Borrowing rate
Budget line
Capital
Capitalized
Consol
Consumer capital
Deposit rate
Future value
Hotelling's law
Impatient
Interest rate
Intertemporal
Life cycle
Marginal rate of time preference
Market for loanable funds
Nonrenewable resources
Patient
Perpetuity
Present value
Rate of return
Rate of time preference
Reservation price
Separation theorem

CASE STUDY: DO HIGH PRICES MEAN WE'RE RUNNING OUT OF MINERALS?

In an empirical study, Margaret Slade[1] estimated the price path of minerals over time. She noted that resource prices are observed to rise and fall over time and that the behavior of prices depends on the various components of resource costs. For example, the technological change in the use of large earth-moving equipment for strip mining ore bodies reduced mining costs in the first part of the twentieth century. She hypothesized that the price paths would be U-shaped and found strong support for this hypothesis in the prices of copper, iron, nickel, silver, and natural gas.

A Why would the price path of a mineral be U-shaped over time? In particular, what are the components of costs that would give rise to a U-shaped price path?

B Do rising prices reflect scarcity and falling prices reflect abundance of a mineral over time? Why or why not?

[1] Margaret Slade (1982), "Trends in Natural-Resource Commodity Prices: An Analysis of the Time Domain," *Journal of Environmental Economics and Management*, **9**: 122–137.

EXERCISES

Multiple-Choice

Choose the correct answer to each of the following questions. There is only one correct answer to each question.

1 Income stream *A* consists of \$1 000 in each of three consecutive years (starting today) and income stream *B* consists of \$4 000 two years from today. Then
  a Income stream *A* has a larger present value for an annual interest rate of 0%.
  b Income stream *A* has a larger present value for all annual interest rates greater than 30%.
  c Income stream *B* has a larger present value for all annual interest rates greater than 0%.
  d The present value of the two income streams are equivalent for an interest rate equal to 10%.
  e None of the above.

2 Georges is indifferent between an annuity of \$10 000 and a lump-sum payment of \$200 000, from which we can conclude:
  a The interest rate is at least 5 per cent.
  b Georges expects to live at least another 20 years.
  c Georges expects to live at least another 15 years.
  d Both **a** and **b**.
  e Insufficient information to determine.

To answer questions **3**, **4** and **5**, refer to Figure 5.1. Shown in the diagram are Sean's budget line (*CD*) and his indifference curve. Sean's income (I_0, I_1) is given by point *A* and his consumption (C_0, C_1) is given by point *B*. Assume consumption in periods 0 and 1 are normal goods.

3 Which of the following is true about Sean's intertemporal consumption decision?
  a His present value of consumption exceeds his present value of income.
  b He is a borrower in period 0.
  c He could increase his present value of consumption by consuming less in period 0.
  d Since he is not spending all of his income in period 1, he is not maximizing his utility.
  e None of the above.

4 If the interest rate increases, then Sean
  a Will consume less in period 1..
  b Will increase his consumption in both periods.
  c May become a saver.
  d Will consume more in period 0.
  e None of the above.

5 Suppose that the price of goods in period 1 doubles.
  a. Sean's budget line will shift downwards in a parallel fashion.
  b. Sean's budget line will shift upwards in a parallel fashion.
  c. Sean's budget line will pivot upwards around point A, becoming flatter.
  d. Sean's budget line will pivot downwards around point A; becoming steeper.
  e. none of the above.

FIGURE 5.1

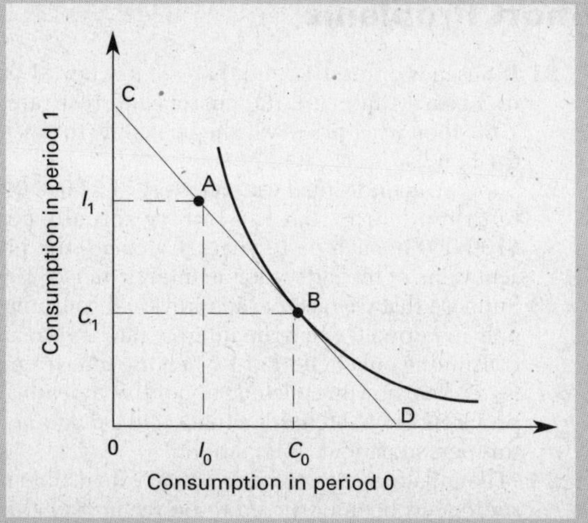

FIGURE 5.2

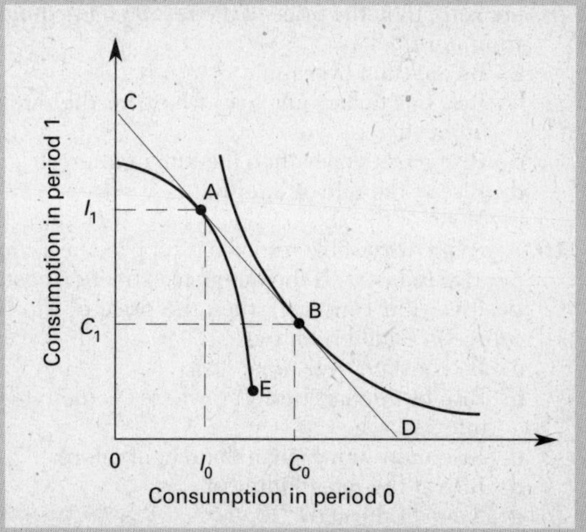

6 If Eleanor consumes less than her income in period 0 at the current interest rate, and consumption in periods 0 and 1 are normal goods, then
a An increase in the interest rate will lead Eleanor to continue to save some of her income in period 0.
b A decrease in the interest rate will lead Eleanor to consume less of her income in period 1.
c A decrease in the interest rate may lead Eleanor to borrow some income in period 0.
d All the above.
e None of the above.

7 Suppose Suzanne is a borrower at current interest rates. Then
a For an increase in the interest rate, the income effect increases consumption in both periods.
b For an increase in the interest rate, the substitution effect reinforces the income effect to increase consumption in period 1.
c For a decrease in the interest rate, the substitution effect reinforces the income effect to increase consumption in period 0.
d For a decrease in the interest rate, the substitution effect increases consumption in period 1.
e None of the above.

8 Which of the following is true:
a An increase in the marginal productivity of capital goods, *ceteris paribus*, will decrease a firm's demand for loanable funds.
b An increase in the price of capital goods, *ceteris paribus*, will increase a firm's demand curve for loanable funds.
c An increase in the expected wages for high-skilled jobs, *ceteris paribus*, will increase an individual's demand for loanable funds.
d A tax on interest earned on savings accounts will increase the supply of loanable funds.
e None of the above is true.

9 A certain exhaustible resource is supplied by a competitive industry. If the marginal extraction costs are zero, then the price of the resource in equilibrium must
a Be constant over time.
b Rise by i dollars per year, where i is the rate of interest.
c Rise more slowly then the rate of interest.
d Rise at the rate of interest.
e None of the above.

10 A certain exhaustible resource is supplied by a competitive industry. If the marginal extraction cost is positive (but constant), then the price of the resource in equilibrium must
a Be constant over time.
b Rise by i dollars per year, where i is the rate of interest.
c Rise more slowly than the rate of interest.
d Rise at the rate of interest.
e None of the above.

True-False

11 A firm with earnings of 100 in each of three periods has a lower present value of profits than a firm with earnings of 180 in period 1, 100 in period 2, and 0 in period 3 if the discount rate equals 25%.

12 The present value of $100, received one year from today, is a sum of money, $x, such that if an individual borrowed $100 today, he or she would have to pay the lender $x one year from now.

13 An individual will consume more in period 1 than in period 0 if the marginal rate of time preference of consumption in period 1 for consumption in period 0 is less than $1 + i$ at the point where consumption in the two periods is equal.

14 If there are only two periods, 0 and 1, an increase in the interest rate will always lead to an increase in consumption in period 1.

15 If there are only two periods, 0 and 1, the substitution effect of an increase in the interest rate will reduce consumption in period 0 and increase consumption in period 1.

16 If an individual has a constant marginal rate of time preference, then he or she is indifferent between consumption today and consumption tomorrow.

17 An impatient person is willing to forgo current consumption for future consumption only when the interest rate is positive.

18 An increase in the price of a capital good will reduce the demand for loanable funds.

19 If an individual is a saver at current interest rates, then the substitution and income effects for an increase in the interest rate will reinforce each other to reduce consumption in period 1.

20 The opportunity cost of extracting a barrel of oil from the ground today is the present value of the income received if it were extracted tomorrow.

Short Problems

21 If Susan is offered a bond that will pay her $1 000 in 3 years' time, and the current interest rate is 10%, then what price will she be willing to pay for the bond?

22 Suppose an individual wins a lottery of $1 000 000, but then learns that the lottery actually pays $100 000 in each of 10 years. Calculate the present value of the lottery for an interest rate of 10%.

23 Suppose that we observe an individual consuming only in period 0 when the interest rate is zero and consuming only in period 1 when the interest rate is r. What can you conclude about this individual's preferences? Sketch this situation in a diagram. Is this person patient or impatient?

24 "The inflation-adjusted price of an exhaustible resource has been observed to be rising over time,

while the cost and demand conditions were unchanged. From this observation alone it follows that the market for this resource is being gradually monopolized over time." Do you agree with the conclusion? Why or why not?

Long Problems

25 What effect will an increase in the interest rate have on the demand curve for automobiles? Explain.

26 Suppose that Ralph owns a very small oil well that holds 50 000 barrels of crude oil. At the moment, the price of a barrel of crude oil is $25 and it is expected to increase to $27.50 next year.

a Given zero extraction costs, what interest rate would make Ralph indifferent between selling his oil now and next year?

b Suppose that extraction costs are currently $5 per barrel and, because of tighter environmental controls on the process, are expected to increase to $10 per barrel next year. How will this affect your answer to part **a**?

c Let's now suppose that the government is seriously considering imposing a stiff tax on crude oil, to be paid by the owner of the oil, in the hopes of encouraging better conservation of the reserves. With zero extraction costs and an interest rate of 12 %, how much need the tax be in order to encourage Ralph to leave his reserves in the ground? What do you think of such a policy as a means of encouraging conservation?

d Comment on the incentive to explore for further reserves stemming from the following: (i) a rise in the price of crude oil; (ii) an increase in the tax on crude oil; (iii) stricter environmental controls on oil spills while extracting.

*27 Tammy is a chicken farmer. The price of chicken is $4 a kilogram. A chicken that is t years old weighs $t^{1/2}$ kilograms. Let the weekly interest rate be i. Assume that the cost of raising chickens is zero.

a How many weeks should Tammy raise her chickens before selling them to the market?

b Now assume that Tammy cannot breed any new chickens until the existing chickens are sold. For example, Tammy has a fixed number of chicken coops and she cannot put more than one chicken in each coop. After the grown chickens are sold, Tammy replaces them with new chicks that she is given for free, and starts all over again. Will Tammy raise her chickens for a longer or shorter period of time than you found in **a**? Explain your answer.

ANSWERS TO CHAPTER 5

Case Study

A Costs of extraction may decrease over time due to technological change, increase over time due to declining grades of the ore, and increase over time due to the intertemporal effect (the opportunity cost of extracting the resource today instead of tomorrow). In the early stages of the life-cycle of mineral extraction, the technological factor may dominate the declining grade and intertemporal effects, giving rise to a declining price path. Eventually, as predicted by Hotelling's law discussed in this chapter, the price path rises as the high-quality ore is depleted and the intertemporal opportunity cost of extracting the resource increases.

B Rising prices often signal that the resource is being depleted. However, even if the resource is becoming more scarce, prices may fall. Improvements in transporting, smelting, and refining the resource may reduce the price of the refined product. The market structure or the regulatory structure of the industry may change; for example, price controls kept the price of petroleum in the United States and Canada artificially low in the postwar period. Finally, substitutes for the resource may reduce the price of the resource.

Multiple-Choice

1 b 2 d 3 b 4 c 5 a
6 d 7 c 8 c 9 d 10 c

True-False

11 T 12 F 13 T 14 F 15 T
16 F 17 T 18 T 19 F 20 T

Short Problems

21 $$PV = \frac{\$1\,000}{(1+i)^t} = \frac{\$1\,000}{(1+0.1)^3} = \$751.30$$

22 If the individual receives only $100 000/year, then the value of the lottery today is its present value:

$$\$100\,000(1 + 1/(1+i) + 1/(1+i)^2 + \ldots + 1/(1+i)^9)$$

At an interest rate of 10%, the present value of the lottery equals approximately $676 000.

23 This individual considers consumption in periods 0 and 1 to be perfect substitutes for each other. The only factor determining when consumption will take place is the interest rate. The indifference curve of this individual is a straight line whose slope lies somewhere between 1 and 1+r. This situation is depicted in figure A5.1. Notice that when r=0, the individual can attain the highest indifference curve (I', passing through point B) when consumption takes place only in period 0. By contrast, when the interest rate is r, the consumer can attain the indifference curve I" (passing through point C) by consuming only in period 1. This individual is impatient given that he will spend all of his income in the first period whenever the interest rate is zero.

24 No. Competitive resource owners maximize the present value of their asset by supplying the resource on the market in the period with the highest net present value income. That is, as long as the present value income is equal in all periods, the resource owner will be willing to supply some of his resource in each period. This implies that the price must rise at the rate of interest over time, even in competitive resource markets.

FIGURE A5.1

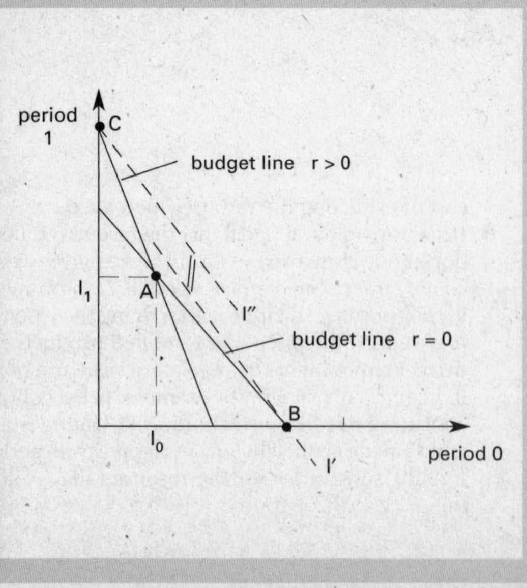

Long Problems

25 Automobiles represent a stock of capital that produces a flow of services. It is the flow of services that gives utility to consumers and the existing stock of cars is valuable only because the flow of services from it is valuable.

The total value of an automobile is equal to the present value of the future net flow of services that the automobile is expected to yield. Let the consumer's value of automobile services in year t be V_t, and let m_t and d_t be the maintenance costs and depreciation of the car during the year t. Then, the value of the services of a particular automobile during the year is

$$N_t = V_t - m_t - d_t.$$

The present value of the flow of services to the consumer equals

$$PV = N_0 + N_1/(1+i) + N_2/(1+i)^2 + \ldots$$

This also represents the maximum price that an individual is willing to pay for the car. An increase in the interest rate, then, reduces the present value of automobile services, and thus the price that consumers are willing to pay. This shifts the demand curve for cars downwards.

26 a Need to equate 25°(50 000) = (27.5°(50 000))/(1 + i), which yields i = 10%.

b In this case, once extraction costs are taken into account it is clear that it is always worthwhile to extract all oil immediately. Solving for the interest rate yields a negative value (–12.5%).

c Equating 25°(50 000)°(1 – t) = (27.5°(50 000))/(1.12) where t is the tax rate per dollar revenue yields t = 1.79%. Using the tax system encourages conservation and yields revenues for the government. However, what will happen next period? It only encourages conservation when the tax is clearly a one-period phenomenon; if it continued next period its conservation properties would be lost. Can the government credibly impose a tax that lasts only one period?

d (i) As the price of crude oil rises, the incentive to explore increases as well. We saw this during the oil-shock years of the early to mid-1970s. Much exploration took place in Canada during that period because of the large increase in the world price of oil. (ii) As crude oil is taxed, it lowers the profitability of crude oil and hence reduces the incentives to explore. (iii) Stricter environmental controls which raise the cost of extracting oil, hence reducing its profitability, reduce the incentive to explore. Notice that the fact that less exploring is undertaken may not be a bad thing from society's perspective. It may well be that the social costs in terms of pollution from crude oil's extracting, refining and burning may be very high, and hence it may be beneficial to reduce the incentive to find more oil and (by implication) increase the incentive to find oil substitutes.

***27 a** The number of weeks that Tammy will raise her chickens maximizes her profits: $\$4t^{1/2}/(1+i)^t$. The first-order conditions for a maximum are:

$$\frac{(4)t^{-1/2}}{2(1+i)^t} - \frac{(4)t^{1/2}\ln(1+i)}{(1+i)^t} = 0$$

which implies $t = \dfrac{1}{2\ln(1+i)}$

b Now there is an opportunity cost from breeding the chickens too long; it is the delay in breeding the next group of chickens that are later sold in the market. This will shorten the optimal breeding time for each set of chickens, relative to the time found in part **a**.

CHAPTER 6

Production and Cost: One Variable Input

Chapter Summary

In this chapter, we abstract from the complexities of the firm's internal organization and concentrate on its production decisions. The firm is treated simply as an organization that buys inputs and transforms them into goods and services for the market.

The Production Function

Basic to all the firm's production decisions is the **production function** of the firm, $y = f(z_1, \ldots, z_n)$, which is the relationship between quantities of inputs (the z_i's or **input bundle**) and the maximum output that can be produced (y). The production function describes the output that can be produced when inputs are used in a **technically efficient** manner. The production technology can be one of several types — inputs can be used in fixed proportions or in variable proportions in production. In **fixed proportions production functions**, also known as **Leontief production functions**, the ratio in which the inputs are used never varies. By contrast, **variable proportion production functions** allow for the substitution among inputs. The **Cobb-Douglas production function**, which is frequently used in economics, allows for substitution among the inputs. In the two-input case, this function has the general form: $y = Az_1^u z_2^v$, where A, u and v are positive constants.

Opportunity Costs

Several cost concepts are important in economics. **Opportunity cost** refers to the value of the next best alternative. It is crucial to distinguish between **sunk costs** which are unavoidable and **avoidable costs**. Sunk costs do not affect economic decisions because they are, well, sunk! Avoidable costs need not be incurred and thus do influence economic decisions. We also distinguish between **fixed costs** that are independent of output and **variable costs** that vary directly with output.

To put the production function in perspective, we must emphasize that the firm wants to maximize profits; that is, it wants to maximize its revenues from sales of output while minimizing its costs of production. Thus, **profit-maximization** implies **cost-minimization**.

Cost-Minimization Problems

In the long run, all factors are variable. The firm's **long-run cost minimization** problem is thus to choose all factors of production in order to minimize costs. In the two-input case, this amounts to choosing z_1 and z_2 to minimize total costs $w_1 z_1 + w_2 z_2$ subject to the constraint that the firm produce some given level of output $y = F(z_1, z_2)$. The firm's **short-run cost minimization problem** recognizes that the short run implies that at least one of the firm's factors of production is fixed (exactly one in the two-input case) and minimizes total costs given some level of the fixed factor.

Production: One Variable Input

As is intuitively clear (and rigorously discussed in later chapters), the decision about which inputs to employ by a firm depends on how "productive" an input is, relative to its cost. For this reason, we isolate increases in the total product or output attributable to a particular input, holding the other input(s) fixed — given by the **total product function**. As first recognized by Malthus, the total product curve is characterized by **diminishing marginal productivity** of a variable input, holding all other inputs fixed in quantity. That is, as *additional* amounts of an input are applied to fixed factors, the *additional* output (or **marginal product**) produced eventually begins to decline. Similarly, the **average product**, the total product divided by the quantity of a variable input employed, will also begin to decline after some level of a variable input. The relationship between the average and marginal products is the following: When the marginal product exceeds (is less than) the average product, the average product rises (falls); when marginal product equals average product, average product is at a maximum. Although technically speaking, the marginal product can be negative, firms would never allow this to happen. We thus assume that firms can always get rid of any excess input rather than allow marginal product to become negative (the **free disposal assumption**).

Cost of Production: One Variable Input

Consider the case in which all inputs but one are fixed in quantity. In this case, the short-run production function is defined by the total product (TP) function, $TP(z_1) = F(z_1, \bar{z}_2, \ldots, \bar{z}_n)$. From the short-run production function, we can derive the **short-run cost function** and the seven short-run cost concepts: the **short-run total cost $STC(y)$, short-run variable costs $VC(y)$, short-run fixed costs FC, short-run average costs $SAC(y)$, short-run average variable costs $AVC(y)$, short-run average fixed costs $AFC(y)$, and short-run marginal costs, $SMC(y)$.** $STC(y)$ equals the sum of $VC(y)$ and FC. The variable-cost function is found simply by turning the total product function on its side; more precisely, transform the variable input axis to variable costs by multiplying the input quantities by the input price and then interchange the axes. The $AVC(y)$, variable costs divided by output, has an inverse relationship with the average product: As average product rises, average variable costs fall, and vice versa. An analogous relationship holds between the $SMC(y)$, the additional costs of producing additional output, and marginal product. Adding the fixed costs to the variable costs gives the short run total costs; adding $AFC(y)$, which is the total fixed costs divided by output, to the average variable costs gives $SAC(y)$. Hence, we have the seven short-run cost curves and related production relationships that are necessary for analyzing the firm's production decisions in the short run. In the case of **multi-plant firms**, where a firm can produce its output in more than one plant, total variable production costs are minimized if output is allocated such that the short-run marginal costs are equalized across each plant.

An Application: Traffic Congestion

Many of the issues associated with cost and production functions can be illustrated in a simple model of traffic congestion. Suppose that a commuter can choose between two alternative routes to get him to work. The costs of the commuter are measured in terms of the money value of time spent commuting, which in turn depends on the number of cars on each of the alternative routes. In this case, the output is the total number of commuter trips made on each road.

From this simple model, we find that if there is unrestricted access to both roads — that is, if both roads are common property — then commuters equate their average commuting costs on each route. This equilibrium is sub-optimal from a cost-benefit perspective because it does not minimize the total commuting costs to society. To attain the socially optimal number of cars on each road, commuters should be allocated so as to equalize their marginal commuting costs across all routes. One possible solution to this problem is to levy a toll — that is, to restrict access — on one of the routes in order to shift the private equilibrium to the optimum. Note that we could reinterpret this example to reflect the issues of multiplant production. To minimize total variable costs of production given that output is produced in two or more plants, set the short-run marginal costs of production equal in all plants.

KEY WORDS

- Average product
- Avoidable costs
- Cobb-Douglas production function
- Cost-minimization
- Diminishing marginal productivity
- Fixed costs
- Fixed-proportions production function
- Free disposal assumption
- Input bundle
- Long-run cost minimization
- Leontief production functions
- Marginal product
- Multiplant firms
- Opportunity costs
- Production function
- Profit maximization
- Short-run cost function
- Short-run cost minimization
- Short-run total costs, variable costs, fixed costs, average costs, average variable costs, average fixed costs, marginal costs
- Sunk costs
- Technical efficiency
- Total product function
- Variable costs
- Variable-proportions production function

CASE STUDY: LIFE ON THE FARM

Farming can be a tough business in Canada as well as elsewhere. For many, it constitutes a way of life that is passed from generation to generation — and hence is more than simply a means of earning a living. The growing season is short, the days are long, and the grain yield is a function not only of the effort of the farmer but of factors beyond his or her control like the weather. In recent years because of banner yields, the wholesale prices of grains have been on the decline, causing considerable hardships in farm life in Canada's prairie provinces. Indeed, many farmers are now reporting that the costs of grain farming exceeds revenues.

Grain farmers are not the only people pushed to the brink. Recently, pig farmers have reported that the costs of raising pigs far exceeds the amount received for pigs on the market. As a result, some farmers have actually slaughtered their piglets rather than have to pay for their maintenance before taking them to market.

A If revenues are exceeding the costs of farming, why do we still observe farms in operation?

B If revenues fall when the price of a good falls, what does this tell you about the elasticity of demand for this good? What does this imply for when times are "bad", i.e., when the crop yield is poor or there are few pigs on the market? What is the relationship between the Canadian market and the international market for grain?

C Suppose that during past farming crises the government has provided financial assistance to farmers. How might this affect your answer to part **a**? Provide an economic rationale for such assistance.

D The government has just announced a large bail-out package for Western farmers. What are the potential short and long-run consequences of such a bail-out?

EXERCISES

Multiple-Choice

Choose the correct answer to each question. There is only one correct answer to each question.

Refer to Figure 6.1 to answer questions **1** and **2**.

1 A firm producing y' units of output
- **a** Is minimizing average variable costs of production.
- **b** Is minimizing average total costs of production.
- **c** Faces fixed costs equal to My'.
- **d** Faces a marginal cost smaller than the average total cost production.
- **e** None of the above.

2 In Figure 6.1, which of the following is shown?
- **a** Total fixed costs decline for increases in output.
- **b** Average total costs at y' equals My' divided by Oy'.
- **c** Marginal costs are increasing for all values of output.
- **d** Average variable costs at y' equal the difference between My' and OL divided by Oy'.
- **e** Both **b** and **d**.

3 The law of diminishing returns to a variable input
- **a** Assumes that at least one input is held fixed.
- **b** Refers to the behaviour of the marginal product of the variable input.
- **c** Implies that an increase in the fixed factor would increase total product.
- **d** All the above.
- **e** Only **a** and **b**.

FIGURE 6.1

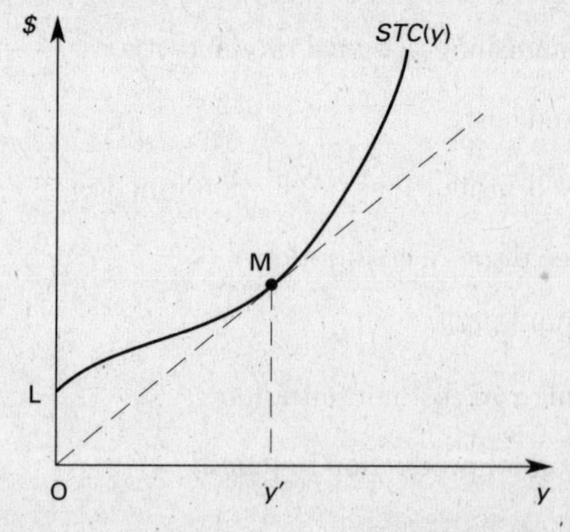

4 Suppose that two dozen bagels can be produced with two workers, and four dozen bagels can be produced with six workers. Then, which of the following is correct?
- **a** Average product is 1/2.
- **b** Average variable costs are rising.
- **c** The marginal product is higher than the average product.
- **d** The marginal product of labor is two (dozen bagels).
- **e** None of the above.

5 The production function $y = \text{Min}(az_1, bz_2)$ implies which of the following?
- **a** Good Y can be produced with variable proportions of input 1 and input 2.
- **b** The production of one unit of good Y requires more of input 1 than input 2 if $a > b$.
- **c** If input 1 and input 2 are being used in the proportion b/a, then an increase in the quantity of only one of the inputs will not increase output.
- **d** If input 1 and input 2 are being used in the proportion b/a, then an increase in the quantity of only one of the inputs will double output.
- **e** None of the above.

6 Which of the following equals the average variable cost?
- **a** The price of the variable input divided by the marginal product of that input.
- **b** Total variable costs divided by the quantity of the variable input hired.
- **c** The additional cost of hiring another unit of the variable input.
- **d** The price of the variable input divided by the average product of that input.
- **e** None of the above.

To answer questions **7** and **8**, refer to Figure 6.2. Assume that input 1 is the variable input in the production of good Y.

7 In Figure 6.2,
- **a** The average product of input 1 is maximized at point A.
- **b** Average fixed costs are constant.
- **c** The slope of AVC equals the slope of SAC at every output.
- **d** None of the above.
- **e** Both **a** and **c**.

8 At point B,
- **a** The average product of input 1 is at a maximum.
- **b** The slope of the total cost curve is less than the slope of the total variable cost curve at the same output.
- **c** The average product is rising.
- **d** The marginal product is less than average product.
- **e** None of the above.

9 Four servings of spaghetti *alle vongole* require 0.8 kilograms of spaghetti, eight tomatoes, 12 large clams, and four garlic cloves. Suppose that a cook has 4.9 kilograms of spaghetti, 60 tomatoes, 54 large clams, and 30 garlic cloves. Then, the maximum number of individuals that he can feed is
- **a** 28
- **b** 24
- **c** 20
- **d** 18
- **e** None of the above.

FIGURE 6.2

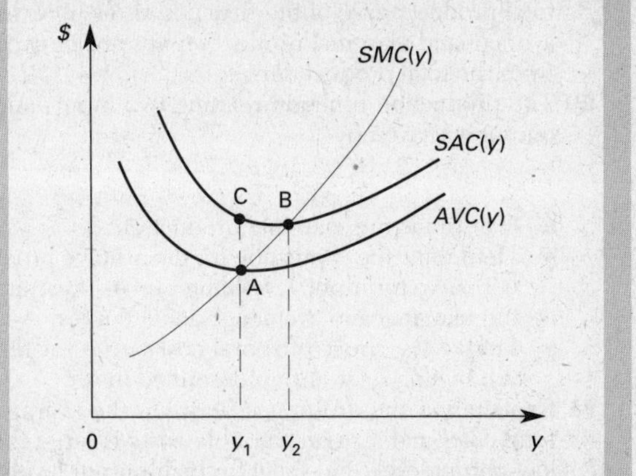

True-False

10 If marginal product is decreasing, then average product must also be decreasing.

11 For a fixed-proportions technology, inputs cannot be substituted for each other in production.

12 The marginal product of input 1 derived from the production function $y = \text{Min}(az_1, bz_2)$, diminishes for increases in input 1.

13 If the average product is declining, then average total costs must be increasing.

14 The short run is that period of time during which some inputs cannot be varied.

15 The slope of the short-run total cost curve equals the slope of the short-run variable cost curve at every output.

16 Average fixed costs are constant for all output levels.

17 A profit-maximizing firm would never operate on the declining portion of the total product curve.

Short Problems

18 Give an intuitive argument in support of the law of diminishing returns.

19 Suppose that a firm produces with one variable factor of production and that marginal product decreases for all levels of the input used. Draw the total product curve of the firm and show how the average and marginal product curves are derived from the total product curve.

***20** The production function relating two inputs and output y is given by

$$y = z_1^{1/2} z_2^{1/2}$$

a Determine the marginal product of z_1.

b Determine the expression for the average product curve for input 1, holding $z_2 = 4$. Illustrate the marginal and average product curves.

c Derive the short-run total cost curve for the production relationship described in **a**.

21 Explain why the difference between the average total costs and average variable costs is large for low-output levels and small for high-output levels.

***22** A wheat farmer in Saskatchewan produces kilograms of wheat, y, using land (input 2) and labour (input 1) according to a production function, where the marginal product of labour is $(2z_2^{1/2})/z_1^{1/2} - 1$. The farmer has 16 hectares of land for wheat production. In addition, she has unlimited amounts of her own labour services for producing wheat (that is, her opportunity cost of time is zero). How many units of her labour will she use, given that she employs all 16 hectares of land? Explain.

***23** It takes Doreen 15 minutes to travel to her soccer practice when the flow of traffic is less than 500 cars per hour; but for a flow of traffic greater than 500 cars per hour, it takes $0.0005X$ hours of travelling time, where X is the flow of traffic per hour. Along an alternative route, it takes 45 minutes of travelling time. Find the toll that will allocate commuters efficiently between the two routes.

Long Problems

24 Suppose that a firm's short-run total cost function is given by

$$STC(y) = a + by$$

where a and b are positive constants and y is output. Only one variable and one fixed factor are used in production.

***a** Find the total variable costs, total fixed costs, average total costs, average variable costs, average fixed costs, and marginal costs.

b Assume that the price of the variable input is w. Find expressions for the total product, average product, and marginal product.

c Do you think that these costs and production relationships are realistic? Why or why not?

25 Suppose that a farmer in Manitoba has a fixed amount of labour and two plots of land, A and B.

a If the marginal productivity diminishes on both plots, what distribution of labour on the two plots of land will maximize output? Use economic intuition as to why your solution is correct.

b Now suppose that the marginal product of labour increases on plot A and diminishes on plot B. Would only plot A be cultivated? Explain, using a diagram.

26 Milkshakes are produced at the local ice-cream parlour with two inputs: Theodore's time, input 1, and the set of fixed ingredients (1 cup of milk, 1 tablespoon of malt, 1 scoop of ice cream), input 2. The number of milkshakes produced can be no greater than Theodore's time multiplied by the speed s (measured in number of milkshakes per hour) at which Theodore works. Theodore also knows that when he makes milkshakes very quickly, he spills a large amount of the ingredients. Hence, his production is constrained by the technological relationship that says that the number of milkshakes he can make *per set of ingredients* can be no greater than $10/s$. In other words, if Theodore makes 10 milkshakes per hour, he can produce one milkshake for every set of ingredients, but if he makes 20 milkshakes per hour, he needs twice the ingredients because one-half of them land on the floor. This production relationship has an upper bound of 1; he cannot make more than one milkshake per set of ingredients. Given these relationships, determine the speed at which Theodore will work as a function of z_1 and z_2 (quantities of inputs 1 and 2) and the production function for milkshakes.

ANSWERS TO CHAPTER 6

Case Study

A There are several reasons why farmers are still farming. First, what we are witnessing may be a short-run phenomenon. As long as the farmers are still covering their variable costs, they may make losses in the short run. (Grain farmers might be in this situation, pig farmers are not even covering their variable costs.) Second, farming is a way of life and hence farmers are less likely to quit while they are still able to eke out a living. Third, farm incomes are subject to quite a bit of volatility due to the nature of the product. Demand is fairly inelastic and so too is supply, this means that prices and revenues can be very volatile. Farmers should be operating, therefore, on a fairly long time horizon, expecting fluctuations from year to year, but obtaining an adequate average income over the long run.

B As mentioned above, if revenues fall when the price falls, this implies that the elasticity of demand for the good is low (inelastic). When the price of the grain rises, therefore, so too will revenues. Part of the difficulty, especially with grain, is that prices are often set on world markets. If the world producers are having a banner crop, it has an impact on all farmers. Thus, if world producers are having a banner crop and Canadian farmers are not (because of, say, weather conditions) this has a tremendous impact on our farmers. They receive a low price for their small quantity of grain. In principle, grain marketing boards try to stabilize prices by storing grain in good years and putting it onto the market in bad-yield years. Recently, because crops have been very good for several years, this strategy has been less effective.

C Clearly, if the Canadian government has had a history of helping out farmers in trouble, then farmers will hang on to their business in the hopes of such help being available again. From an economic perspective, it may make sense for the government to take a long-run perspective in ensuring that the Canadian farm sector does not disappear because of circumstances in the world market. Some argue that it is important that we protect the domestic food supply.

D In the short run, of course, it helps farmers deal with the current cyclical difficulties. In the long run, the potential problem with subsidies is that they are difficult to stop. One might argue that farms that are not viable should be closed or, at least, the farmers should switch into the production of something that will enable them to make a reasonable living. In some sense, market fluctuations perhaps provide the needed encouragement to keep farming operations efficient.

Multiple-Choice

1 b 2 e 3 d 4 b 5 c
6 d 7 a 8 d 9 d

True-False

10 F 11 T 12 F 13 F
14 T 15 T 16 F 17 T

Short Problems

18 Consider the case of land. If the law of diminishing returns did not hold, only cultivated land would be used to produce food; new land would never be brought into production. Alternatively, one can think of a small plot of farmland. Initially, as labour is added to the plot, output and productivity increase. However, if too many labourers come to work on the plot, they begin to get in each other's way, and there is not enough work to keep them all busy. This is when diminishing returns to labour set in.

19 When the marginal product decreases as the input increases, it implies that the slope of the total product curve declines throughout, as shown in Figure A6.1. The average product at a point is given by the slope of a ray from the origin to that point on the total product curve. Note that the slope of a ray from the origin falls as z_1 increases. Furthermore, $AP(z_1) > MP(z_1)$ at every z_1.

*__20 a__ If $z_2 = 4$, $y = z_1^{1/2}(4^{1/2}) = 2z_1^{1/2}$. Average product and marginal products are given by $AP_1 = 2z_1^{1/2}/z_1 = 2/z_1^{1/2}$ and $MP_1 = 1/z_1^{1/2}$. To plot AP_1 and MP_1, let $z_1 = (4, 9, 16)$. At these values, $MP_1 = (1/2, 1/3, 1/4)$ and $AP_1 = (1, 2/3, 1/2)$, as shown in Figure A6.2.

b The short-run total cost is the sum of the variable costs and the fixed costs. Variable costs are found by inverting the production function and multiplying z_1 by the wage rate. That is,

FIGURE A6.1

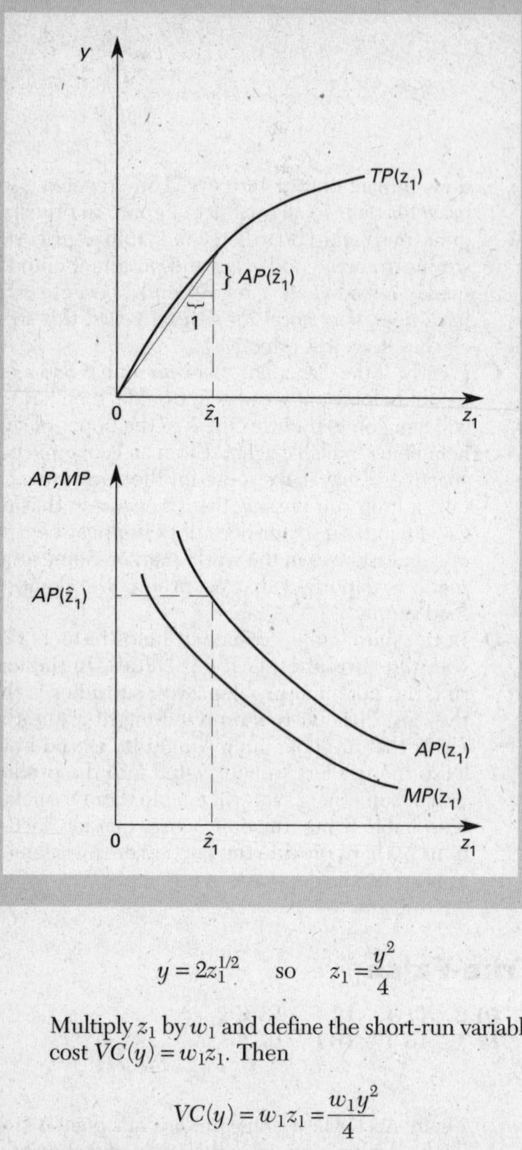

$$y = 2z_1^{1/2} \quad \text{so} \quad z_1 = \frac{y^2}{4}$$

Multiply z_1 by w_1 and define the short-run variable cost $VC(y) = w_1 z_1$. Then

$$VC(y) = w_1 z_1 = \frac{w_1 y^2}{4}$$

The fixed input is z_2, so fixed costs are found by multiplying 4 ($= z_2$) by its price w_2; thus, $FC = 4w_2$. Total costs are

$$STC(y) = VC(y) + FC = \frac{w_1 y^2}{4} + 4w_2$$

21 The difference between the short-run average total costs and the average variable costs is the average fixed costs. That is,

$$SAC(y) = AVC(y) + AFC(y)$$
$$SAC(y) - AVC(y) = AFC(y)$$

As output increases, $AFC(y)$ declines, and $SAC(y) - AVC(y)$ goes to zero.

FIGURE A6.2

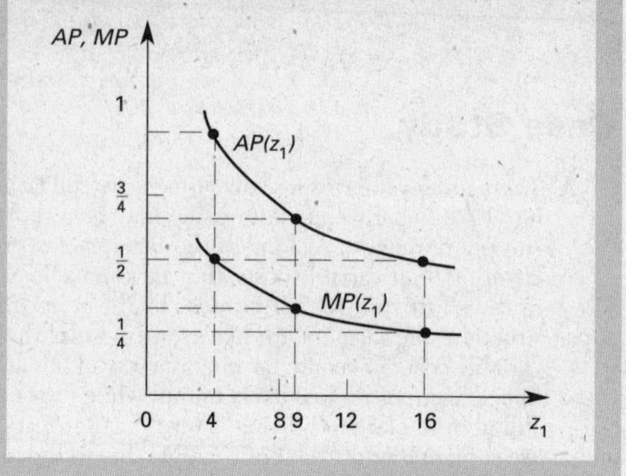

***22** The farmer will use an amount of labour such that $MP_1 = 0$. For $z_2 = 16$, $MP_1 = (2)(4)/z_1^{1/2} - 1 = 0$, which implies $z_1 = 64$. If she were to use more than 64 units of labour, the MP_1 of labour would be negative and output would decline. If she used fewer than 64 units, MP_1 would be positive; more output could be produced at zero opportunity cost.

***23** Doreen, like the other commuters, will equate the average commuting costs of the two routes. That is, since the opportunity cost of time is the only cost, we can simply equate $0.0005X = 0.75$ to get the number of commuters on the first route. $X = 1\,500$ commuters will use the first route. Since total cost of time is $(0.0005X)X$ for X commuters (for $X > 500$), the socially efficient number equates the marginal commuting costs; that is, $0.001X = 0.75$, or $X = 750$. At $X = 750$, the average commuting cost for the first route is $(0.0005)(750) = 0.375$. To ensure that the average commuting cost of the first route equates with the average commuting cost of the alternative route at $X = 750$, a toll of $t = 0.75 - 0.375 = 0.375$ must be imposed on the travellers of the first route.

Long Problems

24 *a Total variable costs $= by$, total fixed costs $= a$, average total costs $= (a + by)/y$, average variable costs $= b$, average fixed costs $= a/y$, and marginal costs $= b$.

b Let z_1 be the quantity of the variable factor. To find the product curves, we must invert the variable cost curve, where $VC(y) = wz_1$. Then, since $VC(y) = by$, $wz_1 = by$ and, therefore,

$$y = \frac{wz_1}{b}$$

Then, $AP(z_1) = y/z_1 = w/b$ and $MP(z_1) = \Delta y/\Delta z_1 = w/b$.

c These production relationships are not realistic in that they do not exhibit diminishing marginal productivity. In this case, the marginal product w/b is a constant and therefore is independent of output.

25 a If marginal product of labour (input 1) diminishes on both plots, the farmer will want to allocate labour to the two plots until the marginal products are equal. To see this, suppose that $MP_1^A > MP_1^B$. Then by transferring labour from plot B to plot A, total output can be increased. As this transfer continues, MP_1^A falls and MP_1^B increases; output is maximized at $MP_1^A = MP_1^B$. The argument is similar for $MP_1^A < MP_1^B$.

b If the marginal product increases on plot A and diminishes on plot B, then (1) only A will be used, (2) only B will be used, or (3) both plots will be cultivated. The three possibilities are plotted in Figure A6.3, in which the marginal product of labour on plot A is measured from left to right, and the marginal product of labour on plot B is measured from right to left.

(1) Only plot A is cultivated. In Figure A6.3a, the MP_1^A increases in z_1 and MP_1^B declines in z_1. Because $MP_1^A > MP_1^B$ for every unit of labour, all labour is used on plot A.

(2) Only plot B is cultivated. As shown in Figure A6.3b, the marginal product of labour on plot B, though declining in z_1, is greater than the marginal product of labour on plot A.

(3) Both plots are cultivated. In Figure A6.3c, the two marginal product curves cross; z_1^{A*} units of labour are used on plot A, and z_1^{B*} units are used on plot B. To see that this allocation maximizes output, consider an increase in labour on plot A — say, to $z_1^{A'}$. Since $MP_1^B > MP_1^A$ in this case, a transfer of labour from plot A to B would increase output. If labour were reduced — say, to $z_1^{A''}$ — $MP_1^A > MP_1^B$ and again total output could be increased with a reallocation of labour. Hence, output is maximized at point E.

26 There are two constraints to this production relationship. Let m be the total number of milkshakes produced and s be the speed (milkshakes per hour) at which Theodore works. Then $m \le sz_1$ implies that the number of milkshakes produced can be no greater than Theodore's time multiplied by his speed. The second constraint, $m/z_2 \le 10/s$, is a "technological relationship" which says that the number of milkshakes made per set of ingredients can be no greater than 10 divided by the speed. The speed s at which the maximum number of milkshakes can be produced, given these two constraints, is found by equating $m = sz_1$ and $m = 10z_2/s$. That is,

$$sz_1 = \frac{10z_2}{s}$$

and so

$$s^* = \left(\frac{10z_2}{z_1}\right)^{1/2}$$

Substituting s* into either of the constraints yields the production function

$$m^* = (10z_1z_2)^{1/2}$$

FIGURE A6.3

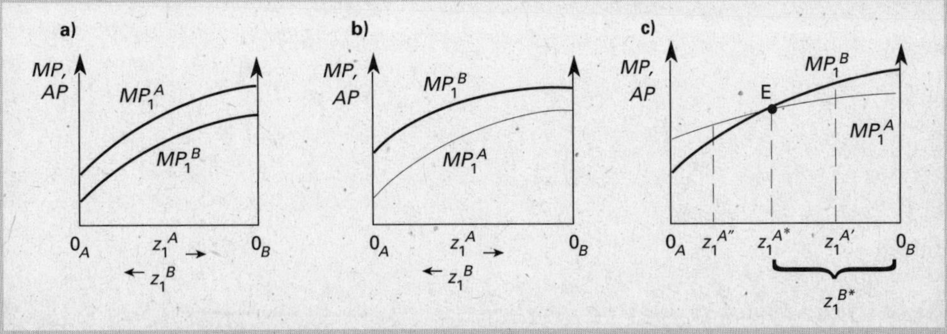

CHAPTER 7

Production and Cost: Many Variable Inputs

Chapter Summary

Many Variable Inputs

We now explore a firm's input and output decisions when it has sufficient time to vary *several* production inputs to achieve the lowest possible production costs for every output. The production function of the firm in the long run can be described by **isoquants**, which are curves of all combinations of inputs that yield the same output level. By fixing the quantity of output, we can examine the firm's **input substitution**. The slope of the isoquant is called the **marginal rate of technical substitution** (MRTS) since it measures the rate at which one input may be substituted for another. Isoquants are usually characterized by a **diminishing marginal rate of technical substitution**, which implies that increasing amounts of one input must compensate for decreasing amounts of other inputs to keep output constant. Two special cases of input substitution — **perfect substitutes** and **perfect complements** in production — are represented by straight-line and right-angled isoquants, respectively.

Production functions can exhibit constant, increasing, or decreasing returns to scale. If **constant returns to scale** (CRTS) prevail, an increase in the **scale of production** by the constant a — that is, a times the quantities of *all* inputs used in production — results in a times the original level of output; output increases more than a times for **increasing returns to scale** (IRTS) and less than a times for **decreasing returns to scale** (DRTS).

The Cost-Minimization Problem and Derivation of the Long-Run Cost Function

In the long run, the firm can vary *all* inputs in production. To derive the long-run cost function, an important ingredient in model development in later chapters, we need to determine the combination of inputs that minimizes the costs of producing every output level, i.e., the long-run cost-minimization problem. The algebraic solution to this problem is a set of **conditional input demand functions** that give the cost-minimizing level of inputs as a function of input prices and the output level. Substitution of these input demands into the cost identity (sum of inputs weighted by their respective prices) yields the **long-run cost function**.

This algebraic solution can be illustrated on an isoquant–isocost diagram. An **isocost line** gives the combinations of inputs that can be purchased at a particular outlay or cost, given input prices. The relevant isoquant is the one that represents the quantity of output that the firm must produce. The **feasible input bundles** are all of those input bundles that lie on or above this isoquant because these represent input combinations that can produce the given quantity. When isoquants are smooth and convex, and the solution to the cost-minimization problem is interior, then the cost-minimizing combination of inputs that produce a given level of output is described by two conditions: The **first principle of cost minimization** states that the optimal input bundle must lie *on* the relevant isoquant; the **second principle of cost minimization** is that the marginal rate of technical substitution, also defined as the ratio of the marginal products of input 1 to input 2, must equal the ratio of the prices of input 1 to input 2.

Comparative Statics

Comparative statics analysis reveals interesting information about the relationships among output, inputs, and input prices. While holding output constant, one can show that if the price of an input that is used in positive amounts rises, then the minimum cost of producing that output will also rise. In addition, the amount of the input in question that is used decreases and the other input increases. If the prices of *all* inputs increase by the same factor, then the cost-minimizing bundle of inputs will remain unchanged, and the minimum cost of producing an output will rise by the same factor.

Suppose, instead, that we hold input prices constant but allow output to change. As output increases, holding input prices constant, the cost-minimizing combinations of inputs map out the **output expansion path**, from which the long-run total cost function is derived. If the quantity demanded of an input rises, the input is said to be a **normal input;** if it falls, it is an **inferior input**. If the firm has a **homothetic production function**, the output-expansion path is a ray through the origin. In this case, the long-run cost function can be expressed in terms of a scale factor a; that is, when all inputs increase by the same scale a, the new input bundle is on the output expansion path. The costs of the inputs used to produce this new output equals a times the costs of the inputs at the old output.

The **long-run marginal costs** $LMC(y)$ and the **long-run average costs** $LAC(y)$ have the same relationship as their short-run counterparts described in Chapter 6. Another important relationship is between the returns to scale and the $LAC(y)$ curve. For increases in output, the $LAC(y)$ curve declines, increases, or stays constant under IRTS, DRTS, and CRTS, respectively.

Relationship Between the Short-Run and Long-Run Curves

For every output level, there is a cost-minimizing combination of inputs and, hence, an optimal plant size or a level of the fixed input that is optimal for that output during production in the short run. For example, at some output — call it y' — there is a short-run cost curve that is tangent to the long-run cost curve. For output levels larger or smaller than y', short-run costs exceed long-run costs because there is a larger or smaller use of the fixed factor that would produce the output at lower costs in the long-run. The point where the long- and short-run costs are tangent, so are the $SAC(y)$ and $LAC(y)$ curves at y'. Again, at higher and lower levels than y', $SAC(y)$ exceeds $LAC(y)$. At y', the long- and short-run marginal costs are equal. For larger output levels, the cost increases from additional output are smaller in the long run than in the short run [$(LMC(y) < SMC(y))$], but for smaller output levels, the *cost savings* are larger in the long run than in the short run [$LMC(y) > SMC(y)$].

Costs and the Market Structure

A review of these various long-run relationships provides us with a basic **theory of market structure** which provides some insight into the conditions under which we would expect to find firms. If the production technology exhibits DRTS throughout, we would expect the good to be produced at the smallest possible scale, that is, by the household. For CRTS, there is neither an advantage nor a disadvantage to producing at a larger scale and, hence, no compelling reason to observe firms. However, for IRTS, there is a definite disadvantage from small-scale production, and we would expect to see a few large firms. Finally, if the $LAC(y)$ curve is U-shaped and the output corresponding to the minimum value is relatively small, we might expect to see many small firms in the market. Alternatively, if the minimum value of the $LAC(y)$ curve is relatively large, we might expect to see a monopoly or an oligopoly.

KEY WORDS

Conditional input demand functions

Constant returns to scale

Decreasing returns to scale

Diminishing marginal rate of technical substitution

Feasible input bundles

First principle of cost minimization

Homothetic production functions

Increasing returns to scale

Inferior inputs

Input substitution

Isocost line

Isoquant

Long-run average costs (*LAC*)

Long-run cost function

Long-run marginal costs (*LMC*)

Marginal rate of technical substitution (*MRTS*)

Normal inputs

Output expansion path

Perfect substitutes

Perfect complements

Returns to scale

Scale of production

Second principle of cost minimization

Theory of market structure

CASE STUDY: IS THE END OF THE WORLD IN SIGHT?

In the early 1960s, the Club of Rome published a report, *The Limits to Growth*,[1] that created great anxiety among politicians, academicians, and the general population for the following decade. Using computer models of the world economy, the Club of Rome prophesied that doomsday was near at hand. Developing nations of the world were rapidly depleting the earth's natural resources, and without resources, production of consumption goods was impossible. The Club made a strong warning to conserve our natural resources or accept the consequences of our extravagant behaviour.

Panic struck many countries around the world. In Japan, land speculation and inflation increased, and policies of rapid industrial growth met resistance from environmental groups and the general public. Many people, however, were sceptical of the report, arguing that it promoted unnecessary panic. J. Stiglitz wrote a paper[2] showing that if assumptions different from those adopted by the Club of Rome were made, the world could go on indefinitely with everyone enjoying some constant level of consumption, even with a finite stock of resources! Although Stiglitz did not deny that human activity may indeed result in the demise of the world, his paper suggested that it would not necessarily result from exhaustion of our natural resources.

A Given the Club of Rome's conclusions, what do you think the long-run production function assumed in their report looked like? Explain.

B Describe a production function relationship alternative to the one in question **A**, which Stiglitz may have had in mind. If this represented the true "production function" for the world economy, why would resource exhaustion be less of a problem? Do prices of inputs have anything to do with the argument? Explain.

C It would seem that a reasonable conclusion to make from this debate is something in between the argument of the Club of Rome and that of Stiglitz. Indeed, conventional supplies are nonrenewable, but this does not necessarily imply that future economic growth must be limited. You gave one argument for this in question **B**. Suggest other reasons why a declining resource base may not stifle future growth. What other changes might take place in the economy?

EXERCISES

Multiple-Choice

Choose the correct answer to each question. There is only one correct answer to each question.

1 For a given output, long-run average cost, $LAC(y)$, equals short-run average cost, $SAC(y)$, and $LAC(y)$ is greater than long-run marginal cost, $LMC(y)$. Then

- **a** The $LAC(y)$ curve is rising.
- **b** The $LAC(y)$ curve is falling.
- **c** The $SAC(y)$ curve is at its minimum.
- **d** $SAC(y)$ equals $LMC(y)$.
- **e** Only **c** and **d** are true.

2 The production function $y = z_1 + 2z_2 + 5$ exhibits which of the following?

- **a** IRTS
- **b** CRTS
- **c** DRTS
- **d** Diminishing marginal product of labour
- **e** None of the above

3 If the marginal rate of technical substitution of input 2 for input 1, $MRTS(z_1, z_2)$, is 1/3 in firm A but 2/3 in firm B, then

- **a** Only firm A is minimizing its production costs.
- **b** Only firm B is minimizing its production costs.
- **c** Firm A's amount of input 2 is twice that of firm B.
- **d** Output in firm A could be increased if firm A traded three units of input 1 for two units of firm B's input 2.
- **e** None of the above is true.

[1] D.H. Meadows, D.L. Meadows, J. Randers, W.W. Behrens III (1972). *The Limits to Growth*, New York: Universe Books.

[2] J. Stiglitz (1974). "Growth with Exhaustible Natural Resources: Efficient and Optimal Growth Paths," *The Review of Economic Studies*, Symposium on the Economics of Exhaustible Resources: 139–152.

FIGURE 7.1

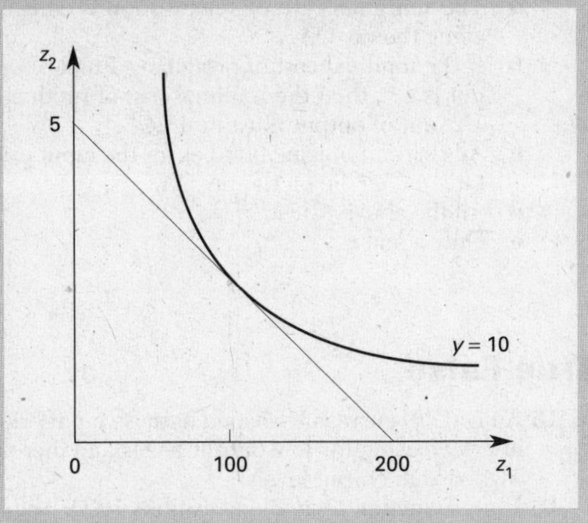

FIGURE 7.2

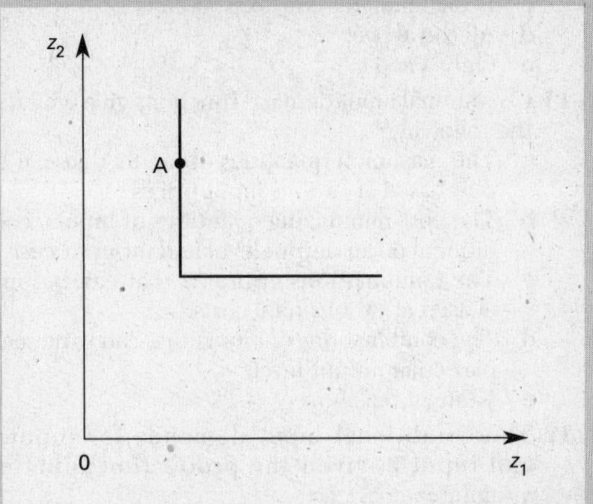

For questions **4** and **5**, refer to Figure 7.1.

4 If the price of input 1 is $10 per unit, then
- **a** Five units of input 2 will minimize the cost of producing 10 units of output.
- **b** The price of input 2 is $400.
- **c** There must be IRTS.
- **d** The total outlay (cost) of 10 units of output is $1 000.
- **e** None of the above.

5 If the firm is currently operating at a plant size of five units of input 2 while producing 10 units of output in the short run, then
- **a** It would be minimizing the costs of producing 10 units of output in the long run.
- **b** It could reduce the production costs of producing 10 units of output in the long run by building a smaller plant.
- **c** It could reduce the production costs of producing 10 units of output in the long run by building a larger plant.
- **d** 100 units of input 1 minimize the short-run variable costs of producing 10 units of output.
- **e** Both **b** and **d** are true.

6 At point A on the isoquant in Figure 7.2, which statement is true?
- **a** The marginal products of both input 2 and input 1 are negative.
- **b** The marginal products of both input 2 and input 1 are zero.
- **c** The marginal product of input 2 is zero, and the marginal product of input 1 is positive.
- **d** The marginal product of input 2 is positive, and the marginal product of input 1 is zero.
- **e** None of the above is true.

7 Suppose that a producer minimizes the cost of producing a certain output level with 200 units of labour and 100 units of capital. Then
- **a** The per-unit price of capital per unit must be twice the per-unit price of labour.
- **b** Labour per unit must be twice as expensive as capital per unit.
- **c** The marginal rate of technical substitution of capital for labour must equal 2/1.
- **d** The marginal rate of technical substitution of capital for labour must equal 1/2.
- **e** None of the above is true.

8 Suppose that the production function is $y = az_1 + bz_2$, so the marginal rate of technical substitution of input 2 for input 1 is a/b. If w_1 is the price of input 1, w_2 is the price of input 2, and $w_1/w_2 > a/b$, then
- **a** Input 1 and input 2 are complements in production.
- **b** Only input 2 will be used to minimize the cost of producing any output level.
- **c** Only input 1 will be used to minimize the cost of producing any output level.
- **d** The marginal cost of production is rising.
- **e** None of the above is true.

9 Suppose that the production function for good Y is given by

$$y = \min(2z_1, 3z_2)$$

Then
- **a** $LMC(y)$ is constant for all output y.
- **b** The ratio of input 1 to input 2 required by the production process is 2/3.
- **c** The ratio of input 1 to input 2 required by the production process is 3/2.
- **d** Both **a** and **b** are true.
- **e** Both **a** and **c** are true.

10 The marginal rate of technical substitution of input 2 for input 1
- **a** Equals the absolute value of the slope of the isoquant at every point.
- **b** Is the amount of input 2 that can be replaced

by a unit of input 1 to keep output at the same level.
c Is declining for convex isoquants.
d All the above.
e Only **a** and **c.**

11 Conditional input demand functions give which of the following?
a The maximum quantities of inputs that can be purchased at various input prices.
b The cost-minimizing quantities of inputs, conditional on an output level and input prices.
c The combinations of inputs that can be purchased at various total costs.
d The combinations of inputs that can produce a particular output level.
e None of the above.

12 The conditional input demands for input 1 and input 2, given the production function $y = \min(az_1, bz_2)$, are
a $z_1 = ay, z_2 = by$
b $z_1 = by, z_2 = ay$
c $z_1 = y/a, z_2 = y/b$
d $z_1 = y/b, z_2 = y/a$
e None of the above.

13 At point A in Figure 7.3, which statement is true?
a The marginal productivity per dollar of input 1 exceeds the marginal productivity per dollar of input 2.
b The marginal productivity per dollar of input 2 exceeds the marginal productivity per dollar of input 1.
c Total costs of producing y^* units of output are minimized.
d The ratio of the marginal product of input 1 to input 2 exceeds the ratio of the input prices of input 1 to input 2.
e None of the above.

14 If the production function in Figure 7.4 is homothetic, then
a The marginal rate of substitution is constant along the ray OA.
b If the minimal cost of producing 1 unit of output is C^*, then the minimal cost of producing 1/2 unit of output must be $1/2C^*$.
c All cost-minimizing bundles for the input price ratio w_1^*/w_2^* lie on the ray OA.
d All the above.
e Only **a** and **c**.

True-False

15 An $LAC(y)$ curve is U-shaped because input prices are decreasing for low output levels and increasing for high output levels.

16 If a production technology exhibits IRTS, then a 10% increase in output will result in less than a 10% increase in the long-run total costs of production.

17 If an equal percentage increase in the use of all inputs results in a smaller percentage increase in the quantity produced, a firm's production function is said to exhibit decreasing returns to scale.

18 Since short-run and long-run marginal costs are equal at the point at which the short- and long-run costs curves are tangent, the $LMC(y)$ curve has the same slope as the $SMC(y)$ curve.

19 To minimize the costs of producing a given amount of output, the marginal products of all inputs must be equal.

20 If a production process uses the two inputs of labour and capital, then an increase in the wage rate will cause a firm to increase its use of capital, with output held constant.

FIGURE 7.3

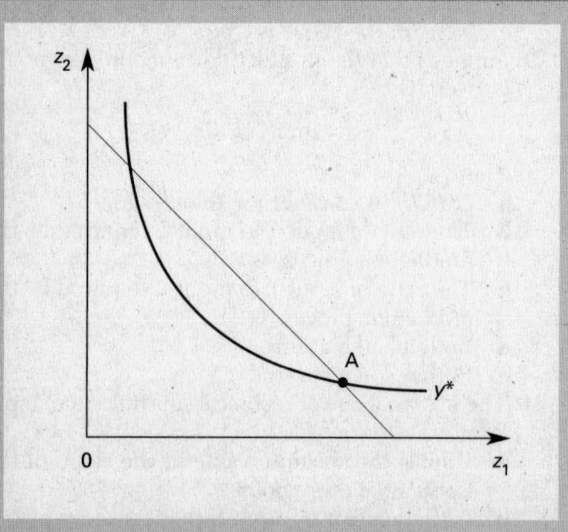

FIGURE 7.4

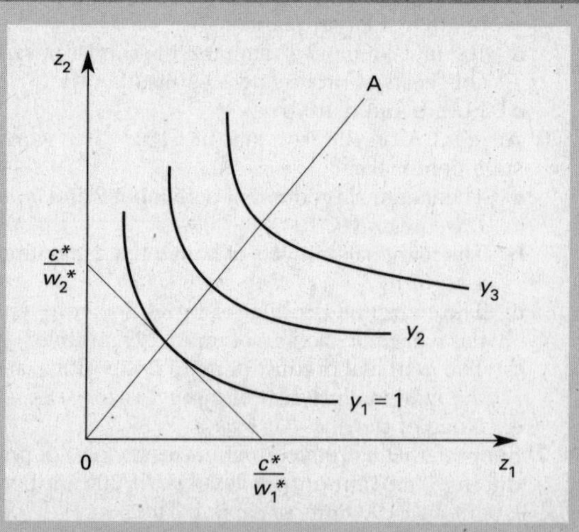

21 For strictly convex isoquants, an increase in the wage rate results in an increase in the use of capital, holding total costs constant.
22 The isoquants for a production technology characterized by fixed proportions are straight lines.
23 DRTS implies that the $LAC(y)$ curve is decreasing.
24 Any input bundle on an isocost curve yields a higher output than any point below the isocost curve.
25 The costs of producing a given level of output falls when the price of an inferior factor of production increases.
26 The flatter the long-run average cost curve is to the left of the output that minimizes average cost, y_{min}, and the smaller y_{min} is relative to the total market, the more competitive the market is likely to be.
27 Isocost curves are homogeneous of degree one in input prices.
28 The $LMC(y)$ curve necessarily intersects the $LAC(y)$ curve where the average product of labour reaches a minimum.

Short Problems

29 You observe that a firm has increased its output during a particular month in response to an increase in demand and that it has experienced an increase in the average cost of production. Assuming that neither technology nor input prices have changed, can you tell whether the firm is producing in a region of increasing, constant, or decreasing returns to scale? Explain.

*30A firm minimizes its production costs subject to a quantity constraint $y = y^*$ (or, alternatively, maximizes output subject to costs equal to C^*). The firm produces its product with input 1 and input 2, which cost w_1 and w_2 per unit, respectively. Set up the general long-run cost-minimization problem and find the two conditions which characterize the solution.

31 If a firm's production technology is characterized by CRTS for all output levels, then can the firm's $SAC(y)$ curve be U-shaped? Explain, using diagrams.

32 Homothetic production functions have the property that the slopes of the isoquants are equal along a ray from the origin. Why does this imply that the cost-minimizing bundles of inputs lie along a ray from the origin for a particular ratio of input prices?

33 Explain how particular characteristics of the production technology for a good can influence the existence of firms and the market structure in that industry.

Long Problems

*34 Suppose that a firm produces a product with two inputs, labour (input 1) and capital (input 2). Labour costs \$3 per unit and capital costs \$5 per unit. The firm's production function is $y = z_1^{1/3} z_2^{1/2}$.

a Calculate the profit maximizing input combination for the firm and the profit maximizing output.

b Minimize the long-run costs of this firm subject to the constraint that it produces the output determined in part **a**.

c Compare your answers in **a** and **b**.

35 Suppose that the long-run total cost of producing 100 units of output is \$1 000. Labour (input 1) costs \$10 per unit, capital (input 2) costs \$10 per unit, and these are the only two inputs used in production. The firm is currently producing 100 units of output and is using the cost-minimizing combination of 50 labour and 50 capital.

a On an isoquant diagram, show that an increase in output from 100 units to 150 units will result in higher short-run total costs, average costs, and marginal costs than in the long-run counterparts.

b Show that a decrease in output from 100 units to 50 units will result in higher short-run total costs and average costs than in the long-run counterparts, but will result in marginal costs that are lower in the short run than in the long run.

c Give an intuitive explanation for these relationships between the short- and long-run cost curves.

36 The table shows a relationship between output y and long-run total cost $TC(y)$ for a firm.

y	$TC(y)$	y	$TC(y)$
100	100	400	300
200	150	500	425
300	200	600	600

a Draw a set of appropriate isoquants and isocosts, assuming two inputs 1 and 2.

b In another diagram, draw the $LAC(y)$ and $LMC(y)$ curves of the firm.

c In the diagram for question **b**, draw the $SAC(y)$ curve when input 2 is optimally chosen for 600 units of output.

37 Show how you would derive the firm's $TC(y)$ curve given constant factor prices of \$100/unit of input 1 and \$200/unit of input 2 and a set of convex isoquants for the firm. Also assume that the firm's production technology is homothetic and initially exhibits IRTS for low output levels and eventually exhibits CRTS for *all* higher output levels. What do the corresponding long-run marginal cost curves look like? Explain.

*38 Four production functions are

$$y = z_1^{1/2} z_2^{1/2} \quad (1)$$

$$y = 2z_1 + \frac{z_2}{2} \quad (2)$$

$$y = 2z_1^{1/4} + \frac{z_2}{2} \quad (3)$$

$$y = \min(z_1, z_2) \quad (4)$$

a Determine whether the production functions exhibit increasing, decreasing, or constant returns to scale for all levels of output. Explain.
b Determine which of the production functions are homothetic.

39 Suppose that 10 units of a good can be made with one of three fixed-proportion technologies: Process A uses 10 units of capital (input 1) and two units of labour (input 2); process B uses five units of capital and eight units of labour; process C uses two units of capital and 15 units of labour.
a Draw the "kinked isoquant" curve for 10 units of output.
b Can 10 units of output be made with 3 1/2 units of capital and 11 1/2 units of labour? If so, how can this be achieved? Can 10 units of output be made with 9 1/6 units of capital and three units of labour? If so, how can this be achieved?
c What do your answers in **b** imply about the restrictiveness (or unrestrictiveness) of the assumption of smooth isoquants?

ANSWERS TO CHAPTER 7

Case Study

A The long-run production function exhibited fixed proportions, where no or little substitution between exhaustible resources and other inputs is possible.
B Stiglitz allowed for greater substitutability between resources and other inputs, a characteristic of the Cobb–Douglas production function, for example. In this case, diminishing resources could be replaced by other inputs: for example, capital. As a resource is exploited, its price rises, encouraging firms to replace it with other inputs.
C The long-run production function is based on existing technology. New types of technology (for example, replacing oil with solar power) could enable the world to circumvent the problem of a shrinking resource base.

Multiple-Choice

1 b 2 c 3 d 4 b 5 b 6 c 7 e
8 b 9 e 10 d 11 b 12 c 13 b 14 e

True-False

15 F 16 T 17 T 18 F 19 F 20 T 21 T
22 F 23 F 24 F 25 F 26 T *27 T *28 F

Short Problems

29 No, it is not possible to tell. Recall that returns to scale deal with the long run because such returns ask how output changes when *all* factors of production are variable. A month may not be long enough for all inputs to vary. If the firm were operating at point A in Figure A7.1 and moved along SAC_I to point B, then it would be on the IRTS section of the $LAC(y)$ curve. If it started at point C on SAC_{II} and moved to D, then it would be on the CRTS section of the $LAC(y)$ curve. SAC_{III} indicates a situation in which the firm would be on the DRTS portion of the $LAC(y)$ curve.

***30** Min $w_1z_1 + w_2z_2$, subject to $y = f(z_1, z_2)$. Set up the Lagrange multiplier: $L = -w_1z_1 - w_2z_2 + \lambda(y - f(z_1, z_2))$ which is maximized with respect to the three variables z_1, z_2, λ, yielding three first-order conditions: 1) $-z_1 - \lambda f_1 = 0$, 2) $-z_2 - \lambda f_2 = 0$, 3) $y = f(z_1, z_2)$. From 1) and 2) we get that $w_1/w_2 = f_1/f_2$, where $f_1/f_2 = \text{MRTS}(z_1^*, z_2^*)$, which is the first condition for cost minimization, and the second is simply the condition 3) evaluated at the cost-minimization bundle.

31 Yes. Figure A7.2 illustrates a production technology that exhibits CRTS and the short-run average cost curves are U-shaped.

32 Consider a ray from the origin for a homothetic production function. Along the ray, the $\text{MRTS}(z_1, z_2)$ is constant. Let that constant be given

FIGURE A7.1

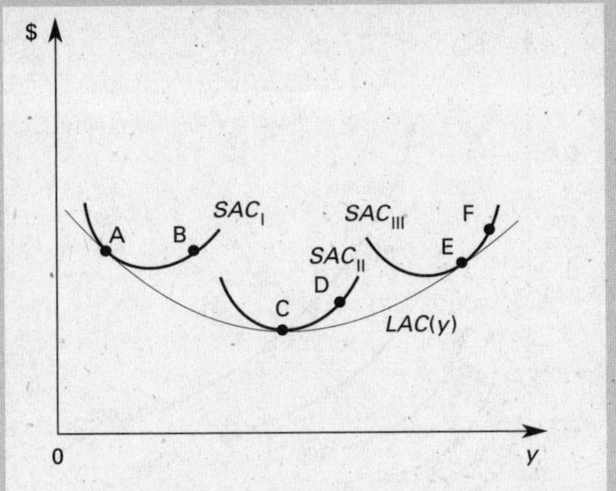

FIGURE A7.2

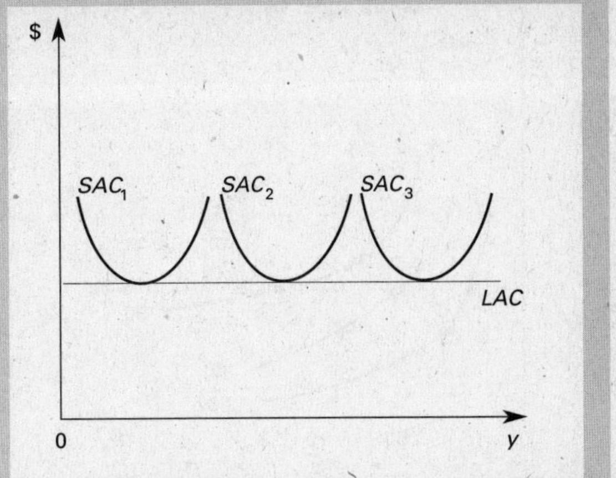

by some ratio of input prices w_1/w_2. Since $MRTS(z_1, z_2) = w_1/w_2$ along the ray from the origin, then these input bundles are cost-minimizing for that input price ratio.

33 If the production technology exhibits IRTS for all levels of output, then only one firm can be sustained in the industry. Since average costs of production fall as output increases, the firm has an incentive to capture all the demand in the market at any given price in order to have the largest output possible. For CRTS, there is no obvious incentive for firms to enter because a good can be produced at the same average cost regardless of the scale of production. If the production technology exhibits DRTS, then the good is best produced at the smallest possible scale; for example, by the household. For an initial range of IRTS that is not too large, firms will arise. Where the efficient scale is small, a competitive market will develop; where the scale is large, oligopoly is likely to be the market structure.

Long Problems

°**34 a** Set up the profit function and maximize it with respect to z_1 and z_2:

$$\max_{z_1, z_2} \pi = 10(z_1^{1/3} z_2^{1/2}) - 3z_1 - 5z_2.$$

The first-order conditions are

$$\partial\pi/\partial z_1 = (10/3)(z_1^{-2/3})(z_2^{1/2}) - 3 = 0 \quad (1)$$
$$\partial\pi/\partial z_2 = 5(z_1^{1/3})(z_2^{-1/2}) - 5 = 0 \quad (2)$$

Rearranging the equations and dividing (1) by (2) and solving for z_1 gives $z_1 = 9/10(z_2)$, which can be substituted back into either equation. From (2) we get:

$5(z_1^{1/3})(9z_1/10)^{-1/2} - 5 = 0$ or $z_1^{-1/6} = (9/10)^{1/2}$ or $z_1 = (9/10)^{-3} = 1.37$

Therefore $z_2 = (9/10)(1.37) = 1.23$, and $y = (1.37)^{1/3}(1.23)^{2/3} = 1.23$

b Now the problem is:

$\min_{z_1, z_2} (3z_1 + 5z_2)$
Subject to $y = z_1^{1/3} z_2^{1/2} = 1.23$, or
$z_1 = (1.23/z_2^{1/2})^3$

which can be written as the unconstrained problem: $\min_{z_2} 3(1.23/z_2^{1/2})^3 + 5z_2$

The first order condition is
$-(9/2)(1.23)^3 z_2^{-5/2} + 5 = 0$, which implies that $z_2 = 1.23$.

Thus $z_1 = [1.23/(1.23)^{1/2}]^3 = 1.37$.

c Parts **a** and **b** represent two ways of solving the same problem. Profit maximization is identical to cost minimization whenever the appropriate output level is chosen.

35 a The isoquants $y = 100$ and $y = 150$ are shown in Figure A7.3 In the long run, the costs of producing 150 units of output are given by the isocost curve *AB*. In the short run, capital is fixed at 50, and costs of production are given by isocost *CD*, which are larger than the long-run costs. Since average costs = total costs/output, $LAC(y) < SAC(y)$ for $y = 150$. The marginal costs of producing the additional 50 units of output in the long run are

$$\frac{\text{costs given by } AB - 1\,000}{50}$$

In the short run, the marginal costs are

$$\frac{\text{costs given by } CD - 1\,000}{50}$$

Hence, $SMC(y) > LMC(y)$.

FIGURE A7.3

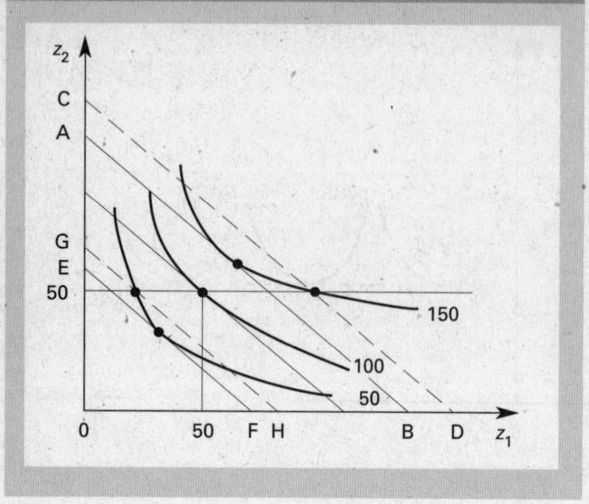

FIGURE A7.4

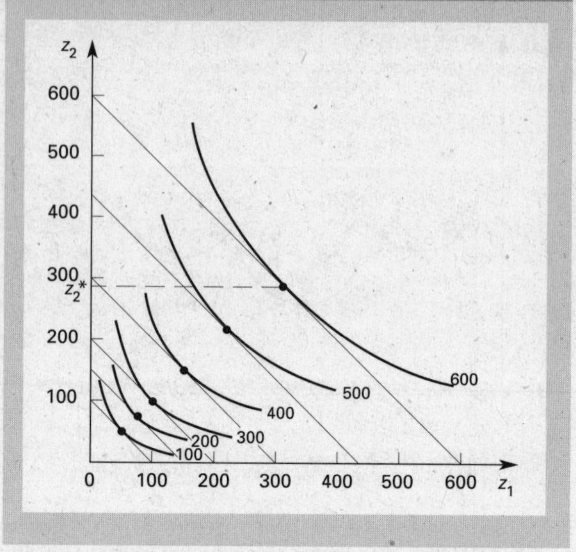

b The long-run cost of producing 50 is given by isocost curve *EF*; the short-run cost of producing 50 is given by *GH*. As before, $\text{STC}(y) > \text{LTC}(y)$. Note that the $LMC(y)$ is

$$\frac{1\,000 - \text{costs given by } EF}{50}$$

and the $SMC(y)$ is

$$\frac{1\,000 - \text{costs given by } GH}{50}$$

Since costs for *EF* are less than costs given by *GH*, $LMC(y) > SMC(y)$.

c In the short run, the relationships described hold because capital is not flexible. In the long run, inputs can be adjusted to lower costs. For increases in output, $SMC(y) > LMC(y)$ because the *increase* in costs is greater in the short run; for decreases in output, $SMC(y) < LMC(y)$ because the *cost-savings* from decreasing output are less in the short run than in the long run.

36 a Let $w_1 = w_2 = \$1$. Then the isocost–isoquant map can be drawn as in Figure A7.4.

b The $LAC(y) = LTC/y$ and $LMC(y) = \Delta LTC/\Delta y$ schedules are shown in the table.

Q	*LAC*(*y*)	*LMC*(*y*)
100	1	1
200	0.75	0.50
300	0.66	0.50
400	0.75	1
500	0.85	1.25
600	1	1.75

The $LAC(y)$ and $LMC(y)$ curves are plotted in Figure A7.5. $LMC(y)$ is plotted in between quantity values; for example, the $LMC(y)$ between 100 and 200 units of output is plotted at $y = 150$.

c When z_2 is optimally chosen for $y = 600$, the cost-minimizing level is given by z_2^* in Figure A7.4. For any output greater or less than $y = 600$, $SAC(y)$ will exceed $LAC(y)$. For $y > 600$, $SMC(y)$ will exceed long-run marginal costs, and for $y < 600$, $SMC(y) < LMC(y)$. These relationships are shown in Figure A7.5 by $SAC(y)$ and $SMC(y)$.

FIGURE A7.5

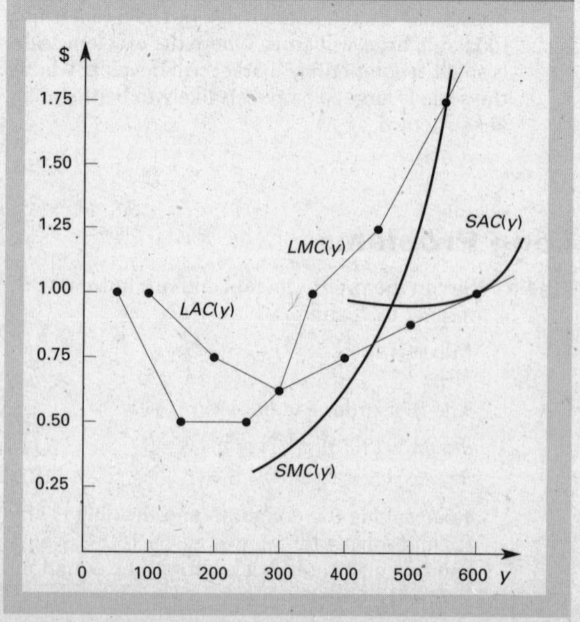

37 An example of a production function that satisfies the technological requirements is shown in Figure A7.6. At an output of 10, five units of labour (input 1) and one unit of capital (input 2) are required. The scale is doubled and output increased by $2^1/2$ times. The scale increases by 50% from 10 labour and two capital, and output increases to 40 (75%). Beyond this point, an increase in the scale by some proportion increases output by the same proportion. For simplicity, the production function is assumed to be homothetic, so the expansion path is a straight line from the origin.

Because the production function is homothetic, we know that the costs of production increase proportionately with the scale of production. The costs are

$$TC(10) = 700$$
$$TC(25) = 1400$$
$$TC(40) = 2100$$
$$TC(53.3) = 2800$$
$$TC(66.7) = 3500$$

The cost function is graphed in Figure A 7.7a. Average costs initially decline up to 40 units of output and are constant afterwards. Marginal costs fall initially and then increase up to 40 units of output, and are constant thereafter. The $LMC(y)$ and $LAC(y)$ schedules are shown in the table.

Q	*LMC*(*y*)	*LAC*(*y*)
10	70	70
25	46.6	56
40	46.6	52.5
53.3	52.5	52.5
66.7	52.5	52.5

FIGURE A7.6

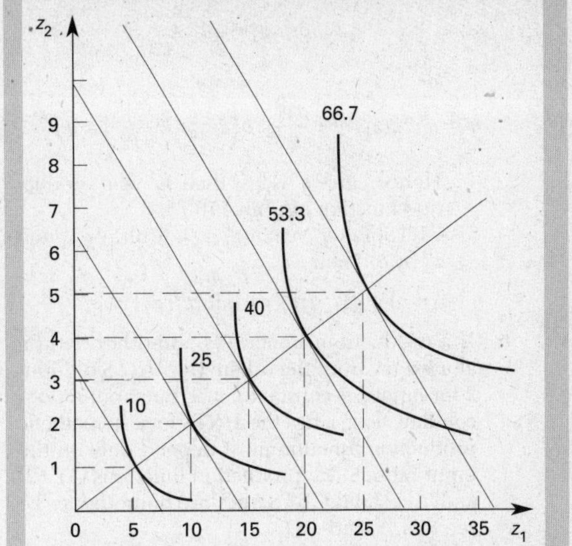

The long-run marginal and average cost curves are graphed in Figure A7.7b.

***38 a** (1) CRTS. Let $y^0 = (z_1^0, z_2^0)^{1/2}$. Multiply z_1^0 and z_2^0 by a. Then the new output is

$$y' = (az_1^0 az_2^0)^{1/2} = a(z_1^0 z_2^0)^{1/2} = ay^0$$

(2) CRTS. Let $y^0 = 2z_1^0 + z_2^0/2$. Multiply z_1^0 and z_2^0 by a. Then the new output is

$$y' = 2az_1^0 + \frac{az_2^0}{2} = a\left(2z_1^0 + \frac{z_2^0}{2}\right) = ay^0$$

FIGURE A7.7

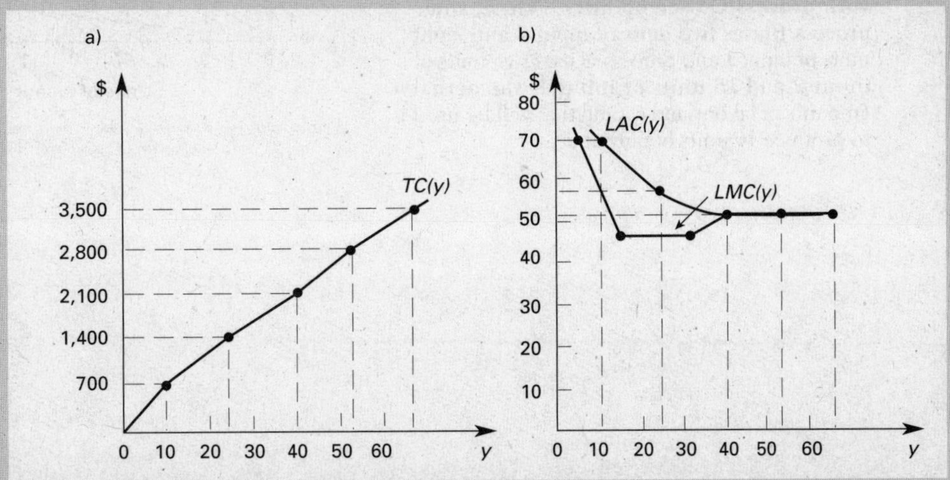

(3) DRTS. Let $y^0 = 2(z_1^0)^{1/4} + z_2^0/2$. Multiply z_1^0 and z_2^0 by a. Then the new output is

$$y' = 2(az_1^0)^{1/4} + \frac{az_2^0}{2}$$

so

$$y' = a^{1/4}2(z_1^0)^{1/4} + \frac{az_2^0}{2} < a\left(2(z_1^0)^{1/4} + \frac{z_2^0}{2}\right) = ay^0$$

Hence, since y' is less than ay^0, the production function exhibits DRTS.

(4) CRTS. Let $y^0 = \min(z_1^0, z_2^0)$. Multiply z_1^0 and z_2^0 by a. Then

$$y' = \min(az_1^0, az_2^0) = a\min(z_1^0, z_2^0) = ay^0$$

b If a production function is homothetic, then along a ray from the origin, the *MRTS* of input 2 for input 1 is constant. Since the input ratio is constant along a ray, the *MRTS* for a homothetic production function must depend only on the input ratio. Since production functions (1), (2) and (4) exhibit CRTS, they are homothetic. To see this, consider (1).

$$MRTS = \frac{MP_1}{MP_2} = \frac{z_2}{z_1}$$

To check whether production function (3) is homothetic, the *MRTS* is derived:

$$MRTS = \frac{MP_1}{MP_2} = \frac{0.5z_1^{-3/4}}{0.5} = \frac{1}{z_1^{3/4}}$$

Since *MRTS* depends on the absolute rather than relative amount of the input, it is not constant along a ray from the origin; therefore, the production function is not homothetic.

39 a The isoquant is given by ABC in Figure A7.8.

b If $3^1/2$ units of capital and $11^1/2$ units of labour are used, then a combination of processes B and C is used. Let λ be the proportion of the 10 units of output that is produced using process B, and $1 - \lambda$ the proportion of output produced with process C (See point D). Then, since process B uses five units of input 2 and eight units of input 1 and process C uses two units of input 2 and 15 units of input 1, the actual amounts of labour and capital that will be used to produce 10 units of output are

$$z_1 = 8\lambda + (1 - \lambda)15 = 15 - 7\lambda$$

and

$$z_2 = 5\lambda + (1 - \lambda)2 = 2 + 3\lambda$$

Substitute $z_2 = 3^1/2$ and $z_1 = 11^1/2$ into these expressions to get $\lambda = {}^1/2$. That is, half of the 10 units of output are produced using process B and half with process C; this combination requires $3^1/2$ units of input 2 and $11^1/2$ units of input 1.

To use 3 units of labour and $9^1/6$ units of capital, processes A and B are needed. Now let λ be the proportion of output produced with process A. Then,

$$3 = 2\lambda + (1 - \lambda)8 = 8 - 6\lambda \quad \text{and} \quad \lambda = 5/6$$

and

$$9\,1/6 = 10\lambda + (1 - \lambda)5 = 5 + 5\lambda \quad \text{and} \quad \lambda = 5/6$$

Hence, 5/6 of the 10 units of output are produced with process A and 1/6 with process B. See point E in Figure A7.8.

c The answers in **b** give a justification for the assumption that isoquants are smooth.

FIGURE A7.8

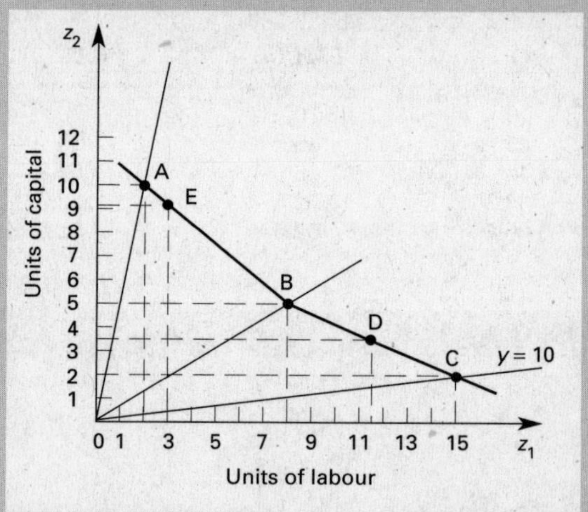

CHAPTER 8

The Theory of Perfect Competition

Chapter Summary

A Competitive Model of Exchange

Perfect competition is a good benchmark for understanding our price system. The formal theory is built on the assumption of the existence of a large number of price-taking buyers and sellers, perfect information, a homogeneous product, and perfect mobility. One is hard-pressed to come up with real-world examples that have these characteristics of the ideal, perfectly competitive market. Some agricultural markets appear to come closest; but in the case of wheat, for example, the existence of a small number of large, price-setting grain companies makes that example questionable. Then why bother with perfect competition?

Many of the reasons for studying perfect competition can be seen in the context of a simple exchange economy — an economy in which goods are traded but not produced. Consider two groups of individuals on an island: one group is endowed with bananas and the other with fish. Each individual has a **reservation price** which indicates the maximum that he or she is willing to pay for each good. By examining their reservations prices for each unit of bananas or fish we can construct the **market demand function** for these goods. Similarly, each individual has to decide whether to place their goods on the market which again will be characterized by reservation prices. As long as the individual can obtain at least his or her reservation price for the endowed good, it will be offered to the market. From this exercise, we can create the **market supply function**. In this hypothetical market, a **Walrasian auctioneer** will announce prices for each good, say bananas; as the price increases more bananas will be put onto the market and fewer bananas will be demanded. **Excess demand** arises when the price is too low and **excess supply** arises when the price is too high. At some price, quantity demanded will equal quantity supplied achieving a **competitive equilibrium**. In this equilibrium, the allocation is **Pareto-optimal** in that no one can be made better off without making someone else worse off.

Potential Difficulties with the Competitive Equilibrium

All individuals are assumed to be price takers and hence cannot influence price. In our island example, the fish owners could have, for instance, banded together (formed a cartel) and demanded a higher price for their fish. The more individuals in the market, the less likely that such behaviour will occur. Although the Walrasian auctioning process rarely exists, the assumption of perfect information ensures that consumers will buy from the cheapest seller — hence encouraging all sellers to offer their goods at the lowest feasible price.

Just how applicable is this model of perfect competition? We already understand that models do not have to capture all the complexities of the real world to be useful. In providing an abstraction of the salient features of markets that look like perfect competition, the forces at work in this model appear very much like the ones that direct the allocation of resources in a capitalistic price system. **Experimental economics** has provided strong support for the robustness of the competitive model. In simple environments of economic trading, the outcomes predicted by the competitive models are often attained, even when the assumptions of many traders and perfect information are relaxed.

The Short-Run Supply Decision

The perfectly competitive firm is assumed to maximize profits. The short-run **profit function** may be written as the difference between the firm's **total revenue function** and its short-run costs. The solution to the profit maximization problem gives the **short-run supply function** for the firm as long as price is above the average variable cost curve (otherwise, the firm is better off shutting down). Profits are maximized whenever **marginal revenue** equals the **short-run marginal cost** of production. Because marginal revenue is identical to price in perfect competition, price equals short-run marginal costs is the profit maximizing rule as long as the firm is on the upward sloping part of its marginal cost curve. The industry short-run supply curve is the horizontal summation of the firm's short-run supply curves. The **short-run competitive equilibrium** is described by the intersection of the aggregate demand and the short-run supply curves. This equilibrium is efficient because there are no gains from further trading. The **total surplus** which consists of **consumers' surplus** and **producers' surplus**, is maximized under this allocation.

The Long-Run Competitive Equilibrium

As in the short run, the long-run equilibrium is characterized by demand equals supply; however, the industry **long-run supply function** is more complicated to derive. As in the short run, each firm makes its long-run plan by equating its **long-run marginal cost** and the price. The difference is that the industry long-run supply is not simply the horizontal summation of the firms' long-run marginal cost curves. In the long run, firms can enter the industry if economic profits are being made by established firms. Similarly, established firms can exit the industry if they are making losses. In the former case, profits are reduced to zero by the entry of new firms and the expansion of output; in the latter case, the exit of firms and the consequent reduction of output raises profits to zero. Hence, the long-run equilibrium for the industry is not achieved until economic profits equal zero. In long-run equilibrium, then, price equals **minimum average cost**, which in turn equals $LMC(y)$, $SAC(y)$, and $SMC(y)$ and output is at the **efficient scale of production**. That is, all firms must operate at the minimum of their $LAC(y)$ curves in the long-run equilibrium.

What does this equilibrium condition tell us about the long-run supply curve of the industry? It depends on whether the prices of inputs as industry output expands stay constant, increase, or decrease; that is, if the industry is a constant-cost, increasing-cost, or decreasing-cost industry, respectively. Consider a constant-cost industry. Starting at some long-run equilibrium, suppose there is a shift in the demand curve to the right. Established firms will equate their $SMC(y)$ to the increased price and contemplate a further increase in output in the long run. However, entrants will also see that there are profits to be made by following this same rule and will enter the industry. By the very nature of a constant-cost industry, the expansion of output by both the established firms and entrants *will not increase the costs of production*. Entry will continue until price is once again equal to **efficient average cost**, yielding a long-run industry supply that is horizontal at the minimum of the $LAC(y)$ curve. Similar analysis indicates that the long-run industry supply curve for an increasing-cost industry is positively sloped, whereas a decreasing-cost industry is characterized by a negatively-sloped industry supply curve.

KEY WORDS

Competitive equilibrium	Market supply function
Consumers' surplus	Minimum average cost
Efficient average cost	Pareto-optimal
Efficient scale of production	Producers' surplus
Excess demand	Profit function
Excess supply	Reservation price
Experimental Economics	Short-run competitive equilibrium
Long-run supply function	Short-run marginal cost
Long-run marginal cost	Short-run supply function
Marginal revenue	Total surplus
Market demand function	Walrasian auctioneer

CASE STUDY: THE MARKET FOR TAXI CABS

Several interesting insights may be gained from examining the taxi-cab market. On the face of it, this market boasts many of the features of a competitive market — a large number of buyers, potentially a large number of sellers (in the absence of regulation), information that is relatively easy to obtain, and a fairly homogeneous product. However, in virtually every Canadian city, this market is regulated on the supply side. The number of taxis is dictated by the number of licenses (or medallions) issued by the city. These licenses are typically allocated to the original participants in the market, and thereafter must be purchased or leased by new entrants. In order to provide taxi services, the individual must be in possession of a license. Several explanations have been offered regarding why such regulation is in place: to promote safety by setting conditions for the ownership of licenses; to prevent too many taxis on the road which might contribute to congestion and accidents; and, as a way of conferring on taxi drivers some monopoly profits.

Regardless of the reason for regulation, the fact of the matter is that neither consumers nor suppliers seem particularly happy with the current situation. Consumers complain about too few taxis on the street and taxi-cab owners complain about the cost of acquiring the right to operate their cabs. Indeed, it currently costs about $90 000 to obtain a license in Toronto. Attempts to remedy this situation by increasing the number of licenses on the market do not meet with approval from both sides. Recently, the city of Toronto announced that it would increase by about 10 per cent the number of taxi-cab licenses issued in the market — which met with considerable disapproval on the part of incumbent taxi-cab owners. To see why they reacted in such a manner, the following exercise looks at a simplified version of this market, including an analysis of who is likely to benefit and who is likely to lose from such a scheme.

Let's suppose that in Honey Harbour, a representative individual's demand for taxi rides is $q=10\text{-}p$ per day and that there are 1 000 individuals in the village. The marginal cost of a taxi ride is constant and equal to $8.00; the maximum number of rides that any one taxi can offer in a day is 32.

A What is the competitive equilibrium price and number of taxi cabs operating in Honey Harbour?

B Suppose now that the municipality of Honey Harbour decides to introduce a policy of licenses for taxi cabs. It gives one license to each taxi in the market. What is the immediate impact of this policy?

C Over time, the number of individuals demanding taxi rides increases by 10% (costs, however, remain the same). How does this affect the market for taxi-cab rides?

D In a competitive market, how much would a potential taxi-cab operator be willing to pay to lease a license for a year? Given an annual discount rate of 5%, how much would this individual be willing to pay to buy this license?

E Who are the winners and losers associated with Honey Harbour's licensing policy?

F Explain why the taxi-cab drivers in Toronto are unhappy with the decision to increase the number of licenses in that city.

EXERCISES

Multiple-Choice

Choose the correct answer to each question. There is only one correct answer to each question.

For questions **1** and **2**, refer to Figure 8.1. In the short run, a representative profit-maximizing firm operates at a plant size with short-run average cost curve $SAC(y)$.

1 If a firm faces a price p_1 in the short run, it will do which of the following?
- **a** Make positive profits.
- **b** Incur a loss equal to DE times OA.
- **c** Exit from the industry and make no loss at all
- **d** Incur a loss equal to GD times OA.
- **e** None of the above.

2 If all firms in the competitive industry have cost curves as shown in the figure, then in long-run equilibrium
- **a** There will be more firms in the industry than in short-run equilibrium.
- **b** Firms will make positive profits.
- **c** Prices will rise to the minimum of the $LAC(y)$ curve.
- **d** Firms will make a loss equal to GD times OA.
- **e** None of the above.

3 If a perfectly competitive firm earns a profit of $1 000 per year and faces CRTS in production, which of the following is true?
- **a** In the long run, it can double its profits by doubling all its inputs.
- **b** It can raise prices as its profits begin to erode.
- **c** It can make the same profit in the long run.
- **d** It will make no profits at all as firms enter the industry.
- **e** None of the above.

4 An allocation of goods among individuals and resources among firms is said to be Pareto-optimal if
- **a** Consumers' surplus is maximized.

FIGURE 8.1

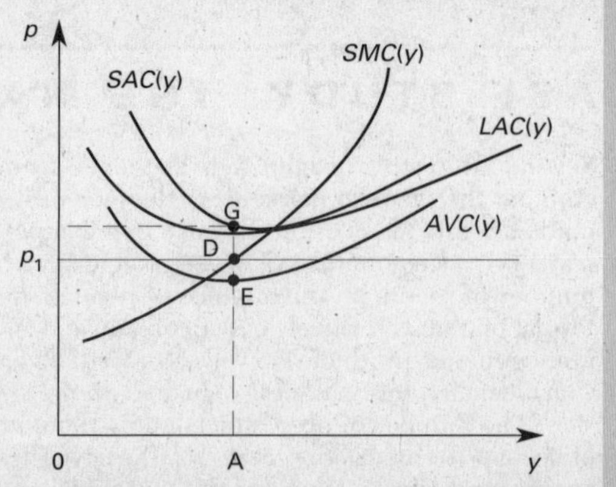

b It is not possible to make someone better off without making anyone else worse off.
c It is possible to make someone better off without making anyone else worse off.
d The utilities of all individuals are equal.
e Only **a** and **b**.

5 Suppose that you observe that $p = 10$, and you know that a firm's total cost function is $TC = 100 + y^2$. From this we may conclude that, in a perfectly competitive market,
a This firm would supply 5 units of output.
b This firm would supply 10 units of output.
c In the long run, this firm would exit the market.
d Both **a** and **c**.
e None of the above.

6 Suppose, again, that you observe $p = 10$, and you know that a firm's total cost function is $TC = a + y^2$. If the market is in long-run equilibrium, then
a $a = 50$
b $a = 25$
c $a = 0$
d $a = -25$
e None of the above.

7 Which of the following is *not* an assumption of perfect competition?
a The number of suppliers is large enough that no one produces a significant proportion of the output, and all demanders and suppliers are price-takers.
b All individuals have perfect knowledge.
c The products sold by all firms in the market are homogeneous.
d Each firm faces a downward-sloping demand curve.
e All the above are assumptions of perfect competition.

8 If an industry is an increasing-cost industry, then
a The long-run industry supply curve is positively sloped.
b The long-run industry supply curve is negatively sloped.
c The supply curve for inputs used in the production is horizontal.
d The short-run average cost curve cannot be U-shaped.
e None of the above.

9 Which of the following is *not* true about a perfectly competitive firm?
a In the short run, it may produce where AVC is downward-sloping.
b In the long run, it will produce where LAC is rising in an increasing-cost industry.
c In the short run, it would never produce where SMC is downward-sloping.
d In the long run, it will produce at a point where there are CRTS in production.
e All the above are true.

True-False

10 Since long-run economic profits for a competitive firm are always zero, it will never pay a competitive firm to adopt a cost-reducing innovation.

11 The short-run supply curve of the firm coincides with its marginal cost curve for all prices.

12 The greater the increase in demand, the higher is the long-run price of a good produced in a competitive increasing-cost industry.

13 If each firm is initially earning positive profits in a perfectly competitive industry, then there will be entry of new firms, price will fall, and the output of each firm will fall in the final long-run equilibrium.

14 Since every firm in a competitive industry earns zero economic profit in long-run equilibrium, then a fall in the market price would mean that no firms could survive in the long run.

15 If all firms minimize costs and face the same input prices but different production functions, then all firms will use inputs in the same proportion.

16 The horizontal summation of the $LMC(y)$ curves of individual firms is not the long-run supply curve for the industry.

17 If two individuals have identical preferences, there are no benefits from trade.

18 The competitive equilibrium price depends on the initial distribution of resources.

19 If all firms have constant marginal costs, then total surplus in the market consists solely of consumers' surplus.

20 In a Pareto optimal allocation, the initial distribution of resources does not matter.

Short Problems

21 Consider a competitive industry with a long-run demand curve

$$y_d = 40 - 2p$$

and long-run supply curve

$$y_s = 4p - 20$$

a Find the equilibrium price and quantity.
b Suppose that consumers must buy the product from a third person who charges \$6 per unit for his services. Find the new equilibrium quantity and price.

22 Discuss why "scalping" at sports events (individuals buying several tickets in advance and selling them at very high prices just before a game) may be desirable from an efficiency point of view.

23 The demand and supply curves for wheat in a bad and good year are shown in Figure 8.2. The demand curves are the same in the two years.
a What would happen to total expenditures on

FIGURE 8.2

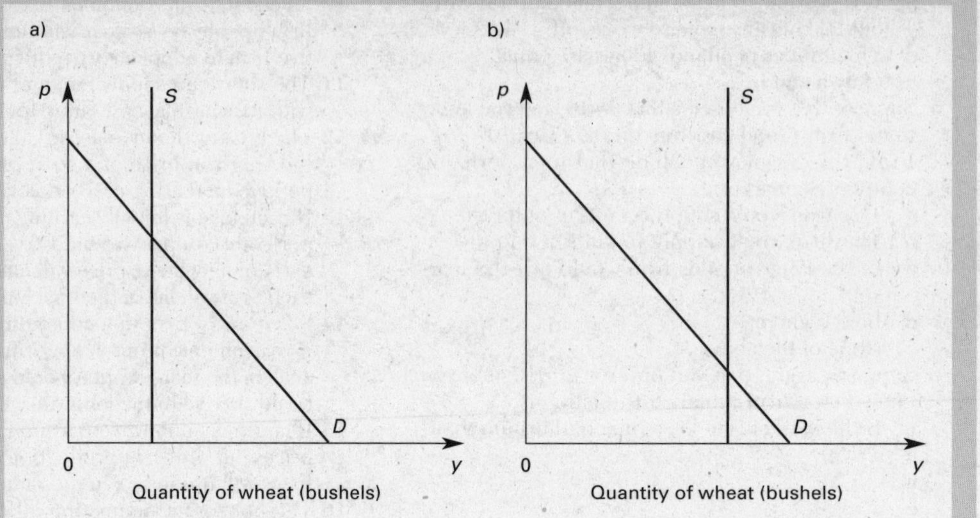

wheat if supply were to increase slightly in the bad year shown in Figure 8.2a?

b What would happen to total expenditures on wheat if supply were to increase slightly in the good year shown in Figure 8.2b?

Long Problems

24 The table gives a relationship between the quantity of feed fed to a hen and the dozens of eggs obtained.

Feed fed (kilos)	0	4	8	12	16	20
Eggs obtained (dozens)	2	12	20	26	30	32

Assume that all other inputs are held constant and that their total cost is \$5. Suppose that the cost of feed is \$2 per kilo and the price of eggs is \$2 per dozen. Assume that eggs and feed are sold in a competitive market.

a Calculate the following:
(1) The profit-maximizing number of eggs to produce.
(2) The profit-maximizing amount of feed to give a hen.

b Derive the marginal and average product curves for feed and the marginal and average cost curves. Plot the marginal and average products on one diagram and the marginal cost, average total cost, and marginal revenue functions on another diagram. Indicate your answer in **a**(1) by a point *C*.

25 Industry Y is a perfectly competitive, constant-cost industry. It is currently in a position of long-run equilibrium. Market demand in the industry is given by

$$y = 1500 - 25p$$

The short-run market supply curve is given by

$$y_s = 15p - 100 \quad \text{for } p \geq 10$$
$$= 0 \quad \text{for } p < 10$$

There are 25 firms in the industry.

a Calculate the equilibrium market price and quantity and the equilibrium quantity produced by each firm.

b Each firm is currently operating at the optimal plant size. What must be the minimum short-run average variable costs for this plant and what is the efficient average cost? Explain.

c Now suppose that the government imposes a tax of \$10 on producers for each unit of the commodity produced.
(1) Illustrate on a diagram the loss in consumer surplus plus producer surplus as a result of this tax. If the consumer surplus is to be an accurate measure of willingness to pay, what must be true?
(2) What will happen to the price paid by consumers in the long run? Explain.

26 Grand Grain, Inc. produces a breakfast cereal in a constant-cost, perfectly competitive industry. Its average cost curve is U-shaped. The firm is currently operating at $y = 10$. The minimum of the long-run average cost curve is at $y = 10$ with average costs equal to \$30.

a What is the long-run equilibrium price of cereal? Explain.
b The price falls to $22. Should the firm shut down in the long run? Why or why not? Should it shut down in the short run? Why or why not?
c Suppose that the rent of the land on which the factory stands falls in the next period. If the price of cereal is $30, how does this rent decrease change the quantity that the firm produces in the short run? Explain and illustrate the effect of this rent decrease on the short-run cost curves.
d What effect will an increase in the price of wheat (an input) have on the long-run output of each firm? On the number of firms in the long run? On the long-run industry output? Explain.
e The producers of Nutty Bread, who use the Grand Grain breakfast cereal as an ingredient, receive a per-unit subsidy from the Department of Agriculture. The subsidies come from general tax funds. How will this affect the equilibrium price and industry output for breakfast cereal in the long run? Explain, using diagrams.

27 Suppose that an advance in microchip technology reduces the average cost of producing computers by $100 at every output level. Assume that the long-run average cost curve is U-shaped and the computer industry is a constant-cost industry. Also assume that the minimum of the long-run average cost is at 400 units of output per year.
a If the inventor of the new chip offered her invention to firms at a per-unit cost of $50, what would be the long-run effects on price and quantity produced by the firm and the industry as a result of the invention? Describe the effects, using diagrams.
b Suppose that the inventor were to charge a fixed total royalty of $20 000 per year to each firm using the invention instead of the $50 per-unit royalty. Show the effect that this fee will have on the average and marginal cost curves of each firm. Under which royalty payment scheme would the long-run price of computers be lower? Explain.

***28** Suppose that Jane's demand function for butter per month is: $y = (10p_m - 3p_b)/2$ where p_m represents the price of margarine and p_b is the price of butter per kilogram.
a Given that margarine is $2 per kilogram and the price of butter is $4, how much butter is demanded by Jane in one month?
b Calculate and interpret $\partial y/\partial p_m$ and $\partial y/\partial p_b$.
c Suppose that the market consists of 100 individuals just like Jane and the market supply of butter is $y = 100 + 30p_b$. Calculate the equilibrium price and output in this market (given that the price of margarine is $2).
d Suppose that the price of margarine were to increase by $1 per kilogram, calculate the new equilibrium price and quantity for butter.
e Calculate the change in producers' and consumers' surplus arising from this increase in the price of margarine.

***29** Suppose that Peter and Elaine are stranded on a desert island. Peter has found and claimed 12 coconuts while Elaine has acquired the only 6 bananas on the island. Peter's preferences for coconuts and bananas may be expressed as $U(x_c, x_b) = x_c^2 x_b$ while Elaine's is $U(x_c, x_b) = x_c + x_b$.
a. Does the current situation represent a Pareto optimum? Explain.
b. Calculate the only Pareto optimal allocation that is also a competitive equilibrium.
c. Suppose that the allocations were reversed: Peter had the 6 bananas and Elaine had the 12 coconuts. How would this affect the Pareto optimal allocation?

ANSWERS TO CHAPTER 8

Case Study

A The market demand function is $q = 10\ 000 - 1\ 000p$. Remember that in equilibrium, $p = mc$. Substituting $p = 8$ into the market demand function yields total demand of 2 000 rides per day (the residents of Honey Harbour like to take taxis!). Since each cab can at the most offer 32 rides per day, this means that the market will have 2 000/32 = 62.5 taxi cabs (you can think of this as 62 full-time taxis and one half-time taxi).

B Honey Harbour thus issues 62.5 licenses. There is no real immediate impact of this policy since all taxi owners are given, *gratis*, their licenses.

C The number of individuals increases to 1 100 and the new market demand becomes $q = 11\ 000 + 1\ 100p$. Now the constraint is on the supply side — no matter the price, only 2 000 rides may be provided in one day. Thus, $2\ 000 = 11\ 000 + 1\ 100p$ means that $p = 8.18$ (an increase of 18 cents). Taxi owners thus gain an economic profit of (0.18)(32) = $5.76 per day which amounts to $2 102.40 per year. Note that this profit occurs because entry is no longer permitted in this market.

D A potential taxi operator would be willing to pay up to the expected profit per year to lease the license, which is \$2 102.40. To buy this license, he or she would be willing to pay the present value of an infinite future stream of payments of \$2 102.40 which is 2 102.40/.05 = \$42 048.

E The winners are clearly the incumbent taxi owners who were given free of charge a valuable asset in the form of the license. Consumers lose because the price of taxi rides will increase as demand increases unless the number of licenses is adjusted. Potential entrants into the market also lose because they now have to pay an entry fee in order to acquire the right to operate a taxi in Honey Harbour.

F All license owners would be opposed to such a policy because as the number of licenses increases, their price would fall. Thus, the value of the asset that is the license would fall as well.

Multiple-Choice

1 d 2 c 3 d 4 b 5 d
6 b 7 d 8 a 9 b

True-False

10 F 11 F 12 T 13 T 14 F 15 F
16 T 17 F 18 T 19 F 20 T

Short Problems

21 a Quantity demanded equals quantity supplied, where

$$40 - 2p = 4p - 20$$

from which $p^* = 10$. Substitute $p = 10$ into either the demand or supply equation to get equilibrium quantity $y^* = 40 - 2 \times 10 = 20$.

b If consumers must pay \$6 to a third person, then the price paid by consumers is $p = p_s + 6$, where p_s is the price received by suppliers; p_s is substituted for p in the supply function. Demand and supply curves become

$$y_d = 40 - 2(p_s + 6) \quad \text{and} \quad y_s = 4p_s - 20$$

Equating y_d and y_s gives

$$40 - 2(p_s + 6) = 4p_s - 20$$
$$p_s = 8$$

The price paid by consumers is $p^* = 8 + 6 = 14$, and quantity demanded and supplied in the market is found by substituting $p = 14$ into the demand curve: $y^* = 40 - 2(8 + 6) = 12$. This solution is illustrated in Figure A8.1

22 Suppose that, in the absence of scalping, the price of tickets is at $\bar{p}$, which is below the equilibrium price in Figure A8.2; that is, y_d individuals want tickets and y_s tickets are available. Under a first-come, first-served rationing scheme, the individuals with the lowest surplus may be the lucky ones to get the tickets. Alternatively, if a scalper gets the tickets and sells them to the individuals willing to pay the highest prices for the tickets, then total surplus from the sale of y_s tickets could be as large as the shaded area.

FIGURE A8.1

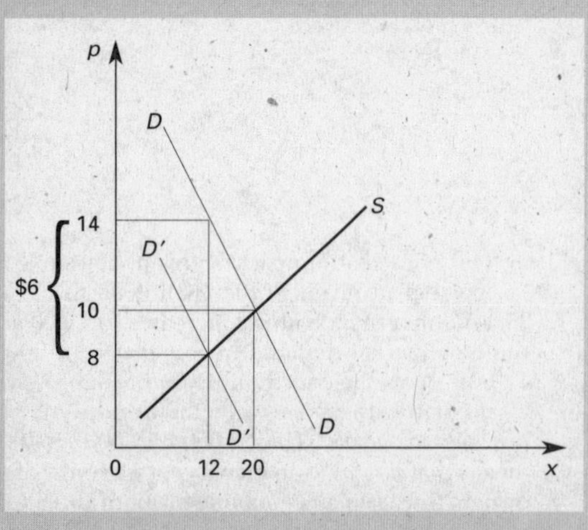

FIGURE A8.2

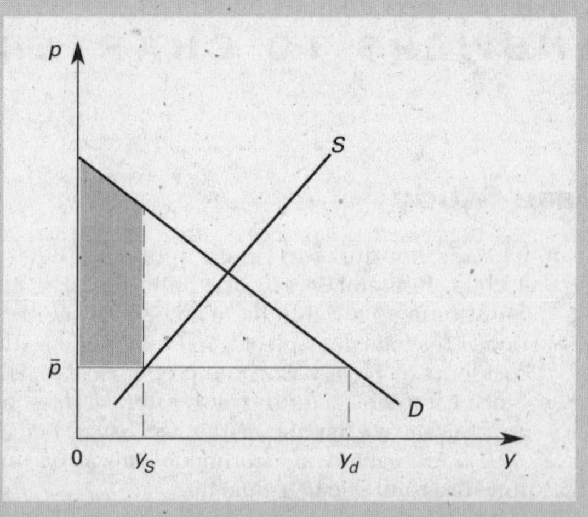

23 a Since the intersection of demand and supply is on the elastic portion of the demand curve, total expenditures increase when supply curves increase and equilibrium price falls.

b The intersection of demand and supply is on the inelastic portion of the demand curve. When equilibrium price falls, total expenditure falls.

Long Problems

24 Multiply the quantities of feed by $2 and add $5 to get the total costs. Multiply the quantities of eggs by $2/dozen to get total revenue.

Total costs	5	13	21	29	37	45
Total revenues	4	24	40	52	60	64

a To find the profit-maximizing number of eggs to produce and amount of feed to use, derive the marginal cost and marginal revenue schedules. (*Caution:* Eggs are not increasing in *unit* increments; for example, the marginal cost between 2 and 12 dozen eggs is (13 – 5)/(12 – 2) = $0.80).

Quantity	2	12	20	26	30	32
Marginal costs	0.80	1.00	1.33	2.00	4.00	
Marginal revenue	2.00	2.00	2.00	2.00	2.00	

(1) The profit-maximizing output level is where $p = MC(y)$ or between 26 and 30 units (or the average, 28).

(2) The profit-maximizing feed is the amount required to produce between 26 and 30 units; that is, between 12 and 16 kilos of feed (or the average of 14 kilos).

b The marginal and average product curves are plotted in Figure A8.3a. For example, the marginal product between 0 and 4 units of feed is (12 – 2)/(4 – 0) = 2.5; the average product of 4 units of feed is 12/4 = 3. The cost curves are plotted in Figure A8.3b.

Feed	0	4	8	12	16	20
Marginal product		2.5	2	1.5	1	0.5
Average product	∞	3	2.5	2.2	1.9	1.6
Quantity	2	12	20	26	30	32
Marginal costs		0.8	1	1.3	2	4
Average costs	2.5	1.1	1.1	1.1	1.2	1.4

25 a Equilibrium market price and quantity are found by equating supply and demand.

$$1500 - 25p = 15p - 100$$
$$p = 40$$
$$y = 15 \times 40 - 100 = 500$$

The equilibrium quantity per firm is 20.

b The minimum short-run average variable cost is 10; at any price below 10, the firms refuse to supply the market and output is zero. The efficient average cost is 40.

c (1) The loss in surplus is given by the shaded area in Figure A8.4. For consumer surplus to be an accurate measure of willingness to pay, the income effect must be zero.

(2) Each firm's cost curves increase by $10 at every output, so the efficient average cost increases from $40 to $50. In the long run, firms will drop out of the market until the price increases to $50.

26 a It is $30. The long-run price equals the minimum of the $LAC(y)$ curve because competitive firms cannot earn economic profits in the long run.

FIGURE A8.3

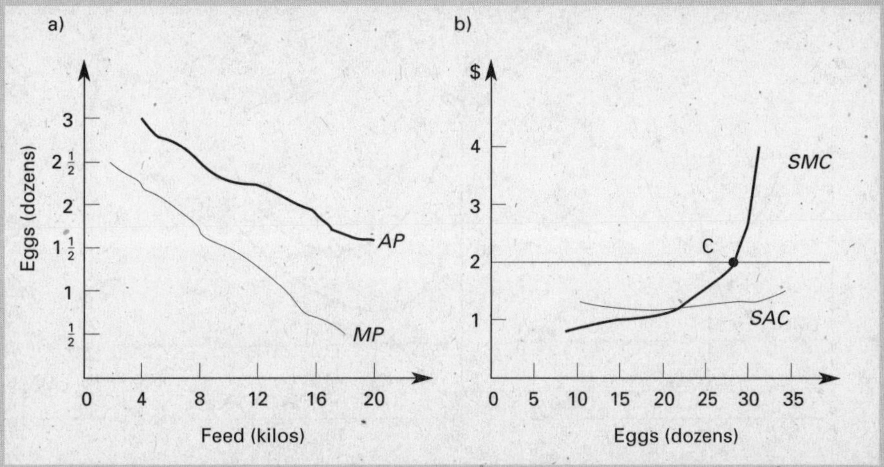

FIGURE A8.4

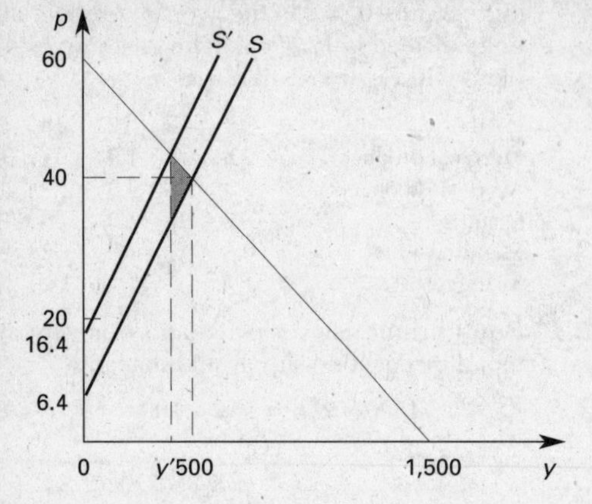

b The initial equilibrium is shown in Figure A8.5a. If the price falls to \$22, the firm will want to exit from the industry in the long run because it is making negative profits. In the short run, the firm will not shut down if it is covering its variable costs.

c Rent on land is a fixed cost of production. The decrease in the rent will result in a shift of the $SAC(y)$ curve from SAC_0 down the $SMC(y)$ curve to SAC' in Figure A8.5b. This does not change the supply curve of the firm. Hence, the short-run market price and the quantity produced by the firm do not change, as shown in Figure A8.53b.

d An increase in the price of wheat will increase the $LMC(y)$ and $LAC(y)$ curves. This change is indicated in Figure A8.5c for the case in which the minimum of the $LAC(y)$ curve does not change. (This may not always be the case.) Since firms are making negative long-run profits, firms will drop out of the industry; the industry supply curve will shift to the left; industry quantities will fall; and the market price will rise to p'. The firm quantity will stay the same (in this case). However, if the minimum of the $LAC(y)$ curve had fallen to $y < 10$ or increased to $y > 10$, then the firm quantity would have fallen or increased, respectively.

e The subsidy will increase the production of Nutty Bread and thus the demand for Grand Grain cereal. The increase in demand will result in profits to the firms; more firms will enter the industry until price falls to its original level at a higher output, y', because the industry is a constant-cost industry. This equilibrium solution is illustrated in Figure A8.6.

27 The effect of a \$100 per unit decrease in costs is shown in Figure A8.7. LMC_0 and LAC_0 fall by \$100 at every output level (to LMC' and LAC', respectively). The minimum of the $LAC(y)$ curve remains at 400.

a If the inventor offers her technology for \$50 per unit, then LMC_0 and LAC_0 will fall at every output by only \$50 to LMC_a and LAC_a rather than by the full \$100, as shown in Figure A8.8. The equilibrium price falls to $p_0 - 50$; firm quantity stays at 400; market quantity rises from $400n_0$ to $400n_a$, where $n_a > n_0$.

b If a fixed fee of \$20 000/year is charged, LMC' — the $LMC(y)$ curve under the new technology, with no license fee — will not change. However, the LAC' slides up LMC' to LAC_b. At $y = 400$, the average cost increases by \$50.

FIGURE A8.5

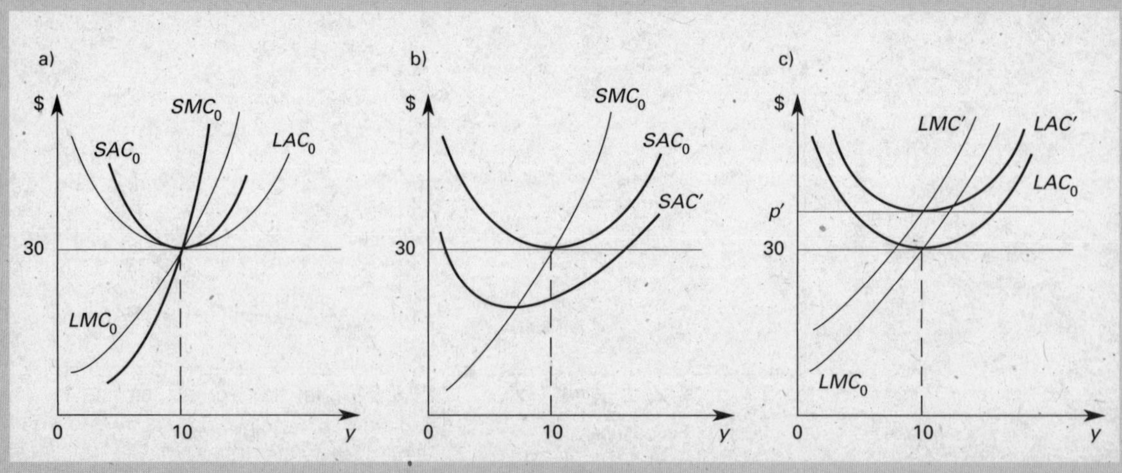

FIGURE A8.6

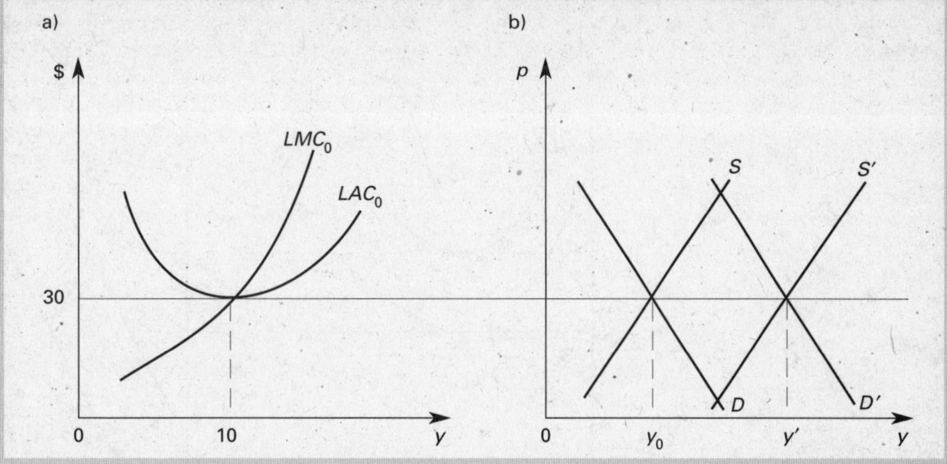

FIGURE A8.7

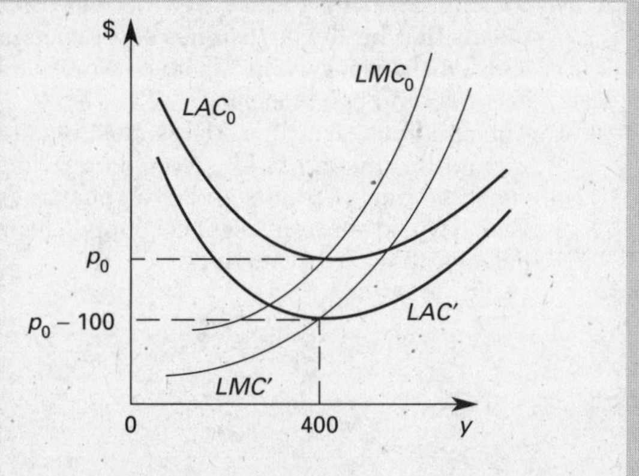

The long-run average and marginal cost curves under the new technology with no license fee — LAC' and LMC' — and under the new technology with the \$20 000 fee — LAC_b and LMC' — respectively, are shown in Figure A8.9. Note that the firm and market quantity (y_b and n_by_b, respectively) are larger under the lump-sum royalty than under the per-unit royalty in Figure A8.9a (400 and $400n_a$, respectively). Also, the market price under the lump-sum fee, p_b, is lower than the price under the per-unit fee, $p_0 - 50$.

*28 a $y = 10 - 1.5(4) = 4$ kilograms of butter.

b $\partial y/\partial p_m = 5$, gives the cross-price elasticity of demand for butter. As the price of margarine increases by \$1, the quantity of butter demanded increases by 5 kilograms, *ceteris paribus*. Margarine and butter are thus substitute products. $\partial y/\partial p_b = -3/2$ which implies that the demand curve for butter has a negative slope and thus butter is an ordinary good. As the price of butter increases by \$1, the demand for butter falls by 1.5 kilograms, *ceteris paribus*.

c The market demand for butter is $y = 1000 - 150p_b$, setting demand equal to supply yields a price of \$5 per kilogram and an equilibrium quantity of 250 kilograms of butter in total (or 2.5 kilograms per individual).

d If the price of margarine increases by one dollar, the market demand is $y = 1500 - 150p_b$, the new equilibrium price is \$7.78, and 333 kilograms of butter is the new equilibrium quantity.

e The change in producers' surplus is given by the areas $A + B + C$ in Figure A8.10. Areas $A + B = (7.78 - 5)(250)$, and $C = (7.78 - 5)(333 - 250)(0.5)$, which gives a total value of \$810.37. The change in consumers' surplus is given by the area $(D - A) = 729.26 - 417.5 = \$311.76$.

*29 a No. At the current situation, Peter derives no utility from his bundle. If Elaine were to give him one banana in exchange for one or more coconuts, Peter would be better off and, because Elaine considers bananas and coconuts as perfect substitutes, she would be no worse off (she, indeed, would be better off if she obtained more than one coconut). Indeed, Peter would be better off with one of each good rather than 12 coconuts and zero bananas.

b There are a few different ways of tackling this problem. We know that in equilibrium, the price is such that demand equals supply. We also

FIGURE A8.8

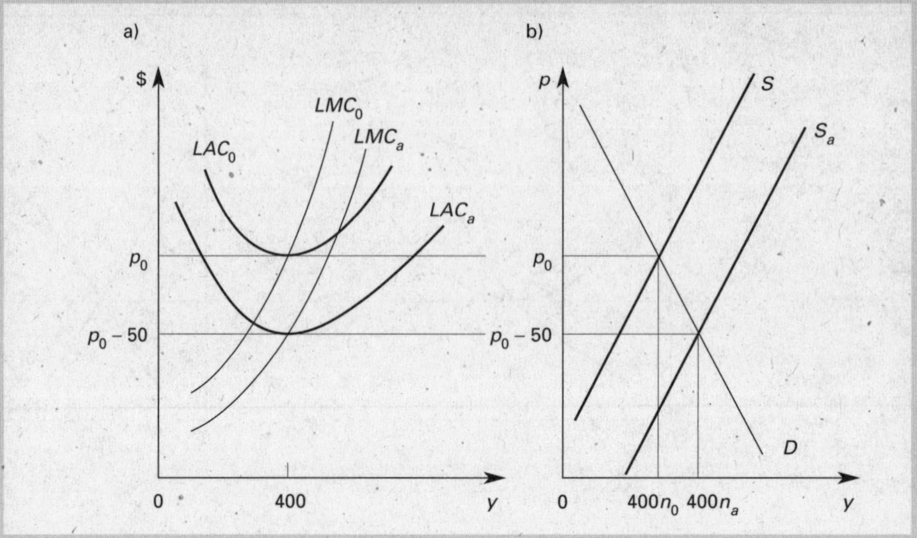

know that with Peter's preferences, the equilibrium must be one in which Peter consumes some of both goods. In equilibrium the marginal rate of substitution between bananas and coconuts must equal the price ratio for all individuals. The MRS, which equals the ratio of marginal utilities for the two goods, is $(2x_c)/x_b$ for Peter and one for Elaine. We know that these MRSs must be equal in equilibrium. Hence, the only possible prices in equilibrium is one where bananas and coconuts trade one for one. Setting Peter's MRS equal to one means that he thus consumes eight coconuts and four bananas while Elaine consumes four coconuts and two bananas.

c The condition that their MRSs must be equal in equilibrium still holds. Now, Peter would consume four coconuts and two bananas and Elaine would consume eight coconuts. The initial allocation clearly matters.

FIGURE A8.9

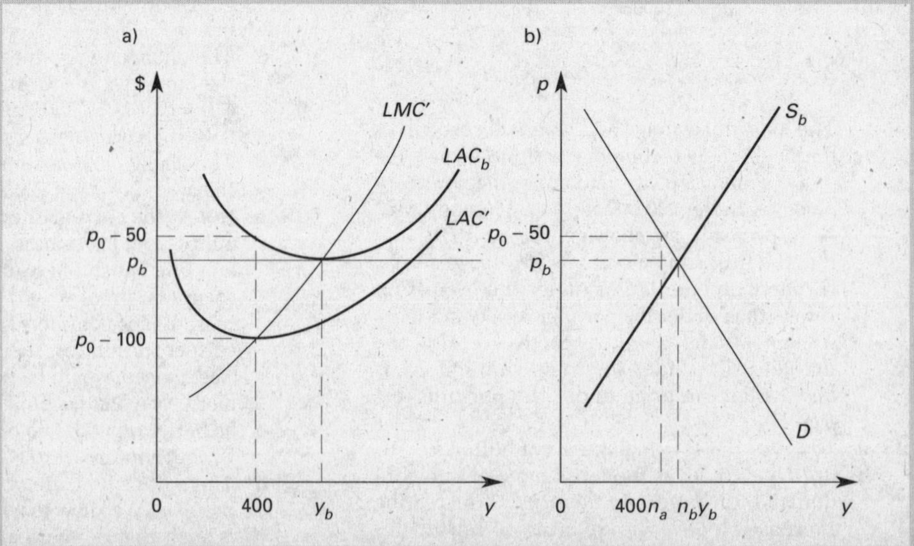

FIGURE A8.10

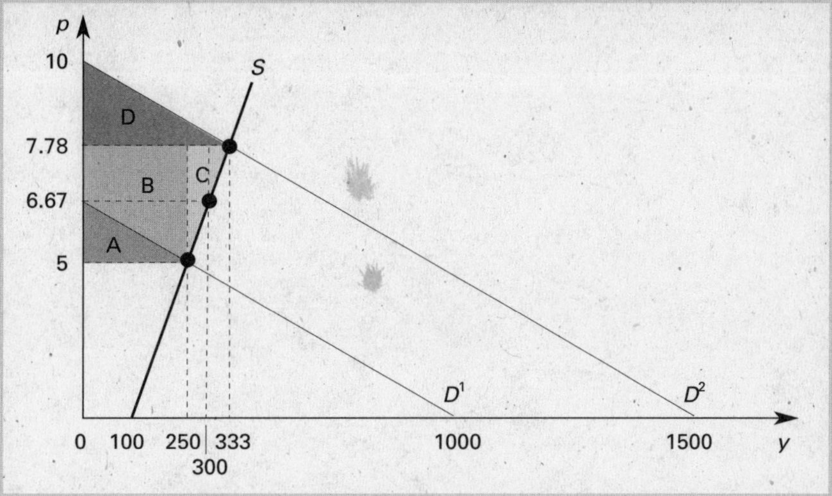

CHAPTER 9

Applications of the Competitive Model

Chapter Summary

Although based on simplifying and often unrealistic assumptions, the competitive model developed in Chapter 8 may be used to gain valuable insights into the behaviour of economic agents. This chapter focuses on several applications of this simple yet powerful model.

Comparative Statics in the Basic Model

When the price of a good changes, consumers (producers) move along their demand (supply) curves — we say that quantity demanded (supplied) changes. When any other exogenous variable changes (like income or the price of other goods in the case of demand, or input prices and technology in the case of supply) the entire demand (supply) curve shifts.

Applications of the Basic Model

One has to be careful when applying the basic model to take account of the fact that demand and supply curves tend to be more responsive to changes in prices over time. That demand curves are more elastic over time is known as the **second law of demand** and reflects the fact that more substitutes are available over time. Think about the demand for gasoline. Over time, as the price of gasoline increases individuals are more likely to use more fuel-efficient vehicles (or start to ride a bicycle or take public transportation) in comparison to the short run. Firms, too, will tend to look for alternative ways of producing their output when faced with rising input prices.

Perhaps less obviously, other phenomena may be better understood using the simple model of demand and supply. For instance, houses in colder climates tend to be warmer inside than those in milder climates; economic crimes, like theft, tend to be inversely related to conditions in the economy.

Much insight can be gained from examining agricultural policies using the competitive framework, as reflected in the case study presented below. One policy that has been used quite regularly in the past is quotas. An agricultural quota gives a farmer the "right" to produce a given quantity of a particular product. Effectively, quotas confer a valuable asset on the initial participants in the market as they are typically allocated free of charge. The number of quotas allocated is less than the competitive equilibrium output, and hence the initial holders of the quota may gain an **economic rent** or a return over and above their opportunity costs. One of the problems with trying to disband the quota policy is that subsequent owners of quotas have to buy them at a price which reflects the economic rent associated with the asset. As such, only the initial holders of the quota gain the economic rent; as a result, quotas typically only benefit the original farmers. This problem is known as the **transitional gains trap** and is one of the principal reasons why quota policies are very difficult to disband. You should notice a similarity between agricultural quotas and other policies such as the licensing of taxi cabs as described in the case study of Chapter 8.

Rent-control policies impose a **price ceiling** on the price for rental accommodation. Several problems arise from these policies. In the short run, criteria other than price are used to decide who should get an apartment. In the long run, rent controls have a direct impact on the amount of new apartments constructed and the up-keep of existing dwellings. Another market impediment is a **price floor** in which sellers are not permitted to charge a price lower than some specified level. International cartels, like OPEC, usually price in this manner.

Policies like taxes and tariffs may also be analyzed using demand and supply curves. A per-unit tax imposed on sellers shifts the supply curve up by the amount of the tax. The same tax may be imposed on consumers and would result in their demand curve shifting down to the left. Either way, the tax results in a wedge between the amount paid by a consumer and the amount received by the supplier — leading to a loss in total surplus known as the **deadweight loss** associated with a tax. Note that, irrespective of whether the tax is imposed on the supplier or the consumer, the short-run equilibrium price and output will be identical. Who pays the burden of the tax depends upon the relative elasticities of demand and supply. The lower (the absolute value of) the elasticity of demand relative to the elasticity of supply, the higher the proportion of the tax paid by consumers. Tariffs, like taxes, result in a deadweight loss.

The amount of capital goods purchased by the firm is its **investment demand**; it is this demand which generates the firm's demand for loans. The demand for capital goods is inversely related to the rate of interest which, in turn, means that the firm's demand for loanable funds is also inversely related to the interest rate. The supply of funds is provided by savers, and is positively related to the interest rate.

The tools of economic analysis may be used to analyze aspects of criminal behaviour. In particular, the idea that the quantity of crime depends on costs and benefits can yield some valuable insights into how society may control criminal activity. Several examples can illustrate this point. For instance, in recent years the province of Ontario experimented with the use of photo-radar equipment to control excessive speeding on its major highways. The result was startling. Wherever the radar equipment was installed or was suspected of being in place, speed was dramatically reduced. The fact that a costly speeding ticket was virtually guaranteed with this system had a profound impact on the speed driven. Many provinces have introduced tough drinking and driving laws — which impose severe penalties on drivers who drink — which has affected the drinking and driving behaviour of many people.

KEY WORDS

Deadweight loss

Economic rent

Investment demand

Price ceiling

Price floor

Second law of demand

Transitional gains trap

CASE STUDY: THE MARKET FOR AGRICULTURAL COMMODITIES

The market for agricultural products in North America is characterized by many price-taking farmers and consumers. This competitive market captures the attention and concern of policy-makers because of the volatility in prices, and hence in incomes, that farmers face owing to random and often uncontrollable effects on their crops, especially by the weather. Even when farmers are fortunate enough to harvest a bumper crop, farm income suffers because the demands for most agricultural products are price-inelastic. An increase in the supply of a particular crop decreases the price and the farmers' incomes from that product.

In response to these problems, the government has proposed various schemes. We examine some of them in this case study. In considering the effects of these programs, let the initial competitive price of the agricultural commodity be $4 per kilogram. For each of the three proposed schemes, analyze the short-run implications for the industry before entry or exit can occur.

Scheme 1 — The government imposes a price floor of $6 per kilogram on the agricultural commodity. Any quantity not sold to the public at that price is purchased by the government and destroyed.

Scheme 2 — The government ensures that farmers will receive $6 per kilogram by offering a per-unit subsidy on every unit of the commodity sold.

Scheme 3 — Quotas are imposed on farmers' output of corn to raise the equilibrium price to $6 per kilogram.

A Which program has the largest impact on the output of corn compared with the initial competitive equilibrium? Compare the change in quantity supplied by the farmers under each system.

B The original goal of these programs was to stabilize farm income. Which program has the largest impact on the revenues received by farmers?

C Which program is the most expensive for the government (and hence, the taxpayers) to implement? What are the social costs of the program?

EXERCISES

Multiple-Choice

Using Figure 9.1, answer the following three questions.

1 If output is restricted to 200 (thousand) chickens, market price will be:

a p_1
b p_2
c p_3
d p_4
e None of the above.

2 Compared to the competitive equilibrium,

a Consumers lose, producers gain and society on balance is better off.
b Producers lose, consumers gain and society on balance is better off.
c Consumers lose, producers gain and society on balance is worse off.
d Producers lose, consumers gain and society on balance is worse off.
e Cannot say without further information.

FIGURE 9.1

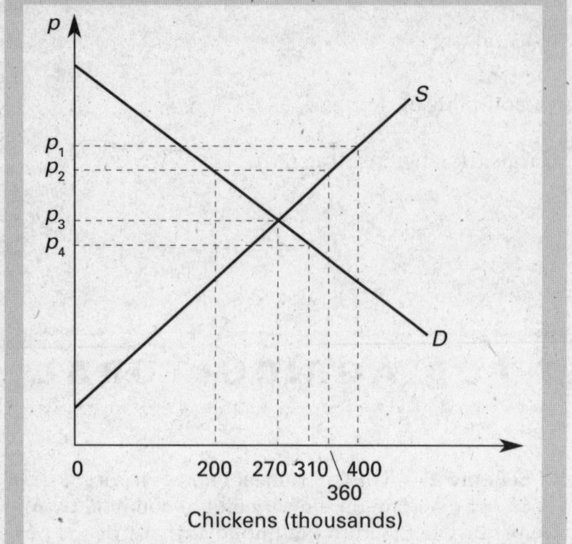

FIGURE 9.2

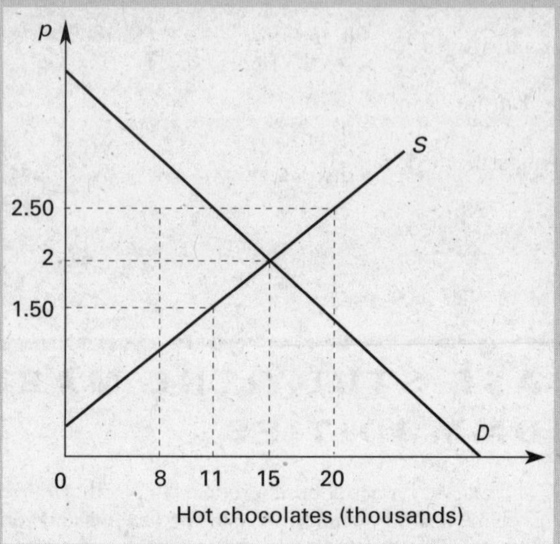

3 Suppose that the quota is now increased to 400 (thousand) chickens; then the market price becomes
- **a** p_1
- **b** p_2
- **c** p_3
- **d** p_4
- **e** None of the above.

Figure 9.2 shows the market demand and supply for hot chocolate at the Québec winter carnival. Answer the following two questions.

4 Suppose that the Government of Québec decides to impose a price ceiling on hot chocolate of $1.50 per cup. This will result in
- **a** An excess demand of 9 000 hot chocolates.
- **b** An excess supply of 4 000 hot chocolates.
- **c** An increase in consumers' surplus and a decrease in producers' surplus
- **d** Both **a** and **c.**
- **e** Both **b** and **c.**

5 Again, refer to Figure 9.2 and suppose, instead, that the producers banded together and decided to set a price floor of $2.50 per cup. In comparison to the competitive equilibrium this will result in:
- **a** An excess demand of 7 000 hot chocolates.
- **b** An excess supply of 12 000 hot chocolates.
- **c** An excess supply of 5 000.
- **d** An excess supply of 9 000.
- **e** None of the above.

6 Which of the following are consequences of a rent control policy?
- **a** Low-income people are guaranteed affordable accommodation.
- **b** Builders are induced to construct affordable accommodation.
- **c** Builders switch from building rental to other types of accommodation.
- **d** Both **a** and **b**.
- **e** All of the above.

7 If consumers have a perfectly elastic demand for a good and producers have a perfectly inelastic supply, then a per-unit tax of $1 in the short run will
- **a** Be paid only by consumers.
- **b** Be paid only by producers.
- **c** Be shared by consumer and producers.
- **d** Be paid by either consumers or producers depending upon whom it is imposed by the government.
- **e** Have an indeterminate impact.

8 In the market for loanable funds, an increase in the rate of interest
- **a** May be caused by an increase in demand.
- **b** Will result in a decrease in the quantity of funds demanded.
- **c** Will cause a shift in the supply of loanable funds.
- **d** Both **a** and **b**.
- **e** All of the above.

9 In the short run, an excise tax imposed on perfectly competitive firms is passed entirely onto the buyers in the form of a higher price if
- **a** Demand is perfectly price-inelastic.
- **b** Supply is perfectly price-elastic.
- **c** Demand is perfectly price-elastic.
- **d** Both **a** and **b**.
- **e** None of the above.

10 Rent controls that constrain the rent on apartments below the competitive price
- **a** Result in a Pareto-efficient allocation.
- **b** Are more equitable since all lower-income individuals will get housing.
- **c** Result in an excess demand for housing.
- **d** Will increase the supply of housing in the long run.
- **e** None of the above.

True-False

11 If the price of bread increases, its own demand will shift to the left and the demand for bread substitutes will shift to the right.

12 The demand curve for personal computers has increased because of technological improvements.

13 Over time, the impact of an increase in the price of electricity on the demand for natural gas will start to diminish.

14 The amount of illegal parking in the city would fall to zero if the culprit was guaranteed a parking ticket.

15 If demand and supply both increase, price and equilibrium output will rise.

16 A reduction in the price of personal computers leads to an increase in the quantity demanded of floppy disks.

17 If a lump-sum tax is placed on firms in a competitive industry, the entire tax will be passed on to the consumers in the form of a higher price in the short run, but none of the tax will be passed on to the consumer in the long run.

18 If all individuals have identical linear demand curves, then the price elasticity of market demand in absolute value is higher at every price level than the absolute value of the price elasticity of the individual demands.

19 A lump-sum subsidy to bread producers will shift the market demand for flour further to the right in the long run than will a per-unit subsidy on bread, if the total payments given to bread producers are equivalent under the two subsidy programs.

20 The long-run price of wheat under a lump-sum subsidy paid to wheat farmers will result in a higher price of wheat in the long run than would a per-unit subsidy paid to wheat farmers, if the total subsidies paid to each farmer are equivalent under the two subsidy arrangements.

Short Problems

21 In January 1998, most of Quebec and Eastern Ontario was hit by a severe ice storm. Some local stores took advantage of the situation by increasing the price of candles, wood and other supplies while other store-owners opened their doors and virtually gave away anything that would assist the victims. In Ottawa, for instance, some coffee shops were giving away free coffee and hot drinks. Analyze the impact of the storm on the demand for, say, candles in the short and long runs, and on the demand for goods from any particular store in the short and long runs.

22 The savings rate in Canada is one of the lowest in the Western world. To encourage savings, the federal government has introduced several policies including Registered Retirement Savings Plans (RRSPs) which allow individuals to defer paying taxes on a portion of their income until such time as they cash-in this money (presumably at the time of retirement) and the recent 20% bonus given on Registered Educational Savings Plans (RESPs) up to $2 000 per annum. Using the market for loanable funds analyze the potential impact of these policies on the interest rate and investment demand. Comment on their potential impact on economic growth in Canada.

23 The only socially acceptable level of crime is zero. Discuss.

24 Compare the effect of a $1 per litre tax on gasoline with a sales (*ad valorem*) tax of t% of total gasoline expenditures on equilibrium price and quantity, assuming that the gasoline market is competitive. Using a diagram, show when the two types of taxes will result in an identical equilibrium price and quantity.

25 Discuss this statement: Price controls are useful to provide adequate housing for those in the lower income levels who would not otherwise be able to afford it.

26 Suppose that a per-unit tax of $1 is placed on producers in a competitive market. Using diagrams, indicate whether none, some, or all of the tax is passed on to the consumer in the form of a higher price in the short run for each case.

- **a** Demand is perfectly price-elastic.
- **b** Demand is perfectly price-inelastic.
- **c** Supply is perfectly price-elastic.

Long Problems

27 Rent controls still exist on many apartments in the city of Toronto. Let's suppose that the demand for apartments in Toronto each month is represented by $y = 500\ 000 - 250p$ and supply is $y = 250p$.

- **a** In the absence of rent control, determine the equilibrium month rent and number of apartments.
- **b** Suppose that, in response to much pressure from apartment dwellers, the city of Toronto imposes a policy of rent control. Landlords cannot charge any more than $1000 per month for their apartments. What is the immediate impact of this policy?
- **c** Over time, the demand for apartments increases as the population of the region grows. Let's say that the demand grows by 20%. Calculate the new equilibrium situation and analyze the impact of the rent control policy in the short run.
- **d** Discuss the impact of rent controls over time

with particular emphasis on the supply of rental accommodation. Who are the likely winners and losers from this policy (be sure to discuss the likelihood of "bribes" for apartments and the amount that prospective tenants would be willing to pay).

e Suppose now, that the government wants to remove rent controls and is considering doing so in three ways: i) "cold turkey" approach where landlords are immediately allowed to charge market rent; ii) allowing landlords to increase rent by 5% per year until market rent is achieved; iii) removing the controls after someone moves out of the apartment, but not otherwise. Analyze the impact of each of these policies; include a discussion of their distributional impact.

***28** When discussing whether a per-unit tax should be payed directly by consumers at the cash register or by sellers, many consumer groups were up in arms protesting that consumers pay too much taxes at the moment and that firms should be paying the tax. Carefully analyze this situation supposing that demand is represented by $y = 11 - p$ and supply is $y = 2 + 2p$, and that the tax in question amounts to $1 per unit. Determine the equilibrium price and output before the tax, if the tax is paid by consumers and if the tax is paid by producers. Determine the relationship between the elasticity of demand (in absolute value terms), the elasticity of supply and the incidence of the tax.

29 In the economic analysis of crime we find that, *ceteris paribus*, the amount of crime undertaken depends inversely upon the expected penalty associated with the crime. The expected penalty is the product of the probability of getting caught and the fine (or a monetized value of the punishment). Thus, the expected penalty may be increased in two ways — by increasing the probability of getting caught and by increasing the fine. Do you think that it matters which of these strategies is implemented? Discuss the relative merits of the following pairs of probabilities and fines (which are set to preserve the expected penalty) for the indicated crimes (or misdemeanors): i) illegal parking (0.8, $50) or (0.01, $5 000); ii) bank robbery (0.5, 5 years) or (0.1, 25 year) ; iii) tax fraud (0.8, $100 000) or (0.5, $160 000). (Note, in the case of bank robbery and tax fraud, the fines are net of any gains obtained from the act.)

30 In the 1960s, the governments of the United States and Canada imposed price controls on natural gas. The price of natural gas was set below the world price.

a Using a diagram, show the short-run effects of the price ceiling on natural gas in the domestic market for natural gas and on one of the domestic firms.

b During this time, the prices of goods using natural gas — for example, electricity — were not controlled. Would you expect the price ceiling on natural gas to cause electricity to be cheaper than it otherwise would be in the short run? Use diagrams to answer this question. Assume that natural gas is used as a variable input in the production of electricity.

31 A common agricultural policy is to assign quotas on egg production such that each producer is allowed to sell eggs only up to the amount allotted under his or her quota. Assume that eggs are produced in a perfectly competitive, constant-cost industry, individual quotas are set at a level less than the former output levels, and the government does not purchase any eggs from the producers.

a Using diagrams, determine the short-run effects of this quota scheme on the egg market and on an egg farmer. Would a farmer have the incentive to cheat by producing more than his or her quota? Explain.

b If quotas are placed on the output of individual farmers but not on the industry output, then what will be the long-run effects? Explain, using diagrams.

c Briefly discuss the advantages and disadvantages of such a quota system.

32 The federal government finds it necessary to increase its tax revenues. It decides that part of this increase will come from the imposition of a tax on a competitive industry that formerly has not been taxed. Two proposals are under consideration regarding the form of the tax:

(1) A licensing arrangement by which every firm in the industry must pay a flat fee of $\$F$ per year

(2) A tax on sales by which each firm would be required to pay a tax of $\$t$ on each unit produced and sold

Analyze the long-run effects of these alternative taxing schemes on

a Market price

b Output per firm

c Output of the industry

d The number of firms in the industry

ANSWERS TO CHAPTER 9

Case Study

A The results of the three schemes are illustrated in Figure A9.1. Under scheme 1, shown in Figure A9.1a, the price floor of $6 per kilo implies that although y_2 units are supplied, only y_1 units are demanded. The government must enter the commodity market and purchase the excess supply $(y_2 - y_1)$. Thus, although output has increased, the quantity actually consumed has fallen dramatically. Under scheme 2 in Figure A9.1b, the supply curve shifts to S'. In these conditions, both the quantity supplied and the quantity demanded increase to y_2 as the consumer price is allowed to fall under p_1. Under scheme 3 in Figure A9.1c, the government must ensure that output never rises above y_1 to guarantee a price of $6 per kilo. Thus, it is only when quotas are imposed that output actually falls relative to the competitive equilibrium commodity; scheme 3 reduces the output.

B When either a price floor or a per-unit subsidy is introduced, farmers receive $6 per kilo on the quantity that they supply to the market, y_2. Thus, each of the first two schemes raises farmers' incomes compared with the competitive equilibrium of $4 per kilo and output y_0. Under a quota system, the price per bushel is still $6, but output is only y_1, so the increase in revenues is much lower than under the first two schemes. The quota system will, however, yield higher revenues than the competitive equilibrium if demand is inelastic with respect to price.

C The cost to the government of a price-floor scheme is determined by the amount of excess supply it must purchase — in this case, $y_2 - y_1$ — at the price of $6 per kilo. In the per-unit subsidy case, the government must make up the difference between the producer price ($6 per kilo) and the consumer price (p_1 per kilo) on the total number of units sold, y_2. The total costs of each of these schemes, if we ignore administrative costs, are represented in Figures A9.1a and A9.1b, respectively, by the shaded region. The actual total cost of each scheme depends on the elasticities of the demand and supply functions. So, it is impossible to say which scheme is more expensive without more information. By imposing quotas, the government avoids having to make direct payments to the farmers; however, administration costs and welfare costs are involved in the artificial restriction of output.

There are inefficiency costs from substituting nonprice allocation mechanisms for price mechanisms. These costs are the loss in total surplus, illustrated by the cross-hatched areas in the diagrams.

FIGURE A9.1

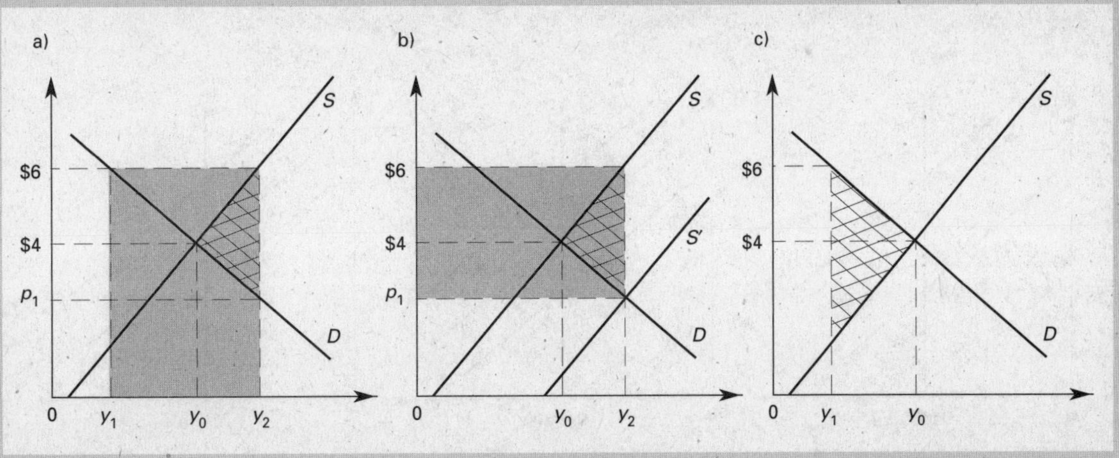

Multiple-Choice

1 a 2 c 3 b 4 c 5 c
6 c 7 b 8 d 9 d 10c

True-False

11 F 12 F 13 F 14 F 15 F
16 F 17 F 18 F 19 T 20 F

Short Problems

21 In the short run the demand for items like candles increased dramatically, as depicted in Figure A9.2a. Notice that the supply of candles is likely to be quite inelastic in the short run. As a result, the large increase in demand would result in a substantial increase in price (from p_1 to p_2 for instance) but not much increase in quantity actually purchased (no increase in the diagram). For the sake of exposition, we are assuming here that the grocery store market is localized, which is a sensible assumption to make at least at the time of the ice storm. Grocers who took advantage of the situation to increase prices dramatically would have found themselves gaining in the short run, but in the long run we would expect that the demand curve facing this localized market would shift in to become even smaller than it was prior to the storm — as depicted in Figure A9.2a. In other words, grocers who took advantage of the situation would find themselves with a short-run gain but a long-run loss as customers took their business elsewhere. Grocers who did not take advantage of the situation would then gain in the long-run from this additional business, as depicted in Figure A9.2b. Of course, the ability to take one's business elsewhere depends upon the availability of grocery stores elsewhere. In small communities where this option is not feasible, one would expect to observe demand returning to a position like D^3 in Figure A9.2c because after the storm individuals are likely to have increased their demand for certain items like candles in order to be prepared for any future crisis.

22 Figure A9.3 depicts the market for loanable funds before and after these policies to encourage savings. The original equilibrium interest rate is r_1. After the policies are implemented, savings increase which leads to an increase in the supply of loanable funds, to S^1. The new equilibrium interest rate thus falls to r_2. Notice that, as a result, the equilibrium quantity of funds loaned in the market has increased, hence the quantity of investment demand has increased. In the long run, an increase in the quantity of investment demand is likely, *ceteris paribus*, to lead to growth in the economy. (However this is a complicated phenomenon which you will treat with much greater depth in your macro economics course.)

23 The social costs associated with having zero crime would be prohibitively high. Instead of undertaking all sorts of, say, social programs, government would have to devote an inordinate amount of resources to crime prevention. In addition, certain crimes just cannot be stopped (how do you prevent people from illegally parking? How can you stop all pickpockets? What about so-called crimes of passion?). The expected penalty will have an impact on the amount of crime undertaken; this is composed of two parts, the probability of getting caught and the

FIGURE A9.2

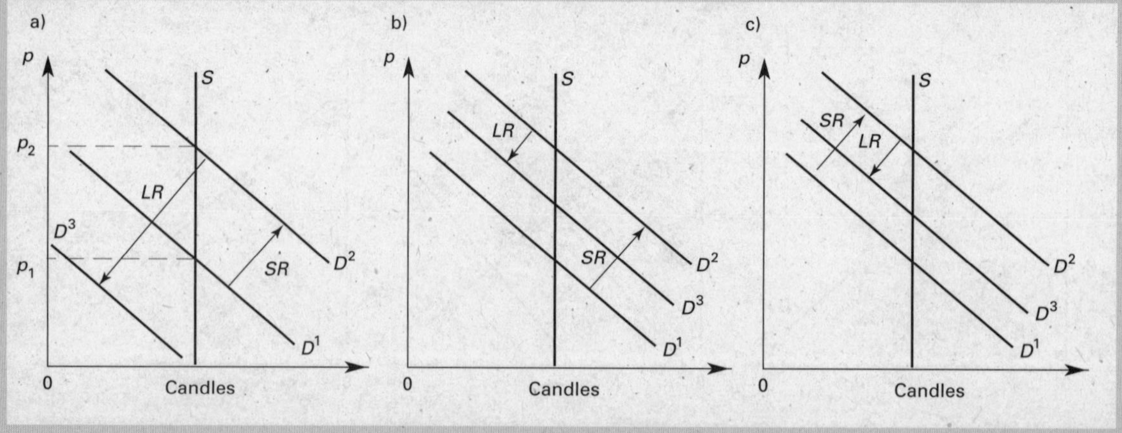

FIGURE A9.3

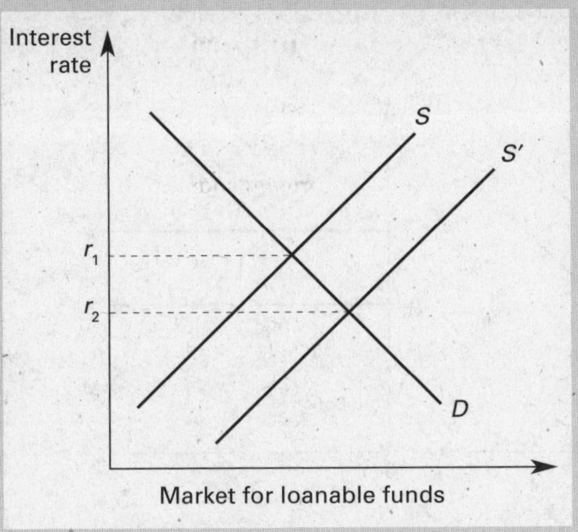

fine. By setting the probability of getting caught close to one, much crime would be eliminated — but think about the costs associated with doing this! Of course, setting the penalty too high would also cause problems. People may simply be unable to pay the fine (this is the so-called "judgement proof" problem); also, punishments have to be seen to "fit the crime." A \$5 000 parking fine would seem ridiculous.

24 Assume that the taxes are placed on the consumer. A tax of \$1 per litre has the effect of shifting the demand curve down by \$1 at every quantity. This is shown by demand CD in Figure A9.4a. In this case, the new equilibrium quantity is y^*. The price paid by consumers is p^*. An ad valorem (sales) tax has the effect of pivoting the demand curve. The demand curve under the ad valorem tax is EB in Figure A9.4b. The two demand curves will yield identical solutions when they intersect the supply curve at the same point, as shown in Figure A9.4b.

25 Price controls in the housing market result in a shortage of available housing. Price controls help the low-income individuals who are fortunate enough to receive adequate housing, but there will be some (and perhaps many) who will be unable to purchase the housing.

26 a A tax of \$1 will shift the supply curve upward by \$1. If demand is perfectly elastic, the price will not change. None of the tax is passed on to consumers. This situation is illustrated in Figure A9.5a.

b Figure A9.5b shows the case in which demand is perfectly inelastic. The entire tax is passed on to consumers.

c As before, the tax shifts the supply curve upward by \$1 at every quantity. The minimum price that firms will accept for the product, given the tax, is $p_0 + 1$. The consumer pays the entire tax, as shown in Figure A9.5c.

Long Problems

27 a $500\ 000 - 250p = 250p \Rightarrow p = \$1000$, $q = 250\ 000$ apartments.

b Because the rent control is exactly at the equilibrium price, no short-run impact of the policy (although this overlooks the problems associated with apartment turnover which we

FIGURE A9.4

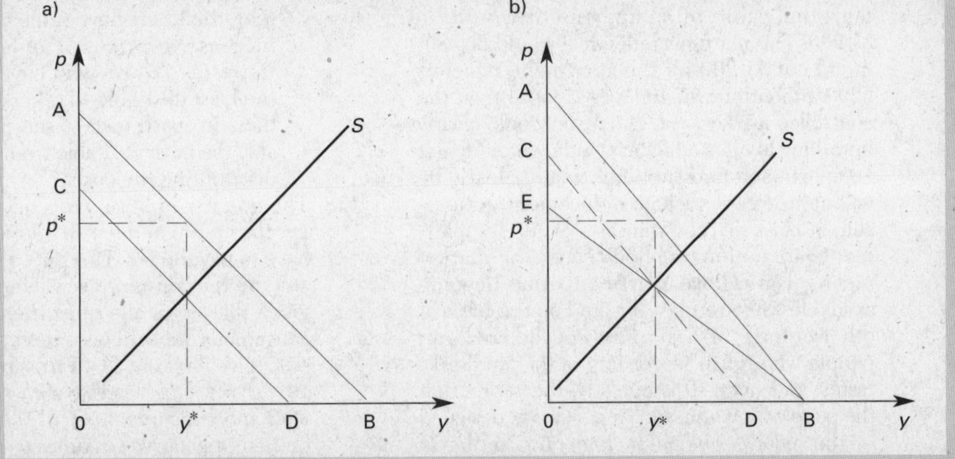

FIGURE A9.5

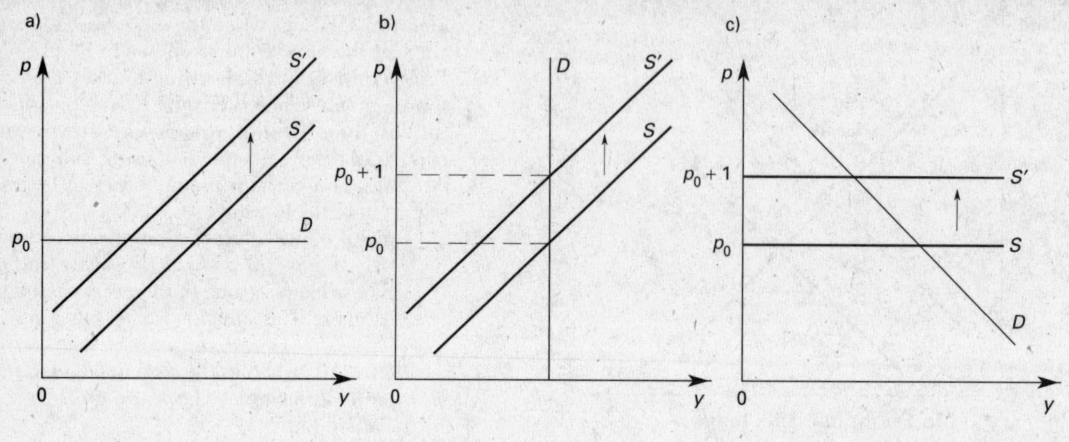

have ignored here. For instance, when we look at average turnovers, we find that fewer people will give up a rent-controlled apartment, especially when they think that the market has the potential to grow. The costs associated with searching and finding an apartment rise as a result.).

c Demand becomes $y = 600\ 000 - 250p$; in the absence of price controls equilibrium rent would be \$1 200 and output would be 300 000 apartments. With a rent controlled price of \$1 000, 350 000 apartments would be demanded but only 250 000 apartments would be supplied, leaving an excess demand for 100 000 apartments.

d Over time, the people who have an apartment are the winners, the people who would like to have one but cannot are potential losers. Indeed, if 300 000 apartments were on the market, the marginal value of an apartment would be \$1 200. This marginal individual would be willing to pay \$1 200 for the apartment, which is \$200 a month or \$2 400 a year more than the controlled market rent. He or she would clearly be willing to offer a financial inducement to get an apartment, and suppliers would clearly be willing to accept such an inducement. As a result, a "black market" may arise whereby apartments are no longer allocated by the market mechanism. Those apartments that become available will often be allocated on the basis of other criteria: bribes, friends of the landlord, people who "fit in" according to the landlord's tastes, and so on. It is unlikely, therefore, that the people for whom such a policy was designed — the "poor" — would be high on a landlord's list for available apartments.

The supply of rental accommodation will fall over time. Owners, who cannot obtain an adequate rent, will stop maintaining their buildings, allowing them to deteriorate and perhaps disappear altogether over time. Another strategy that occurred in places like Toronto was that rental units were converted to condominiums and sold to clients, thus circumventing rent controls.

e Removing rent controls is tricky. If current tenants had to pay a "bribe" for the apartment (equal to the amount they would have been willing to pay in the absence of controls) then the policy results in a *transitional gains trap*. Basically, removing controls would confer an immediate loss on these individuals if the cold-turkey policy i were implemented. Policy ii has some appeal as it smooths the costs associated with deregulating the market over time. To this extent, the losers have some time to adjust to the increase in prices. The last policy iii is the "fairest" to those who have apartments but is the least desirable to others. It still encourages those in apartments to stay put. Policy ii is probably the most desirable from the point of view of distributing the costs.

***28** The no-tax equilibrium occurs where $11 - p = 2 + 2p$, thus $p = 3$ and $y = 8$. Suppose that consumers have to pay the tax. This puts a wedge between the amount the consumer is willing to pay for the good given that he or she must then pay the tax. Thus, consumer's demand becomes $y = 11 - (p^d + t)$ or $10 - p^d$ (given a tax of \$1). Firms receive p^d. Equating $10 - p^d = 2 + 2p^d$ leads to a $p^d = 8/3$. Thus, firms get \$8/3 and consumers pay \$11/3. If firms pay, then their supply curve becomes $y = 2 + 2(p^s - t) = 2p^s$. Consumers pay p^s, which is determined by $11 - p^s$

FIGURE A9.6

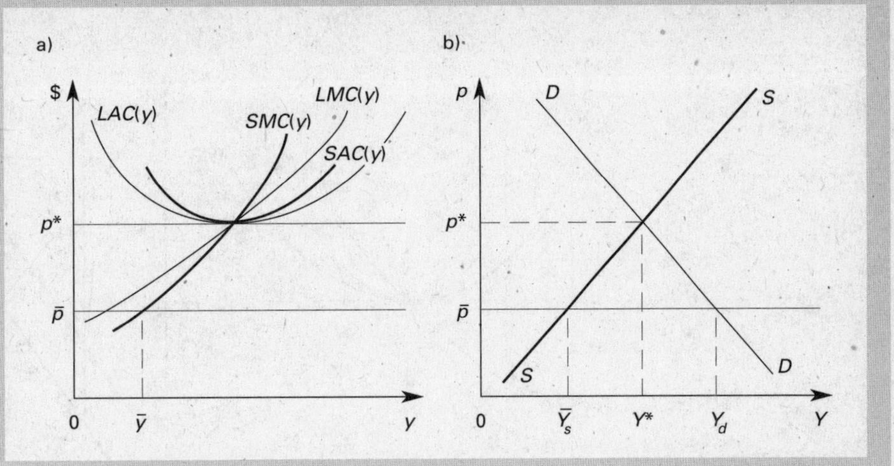

$= 2p^s$; p^s is thus \$11/3. Firms received \$11/3 and pay \$1 per unit, the effective price for firms is thus \$8/3. Notice, therefore, that irrespective of who actually pays the tax, both consumers and producers end up paying the same proportion of the tax. We can determine the proportion of the tax payable by consumers and producers by comparing their price elasticities at the equilibrium. Demand elasticity at the equilibrium point is 3/8 (in absolute value terms); supply elasticity is twice as high at 6/8. Suppliers will therefore pay twice as much of the tax than consumers will. Suppliers thus pay 2/3 of the tax and consumers pay 1/3 of the tax. Referring to our answers above, you can immediately see that this is indeed the case.

29 i) For illegal parking it seems totally unacceptable to have a fine as high as \$5 000. One cannot imagine any judge actually levying such a fine. In some sense, the penalty has to be seen to "fit the crime" (as discussed in question **23**). It is also unlikely that the perpetrator is actually able to afford such a fine. Having a high probability and low fine is likely to be the best strategy. Remember, too, that it is not very costly to catch people who illegally park.
ii) Bank robbers can be very costly to catch. Here, society needs to balance the costs associated with increasing the probability of being caught with the benefits therefrom. A high prison term with a lower probability of getting caught is arguably the best mix.
iii) For tax fraud, it is not as clear cut. Again, the social costs associated with increasing the probability of getting caught have to be taken into account. The issue regarding the payment of the fines is certainly one which needs consideration. To the extent that it is higher income firms or individuals who are likely to undertake tax fraud (since the gains from so doing are presumably higher), then the payment of fines is less of an issue.

30 a The firm is shown in Figure A9.6a and the market in Figure A9.6b. In the absence of price controls, equilibrium price is p^*. Under the price control at $\bar{p}$, the firm equates $\bar{p}$ with $SMC(y)$ and produces $\bar{y}$ units of output. Market quantity supplied is $\bar{Y}_s$; quantity demanded is Y_d.

b Since natural gas is an input into the production of electricity, the supply curve for electricity will be affected by the price control. Suppose, for simplicity, that one unit of natural gas is used to produce one unit of output. Then the supply curve for electricity shown in Figure A9.7 is given by $S'AB$. As shown, there are two effects on the supply curve. First, a reduction in the input price of electricity reduces costs of

FIGURE A9.7

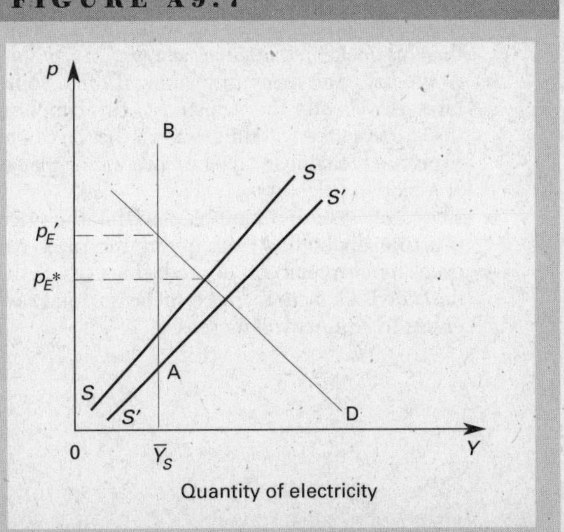

FIGURE A9.8

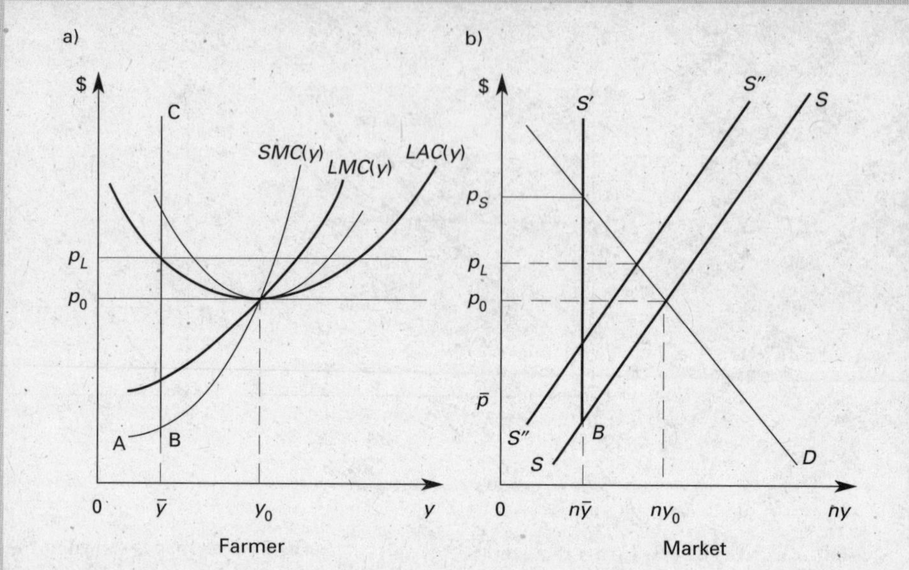

production thereby shifting the supply curve to the right. Second, the quantity of electricity is restricted to $\bar{Y}_s$ units because of limited quantities of natural gas. Price of electricity rises from $p_E{}^*$ to $p_E{}'$.

31 a In Figure A9.8, the firm is shown to be in long-run equilibrium, producing y_0 eggs at price p_0; industry output is ny_0. Individual quotas of $\bar{y}$ are then imposed. In the short run, the supply curve of the firm changes from $SMC(y)$ to ABC; industry supply changes from SS to SBS'. Market price and quantity are p_s and $n\bar{y}$ respectively, under the quota. At a price p_s, each farmer would like to increase profits by producing more than his quota; in particular, where $p_s = SMC(y)$.

b In the long run, firms are making profits. Some farmers will enter the industry. As this happens, the supply curve will shift to $S''S''$; that is, where firms are breaking even when producing $\bar{y}$ eggs at a market price of p_L.

c The quota system is inefficient in that the price is artificially high: At the quota, the price exceeds the marginal cost of producing eggs. Since demand is likely to be price-inelastic, total revenues to farmers will increase.

32 The initial equilibrium before either proposal is imposed on the firm is given by p_0,y_0, and n_0y_0; and n_0 firms are in the market. The cost curves are LAC_0 and LMC_0, and the supply and demand curves are S_0 and D in Figure A9.9.

(1) Under the flat-free charge, F increases the $LAC(y)$ curve only. The $LAC(y)$ curve slides up the $LMC(y)$ curve to LAC'. Firms exit the industry in the long run; the supply curve shifts to S'; price rises to p'; firm quantity rises to y'; and market quantity drops to $n'y'$, $n' < n_0$. The equilibria before and after the lump-sum tax are illustrated in the figure.

(2) Under the excise tax, the $LAC(y)$ and $LMC(y)$ curves shift up by t to LMC' and LAC', as in Figure A9.10. Again firms exit the industry; supply shifts to S' and price rises to p' (where $p' = p_0 + t$); firm output remains unchanged; and industry output falls to $n''y_0$, where $n'' < n_0$.

FIGURE A9.9

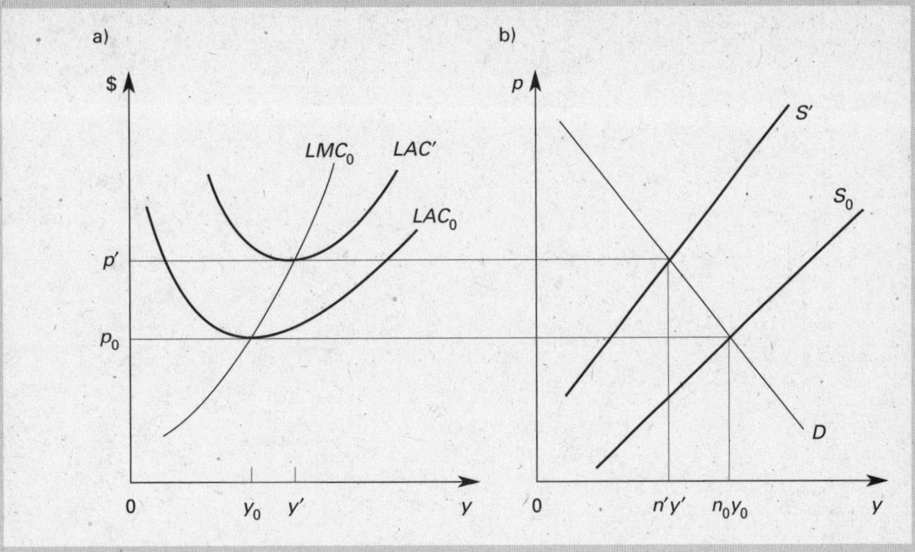

FIGURE A9.10

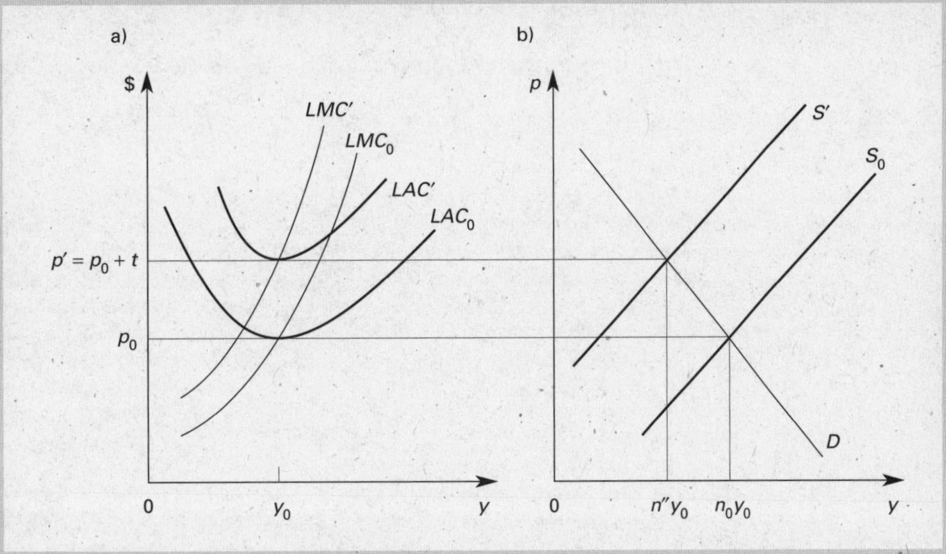

CHAPTER 10

Monopoly

Chapter Summary

Monopoly Defined

Monopoly is a market structure that is the polar extreme of competition. In theory, it refers to a single firm that is producing a good for which no close substitutes exist. In practice, a monopoly is not always easy to identify because close substitutes for a good are often difficult to define. For example, until recently the telephone company had a clear monopoly in providing telephone services to subscribers, but it is now subject to competition in its long-distance market. A single firm providing electricity in a town is a clearer example of a monopolistic market.

Pricing Behaviour of Monopoly

After a monopoly has been identified, its pricing behaviour is relatively easy to predict. As with a competitor, we assume that a monopolist is a profit maximizer and, hence, that it chooses the output level that equates marginal revenue and marginal cost. Unlike a competitor, the monopolist faces the **market demand curve** and a **marginal revenue curve** which lies under the demand curve. The monopolist's **total revenue** function $TR(y)$ is price times output or $D(y)y$. **Average revenue** thus equals price or $D(y)$, and **marginal revenue**, $MR(y)$ equals $TR'(y) = D(y) + D'(y)y$ for small changes in output. Since $D'(y)$, the slope of the demand curve, is negative, marginal revenue lies below demand.

The monopolist's **profit-maximizing problem** is to choose output (y) to maximize profits $\pi(y)$ defined as total revenue minus total costs: $TR(y) - TC(y)$. Solving this problem yields y^* which occurs where $MR(y) = MC(y)$ as long as $\pi''(y^*)$ is negative. Thus, profit maximization implies that the monopolist operates where marginal revenue equals marginal cost at the point where the marginal cost curve is upward sloping. The monopolist sets a price higher than marginal cost and thus it contravenes the **efficiency criterion**. The monopolist prices too high and produces too little in comparison to the perfectly competitive solution, resulting in a **deadweight loss of monopoly**. This outcome is an example of a **market failure**: there are unrealized gains from trade that no one — neither the consumer nor the monopolist — is able to capture.

Sources of Monopolies

How does a monopoly come about? There are several sources: The government may create a **franchise monopoly**; a firm may discover a new product and obtain the right to be a **patent monopoly** — a patent gives the firm monopoly rights for 17 years; a firm may have exclusive rights to a low-cost resource — a **resource-based monopoly**; a firm may be a **natural monopoly** by nature of the production technology; one firm may emerge and become a **monopoly by good management**; or the monopolist just may have been at the right place at the right time to be able to deter the entry of other firms into the market. The **Sylos postulate** suggests that potential market entrants take the output of existing firms as given. Thus, the decision of whether or not it is worthwhile to enter the market depends only on the **residual demand function**, that portion of market demand not supplied by the monopolist.

Regulation of Monopolies

The social desirability of a monopoly and the type of government action used against it depend partly on the source of the monopoly. For example, although recognizing that public utilities are natural monopolies, the government may want to limit their profits. A common mechanism used is an **average-cost-pricing policy**, in which the price is set equal to the average cost of production. Since price equals average cost rather than marginal cost, an inefficient amount of output is produced. Moreover, the monopolist does not have the incentive to minimize production costs. Another common policy is **rate-of-return regulation** in which the regulator determines the allowable rate of return on capital. This policy many result in an inefficient mix of capital and other inputs. Too much capital will be used in production relative to the efficient mix of inputs. In a more efficient mechanism, which requires considerable information on the part of the government, the regulatory agency gives a subsidy equal to the consumer surplus less the total revenue generated by the sales earned at the current price.

Patent Policy

Innovation is important in a changing world. Patent monopolies play a significant role in encouraging innovation. Patents confer a monopoly right on their holders in order that the inventor may capture the benefits stemming from the innovation — thus solving the **appropriability problem**. In the absence of patents, anyone would be free to benefit from an invention, resulting in very little incentive to conduct the costly research and development (R&D) necessary for most innovations. The optimal policy sets the duration of the patent in order to balance two conflicting forces: patents have to be long enough to encourage innovation and yet not so long as to prolong the period of losses associated with monopoly power. Suppose that a new product is created. Its **social value** is the sum of present and future total surplus, its **social cost** is its R&D costs. Now, taking into account all new products, because one patent policy applies to most innovations, account must be taken of their **aggregate social value** and **aggregate social cost**. The optimal policy maximizes the difference between these two numbers. This maximum will occur where the **marginal social benefit** of increasing the patent by one period equals its **marginal social cost**.

In a static, nonchanging world such as the one we have studied so far, monopolies are associated with inefficiency; however, in a dynamic world, patent monopolies may actually help to reduce inefficiency. An inventor compares the present value of future monopoly profits with the costs of developing a specific idea or invention. If patents were not allowed so that others can quickly imitate the invention, future monopoly profits would be small, and there would be little private incentive to engage in research. Alternatively, a patent, by making the benefits of an invention **appropriable** for the inventor, extends the period of time over which he or she is able to earn monopoly profits. The optimal patent policy balances this tradeoff between encouraging innovation and minimizing monopoly distortions in the use of the innovation.

KEY WORDS

Aggregate social cost
Aggregate social value
Appropriability problem
Appropriable
Average-cost-pricing policy
Average revenue
Deadweight loss of monopoly
Efficiency criterion
Franchise monopoly
Marginal revenue curve
Marginal social benefit
Marginal social cost
Market demand curve
Market failure
Monopolist's profit-maximizing problem
Monopoly
Monopoly by good management
Natural monopoly
Patent monopoly
Profit-maximizing problem
Rate-of-return regulation
Residual demand function
Resource-based monopoly
Social cost
Sylos postulate
Total revenue

CASE STUDY: R&D AND THE PHARMACEUTICAL INDUSTRY IN CANADA

Sales of prescription drugs in Canada represent only about 2% of global sales. One consequence of being a relatively small player is that very little R&D is undertaken in Canada by the pharmaceutical industry. The pharmaceutical market is made up of two distinct types of firms: those which conduct R&D and produce "brand-name" drugs, and those which produce "generic" drugs that contain the essential ingredients of a brand- name drug but are marketed under another name (e.g., Tylenol and Life-Brand acetaminophen). In Canada, public policy has oscillated between trying to promote more R&D by conferring exclusive patents to brand-name drug companies and trying to promote lower drug prices by granting easier access to the market by generic companies.

In 1968 Canadian patent law was changed in order to promote compulsory licensing for generic drugs. Effectively, this legislation made it compulsory for pharmaceutical companies to licence their patented drugs to generic companies, for a modest license fee that was set by the government. This led the way for the increased production and use of generic drugs in

Canada. The pendulum swung back in favour of the brand-name companies some twenty years later when, with Bill C-22, the *Patent Act* was amended to provide a seven-year period of exclusivity for the brand-name drug, after which time licensing was again compulsory. In exchange, the brand-name companies promised to undertake more R&D in Canada, and the Patented Medicine Prices Review Board was established to monitor drug prices.

Public policy has to juggle two very important considerations. First, pharmaceutical firms must be given the incentive to engage in R&D — i.e., they must be able to gain some monopoly profits from their efforts. But this monopoly power results in high prices. Second, important drugs must be made affordable to the consuming public. As is clear from the above discussion, the Canadian government has grappled with this problem for decades, oscillating between giving strong patent protection to firms and ensuring easy licensing opportunities for generic producers. Using a very simple model in which the demand for a given drug is captured by $p = 10 - y$ (where y is measured in one hundred thousand prescriptions) and marginal costs are a constant \$2, evaluate the pros and cons of the following policies for Canada:

°**A** Strong patent protection, no compulsory licensing.
B Patent protection with compulsory licensing at a fee determined by the government.
C Patent protection with compulsory licensing at a fee determined by the firm.

EXERCISES

Multiple-Choice

Choose the correct answer to each question. There is only one correct answer to each question.

Use the following information to answer questions **1–3**. Three monopolists want to maximize their profits in the long run. The demand curve facing each firm is linear and given by $p = 100 - y$, where p = price and y = quantity. The average cost curve is U-shaped. Sufficient information to make a recommendation has been provided (see table).

	Price (\$)	Qnty	Total Cost (\$)	*LAC* (\$)	*LMC* (\$)
Firm 1	70	—	—	50	40
Firm 2	—	40	600	At minimum	—
Firm 3	80	—	2 000	—	60

1 What should firm 1 do to maximize profits?
a Stay at current position.
b Increase price and reduce quantity.
c Decrease price and increase quantity.
d Exit from the industry.
e None of the above.

2 What should firm 2 do to maximize profits?
a Stay at current position.
b Increase price and reduce quantity.
c Decrease price and increase quantity.
d Exit from the industry.
e None of the above.

3 What should firm 3 do to maximize profits?
a Stay at current position.
b Increase price and reduce quantity.
c Decrease price and increase quantity.
d Exit from the industry.
e None of the above.

4 If regulators guarantee a natural monopolist a return on capital in excess of the cost of capital, what will the owners of the natural monopoly do?
a Substitute from capital to other inputs.
b Choose an input bundle that is not cost-minimizing.
c Reduce investment in the firm.
d All the above.
e None of the above.

5 Equilibrium output will be:
a 8
b 18
c 3
d 5
e 4

6 The deadweight loss of monopoly is:
a 25
b 12.5
c 8
d 16
e None of the above.

7 Maximizing revenue rather than profits would result in a loss of profits of:
a \$15
b \$21
c \$14
d \$5
e \$6

8 Which of the following leads to natural monopoly?
  a The firm owns a patent for its invention.
  b The firm is operated by an extremely efficient entrepreneur.
  c The firm operates in the region of increasing returns to scale.
  d Both **b** and **c**.
  e All of the above.

9 Rate-of-return regulation allows firms to make a certain return on capital. As a result,
  a More capital is typically employed than would otherwise be the case.
  b Firms typically do not use the cost minimizing ratio of inputs.
  c The plush-carpet theorem comes into play.
  d Both **a** and **b**.
  e All of the above.

10 The optimal life of a patent
  a Is 17 years.
  b Is between 17 and 50 years.
  c Equates the marginal social value of the patent with its marginal social costs.
  d Both **a** and **c**.
  e All of the above.

True-False

11 The efficiency loss under perfect price discrimination is larger than under either pure monopoly or ordinary price discrimination.

12 The allocation of resources in a monopolistic industry is inefficient because the monopolist makes excessive profits, and it can be improved by taking away these profits.

13 Ergaminol, an old veterinary compound, has been found to be effective in treating colon cancer; however, the drug costs $6/pill for people and $0.06 for the same amount of the drug administered to sheep (*Consumers' Report*, Oct. 1993, p. 670). The demand for ergaminol by people must be more elastic than the demand for the drug by sheep.

14 A profit-maximizing monopolist facing no entry threat will operate on the elastic portion of the market demand curve.

15 Starting at some long-run equilibrium, if the demand for a monopoly's product falls, the price will fall more in the long run than in the short run.

16 If a particular regulated industry is characterized by rates of return on capital invested in the industry in excess of the price of capital, then one can conclude that the allocation of resources in this industry is efficient.

17 Even if an industry has IRTS over the entire range of output, the sum of the producers' and the consumers' surplus will be maximized by pricing at marginal costs.

18 Since monopoly is a "bad" thing for consumers but a "good" thing for producers, on balance, we cannot be sure that monopoly is responsible for any loss in economic efficiency.

19 A monopoly firm will operate where its total revenue is maximized.

20 The quantity sold by a monopolist that maximizes its sales can never be equal to the quantity that would be sold under profit maximization if marginal costs are positive.

21 The marginal revenue of a good that costs $5 and has an own-price elasticity (in absolute value) equal to 0.2 is –20.

Short Problems

22 Suppose that the government declares a monopolist, with declining long-run average and marginal costs, to be a public utility and decrees that it must serve all who are willing to buy at an established price. The price provides the monopolist with a "fair return," that is, a normal rate of return on capital. Show this output and price diagrammatically. Why is this output level not economically efficient?

*23 The total revenue $TR(y)$ earned by a monopolist as a function of the firm's output is given by $TR(y) = 100y - y^2$. The total costs $TC(y)$ as a function of output are $TC(y) = 10 + 6y$. Current production of the monopolist is $y = 50$. Is the firm maximizing profits? If not, can you suggest an alternative objective that is being satisfied?

24 If the marginal revenue for a good X is negative, what is true about the price elasticity of its demand? Explain.

25 Policy makers often argue for the "rationalization" of industries (that is, for there to be one or a few big firms instead of many small ones) in order to take full advantage of economies of scale. With what types of demand and cost conditions is this most likely to be a valid argument?

26 Define "natural monopoly" and illustrate it on a diagram. In your graph show the following situations: (i) an unregulated monopoly free to maximize profits and (ii) a firm required to sell at marginal cost and receive a lump-sum subsidy needed to cover the loss that it would incur by producing at this rate of output.

27 Many artists have been lobbying the Canadian government to impose a special tax on blank cassette tapes. Discuss why this might be the case. Do you think that such a tax should be levied from society's point of view?

28 Canadian competition law prohibits mergers that unduly lessen competition. However, mergers that fall into this category but are shown to result in cost efficiencies are permitted nevertheless. Suppose that a merger results in a monopoly. Provide a diagrammatic analysis of the circumstances under which this "efficiency defense" makes economic sense.

29 A firm of good X sells its good as a monopolist in Canada but faces a perfectly elastic demand in the world; that is, the firm is a perfect competitor in the world market. If the marginal cost of production decreases, then what will happen to the total quantity *produced*? What will happen to the quantity *sold* in Canada?

Long Problems

***30** Let's suppose that a monopolist faces the demand $p = 100 - 2q$ per month. At the moment, average costs are constant and equal to \$60 per unit.

a Calculate the equilibrium price and output in this market.

b The monopolist engages in R&D and discovers a new process that will cut average costs dramatically to \$8 per unit. Determine how much would the monopolist be willing to spend on R&D in order to discover this innovation.

c Suppose that, rather than being a monopoly, the industry is competitive. Compared to the pre-innovation situation, is society better off or worse off if the industry is competitive? Explain. Compared to the post-innovation situation, would your answer change?

d If everyone faced the same technology, how likely is it that this industry would be monopolistic?

e Suppose that this industry is competitive originally, but that the government has a patent policy that guarantees an innovator all of the returns to the innovation for 20 years. What are the potential consequences of this policy?

***31** Suppose that the technology for providing long-distance telephone service is such that a firm must be able to service 500 000 to allow it to reap all economies of scale. In other words, the minimum efficient scale of the firm occurs at 500 000 and it does not pay any firm to enter at a scale of less than this level. One can represent this situation by an average cost curve that is very steep between 0 and 500 000 units — at which point it becomes flat at a cost of \$0.50 per unit. Suppose, initially, a monopolist serves this market and is faced with a demand curve per month for long-distance telephone service of $p = 25 - 0.01y$ (where y is measured in thousands).

a What is the monopoly price and output?

b Is this monopoly sustainable over time?

c Suppose that entrants adopt the Sylos postulate. Suppose, also, that the incumbent firm would like to deter entry. Can you think of an output policy on behalf of the incumbent monopolist that would stop entry from occurring? What factors must the monopolist take into account when deciding upon whether or not to deter entry?

d Discuss the impact of technological changes that reduce the minimum efficient scale associated with providing long-distance telephone service.

32 Electricity provision is still considered to be a natural monopoly. As such, rate-of-return regulation is imposed on electric utilities to ensure that they do not make any excess profits. Provide a diagrammatic analysis demonstrating why average cost pricing is the "best" pricing strategy given that the firm is operating in the region of increasing returns to scale. Be sure to discuss how marginal cost pricing could be imposed in this case.

33 Suppose that a Canadian firm enjoys a monopoly in the domestic market for hockey pucks under the protection of high import duties, which effectively prevent imports. The world market for pucks is competitive, and the world price is lower than the price charged by the domestic monopolist. The domestic monopolist does not sell in the world market. If the import duty is removed, forcing the Canadian firm to lower its price to the world level, what effect will this have on the purchase of pucks by people in Canada and the production of pucks by Canadian firms? Explain carefully.

34 Good X is produced by a monopolist in the market with a linear demand curve and constant marginal cost equal to zero. The Canadian Competition Bureau is deciding whether or not to break up the monopoly into many perfectly competitive firms. The Bureau will make its decision on efficiency grounds. Suppose that if the market becomes perfectly competitive, the marginal cost will increase to a constant level c. Using a diagram, show that the Bureau will not attempt to break up the monopoly if c is sufficiently large.

35 A monopoly that provides electricity in a small town has two plants for generating electricity. The short-run marginal costs of supplying electricity from each plant are as follows:

Plant 1: $SMC_1 = 15$

Plant 2: $SMC_1 = \dfrac{y_2 + 19}{2}$

where y_1 and y_2 are units of output in plants 1 and 2, respectively. (Each unit is 1 000 kilowatt hours.) The monopolist faces the following market demand curve:

$$p = 40 - \frac{y}{2}$$

where $y = y_1 + y_2$. Find the short-run profit-maximizing price and quantities produced by each plant.

***36** Bell Canada (BC) is a supplier of telephone services. In the long run, the marginal cost of providing telephone services is zero, but there is a fixed installation cost of \$30 per individual. An individual's demand curve for the telephone services is described by

$$y = 100 - 100p$$

where y is the number of message units and p is the price per message unit.

a If price is set at the profit-maximizing level, can the firm cover its costs? Explain, using a diagram.

b If the firm cannot cover costs in **a**, does this mean that telephone service is not socially worthwhile? Explain.

37 Suppose that the government decides to levy a tax on producers of good Y. The amount of the tax levied on each firm is $5 000 per year, *regardless of the output produced by the firm.*

a What would be the effect of this tax on firm output, industry output, and price of Y in the long run if the $LAC(y)$ curve for each firm is U-shaped and if good Y is produced in a competitive market by firms with identical cost conditions? Illustrate your answer.

b What would be the effect of this tax, as in **a**, but with good Y produced by a monopolist? Illustrate your answer.

c Is part or all of the tax passed on to the consumer in the form of higher prices? Explain and comment on the change in consumers' burden of the tax as the market becomes more competitive.

38 Assume that the author of a book receives a royalty equal to 25% of the total revenue from selling the book. The profit-maximizing publisher pays this royalty and all other costs of producing the book. As the only supplier of the book, the publisher is allowed to set the price. The demand curve for the book remains the same every year. Marginal costs of production are constant.

a If the author and publisher were to agree to abolish this 25% royalty and replace it with a fixed annual payment equal to the total annual income that the author was receiving from the royalty, would the price of the book be affected? If so, how? Would the publisher's profits be affected? If so, how? Explain.

b If fixed annual payments are a Pareto improvement over royalties, why are royalties often used?

***39** A city is considering building a bridge to an island that is almost inaccessible. The city has estimated that the demand for crossing the bridge would be given by

$$p = 25 - 0.5y$$

where p is the price and y is the number of trips per year. In the long run, the marginal cost of providing bridge crossings is zero, but the costs of maintaining the toll booth are $500 per year, regardless of the number of crossings.

a Would the monopolist provide the bridge without government assistance?

b Is the bridge socially worthwhile to build? Explain.

c Suppose that the government pays the monopolist a subsidy of $K per bridge crossing, *just* sufficient to induce the monopolist to provide the bridge. Show the effects of this subsidy on a diagram.

d Now suppose that, instead of the subsidy of $K per bridge crossing, the government pays the monopoly an annual lump sum grant of $G. The amount of this grant is independent of the traffic across the bridge and is *just* sufficient to induce the monopoly to provide the bridge. Explain the effects of this grant with reference to your diagram.

e Are the two ways of providing assistance to the monopolist equally costly to the government? Explain. Determine the total subsidy paid by the government in each case.

ANSWERS TO CHAPTER 10

Case Study

***A** With patent protection, the firm will set the monopoly price and output ($6, 4). This firm will make $1.6 million dollars in profits. It will always be willing to license out the technology as long as it can make the same profits. In other words, it would be willing to licence the technology to other firms as long as it could make at least this profit. Suppose it licensed the technology to one other firm, and suppose these two firms act as Cournot duopolists (don't faint, you haven't learned this yet, it is in Chapter 15) — that is to say, the firms each maximize their own profits *given* the output of their rival. The profit of firm 1 is $(10 - y_1 - y_2)y_1 - 2y_1$ (notice that total output on the market is $y_1 + y_2$. This yields a first-order condition of $y_1 = 4 - 0.5y_2$; if firm 2 does the same thing, it will have a first- order condition equal to $y_2 = 4 - 0.5y_1$. Solving these two expressions simultaneously yields $y_1 = y_2 = 2.67$, and $p = \$4.67$. Each firm would thus make a profit of $712 890; firm 1, however, would have to charge $887 110 each period in order to be as well off as it would be in the absence of the licensing arrangement. Would firm 2 pay this license fee? Not likely. Given that collusion is illegal, it is thus unlikely that this firm would find it in its best interest to license the technology. Notice that this result depends crucially on the specified demand and cost curves.

B In **A** we demonstrated that licensing is unlikely to be the preferred option for this firm. A compulsory licensing scheme would thus result in the firm being worse off. The likely effect of such a scheme would be to dampen the incentive to undertake R&D in Canada. Note, however, that if not much R&D were undertaken in Canada anyway, perhaps this solution is not so bad. It is not clear that the patent arose from domestic R&D expenditures. In addition, given that Canada is a very small part of the global market, whether or not the firm can gain monopoly profits here may not have much impact on its R&D decisions. This, of course, is partly an empirical question.

C As demonstrated in **A**, in this particular case, the firm would never choose to license. However, this result is particular to the problem at hand. Suppose, however — and this is often the case — that the monopolist cannot charge the monopoly price for his or her new drug because another, substitute, drug is available and rather than paying a very high price, consumers would be willing to use the less effective but much cheaper drug. In other words, the existence of alternatives puts an upper bound on the price that can be charged hence reducing the profitability of an exclusive patent. The monopolist may be willing to license the new drug to his or her competitor, and both could be better off (consumers, in this case, may be worse off as the price is likely to increase). In any event, you can see some of the issues associated with the licensing provisions.

Multiple-Choice

1 a **2** c **3** d **4** b **5** e
6 c **7** c **8** c **9** e **10** c

True-False

11 F **12** F **13** F **14** T **15** F **16** F
17 T **18** F **19** F **20** T **21** T

Short Problems

22 At point *A* in Figure A10.1, the firm earns a normal rate of return. Output is not economically efficient because $p > LMC(y)$.

***23** No. If profits were maximized, then the quantity produced would equate $MR(y) = 100 - 2y$ and $MC = 6$; that is, $y = 47$. Since $y = 50$, the firm is not maximizing profits; $y = 50$ is consistent with *total revenue* maximization where $MR(y) = 0$.

24 If $MR(y) < 0$, the price elasticity (in absolute value), ε, is less than 1 because $MR(y) = D(y)(1 - 1/\varepsilon)$.

25 Rationalization may be a useful policy when the production technology is characterized by significant economies of scale and when demand is sufficiently small that only a few firms can satisfy demand when operating at the efficient average cost. For example, three firms are operating at 10 units of output, given the costs in Figure A10.2. One firm operating at 30 units of output would have lower average costs.

26 A natural monopoly is a market in which one firm can produce the industry output at a lower cost than can two firms. In Figure A10.3, (p_m, y_m) are the price and quantity of an unregulated monopoly; (p_s, y_s) are the price and quantity of a regulated monopolist. The shaded area represents the subsidy that is paid to the monopolist that sets price equal to marginal cost.

27 Many musicians argue that they are losing royalties because individuals buy blank tapes and illegally record their music (illegally, because technically the musicians have a copyright over their work). However, it is impossible to monitor and stop individuals from taping music for their own personal use. Pirating music and selling it on the market can be and is monitored and punished.

FIGURE A10.1

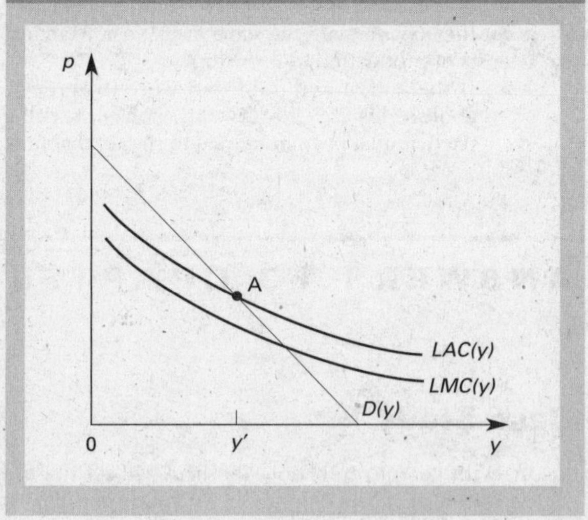

FIGURE A10.2

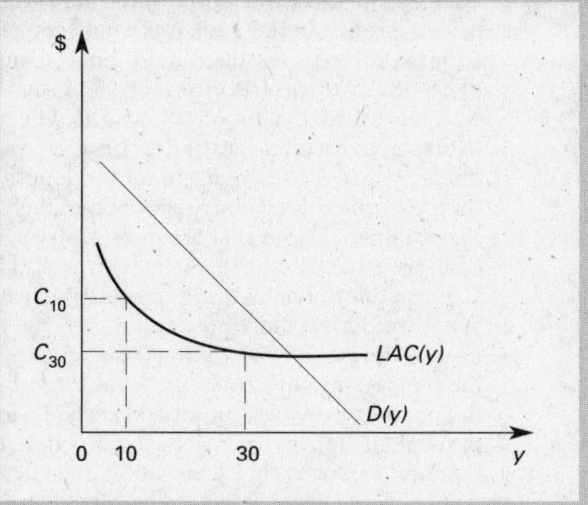

From society's perspective, we have to look at the social benefits and social costs associated with taxing cassettes. As a general rule, taxing a good leads to distortions in the allocation of resources, which is not desirable. However, if the good confers a cost on others (a negative externality as discussed in Chapter 18) then a tax may remedy this situation. As long as the tax is set equal to the amount of damage levied on others (in this case musicians) then it is desirable from society's perspective. One problem with taxing cassettes, however, is the fact that they are used for other reasons as well — like voice recording and dictating messages — a tax on all cassettes would impose a burden on these users.

28 In Figure A10.4. we provide a stylized version of a situation that compares competition to monopoly. Suppose, before the merger, the firms were competitive. Price would be p^c and each of n firms would product Q_c/n. After the merger, one firm emerges and will produce at the optimal scale Q_m. Notice that there is a savings from the merger because the average costs of production are lower. The gain is represented by the area p^cCDAC^m. The deadweight loss associated with monopoly is ABC. As long as the first area is greater than the second area (which will be the case for very small cost savings) then the merger results in a cost savings to society and hence should be allowed.

29 A decrease in the marginal cost will increase total quantity produced. However, since the firm allocates output by equating marginal revenue in the two markets, and the marginal revenue of the world demand is constant, output sold in Canada will not change.

Long Problems

*30 **a** Because AC is constant, then $AC = MC$. Equilibrium is found where profits are maximized, i.e., where $MR = MC$ which happens at $p = \$80$ and $q = 10$; profits are \$200.

b If $MC = 8$ then the new equilibrium price will be \$54 and the new output is 23; profits are \$1058. The firm would spend up to the discounted present value of \$1 058 each year for as many years as it anticipates having the monopoly in this good. The value of this sum depends upon the number of years of exclusive monopoly (the life of the patent) and the discount rate. The incentive to R&D increases with the life of the patent and decreases with the discount rate.

FIGURE A10.3

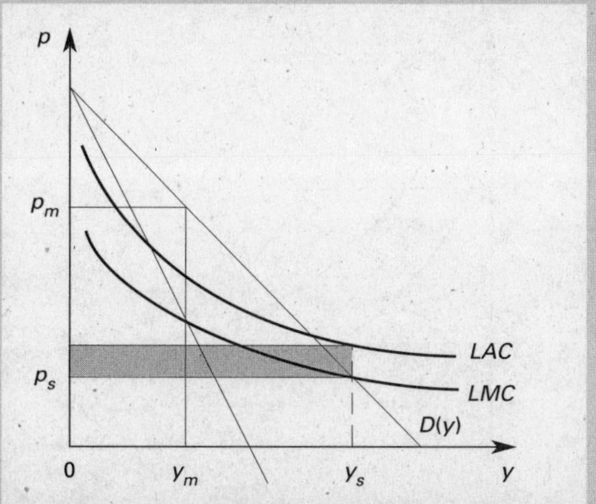

FIGURE A10.4

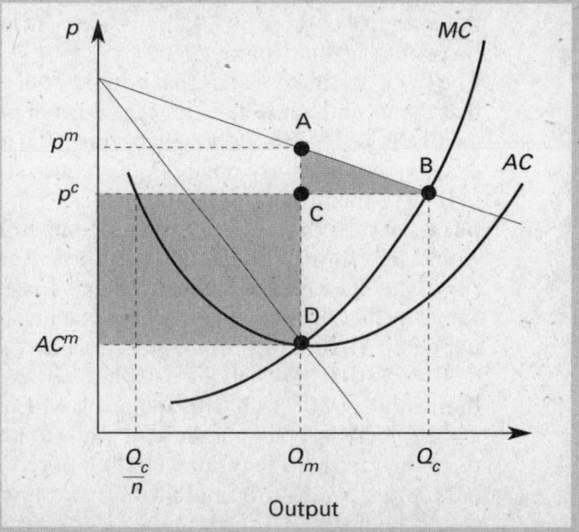

c If the industry is competitive, then with the old technology $p = \$60$ and $q = 20$ (profits are zero). Thus, compared to the pre-innovation situation, consumers are better off. Compared to the post-innovation situation however consumers are worse off. Innovation leads the monopolist to charge a lower price. (This assumes that the competitive firms would not innovate and find the new technology, see part **e** for more details.)

d If everyone faced the same technology then there would have to be some barrier to entry that prevents the other firms from coming into the market. Perhaps the incumbent firm has superior management (monopoly by good management) or is the sole owner of a necessary resource. Basically, without some special advantage, one would not observe monopoly profits persist over time. Notice that after the innovation, costs are much lower. Again, the only way that a monopoly could persist is if it had some special advantage in the market.

e Because a competitive industry makes zero economic profits in the long run, some have argued that its firms would not invest in R&D. However, others argue that it is the presence of expected profits that would encourage such investment. A patent policy that confers a monopoly right on an innovator may encourage firms to race to be the first to discover a lucrative innovation. Notice that such a race may not be beneficial to society since the firms may be duplicating efforts and so on. Some have argued that firms should be allowed to cooperate in the R&D efforts so as to avoid such costly duplication. If this occurs, other problems follow like how does the industry split the profits associated with an invention.

°31 a $p = \$12.75$, $y = 1\ 225\ 000$.

b No. Suppose an entrant entered at 500 (thousand) units and the incumbent remained at 1225, price would fall to \$7.75, still far above the marginal costs of \$0.50, hence entry would be profitable and would occur.

c The Sylos postulate means that entrant believes that the incumbent will maintain its current policy. If this is the case, entry will occur in the absence of a limit-entry policy (as demonstrated in **b**). The incumbent would have to set its output to ensure that, should entry occur, price would fall below \$0.50 and hence the entrant (and the incumbent) would make losses. Knowing this, the theory goes, the entrant would not enter. To find this "limit entry quantity" set $0.50 = 25 - 0.01y$ which occurs when $y = 2450$ then subtract 500 from this quantity, which is $y = 1950$. Now, if the incumbent were to produce, say, 1951 (in thousands) then if entry occurs, price would drop below 0.50 and losses would be made. To see whether this strategy makes sense, the monopolist would have to compare monopoly profits in one period plus "shared" profits after entry to the limit-entry pricing profits. In this case, this would compare \$15 006 250 plus the discounted present value of \$8 881 250 (profits after entry) to the discounted present value of \$9 735 490. Clearly, with a high discount rate option 1 is more profitable. It will also depend upon the length of time for which limit-entry profits are likely to be sustained. (Note that this limit-entry price analysis is based on the naive Sylos postulate. Can you think about why this postulate is naive? What would the monopolist do if, say, the entrant entered anyway while it was pursuing a limit-entry pricing strategy? Would it indeed maintain its previous output and sustain a loss, or would it "move over" and accommodate the entrant? Knowing this, what would the entrant do? What we are uncovering here is the problem associated with strategies that are "credible".)

d As the minimum efficient scale drops from 500 000, the incentive for entrants to enter becomes greater. Smaller firms may come into the market, and the ability of the incumbent to limit-entry price will get weaker

32 Figure A10.5 shows a natural monopoly that is operating in the region of increasing returns to scale. If the firm is forced to price where marginal costs equals price, it would result in p^* which is the socially desirable price. However, notice that such a price would result in a loss to the monopoly of AC^*p^*AB; over time, the monopolist would not offer the service in the market. To deal with this problem the government (regulator) has a few options. It could subsidize the monopolist so that it makes no losses. From a political perspective, sub-

FIGURE A10.5

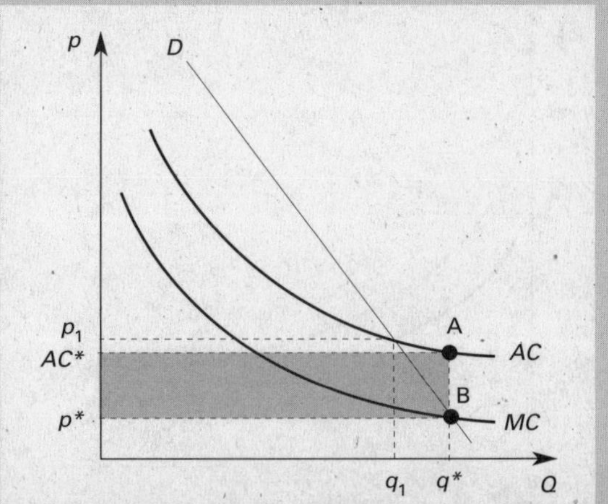

sidizing the monopolist may be difficult to sell. Furthermore, to determine exactly what is the *MC* and *AC* is difficult; the monopolist would have the incentive to exaggerate the magnitude of its losses. The regulator could also allow the monopolist to charge a fixed fee in order to recuperate the loss in addition to the per unit price. A further possibility is to set prices equal to average costs, which is the strategy most often taken for natural monopolies. It is easier to calculate average costs than marginal costs (although a lot of information is still required). Indeed, the strategy most often taken is rate of return regulation in which the return on capital is set so as to give the monopolist a normal return. The information requirements associated with this sort of regulation, while less than straight average cost pricing, are formidable. It may also result in distortions in the input mix chosen by the monopolist.

33 Under the tariff, the monopolist sets p^* and y^* as shown in Figure A10.6. Now consider two alternative possibilities for the world price level, p_A and p_B. If the world price is p_A, then the production of pucks by Canadian firms increases to y_A when the tariff is removed because the new marginal revenue curve intersects the marginal cost curve to the right of the monopoly output. Alternatively, if p_B is the world price, then marginal revenue intersects the marginal cost to the left of the monopoly output, and Canadian production of pucks declines to y_B.

34 Figure A10.7 shows the demand and marginal cost curves of perfectly competitive firms if the monopoly is dissolved. In both a) and b), y_m and y_c are the monopoly and competitive outputs. Also in both cases, $OCBy_m$ represents the resource cost savings from the monopoly and *ABD* measures the dead-weight loss associated with monopoly. In Figure A10.7a, where marginal cost of competitive firms, *c*, is very low, the dead-weight loss outweighs the resource cost savings; in Figure A10.7b, where *c* is high, the cost savings outweigh the dead-weight loss.

35 The horizontal summation of the marginal cost curves is shown in Figure A10.8. At any given output level, the profit-maximizing monopolist will shift production to the plant with lower marginal costs. As shown in the figure, this implies that plant 2 will be used for the first 11 units of output and plant 1 for the rest of the output. That is, equating

FIGURE A10.6

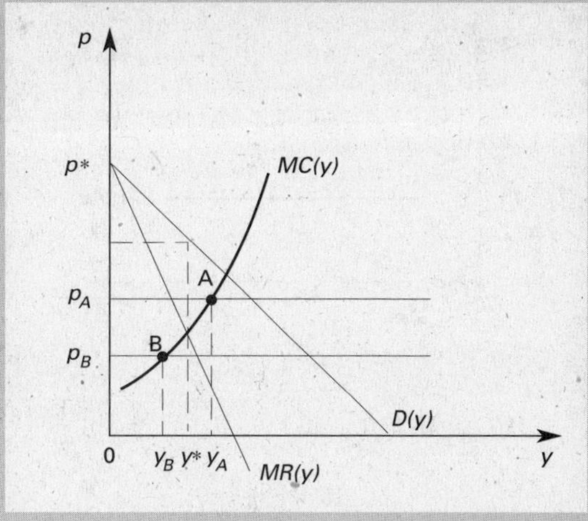

FIGURE A10.7

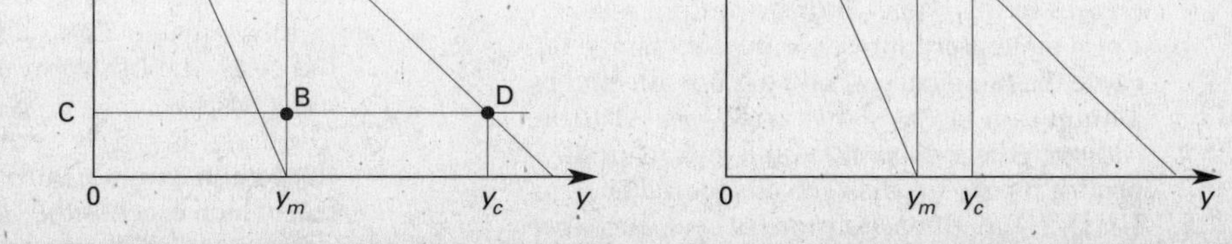

FIGURE A10.8

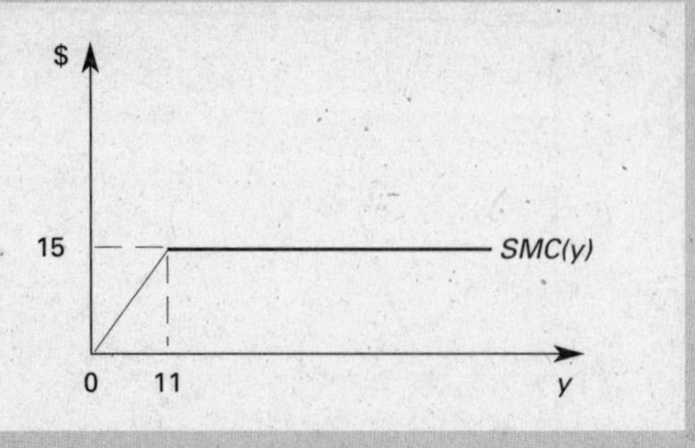

FIGURE A10.9

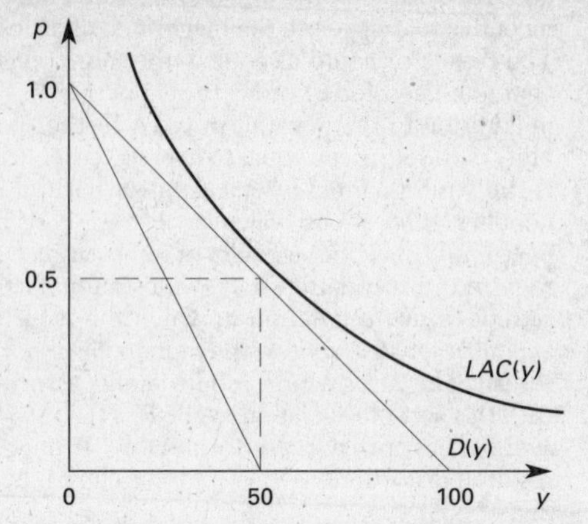

SMC_1 with SMC_2 gives

$$15 = \frac{y_2}{2} + \frac{19}{2}$$

or

$$y_2 = 11$$

To find total output y and, therefore, the output produced in plant 1, y_1, the monopolist equates marginal revenue to marginal cost in each plant (which equals 15). That is,

$$40 - y = 15$$

or

$$y = 25$$

Equations (1) and (2) together imply that $y_1 = 14$, $y_2 = 25$, and $p = 27.5$.

***36 a** Rewriting the demand curve gives $p = 1 - 0.01y$ and $MR(y) = 1 - 0.02y$. Since marginal costs are zero, the monopolist maximizes profits (or minimizes losses) where $MR(y) = 0$; that is, at $1 - 0.02y = 0$ or $y = 50$. Price at this quantity is $p = 0.5$. Total revenues are $25; hence, the firm cannot cover its costs, as shown in Figure A10.9.

b The telephone service is socially worthwhile because the total surplus at the efficient price $p = 0$ is 50 (area under demand curve), which exceeds the installation costs.

37 a When the lump-sum tax is imposed, the average total cost curve slides up the marginal cost curve as shown in Figure A10.10a. In the short run $p < SAC(y)$, so some firms are forced to exit the industry and total industry supply falls. In the long run, price increases to p' (see figure), where firms' economic profits are zero. The number of firms in the industry is smaller; firm output increases from y^* to y'; industry output falls.

b For a monopolist, price would not change because the marginal cost curve is not affected by a lump-sum tax, as shown in Figure A10.10b. Although the monopolist is still making positive profits, the size of these profits has fallen.

c Under competition, consumers bear the entire burden of the tax in the long run; under monopoly, producers do. This is because a lump-sum tax does not change the marginal conditions for profit maximization by a monopolist but does effect the entry–exit decisions of competitive firms.

38 a Under the original agreement, in which the author is paid 25% of revenues, the publisher faces the pivoted demand curve $a'b$ in Figure A10.11. Marginal revenue of this demand, $a'c$, is set equal to marginal costs at quantity y'; the price of the book is p'. Under the lump-sum payment scheme, the marginal revenue of the market demand, ac, is now relevant. The average total costs — $AC(y)$ in the figure — increases by the average lump-sum payment, but marginal costs are not affected. Marginal revenue equals marginal costs at y^*; the price of the book is p^*. In this scheme, the price is lower, output is higher. The publisher is indeed better off because total industry profits have increased (marginal revenue of the market demand equals marginal costs), but the publisher pays the author the same amount as under the old scheme. Hence, the publisher pockets the increase in industry profits.

b Royalties may be used when the demand for the book is uncertain. The author and publisher share the risks under a royalty arrangement, whereas the publisher would bear all the risks under the lump-sum scheme.

***39 a** The monopolist would set $MR(y) = 25 - y$ equal to $MC(y)$ and produce $y = 25$ at $p = 12.5$. Since profits, equal to $25 \times 12.5 = 312.5$, are less than the costs, the bridge would not be built by the monopolist.

b The bridge is socially worthwhile to build because the total maximum surplus (at $p = MC = 0$) is 625, which exceeds the costs of 500.

c A subsidy of K per unit is illustrated by an up-

FIGURE A10.10

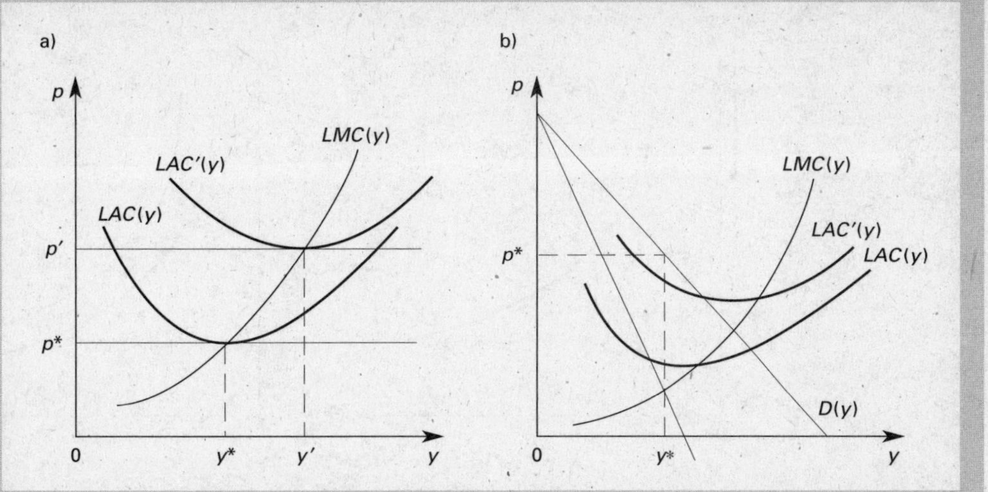

ward parallel shift of the demand curve by K in Figure A10.12a. The K just sufficient to cover costs is at the point where the demand curve is tangent to the average total costs.

d A lump-sum grant is illustrated by a downward shift in the average cost curve in Figure A10.12b. The grant G just sufficient for revenues to cover costs is at the point where the average cost is tangent to the demand curve.

e For the per-unit subsidy in **c**, K must satisfy

$$[p(K) + K]y(K) - 500 = 0 \qquad (3)$$

where $p(K)$ and $y(K)$ are the profit-maximizing price and output, given K. To find $y(K)$ and $p(K)$, $MR = 25 + K - y$ is set equal to $MC = 0$: $25 - y + \mathrm{K} = 0$, which yields $y = 25 + K$. Substituting this expression for y into the demand curve gives $p = 12.5 - 0.5K$. Further substitution of these values into the profit function in Equation (3) yields $K = 6.62$. Given this value of K, $y = 31.62$ and $p = 9.19$. The total payment by the government is $Ky = 6.62 \times (31.62) = 209.32$. The grant G, which just covers costs, is given by the costs (500) minus the maximum achievable profits without assistance (312.5); that is, $G = 187.5$. Hence, the grant program is less costly than the per-unit subsidy.

FIGURE A10.11

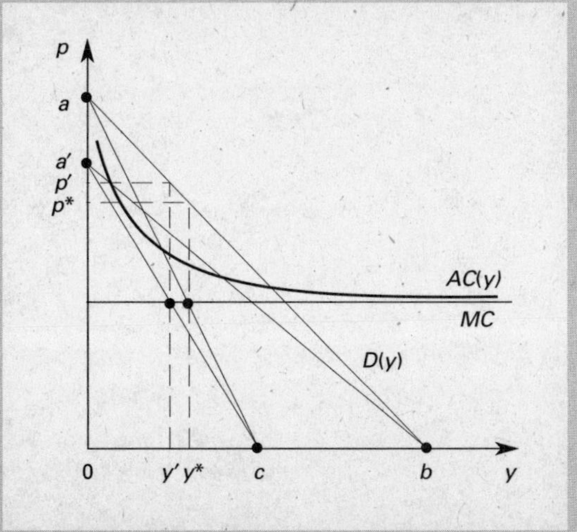

FIGURE A10.12

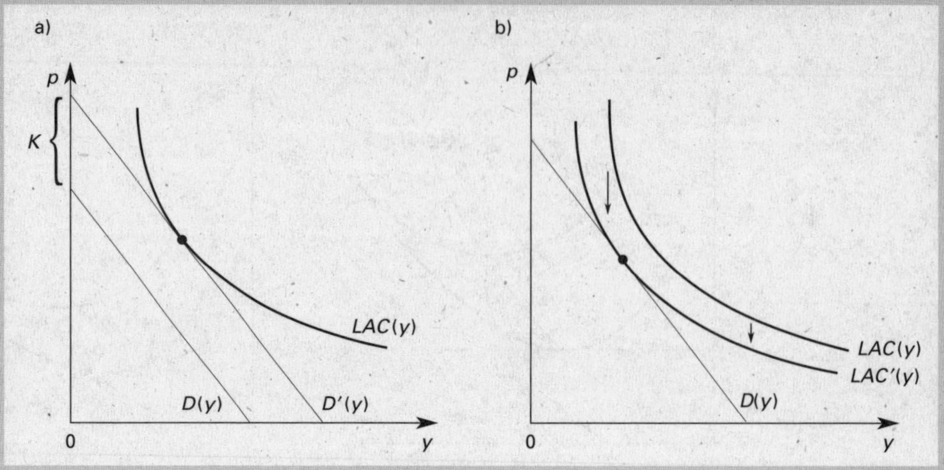

CHAPTER 11

Input Markets and the Allocation of Resources

Chapter Summary

Input Markets

In the previous chapters about output markets, the role of **input markets** in determining the allocation of scarce resources toward competing uses was suppressed. Although the production relationship between inputs and outputs was identified for deriving the cost functions, input prices were held constant for the most part. We now turn to input markets to examine the firm's demand for inputs used in production and the supply of these inputs. In this analysis, output markets, though still important, take a lesser role: Just as input prices "positioned" the firm's cost curve, the output price affects the value of an input, thereby positioning the demand curve for the input.

Perfectly Competitive Input Markets

First, we examine the **perfectly competitive input market**. On the demand side, the employers of inputs are assumed to be firms. Firms of all types may demand a particular input, for example, unskilled workers: farmers in a competitive market or automobile producers with market power. On the supply side are two types of input markets: **primary input markets** and **intermediate input markets**. For primary inputs such as labour and land, the suppliers are individuals, whereas firms are assumed to supply the intermediate input markets. The perfectly competitive input market is based on familiar assumptions: large numbers, perfect information, input homogeneity, and perfect mobility of resources.

The Supply of Inputs

Many of the supply decisions made in input markets are analytically similar to those made in output markets; for example, the producer of an intermediate input sells this input to other firms. As long as the producer of the input is a profit maximizer, the supply of the input is derived in the same way as a firm's supply of some final good.

When an individual sells primary inputs that are either nonrenewable or nonexhaustible, we usually assume for simplicity that the supply of the resource is perfectly price-inelastic.

In the case of primary inputs, for example, an individual selling her own labour services, the individual solves an income–leisure utility-maximization problem to determine how much time to devote to market activities and to leisure. The budget constraint facing the individual takes account of the individual's non-wage (A) and wage income and his or her time constraint. Indeed, the maximum possible income of the individual, his or her **full income**, can be expressed as $A + wT$ were w is the hourly wage rate and T is the total number of hours available. Notice that the wage rate may be interpreted as the **price of leisure**. If an increase in non-work income encourages the individual to take more leisure, leisure is said to be a normal "good"; otherwise, it is inferior. Similarly, an increase in the wage rate may increase or decrease the time allocated to leisure, and consequently, to market activities. If leisure is an inferior good, then an increase in the wage rate will result in an increase in the hours of labour supplied. If leisure is a normal good, an increase in the wage rate may increase or decrease the hours of labour supplied to the market. This ambiguity is attributed to the opposite impact of the income and substitution effects on leisure when it is a normal good: An increase in the wage rate increases the opportunity cost of leisure (substitution effect), whereas the income effect increases the time allocated to leisure. The relationship between the wage rate and the quantity of labour supplied in the market is called the supply curve. Generally, a **labour supply curve** will be positively-sloped; however, if the income effect dominates the substitution effect, an increase in wages may encourage an individual to provide less labour, thus resulting in a "backward-bending" supply curve.

Demand for One Variable Input

A profit-maximizing demander of an input will want to hire units of that input up to the point at which the additional revenue of the output produced by the input equals the money cost of the input, w. The additional revenue provided by the input is the extra output produced by the input times the marginal revenue of that output. The firm's demand for one input, referred to as the **short-run input demand function**, can be derived from this relationship. Call the marginal revenue times marginal product the **marginal revenue product, *MRP*(*z*)**, and the average revenue times the marginal product the **average revenue product, *ARP*(*z*)**. The short-run demand curve for the firm is then defined by the $MRP(z)$ curve below the $ARP(z)$ because, for any wage above $ARP(z)$, the firm is better off not to produce. The firm will choose z until $MRP(z) = w$. This rule is equivalent to the rule $\boldsymbol{SMC(y) = MR(y)}$ for determining the profit-maximizing output.

Does this rule imply an efficient allocation of resources? To answer this question, we must determine how consumers value an additional unit of an input. Because the value to consumers of additional units of output is the output price, the value of an additional unit of input is the **value of the marginal product:** price times the marginal product of that input. Hence, an efficient allocation of resources is characterized by $\boldsymbol{VMP(z) = w}$. Because price equals marginal revenue for a competitive firm, perfect competition in both the input and output markets allocates resources efficiently, whereas a monopolist in the output market demands too few units of the input (and hence, produces too little) since $MRP(z) < VMP(z)$ for the monopolist.

Demand with Many Variable Inputs

The demand for an input when there are many variable inputs, referred to as the **long-run input demand**, is more elastic than the short-run input demand because of the increased flexibility in responding to changes in the price of an input in the long run. If the price of an input falls, the firm will substitute toward the input that has become relatively less expensive. As in consumer theory, the actual change in the quantity demanded of the input due to the change in its price can be decomposed into **substitution** and **output effects.** For both **normal** and **inferior inputs**, the quantity demanded of the input increases for a price decrease due to both substitution and output effects, hence generating a downward-sloping demand function.

Equilibrium in the Input Market

The aggregate demand for an input is steeper than the horizontal summation of individual firms' demands. This situation arises because the increase in the quantity demanded for the input due to a reduction in the input price results in larger production and hence a lower output price. This lower output price reduces the MRP(z) at every level of the input, and so the aggregate quantity demanded of the input is lower than the level implied by the horizontal summation of the firms' demands. The **competitive equilibrium** is found where the aggregate input demand curve intersects the input supply curve.

Monopsony

When only one purchaser of the input exists, there is a **monopsony.** The monopsonist sets the input price. When the supply curve of the input is positively sloped, the monopsonist must raise the input price to attract additional units of the input to the firm. The relationship between the input price and quantity of input supplied is its **market supply function**. The price of an input can be interpreted as **average factor cost** (AFC), hence **total factor cost** (TFC) is price times quantity used. The additional cost of hiring another unit of the input, the **marginal factor cost** $MFC(z)$, increases in z. The monopsonist maximizes profits by hiring units of the input up to the point at which the $MFC(z)$ equals the $MRP(z)$ at an input price that is below the $MRP(z)$. Unless the monopsonist can find a way to perfectly discriminate in setting its input prices, this pricing rule will be inefficient.

What is the source of **monopsony power**? When the perfect-mobility assumption of perfect competition does not hold, a monopsony can arise. One common source of monopsony arises from the **immobility of inputs**. Individuals with very few employment opportunities, workers who would face large moving costs in changing jobs, or owners of inputs requiring large transportation costs are likely to face buyers with monopsony power. If the monopsonist can identify groups of workers with different supply curves, then it might engage in wage discrimination. In the case of two groups of workers, the monopsonist will minimize labour costs of a given number of workers by equating the $MFC(z)$ of group 1 to the $MFC(z)$ of group 2. The profit-maximizing number of workers is then found by equating the horizontal summation of the $MFC(z)$ curves to the $MRP(z)$. The more immobile the labour, the more successful the monopsonist will be in this wage-setting behaviour.

Demand for Capital Inputs

In addition to hiring or renting inputs on a period-by-period basis, firms also buy or rent goods that yield services for more than one period. Such goods, like physical structures and equipment, are called **capital inputs**. As long as the market for loanable funds is perfect, the firm will maximize the present value of profits each period which will determine the demand for these capital inputs.

Human Capital

We can endogenize the individual's lifetime earning by allowing her to make an investment in human capital: training or **foregone income** today, with expectations of some future return. The relationship between the amount of investment that the individual must make today in order to receive some future return is described by the **human capital production function**; the slope is the **marginal product of human capital**.

Using the separation theorem, we can determine the solution to this individual's investment problem without reference to her preferences. To choose the level of human capital that maximizes the present value of income available for consumption, the individual will invest in that level of human capital where her marginal product equals $1 + i$. That is, the future value of investing another dollar on human capital equals the future value of that dollar invested elsewhere.

We can integrate the human capital choice into the life-cycle model. Through each point along the human capital production function, a budget line with slope $-(1 + i)$ can be drawn. The human capital decision that maximizes the present value of income available for consumption is given by that point where the production function is tangent to the budget line. Then, given the income constraint that results from this decision, the individual chooses the utility-maximizing consumption decision, which equates the marginal rate of time preference and $(1 + i)$.

So far, the model assumes that the market for loanable funds is perfect and thus that individuals can borrow against future income — which is based on their human capital — in order to consume presently. Banks need to secure large loans against some asset — like a house. Indeed, when a house is used to secure a loan we call it a **mortgage**. Young people typically only have human capital which cannot be used as security for a loan. Thus, governments often have student loan programmes in order to overcome this imperfection in the market for loanable funds.

KEY WORDS

- Average factor cost
- Average revenue product
- Capital inputs
- Competitive equilibrium
- Foregone income
- Full income
- Human capital
- Human capital production function
- Immobility of inputs
- Inferior inputs
- Input markets
- Intermediate input markets
- Labour supply curve
- Long- and short-run input demand

Marginal factor cost

Marginal product of human capital

Marginal revenue product

Market supply function

Monopsony

Monopsony power

Mortgage

Normal inputs

Output effect

Perfectly competitive input markets

Price of leisure

Primary input markets

Reservation salaries

Substitution effect

Supply curve

Total factor cost

Value of the marginal product

Wealth

CASE STUDY: FREE AGENCY IN PROFESSIONAL SPORTS

The markets for players of professional sports are interesting in their diversity in the way in which players' salaries are determined. In football, the demanders of this labour input are the owners of the teams in the National Football League (NFL). Formerly, the owners operated as a cartel monopsony in that they agreed to follow a set of rules in competing for players for their teams. In particular, the Rozelle Rule stipulated that a team, with a player who wanted to switch teams after the expiration of its contract, would be entitled to compensation from the new team. This rule had the effect of restricting player mobility and was legally challenged by several players, which led to modifications of the rule in 1977.

In contrast to these restrictions, free agency allows players unrestricted mobility in that after the initial contract expires, players are free to play for the team offering the highest bid. Under free agency, markets are more competitive. Free agency is the norm in professional baseball.

A What might be the rationale for the Rozelle Rule in the football contracts?

B Holding constant all other factors that influence wages in football and baseball, what would you expect to be the difference in wages between football and baseball players?

C There is an NFL Players Association which acts as a union for the players. What effect would you expect this players' union to have on the contracts?

EXERCISES

Multiple Choice

Choose the correct answer to each question. There is only one correct answer to each question.

1 If a firm uses two inputs, inputs 1 and 2, then the firm's long-run demand curve for input 1

- **a** Shifts down and to the left when the price of input 1 increases.
- **b** Shifts down and to the left when the price of input 2 decreases.
- **c** Is the marginal revenue product curve for input 1, given a fixed amount of input 2.
- **d** Is flatter than the marginal revenue product curve of input 1.
- **e** None of the above.

2 Suppose that a firm in a perfectly competitive market maximizes profits while the price of the only input is \$5 and the marginal product of the input is 1/2 unit of output. Then, the price of the output must be
  a \$2.50
  b \$10
  c \$1
  d \$0.10
  e None of the above.

3 The demand curve for an input Z will be more elastic in which of the following cases?
  a The more elastic are consumer demands for the goods produced with factor Z.
  b The greater is the decline in the marginal productivity of Z.
  c The more inelastic is the supply of factors of production that are used with factor Z.
  d Only **a** and **b**.
  e None of the above.

4 A monopolist in the output market that is a competitive purchaser of labour is currently setting a price of \$100 per unit and hires labour at \$25 per worker, and the marginal worker produces 0.25 unit. To maximize profits, the monopolist should
  a Stay where it is.
  b Hire more labour (and produce more output).
  c Hire less labour (and produce less output).
  d Reduce its output price.
  e None of the above.

5 A firm purchases labour from a perfectly competitive labour market and is a monopoly seller of its output. Currently, the firm is maximizing its profits at 60 units of output. It faces a demand curve for its product given by $p = 200 - y$. The marginal costs of hiring an additional worker are \$1,200. Thus, the marginal productivity of the last worker hired must be
  a 20 units of Y.
  b 15 units of Y.
  c 8 4/7 units of Y.
  d Not enough information to determine the marginal productivity.
  e None of the above.

6 If the value of the marginal product of labour exceeds the wage rate, then there is probably
  a A monopoly in the output market.
  b A monopsony in the input market.
  c Perfect competition in the input and output markets.
  d Either **a** or **b**.
  e None of the above.

7 Which of the following is *not* an assumption of perfect competition in the input market?
  a All inputs used in production are homogeneous.
  b There are many input demanders and suppliers.
  c All demanders and suppliers of inputs have perfect information.
  d Inputs can be costlessly transported or relocated.
  e All the above are assumptions of the perfectly competitive model.

8 Suppose that at the prices of input 1 and input 2, w_1 and w_2, respectively, a firm's cost-minimizing combination of inputs for producing y_1 units of output is given by point A in Figure 11.1. Then if the price of input 1 increases to w',
  a The firm will demand $z_1^A - z_1^B$ fewer units of the input as a result of the substitution effect.
  b The firm will demand fewer units of input 1 due to the output effect.
  c Input 2 must be an inferior input.
  d Input 1 must be an inferior input.
  e None of the above.

9 If the *MRP* of an input is $MRP(z) = 60 - z/2$ and the supply curve of the input is $S(z) = z/4$, then the wage rate set by a monopsonist is
  a 80
  b 15
  c 60
  d 30
  e None of the above.

10 A perfectly wage-discriminating monopsonist who is also a (nondiscriminating) monopolist in the output market sets
  a $MRP(z) = MFC(z)$
  b $VMP(z) = MFC(z)$
  c $MRP(z) = w$
  d $VMP = w$
  e None of the above.

11 The supply curve of labour will be backward-bending in which of the following cases?
  a If leisure in an inferior good.
  b If the substitution and income effects from an increase in the wage rate reinforce each other.

FIGURE 11.1

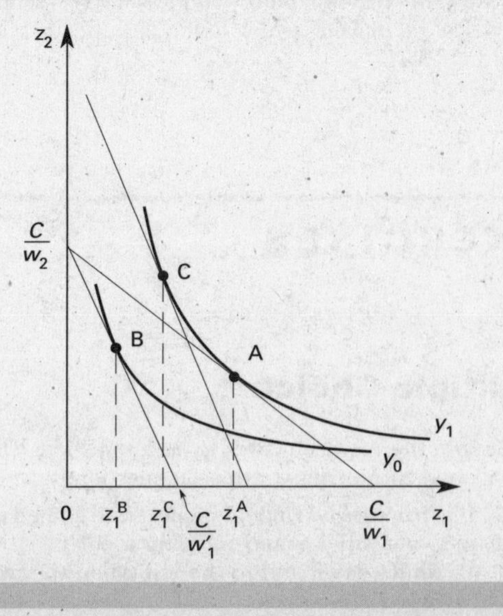

FIGURE 11.2

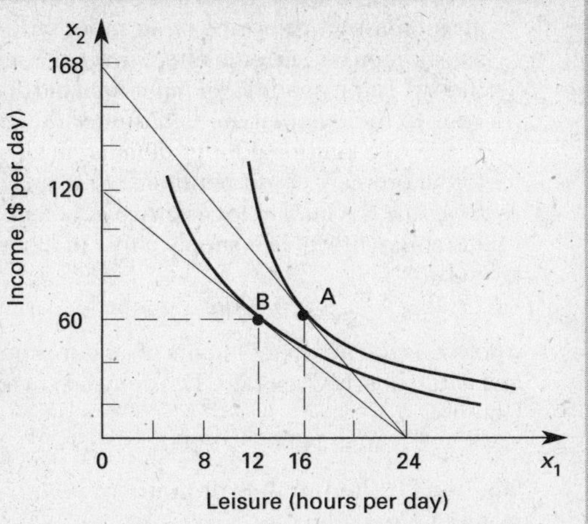

c If an increase in the wage rate results in an increase in the amount of labour supplied on the market.

d If the reduction in leisure due to an increase in the opportunity cost of leisure is less than the increase in leisure due to the corresponding increase in real income.

e None of the above.

Use Figure 11.2 to answer questions **12** and **13**.

12 A utility-maximizing individual

a Is indifferent between the two income–leisure bundles A and B because they contain the same amount of income.

b Will choose to earn $120 income if the wage rate drops to $5 per hour.

c Is facing a wage rate of $7 when choosing bundle A.

d Only **b** and **c** are true.

e None of the above is true.

13 If the individual's wage falls from $7 to $5, which of the following is correct?

a The person will tend to consume less leisure owing to the substitution effect.

b The person will tend to take more leisure because of the income effect.

c The person is on the backward-bending portion of the labour supply curve.

d Leisure is an inferior good.

e None of the above is true.

True-False

14 The more inelastic the supply of inputs of production used with an input Z, the more inelastic is the demand curve for Z.

15 The greater the costs of input Z as a percentage of total production costs, the more inelastic is the demand curve for Z.

16 If firms purchase an input Z up to the point at which the $MRP(z) = w$, then the allocation of resources is always efficient.

17 If only input Z is used in production by a monopolist, the condition $MRP(z) = w$ gives the profit-maximizing choice of input and, with the production function, gives the profit-maximizing choice of output.

18 The input employment condition for a price-taking firm in the input market that is also a price-taker in the output market is $VMP(z) = w$.

19 For a decrease in an input's price, both the substitution and output effects result in negatively-sloped demand curve for the input, whether it is a normal or an inferior input.

20 A firm's short-run demand curve for an input is the $MRP(z)$ curve below the $ARP(z)$ curve.

21 A firm's long-run demand curve for an input is more price-elastic than the firm's short-run demand curve for the input.

22 The aggregate input demand is flatter than the individual firm's demand curve for that input.

23 A firm that is a monopsonist in the input market and a monopolist in the output market and can perfectly wage discriminate in the input market and perfectly price discriminate in the output market will set $VMP(z) = w$.

24 Assume that an individual works five hours per day and earns $50 per day. If the government increases the income tax rate from 0% to 20%, then the individual will certainly increase his work hours to $6^1/4$ to keep his income at the same level.

25 The supply curve for labour will be backward-bending if the substitution effect from an increase in the wage rate is smaller than the income effect when leisure is a normal good.

26 At low wages, the income effect for an increase in the wage is likely to dominate the substitution effect because the individual will want to increase her income by working more to offset the low wages.

27 An increase in the interest rate will result in a parallel shift in the human capital production function.

28 An individual will invest more in human capital the lower is the interest rate.

Short Problems

29 Show that the optimal condition for employment of input Z by a price-taking firm is equivalent to the optimal condition for production of output Y (which uses factor Z) for a price-taking firm.

30 Commodity X is produced by a perfectly competitive industry. In the short run, the only variable input in each industry is Z, also supplied in a competitive industry. With the aid of diagrams, derive the firm short-run demand curve for Z.

31 Why will the aggregate demand curve of firms in a competitive market for an input be less elastic than the summation of the demand curves of the separate firms? (Assume that firms are price-takers in the output markets.)

32 Suppose that a firm is a monopolist in the product market and a monopsonist in the labour market. Show that its choice of wage and employment level is not efficient.

33 Explain why the marginal revenue product for an input is steeper than the firm's long-run demand curve for the input.

34 If the marginal product of labour is $100/z_1$, the marginal product of capital is $50/z_2$, the wage is \$5, the price of capital is \$100, and the price of the product is \$12, how much capital and labour will a perfectly competitive firm demand?

35 In many poorer countries of the world, petroleum workers are paid two or three times more for similar work than are workers in manufacturing. Why would you guess this to be true?

36 Adam Smith wrote that disagreeable jobs have to pay more to attract workers than less disagreeable jobs. Male garbage collectors in Canada earn 5% less than the average male worker. Should we conclude that collecting garbage is a pleasant job?

***37** A monopsonist uses only labour to produce product Y, which she sells in a competitive market at a price equal to 1. Her production and labour supply functions are $y = 6z - 3z^2 + 0.2z^3$ and $w = 6 + 3z$, respectively, where z is the quantity of labour. Determine the values of z and w that maximize profits.

38 Show on a diagram that an individual is less likely to invest in human capital the higher is the interest rate. Illustrate the change in her consumption decision.

39 Suppose the government replaces all scholarships for college students with loans. That is, all students who were eligible for a scholarship may now get a loan for the same amount, however, at the market interest rate. Assume that students only value education as an investment (i.e., going to school increases their market wage). What effect will this new policy have on the number of college students? Explain.

Long Problems

40 In the long run, a firm uses 10 units of labour (input 1) and 100 units of capital (input 2) at a price ratio of $w_1/w_2 = 10$. The firm's total costs are $C = \$1\,000$.

a What are the wage and rental prices? Illustrate the optimal choice of the firm on an isoquant–isocost diagram.

b Show the effect of a capital price increase on labour and capital when output is constant (substitution effect) and when total costs are held constant.

c Compare the substitution and output effects of an increase in the price of an input with the substitution and income effects from consumer theory. Is the conditional input demand analogous to the compensated consumer demand? Is the unconditional input demand analogous to the ordinary consumer demand? Explain.

41 Assume that the market for a particular labour service is competitive. The supply curve of labour is given by

$$z_s = 800w$$

where z_s is the number of hours of labour supplied and w the hourly wage rate. The demand curve for labour is

$$z_d = 24\,000 - 1\,600w$$

where z_d is the number of hours of labour demanded.

a What are the equilibrium wage and number of hours worked?

b Suppose that the government agrees to pay workers of this type one-third of the difference between \$40 and the wage paid by employers for each hour worked; that is, the government pays a *supplement* over and above the wage the workers received from their employers. Given this program, how many hours are worked, what wage rate is paid by employers, and how much do these workers receive in total for each hour worked?

c Assume that a typical worker of this type receives a wage rate of \$6.25 per hour. Show on an income–leisure diagram the effect that the government program in **b** has on the individual's optimal choice of income and leisure, given this wage rate. Will all individuals of this type increase the number of hours that they are willing to work at a particular wage rate as a result of the government program? Why or why not?

42 Assume that the market for a particular labour service is competitive. The supply curve for labour is

$$z_s = 200 + 400w$$

and the demand curve for labour is

$$z_d = 1\,200 - 600w$$

where w is the wage rate per hour, z_s is the hours of labour supplied per day, and z_d is the hours of labour demanded per day.

a What are the competitive equilibrium wage rate and the number of hours worked?

b Consider one of the firms demanding labour in this market. Assume that this firm produces as a monopolist in the output market and faces demand $p = 90 - 2y$. Furthermore, the firm uses only labour and requires 10 hours of labour to produce 1 unit of output for all output. What will be the profit-maximizing number of labour hours hired, z_d, by this monopolist? What are the profit-maximizing price and output?

43 Suppose that a firm's labour demand function (in thousands of worker hours) is of the form

$$z_d = 9 - 0.5w$$

and the supply function it faces is of the form

$$z_s = -6 + 2w$$

a Find the equilibrium z and w.

b Suppose that the government institutes a minimum hourly wage of $6
(1) Find the new profit-maximizing level of w and z.
(2) How many individuals would like to work for the firm but cannot at the minimum wage?

c Suppose that, instead of instituting the minimum wage, the government agrees to pay the firm $3 per hour for each worker it employs. Calculate the new equilibrium w and z and calculate how much the subsidy costs the government.

44 Consider a society with no income taxes. The government decides to impose an income tax equal to 20% of all earnings.

a Use an income–leisure graph to illustrate the effect of this tax on the budget constraint of a representative individual. Assume that the individual has no non-labour income.

b Suppose that leisure is a normal good. Will the tax necessarily result in a decline in work time? Explain, using your diagram. Show the substitution and income effects for this change in the tax rate.

45 Brenda, a poor student, recently hit it lucky in a Prince Edward Island lottery. Her winnings are paid in $1 000 *annual* increments for as long as she lives. She also earns $250 per month working in a local library. Assume Brenda spends all of her annual earnings, and she cannot borrow against her future earnings.

a Draw a diagram of her utility-maximizing choice between leisure and all other goods. Given that Brenda lives a long and happy life, what is the present value of her stream of income earnings from the lottery ticket winnings at a discount rate of 8%?

b Suppose that her wage increases to $350 per month. Show the new optimum.

c Suppose that her lottery earnings increase by $600 per year. Show the new optimum.

d If Brenda is indifferent between a wage or lottery earnings increase, in which case, **b** or **c**, will Brenda work more? Explain.

46 At the present time, Gaston, who owns a garage in town, is trying to decide whether to invest in a new tow truck. His current one, which he bought and paid for years ago, is starting to cost him quite a bit of money on repairs. Indeed, he estimates that it costs him $2 000 per year to keep his old truck on the road; it brings in about $2 500 per year in revenues. He figures that he can keep this old truck going for another five years. With a new truck, Gaston thinks that he can increase the amount of revenue it generates to $4 000 per year. It will cost him, however, $20 000 to purchase a new truck (in five years time, this new truck will cost $21 000 and five years hence, the truck has a salvage value of $5 000). The new truck will last ten years, have zero salvage value after ten years, and will cost about $500 per year to maintain. Let's suppose that the interest rate is 5%, what should Gaston do?

ANSWERS TO CHAPTER 11

Case Study

A One interpretation of the clauses is that they limit competition for the players between the owners of the teams, thus allowing the NFL owners to pay less for the players and capture some of the economic rents of the players. The owners' justification for the contracts is that they help provide a balance between teams; without such contracts, the wealthier teams could offer the highest bid for all the star players.

B Holding all else constant, one would expect wages to be higher in baseball than in football. This is certainly the case, especially at the high end of the salary distribution. The maximum 1987 salaries in football and baseball in the tenth decile of the distribution were $900 000 and $2 412 500, respectively.[1] While median salaries in football and baseball are similar, the average salary in baseball was 80% higher than that in football, owing to the larger variance in baseball salaries.

C Whether or not the union would agree to continue with the restrictive contracts or insist on unlimited free agency depends on the effect that these contracts have on the different players and on the way decisions are made in the union. In any case, one

[1] John A. Bishop, J. Howard Finch, and John P. Fromby, "Risk Aversion and Rent-Seeking Redistributions: Free Agency in the National Football League." *Southern Economic Journal,* (1990, July). **57**, (1).

would expect that the players' union would attempt to reallocate some of the rents from the owners to the players.

Multiple-Choice

1 d 2 b 3 a 4 c 5 b 6 d 7 e
8 b 9 b 10 c 11 d 12 c 13 c

True-False

14 T 15 F 16 F 17 T 18 T 19 T 20 T
21 T 22 F 23 T 24 F 25 T 26 F 27 F
28 T

Short Problems

29 The profit-maximizing condition for employment of factor Z by a price-taking firm is $w = p[MP(z)]$, where w is the wage rate, p is the output price, and $MP(z)$ is the marginal product of the factor of production. Dividing both sides of the condition by $MP(z)$ gives

$$p = \frac{w}{MP(z)} = \frac{w}{(\Delta y/\Delta z)} = \frac{w\Delta z}{\Delta y} = \Delta C/\Delta y = \mathrm{MC}(y)$$

30 Figure A11.1 shows a firm's marginal revenue product and the average revenue product curves for input Z. Given a wage rate w_1, the firm maximizes profits by setting w_1 equal to $VMP(z)$ at point A. If the wage rate exceeds $\overline{w}$, the maximum of the average revenue product curve, the firm will shut down in the short run because variable costs are not covered. Hence, BC, the $VMP(z)$ curve below $\overline{w}$, is the short-run demand curve for a firm in a perfectly competitive industry.

31 Let $D(z)$ in Figure A11.2 be the summation of the value of the marginal product curves (firm demand curves for the input) across all firms in the industry. At an input price of w^*, z^* units of the input are demanded by the industry. Now suppose that the price of the input falls to w'. Each firm will want to hire more of the input until the $VMP(z)$ equals w'; in the aggregate, this increase in the demand for the input and the corresponding increase in the quantity of output supplied will lower the price of the output. Hence, the $VMP(z)$ will fall and the horizontal summation of the new $VMP(z)$ curves will be given by $D'(z)$. At w', only z' units of the input will be demanded; hence, points A and B are points on the aggregate demand.

32 A firm that is a monopolist in the output market and a monopsonist in the input market equates $MRP(z)$ with $MFC(z)$. The profit-maximizing choices of the wage and employment are given by w^* and z^*, respectively, in Figure A11.3. At this point, the value of an additional worker is given by $VMP(z^*)$, whereas the opportunity cost of this individual working is given by w^*. Hence, additional surplus could be realized by moving to point B, where the value of the marginal product from an additional worker equals the opportunity cost of that worker. The shaded area represents the loss in surplus from the monopolist-monopsonist.

33 In Figure A11.4, the $MRP_1(z_2)$ and $MRP_1(z_2')$ curves are the marginal revenue products of input

FIGURE A11.1

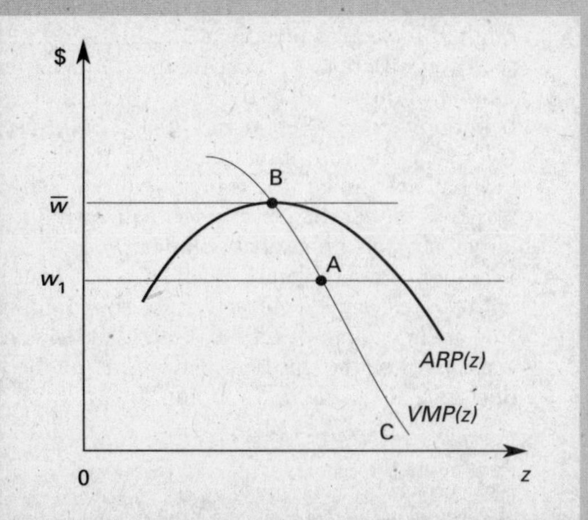

FIGURE A11.2

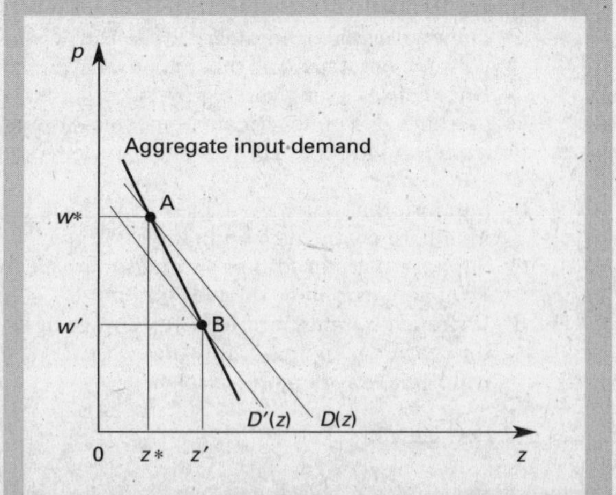

FIGURE A11.3

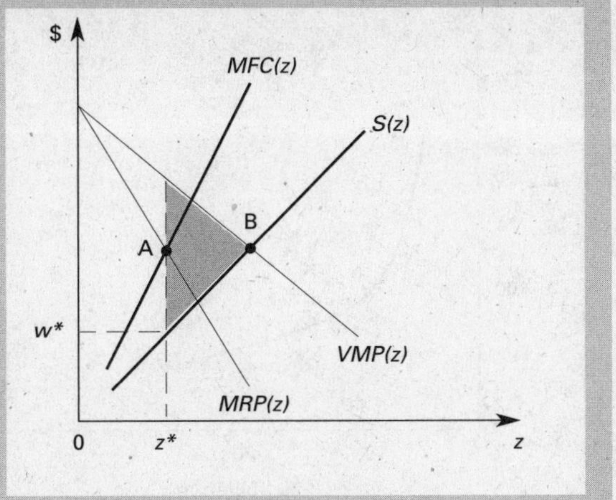

FIGURE 11.4

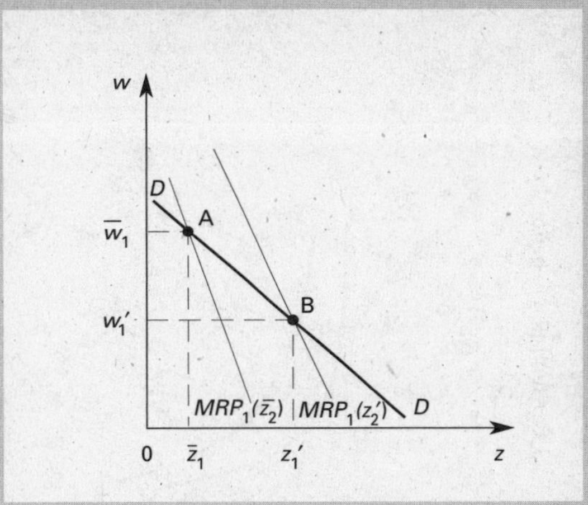

1 when input 2 is held at $\bar{z}_2$ and z_1', for $z_2' > \bar{z}_2$, respectively. The two inputs are used together in production in that a higher value of z_2 increases the marginal product of z_1 at every input level. Initially $\bar{z}_2$ and $\bar{z}_1$ are employed when the price of z_1 is $\bar{w}_1$. A decline in w_1 to w'_1 increases the quantity demanded of z_1 and, because the inputs are complements in production, increases the demand for z_2. This results in an increase in the marginal product of z_1. At a price of w_1', z_1' and z_2' units of the two inputs will be demanded. Points A and B are the firm's long-run demand curve for input 1. So, the demand curve is flatter in the long run since the firm is more flexible in that it can employ more units of a complementary input that may have been fixed in the short run.

34 A perfectly competitive firm will equate the value of the marginal product of labour to the price of labour and the value of the marginal product of capital to the price of capital; that is,

$$\frac{12 \times 100}{z_1} = 5 \quad \text{and} \quad \frac{12 \times 50}{z_2} = 100$$

Hence, $z_1^* = 240$ and $z_2^* = 6$.

35 If workers are paid the value of their marginal product, then petroleum workers would receive higher wages than manufacturing workers because the price (value) of petroleum is higher than the prices of manufacturing products.

36 No. The low wage may reflect a low value of the marginal product of garbage collection, rather than attractiveness of the job.

***37** The monopsonist sets the value of the marginal product equal to the marginal factor cost, and $VMP(z)$ is given by $p[MP(z)] = 6 - 6z + 0.6z^2$. The marginal factor cost is $6 + 6z$. Equating the two expressions gives

$$6 - 6z + 0.6z^2 = 6 + 6z$$
$$0.6z - 12 = 0$$
$$z = 20$$

The wage is found by substituting $z = 20$ into the labour supply:

$$w = 6 + 60 = 66$$

38 In Figure A11.5 is shown an individual's human capital production function (OA), her intertemporal income constraints for zero investment in human capital, the income constraint that is tangent to the human capital production function, and the indifference curves. For a particular interest rate, the individual's optimum is M; she invests in that level of human capital that yields income combination (I_0,I_1), and maximizes utility subject to the corresponding budget constraint by choosing consumption combination N (C_0,C_1). Hence, the individual consumes more than she earns in period 0.

For a higher interest rate, the income line pivots around point O (the income combination with zero human capital), as shown in Figure A11.5, she maximizes the present value of her income by investing in less human capital. This yields income combination, given by point $M'(I_0',I_1')$, and utility is maximized subject to the corresponding budget constraint at point $N'(C_0', C_1')$. The higher interest rate raises the opportunity cost of investing in human capital (rather than some alternative investment), and so she chooses a lower level of human capital.

39 The cost of every dollar spent on education has increased from zero to $1 + i$. Therefore, investment in human capital has become more expensive; consequently, this policy will have the effect of reducing the number of college students. (See explanation and diagram of the previous problem for further intuition.)

FIGURE A11.5

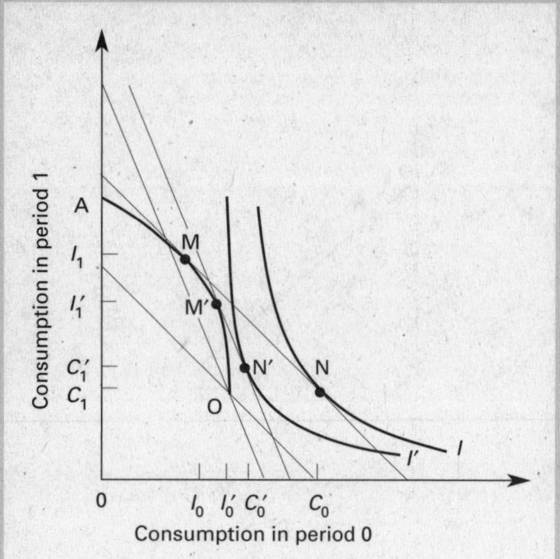

FIGURE A11.6

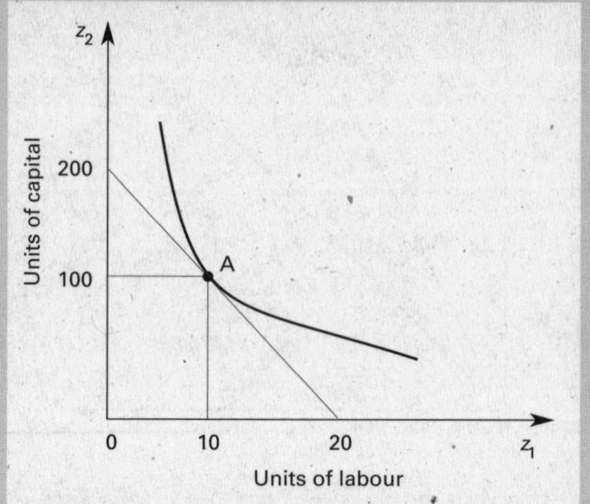

FIGURE A11.7

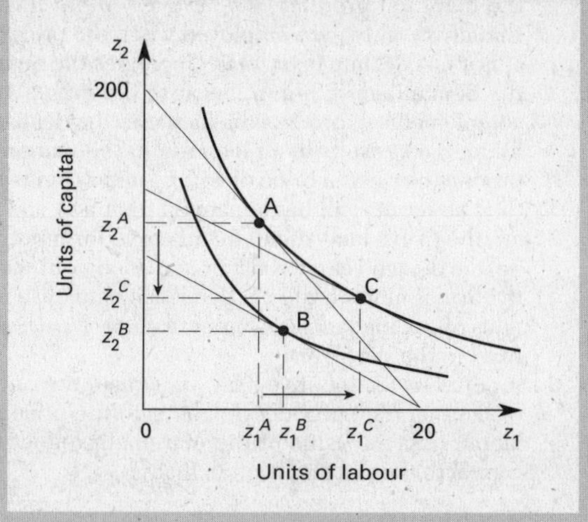

Long Problems

40 a The isocost curve is given by

$$1\,000 = w_2\left(\frac{w_1}{w_2}z_1 + z_2\right)$$
$$= w_2(10 \times 10 + 100)$$

and so

$$w_2 = 5 \quad \text{and} \quad w_1 = 50$$

Figure A11.6 illustrates the firm's labour-capital choice. Note that the firm is in the long run, as denoted by a tangency of the isocost and isoquant curves.

b Figure A11.7 illustrates the increase in the price of capital by a pivot inward of the isocost curve. The substitution effect of *A* to *C* results in a decline in input 2 but an increase in input 1. When total costs are constant, the price increase changes the input bundle from *A* to *B*: Input 2 falls and input 1 increases (in this case).

c As in consumer theory for two goods, the substitution effect for an increase in the price of an input results in a substitution away from that input and in favour of the lower-cost one. In consumer theory, the compensated demand curve is analogous to the conditional demand in producer theory in that both measure only the substitution effect. However, such comparisons of the ordinary consumer demand and a firm's unconditional demand for an input *cannot* be made. To understand this, recall that the consumer's problem is to maximize utility subject to income. This is analogous to only the first stage of the firm's problem: output maximization subject to costs. To find a firm's input demand, a second stage must be solved. In the second stage, the firm chooses the cost-output combination that maximizes profits. That is, along an ordinary demand, the consumer's money income is *constant*; along a firm's demand for an input, total costs vary.

41 a The equilibrium wage rate and number of hours worked are found by equating the supply with demand.

$$800w = 24\,000 - 1\,600w$$

so

$$w = \$10, \quad z_1 = 800 \times 10 = 8\,000$$

b The government pays $(40 - w_1)/3$, where w_1 is the wage paid by the employer. Hence, workers receive $w_2 = w_1 + (40 - w_1)/3 = 40/3 + 2w_1/3$. Then, substituting w_1 (the wage paid by the employer) into the demand curve for labour and w_2 (the wage received by workers) into the supply curve for labour and equating the new demand and supply curves gives

$$800\left(\frac{40}{3} + \frac{2w_1}{3}\right) = 24\,000 - 1\,600w_1$$

Thus, $w_1 = \$6.25$/hour and $w_2 = 40/3 + 2 \times 6.25/3 = \$17.50$. Substituting w_2 into the labour supply gives

$$z_1 = 800 \times 17.50 = 14\,000$$

c When the individual receives a wage of \$6.25 per hour, his income line is given by *AB* in Figure A11.8. The utility-maximizing bundle chosen by the individual is point *E*. Under the government program, his wage increases to \$17.50/hour, and the budget line pivots to *CB*; so the individual chooses point *F*. As indicated, not all individuals will work more under the government program. The reason is that the income effect from the wage increase may outweigh the substitution effect.

42 a The competitive equilibrium wage rate and number of hours worked are found by equating supply and demand:

$$200 + 400w = 1\,200 - 600w$$
$$1\,000w = 1\,000$$
$$w^* = 1$$

and so

$$z^* = 600$$

FIGURE A11.8

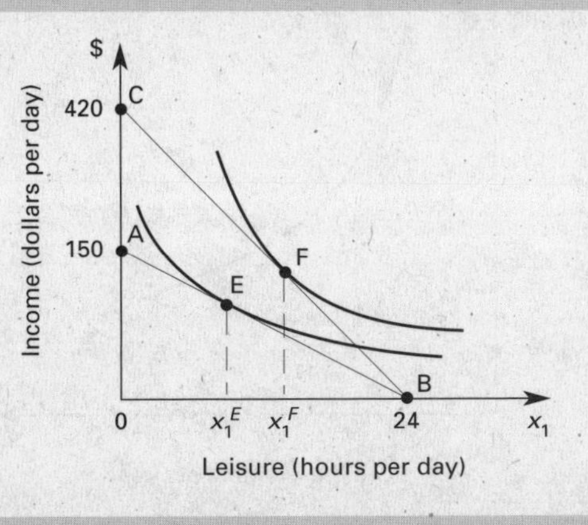

b The monopolist sets the *MRP* of labour equal to the wage rate. The marginal revenue is $MR = 90 - 4y$, and the marginal product is 0.1; hence, $MRP = (90 - 4y)(0.1) = 9 - 0.4y$. Setting $MRP = 1$ (since $w = 1$ from problem **a**) gives $9 - 0.4y = 1$. This implies

$$y = 20, \quad p = 90 - 40 = 50, \quad z_d = 200$$

43 a The profit-maximizing z and w for the monopsonist (the firm is a monopsonist because it faces an upward-sloping supply curve of labour) are found by equating demand and the *MFC*. Rewriting the supply curve gives

$$w = 3 + \frac{z}{2} \quad \text{and } MFC(z) = 3 + z$$

Rewriting the demand curve gives

$$w = 18 - 2z$$

Equating $MFC(z)$ and the labour demand gives

$$3 + z = 18 - 2z$$

so

$$z = 5, \quad w = 3 + \frac{5}{2} = 5.5$$

b (1) If the minimum hourly wage is set at 6, then the $MFC(z)$ of the monopsonist equals 6 up to the supply curve; then at $z = 6$, the $MFC(z) = 3 + z$ as before. Setting the demand equal to the new $MFC(z)$ gives $18 - 2z = 6$; so $z = 6$.
(2) Substitute $w = 6$ into the labour supply: $z = -6 + (2 \times 6) = 6$ individuals would like to work at a wage of \$6, and exactly 6 are hired.

c If the government pays the firm \$3 for every unit of labour hired, then the demand for labour will shift upward. That is, the wage the firms are willing to pay at every quantity of labour is \$3 higher, or

$$w = 18 - 2z + 3 = 21 - 2z$$

Equating the new demand to $MFC(z)$ gives

$$21 - 2z = 3 + z$$

so

$$z = 6, \quad w = 3 + \frac{z}{2} = 6$$

That is, the same solution is reached as in **b**, but the government pays \$3(6) = \$18. The policies in **b** and **c** are illustrated in Figure A11.9. Initial demand is $D(z)$; demand with subsidy is $D'(z)$.

44 a Let w be the daily wage rate for an individual. The income line without the tax is given by DE in Figure A11.9. The effect of the 20% tax is to pivot the income line inward. The maximum income that can be earned is $0.8 \times 365w = 292w$.

b If leisure is a normal good, the tax will not necessarily result in a decline in work time, as

FIGURE A11.9

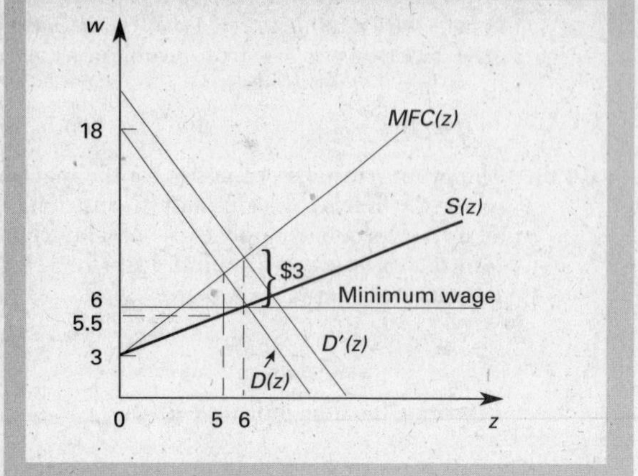

FIGURE A11.10

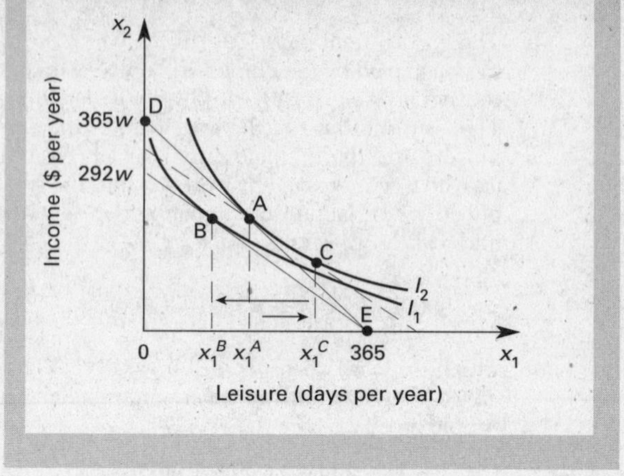

shown in Figure A11.10. The tax lowers the effective wage, resulting in an increase in leisure because of the substitution effect from x_1^A to x_1^C. The decline in real income decreases leisure from x_1^C to x_1^B. If the income effect outweighs the substitution effect, less leisure will be taken.

45 a Since Brenda earns $250 per month, her *maximum* annual income is $3 000. She also receives $1 000 per year from her lottery earnings, so her yearly budget line is *ABC* in Figure A11.11. Point *D* indicates her utility-maximizing bundle. The present value of her stream of income from the lottery is $1 000/0.08 = $12 500.

b If her wage rises to $350 per month, the slope of the budget line increases to $350 (from $250). Maximum income from teaching is now $350 × 12 = $4 200. The new utility-maximizing point is given by *E* in Figure A11.12a.

c If her lottery winnings increase by $600, the income line shifts upward, but the slope of the income line stays the same. The new utility-maximizing point is given by *F* in Figure A11.12b.

d If Brenda is indifferent between the two income increases, as shown in Figure A11.12c, she will choose to work more when the opportunity cost of leisure is higher: that is, when the wage is higher.

46 In principle, capital inputs should be purchased to the point where the present value of their marginal revenue product equals the present value of their costs. However, in many cases, capital inputs are "lumpy" and hence this formula cannot be strictly applied. The point of this result, however, is to show the importance of calculating the present value of the stream of benefits and costs arising from the investment. As long as the net benefit is at least zero, the capital input should be purchased. Now, turning to Gaston's case. Here he has two options (in both options the relevant discount rate is 5%). Option 1 entails keeping the old truck, which yields a net benefit of $500 per year for the next five years ($2 165), then it will cost $21 000 to replace the truck (in PV terms this is $16 454) and it will have a salvage value of $5 000 (in PV terms, $5 000 after 10 years is $3 070). The new truck over the five year period from $t = 6$ to $t = 10$ will generate an annual net return of $3 500 which, in PV terms, is worth $11 873 today. In total, therefore, ten years using option 1 yields a total benefit of $14 038 and a total cost of $13 384. Thus, this option certainly provides a net gain to Gaston. But does it maximize his profits? To answer this question, we need to look at option 2 which entails buying a new truck now ($20 000) which will generate net benefits of $3 500 per year for ten years ($27 026). Clearly, option 2 is preferable.

FIGURE A11.11

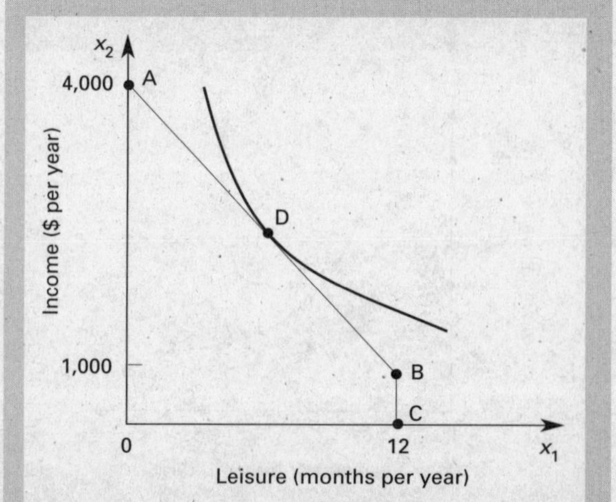

FIGURE A11.12

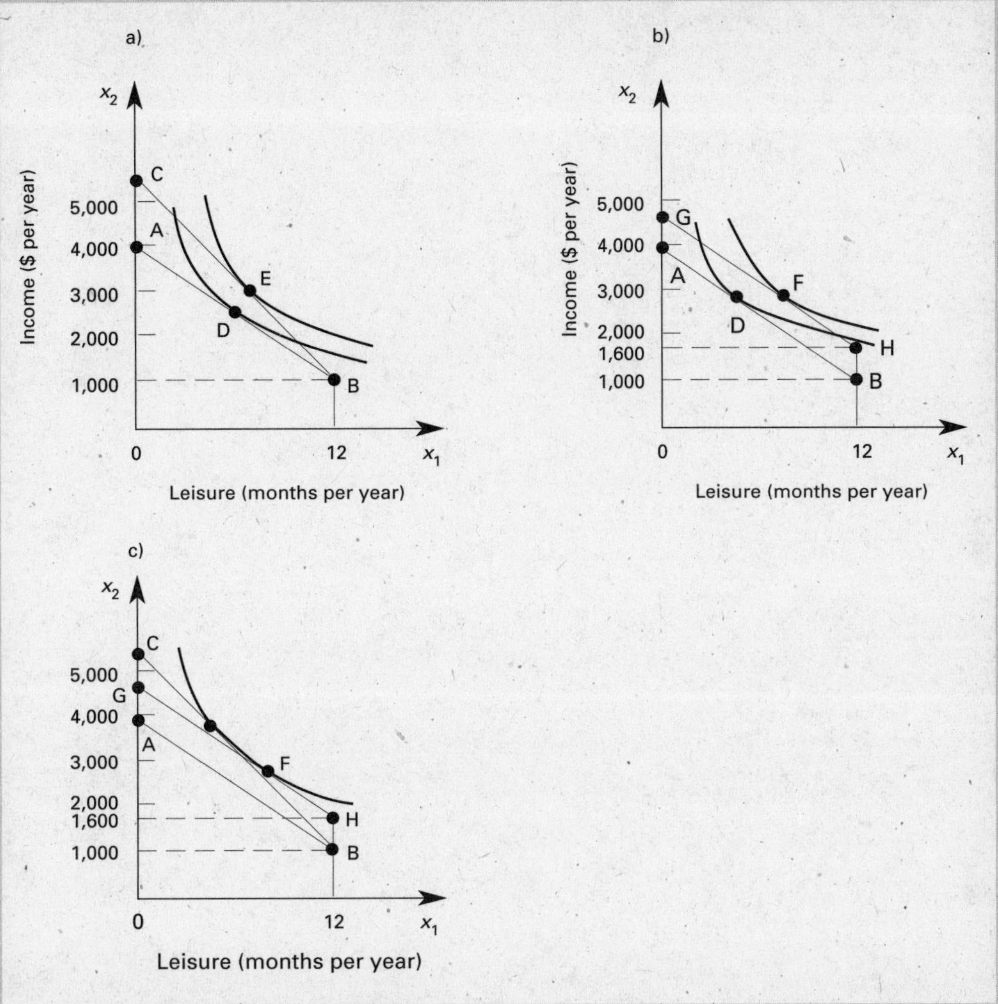

CHAPTER 12

The Distribution of Income

Chapter Summary

Two important questions should be asked about all economic problems. Is the allocation of resources toward competing ends efficient? Is the distribution of the product "just"? We have devoted considerable space to the discussion of efficiency, and, thanks to Pareto, we have reached some important and sometimes surprising conclusions about the ability of markets to allocate resources efficiently. Economists have less expertise on the issue of distribution. Nevertheless, the economist should not stop at the conclusion that markets are efficient without evaluating the distribution of output among individuals.

Lorenz Curve

A common way of measuring income distribution in a population uses the **Lorenz curve** which ranks individuals by income and plots their cumulative number with the cumulative percentage of income received. If, for instance, the distribution is completely equal, then the first 20% of individuals would receive 20% of income, the next 20% of individuals would receive 20% of income, and so on. The curve in this case would be a straight line at a 45-degree angle. The **Gini coefficient** measures income inequality by taking the area between the 45-degree line and the Lorenz curve and dividing it by the area under the Lorenz curve. Complete equality would have a value of zero, while total inequality (in the sense that one individual has all income) would have a value of one.

Productivity Principle

Two philosophical principles of **distributive justice** have been put forth: the **productivity principle** and the **redistributionist principle**. The productivity principle simply suggests that individuals should receive the part of the pie that they produced. When markets are perfectly competitive, each individual is paid her value of the marginal product, and the entire product is exhausted by this distribution. In a sense, the productivity principle justifies the distributional outcome of the competitive market model which satisfies the **product-exhaustion criterion**.

Then why is this principle not widely accepted by economists? If the supply of workers increases, the equilibrium wage as well as the total wage paid to workers falls, when the demand is inelastic. Although labour works as hard, its reward falls under this rule. This outcome is not particularly just in that it simply reflects the fact that *markets reward scarcity*. Rather than being rewarded for the fruits of our labour, the market rewards us according to the scarcity of our talents relative to society's **endowment** of resources.

Redistributionist Principle

The redistributionist principle says that **equity** is a critical component of justice. Under the philosopher John Rawls' **difference principle**, inequality is acceptable only if the plight of the worse-off member of society is improved from some redistribution. Rawls and others have argued that an ethical standard of justice must be impersonal, and this can be achieved by establishing the fiction of an **original position**. In this position, each individual knows all the possible conditions he *can* have in society but does not know the actual position he *will* have. If all individuals are symmetric initially and are risk-averse, then they will prefer an insurance contract that leads to a more equal distribution of income.

If a redistributionist position is accepted as the normative objective in society, economists can analyze whether or not a particular policy will achieve this objective. Three such policies are considered: minimum wage, income maintenance programs, and income and rent taxes.

Minimum Wage

The effectiveness of **minimum-wage legislation** in redistributing income to low-wage earners depends on the structure of the labour market. For a perfectly competitive labour market, the minimum wage will benefit individuals who can hold on to their jobs but will result in unemployment and underemployment, and possibly a lower total income to other workers. However, a moderate minimum wage makes a monopsonist's *MFC* of hiring labour constant, encouraging the monopsonist to hire more workers at the higher minimum wage. If the minimum wage is set too high, the monopsonist may choose to hire less labour. Analysis of the minimum wage gives insight into the effects of unions in redistributing income to workers through wage floors.

A **wage floor** can be analyzed in a two-sector model: a unionized and a nonunionized sector. Unlike a competitive equilibrium, a wage floor in the unionized sector will result in **underemployment** in the sense that labour is not allocated to its most productive use: Too few workers in the unionized sector and too many in the nonunionized sector will be hired compared with the efficient allocation. Moreover, workers will join the union until the expected union wage (the union wage times the proportion of time each member works) equals the wage in the nonunionized sector. In equilibrium, there will be unemployment: More union members will be competing for the limited number of jobs in the unionized sector than will be hired.

Income Maintenance

A **utility-maintenance mechanism** that would provide an unconditional income transfer that leaves all individuals at some minimum standard of living is impossible to implement because utility is not cardinal. If it were possible to implement, it would result in an **efficient transfer mechanism** against which other transfer schemes can be compared. Two other schemes which are less efficient but more practical are the

topping-up mechanism and the **negative income tax**. The first scheme offers a subsidy to an individual whose income falls below some targeted level. This scheme is thus part of an **income-maintenance program**. In practice, welfare programs may **transfer income**, which is conditional on the individual's income. If the individual's income exceeds some target income level, no subsidy is received; otherwise, the individual receives the target income less the income earned. Individuals who would work in the absence of this program may choose not to (or choose not to report the income) and receive the target income. To avoid this disincentive problem, the negative income tax, which is based on an unconditional income transfer and a proportional tax rate, has been proposed. Because everyone receives the subsidy, the work disincentives *may be* less severe and the government's cost *may be* reduced.

For some policies, redistribution is consistent with efficiency (for example, minimum wage in monopsonistic labour markets), whereas many redistribution policies create inefficiency. Although economists do not have the expertise to determine which redistributional principle "should" be followed, they can identify policies that will achieve the desired normative objective and point out possible conflicts between efficiency and equity.

KEY WORDS

Difference principle
Distributive justice
Efficient transfer mechanism
Equity
Gini coefficient
Income-maintenance program
Lorenz curve
Minimum-wage legislation
Negative income tax
Original position
Product-exhaustion criterion
Productivity principle
Redistributionist principle
Topping-up mechanism
Transfer income
Underemployment
Utility-maintenance mechanism
Wage floor

CASE STUDY: THE ECONOMICS OF WORKFARE

The problem of how to provide a social safety net for people unable to make ends meet is complicated. One complication arises from the fact that welfare payments change the incentive for individuals to seek paid employment. Various programs have attempted to overcome this problem by introducing negative income tax schemes. Another way to deal with this issue is through so-called workfare — where certain recipients of welfare payments are compelled to "work" in order to be eligible for them.

In 1996, the Progressive Conservative government of Mike Harris introduced a workfare program in Ontario, following the example of Alberta, Quebec and New Brunswick. Accordingly, all "able-bodied" social assistance recipients without dependents have to work some 17 hours a week in order to be eligible for benefits. At the basic welfare rate of $520 per month, this is tantamount to paying people about $7.06 per hour (slightly above the minimum wage of $6.85 per hour). People without basic literacy and job-search skills are compelled to attend training programs.

Opponents of this scheme have offered several reasons why workfare doesn't work. Unions argue, for instance, that workfare takes jobs away from the regular labour force. Community activists point to the high costs associated with operating the program, arguing that this money could be better spent helping the poor in our communities. Some advocates, by contrast, argue that workfare helps ensure that those who can work do work. In addition, they argue that providing welfare recipients with jobs allows them to gain skills which will enhance their chances of success in the regular labour market.

A Welfare payments effectively impose a wage floor on the labour market. Any wage rate less than these payments will not be accepted. How would such a scheme affect a competitive labour market? What happens when a workfare program is introduced?

B Suppose that labour supply is monopsonistic; would this change your analysis in part **a**?

C Critically discuss the social benefits and costs associated with a workfare program. Can you think of another scheme that might yield the same benefits but has fewer drawbacks?

EXERCISES

Multiple-Choice

Choose the correct answer to each question. There is only one correct answer to each question.

Figure 12.1 applies to question **1** and **2**.

1 A monopsonist in the labour market illustrated by Figure 12.1 will do which of the following?
- **a** Set wage w_3 and hire z' units of labour.
- **b** Set wage w_1 and hire z' units of labour.
- **c** Set wage w_2 and hire z'' units of labour.
- **d** Use an efficient mix of labour and other inputs in production.
- **e** None of the above.

2 If a minimum wage of $\bar{w}$ is set between w_2 and w_3 in Figure 12.1, then
- **a** The monopsonist will hire fewer than z' workers.
- **b** The monopsonist will use an efficient mix of labour and other inputs in production.
- **c** The monopsonist will hire between z' and z'' workers.
- **d** There will be no excess supply of labour at the wage set by the monopsonist.
- **e** None of the above.

FIGURE 12.1

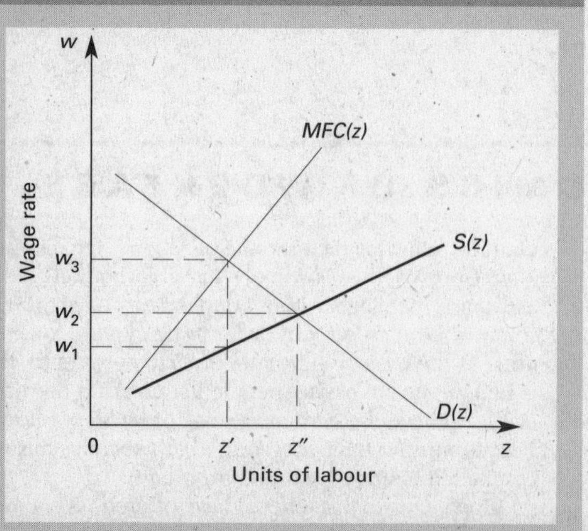

3 When a union of formerly competitive workers forces a monopsonist to push up the wage, the number of workers employed will
- **a** Rise.
- **b** Remain unchanged.
- **c** Fall.
- **d** May do any of the above, depending on the extent to which the wage is raised above the monopsonistic level.

4 The productivity principle asserts that
- **a** Economic equity is served best when all people receive goods in accordance with their needs.
- **b** Economic equity is served best when all people receive goods in equal amounts.
- **c** Economic equity is served best when all people receive goods in accordance with hours worked.
- **d** Economic equity is served best when all people receive goods in accordance with their marginal product.
- **e** None of the above.

5 The productivity principle implies that
- **a** The total product is equal to the sum of the payments to all inputs.
- **b** Inputs are paid according to the product they produce.
- **c** If all markets are competitive, then the allocation of resources is both efficient and equitable.

d All the above.
e Only **a** and **b**.

To answer problem **6** refer to Figure 12.2, which shows two individuals' income lines and indifference curves. The income line in the absence of any government programs is *AB;* under a negative income tax, the income line is *BCD.*

6 Under the negative income tax (NIT),
a The government will receive positive tax revenues of EF from the individual in Figure 12.2a.
b The government will pay a net subsidy of *BC* to the individual in Figure 12.2b.
c The government will receive positive tax revenues of *GH* from an individual in Figure 12.2b.
d Both **a** and **c**.
e None of the above.

7 Consider the following sets of institutions, A, B, and C, and the utilities of three individuals under each institution.

Institution	Utility of 1	Utility of 2	Utility of 3
A	70	40	10
B	40	40	40
C	60	40	20

Suppose that none of the individuals knows which person she will be in the economy, and that each individual has a 1/3 chance of having a particular identity. Then
a According to Rawls' difference principle, the three institutions are equally preferred since the sum of the surplus is the same under all three institutions.
b If the individuals are risk-neutral, then they will be indifferent among all institutions.
c If the individuals are very risk-averse, then they will prefer institution **B**.
d Only **b** and **c**.
e None of the above.

True-False

8 In a monopsonistic labour market, the imposition of a minimum-wage rate above the unconstrained monopsony wage rate must produce an excess of labour supplied over labour demanded at the minimum-wage level.
9 If all markets are perfectly competitive, then the allocation of resources will satisfy the productivity principle.
10 If the market for economists is competitive and the demand for economists is inelastic, then an increase in the supply of economists will increase the collective reward paid to all economists.
11 If an economy adheres to "marginal productivity ethics," then the market reward to an individual will always increase as the amount of effort by the individual increases.
12 In a competitive market, resources are allocated to those uses in which the value of the marginal product is the greatest.
13 The redistributionist principle argues that inequality is justified only if it makes everyone better off.
14 The less market power on the supply side of the labour market, the more efficient the allocation of resources will be under a monopsony.

FIGURE 12.2

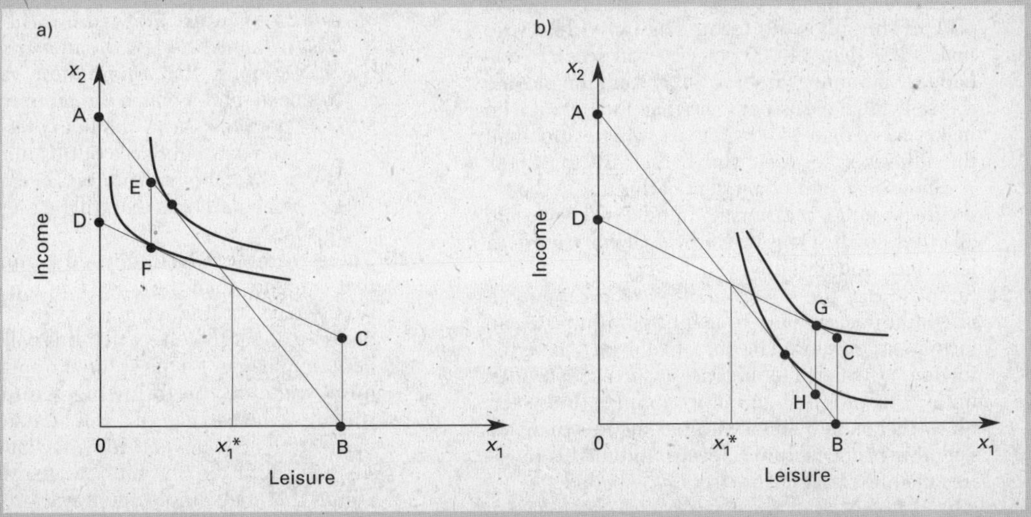

15 An unconditional income transfer requires less money to raise an individual's utility to some target level than would an income transfer conditional on the recipient's income.

16 A redistributionist would prefer a progressive tax over an unconditional tax as a mechanism for collecting government returns.

Short Problems

17 Show how the monopsony model might predict increased employment from the imposition of a minimum-wage law.

18 Graphically show the maximum loss in surplus that the imposition of a minimum wage might cause in a perfectly competitive economy with homogeneous labour and a given labour-demand curve. Explain what the loss in surplus depends upon.

19 Some economists argue that the productivity principle is a justification for the distribution of income that results from a market (or capitalistic) economy but does not provide an ethical principle of justice. Discuss their argument.

20 Two people have the winning lottery number for a \$500 000 jackpot. The winner of the jackpot will be determined by the flip of a coin. However, the two individuals can decide before the coin is flipped what proportion of the \$500 000 the winner of the coin flip should receive. If the two individuals are risk-averse, what proportion of the jackpot will they decide to give to the winner of the coin toss?

21 Suppose that an individual consumes two commodities, *leisure* and *all other goods*, and receives income only from working at a wage rate of \$100 per week. Assume that the individual chooses to consume 30 weeks of leisure and \$2 200 of all other goods.

Now suppose that the government proposes an NIT of the following form. The individual who makes less than \$4 000 per year will *receive* one-half the difference between \$4 000 and the income the individual earns per year. The individual who makes more than \$4 000 per year will *pay* one-half the difference between what he makes and \$4 000.

Show on a graph the effect of this tax on the individual's utility-maximizing bundle of leisure and all other goods. Does the individual work more or less as a result of the NIT?

22 Suppose that the government gives everyone an unconditional income transfer S and imposes an income tax on earned income. Define M^* to be the income at which the income–leisure constraints, under this program and in its absence, intersect. Show that an individual with income less than M^* will always choose more leisure under this negative income tax, if leisure is a normal good.

Long Problems

23 Consider a profit-maximizing firm that is a monopolist in the market for its product Y and a competitor in the market for a particular type of labour Z. The firm's only variable input is Z, and the price of Z is w^*.

a Using a diagram, explain this firm's profit-maximizing choice of output in the market for Y; on another diagram, explain its profit-maximizing choice in the market for Z.

b Suppose that a minimum-wage law is introduced and the minimum wage is higher than the rate the firm had been paying. Using both of your diagrams, analyze the consequences of this minimum-wage law in the labour market and in the Y market.

c Suppose that this particular labour is demanded by both the monopolist and by firms in a competitive market. Furthermore, suppose that the minimum wage is imposed only in the monopoly sector. Using diagrams, show how this minimum wage can result in unemployment in the monopoly sector under the assumptions of inelastic labour supply and perfectly mobile labour.

***24** Consider the market for a particular labour service. Assume that the labour market is monopsonistic. The derived demand curve for labour by the monopsony is

$$z_d = 10 - \frac{1}{2}w$$

The supply curve of labour is

$$z_s = w + 4$$

where w is the wage rate per hour, z_s is the hundreds of hours of labour supplied per day, and z_d is the hundreds of hours of labour demanded per day.

a Show that the monopsonist will set a wage equal to \$2 per hour. Determine the number of labour-hours hired by the monopsonist.

b Now suppose that a minimum-wage law is introduced, under which the minimum-wage rate is \$4 per hour. With the help of a diagram, analyze the consequences of this minimum-wage law in this labour market. Calculate the number of labour hours that will be employed under this law.

25 The government has imposed a minimum wage that is higher than the wage that a particular university pays its student employees. Two students disagree about the effect that this will have on student employment. One student opposes the minimum wage on the following grounds: Though students who can get jobs will be better off, many more students will want to work than the university will pay at the minimum wage. Moreover, she argues that total employment will probably fall.

a Use a diagram to explain the economic reasoning behind this argument. Assume, for the moment, that the first student is correct.

b The other student argues that the university keeps wages at low levels because it knows that if it pays one student more, it will have to pay all students more. The minimum wage will limit the university's power to control wages. This means that the university will hire more labour at a higher wage. Use diagrams and economic theory to explain this argument, now assuming that the second student is correct.

*26 The labour supply function for workers in a union is given by $w = 5 + 3z_s$, and the demand for its services are given by $w = 40 - 2z_d$. What wage will the union set if

a It tries to maximize the total income of its workers.

b It maximizes the surplus of workers in excess of their opportunity costs of working.

27 A monopsonist employs some domestic workers and some foreign workers. The supply curves are such that it is profitable to pay a lower wage rate for foreign labour than for domestic labour.

a Use diagrams to explain the monopsonist's profit-maximizing choice.

b Now the government imposes a quota on employment of foreign workers, which does not allow the monopsonist to employ as many foreign workers as before. With the aid of your diagrams, analyze the effects of this policy.

ANSWERS TO CHAPTER 12

Case Study

A If the welfare payment is less than the competitive wage rate, then it may not have any impact. Notice, however, that this statement abstracts from reality. In fact, some individuals may accept a lower payment in order to stay at home and not incur work-related expenses and time costs. When workfare is introduced, it makes staying at home less desirable for those people who could work but prefer not to because of work-related costs. Hence, more people might find working a desirable alternative. Workfare effectively lowers the welfare payment. If the welfare payment is greater than the competitive wage then it would result in fewer than the optimal number of workers in the market. Workfare, in this case, may help to push some of them back into the workforce. That is, it may reduce the distortion already created by the welfare system.

B In a monopsonistic market, the wage rate is higher than it would be in a competitive market. Welfare payments will have less of an impact on this market because they are almost always likely to be below the going wage rate. Indeed, because the monopsonist sets the wage rate too high relative to the competitive market, welfare payments would help those people who are priced out of the workforce. Workfare in such a case would impose an additional cost on those individuals who cannot find a job because of the monopsonistic nature of the labour market.

C One of the major objections to a workfare program stems from the fact that it forces the less fortunate in society to undergo yet a further humiliation by working for welfare payments. It is also argued that such workers displace the low-paid workers in the market, creating further unemployment. Basically, workfare is predicated on the idea that welfare recipients are people who are choosing not to work. Others view unemployment as an involuntary state. People find themselves unemployed for a number of reasons, and a kind society would provide for these unfortunates. It is also very costly to operate a workfare program. Jobs have to be found, people have to be matched to jobs, and so on. Why not, it is argued, spend the money on trying to help the poor in the community or to try to examine what is causing unemployment. A thorough treatment of this difficult question certainly cannot be provided here. As you work through the problems of this and other chapters, you should be thinking about how the "real world" stacks up against our models and how our models can inform policy makers faced with the difficult task of dealing with problems like poverty and our social responsibility to help those in need. Questions of income distribution, although very difficult, present us with an array of rich challenges.

Multiple-Choice

1 b 2 c 3 d 4 d
5 d 6 a 7 d

True-False

8 F 9 T 10 F 11 F 12 T
13 F 14 F 15 T 16 T

Short Problems

17 The demand curve for labour and the supply curve for labour faced by a monopsonist are shown in Figure A12.1. The monopsonist equates the marginal factor cost to the demand curve for labour and sets a wage rate equal to w^*. If the wage is increased to $\bar{w}$ through minimum-wage legislation, the marginal factor cost curve will become *ABCE*. The monopsonist sets the demand equal to the new *MFC* and hires $\bar{z} > z^*$ units of labour.

18 In the absence of a minimum wage, the equilibrium wage and employment would be w^* and z^*, as in Figure A12.2. If a minimum wage is set at $\bar{w}$, then $\bar{z}_d$ units of labour will be hired. Since the marginal value of another worker, $\bar{w}$, exceeds the opportunity cost of the marginal worker, there is a loss in surplus, given by the shaded area. The loss can vary, depending on the slope of the supply and demand curves.

19 The productivity principle states that income should be distributed to individuals according to the product produced by the individual. Since individuals are paid the value of their marginal products in a competitive market, income is distributed precisely in this manner. However, this method of distribution can lead to economic inequalities that may be ethically unacceptable. For example, this method awards scarcity: The less there is of a factor, the greater is its reward, even if that factor is not putting forth more effort in the production of goods and services in the economy.

20 One-half. Each individual would rather give up one-half of the winnings rather than take the chance of getting zero.

21 If leisure is a normal good (or not highly inferior), the individual will work fewer hours under the NIT, as in Figure A12.3. Under the NIT, the individual's income line is given by *CD*. The income line in the absence of the NIT is *AB*. The individual chooses bundle *E* in the absence of the NIT and bundle *F* under the NIT. In the figure, the NIT increases leisure as a result of both a substitution effect — the opportunity cost of leisure has fallen — and an income effect.

22 Figure A12.4 shows this negative income tax. The government policy of a subsidy-cum-income tax transfer shifts the budget line *AB* upward and decreases the slope, so the final income line faced by the individual is CB′. If the individual chose point *D* before the imposition of this tax — that is, if his income was below M^* — then he will choose a point such as *E* with more leisure. This can be seen by identifying the substitution and income effects of this program. The substitution effect increases leisure from x_1^D to x_1' and, because leisure is a normal good, the income effect increases it to x_1^E.

FIGURE A12.1

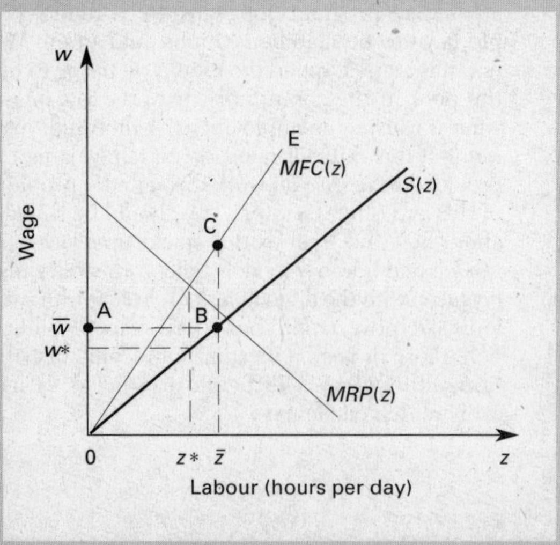

FIGURE A12.2

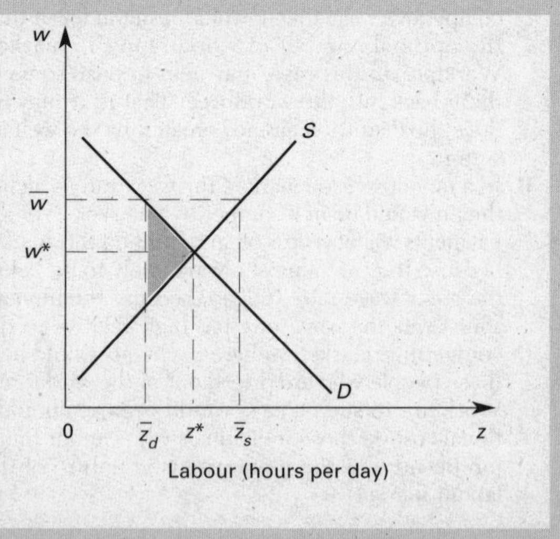

FIGURE A12.3

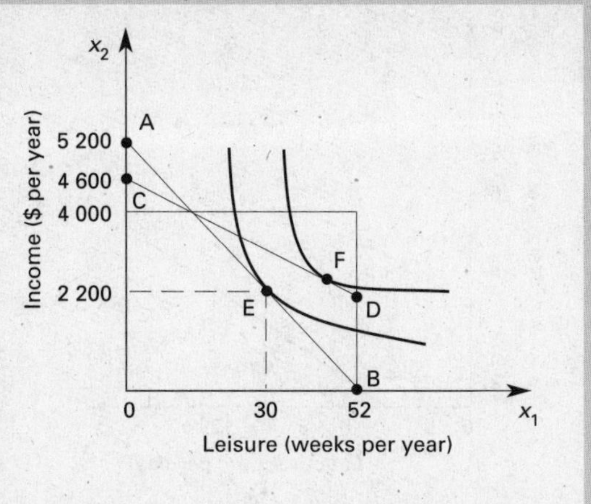

FIGURE A12.4

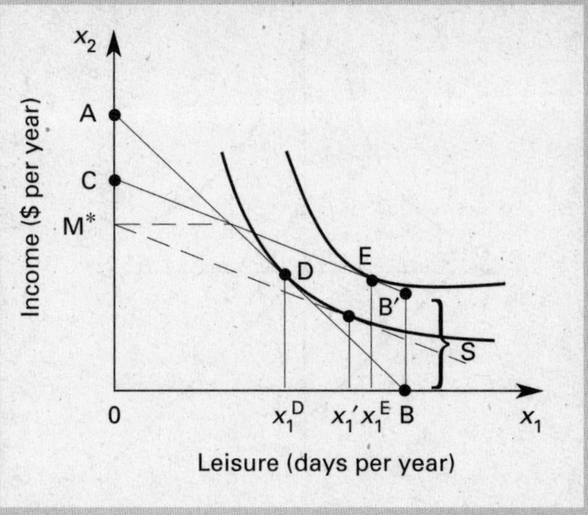

Long Problems

23 a The product market is shown in Figure A12.5a, and the firm's profit-maximizing input choice is shown in Figure A12.5b. In the output market, the firm equates $MC(y)$ with $MR(y)$ and produces y^*. In the input market, the profit-maximizing labour choice z^* satisfies $MRP(z) = w^*$. Of course, z^* is that amount of labour required to produce y^*.

b Under the minimum wage, the firm faces a per-unit labour cost of $\overline{w}$. As indicated in Figure A12.5b, the *MRP* of labour equals $\overline{w}$ at $\bar{z}$. The increase in labour costs shifts the marginal cost curve upward to $MC'(y)$. Marginal cost equals marginal revenue at $\bar{y}$ units of output.

c Individuals will allocate themselves to the two sectors until the wage rate earned in the competitive sector w_c equals the *expected* wage in the monopoly sector; that is, $w_c = \overline{w}\bar{z}/z_m$, where $\bar{z}$ is the number of individuals hired in the monopoly sector at $\overline{w}$ and z_m is the total number of individuals looking for work in that sector. In Figure A12.6, quadrant I shows that labour de-

FIGURE A12.5

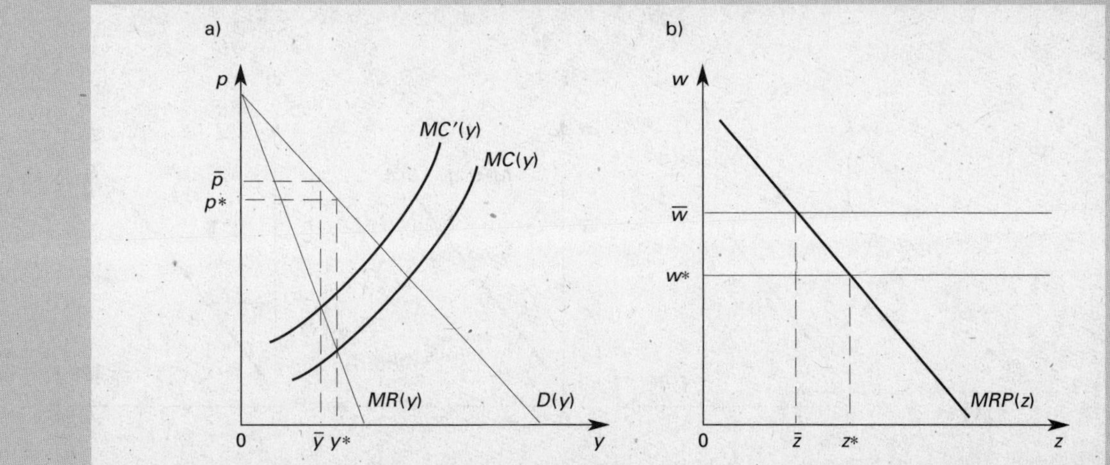

FIGURE A12.6

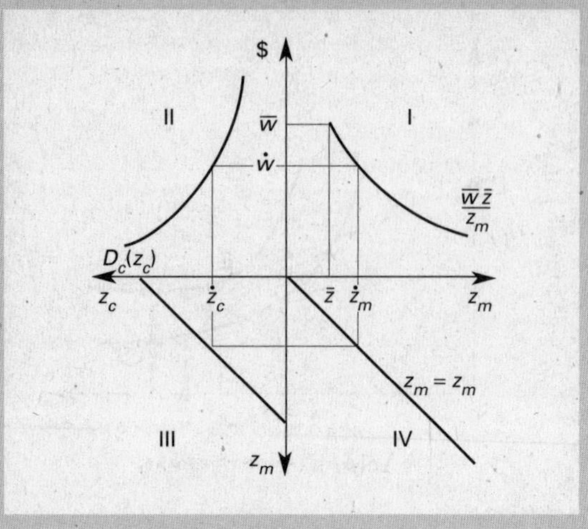

FIGURE A12.7

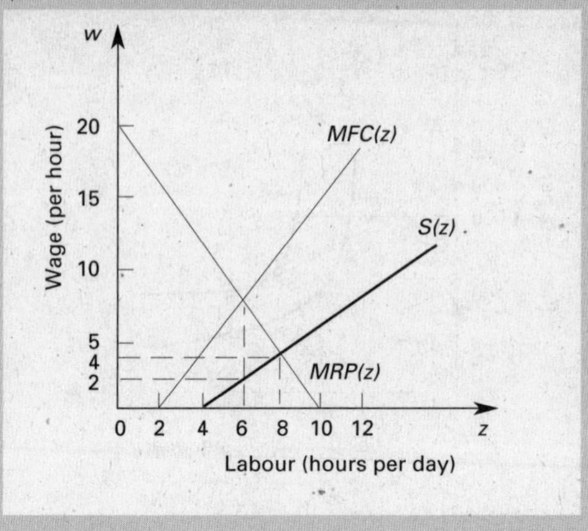

mand of the monopolist as a function of the *expected* wage; in quadrant II is the *aggregate* labour demand of the competitive firms; quadrant III gives the labour supply curve constraint; and quadrant IV projects z_m onto the first quadrant. In equilibrium $\dot{z}_c$ individuals are hired in the competitive market at a wage $\dot{w}$; $\bar{z}$ individuals are hired in the monopoly sector at $\overline{w}$; and $\dot{z}_m - \bar{z}$ unemployed individuals are in the monopoly sector.

***24 a** The monopsonist sets the $MFC(z)$ equal to the MRP of labour. Rewrite the demand and supply curves for z as follows:

$$w_d = 20 - 2z \quad \text{and} \quad w_s = z - 4$$

The marginal factor cost is $MFC(z) = 2z - 4$.

Equating $MFC(z) = MRP(z)$ gives

$$20 - 2z = 2z - 4 \qquad \text{and} \qquad w = 6 - 4 = 2$$
$$z = 6$$

b Given a wage rate of \$4 per hour, the monopsonist will set the $MRP(z)$ equal to \$4 and hire $20 - 2z = 4$, or $z = 8$ workers. The equilibrium wage and employment before and after the imposition of the minimum wage are shown in Figure A12.7. Note that \$4 is conveniently set at the competitive equilibrium wage rate.

25 a The first student thinks either the labour market is competitive, as in Figure A12.8a, or the university is a monopsonist and the minimum wage is considerably higher than the monop-

FIGURE A12.8

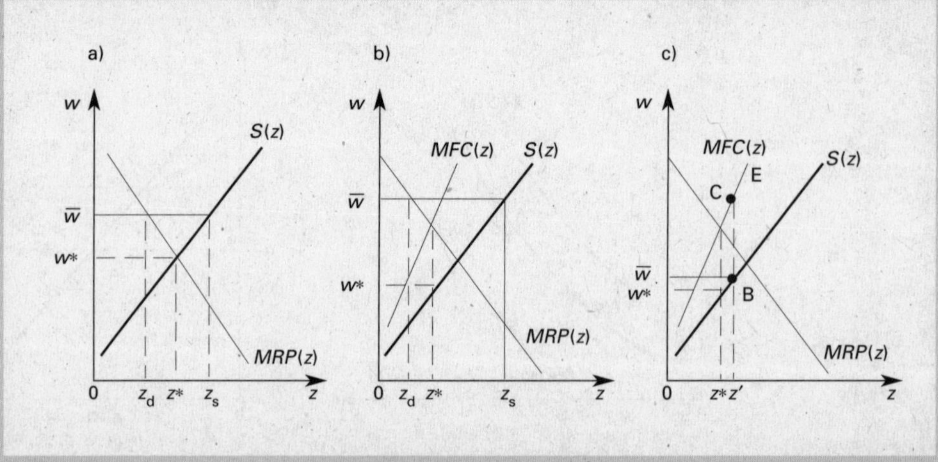

sony wage shown in Figure A12.8b. In both cases, labour employment drops from z^* to z_d, and the number of students willing to work at the new wage is z_s.

b This student thinks that the university is a monopsony. Given the current monopsony wage at w^*, the minimum wage at $\overline{w}$ induces the employer to hire z' units of labour, where $z' > z^*$. The marginal factor cost changes from $MFC(z)$ to $\overline{w}$BCE because of the minimum wage, as shown in Figure A12.8c.

***26 a** Workers are "suppliers" or "producers" of labour services, so they maximize their income by maximizing revenues from sales of their labour services. Revenues are maximized where $MR = 0$. The marginal revenue of the demand for labour is $MR = 40 - 4z$; hence, $40 - 4z = 0$ or $z = 10$ and $w = 40 - 2z = 20$ maximizes income.

b To maximize the "profit" from selling labour, the MR of the demand is set equal to the opportunity cost of labour; that is, $40 - 4z = 5 + 3z$. Thus, $z = 5$ and $w = 40 - 2(5) = 30$. Note that the wage is determined from the demand curve.

27 a The respective supply curves of domestic and foreign workers are illustrated in Figure A12.9a and b. The marginal factor costs mfc_d and mfc_f are horizontally summed to give $MFC(z)$ in Figure A12.9c. $MFC(z)$ is set equal to $MRP(z)$. This value of the marginal worker, MRP^*, is set equal to the marginal factor costs in the domestic and foreign labour markets. Thus, z_d^* domestic workers and z_f^* foreign workers are hired at respective wages of w_d^* and w_f^*.

b If a quota is employed on foreign workers, as shown by $\bar{z}_f$ in Figure A12.9b, then the summation of the MFC curves, $MFC'(z)$, has a steeper slope beyond $\bar{z}_f$ foreign workers. Now, $MRP(z) = MFC'(z)$ at MRP', fewer foreign workers are hired ($\bar{z}_f$) at a lower wage $\overline{w}_f$, and more domestic workers are hired ($\bar{z}_d$) at a higher wage $\overline{w}_d$.

FIGURE A12.12

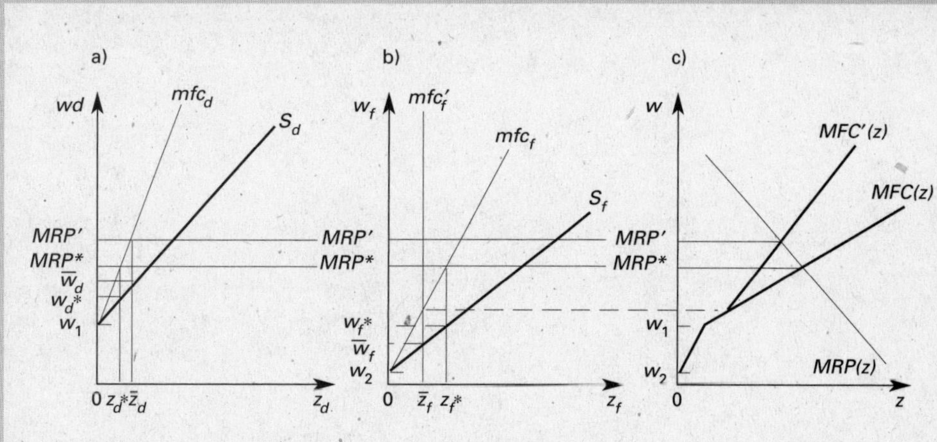

CHAPTER 13

Competitive General Equilibrium

Chapter Summary

General Equilibrium

The efficiency of the **general equilibrium** of the economy is the focus of this chapter. Once again, we examine the extent to which the interaction of self-interested individuals leads to a **natural identity of interests**. We require that the allocation of resources in a general equilibrium be Pareto-efficient; that is, there is no reallocation that can make some people better off without making one or more persons worse off. The leading actors in this drama of the economy are individuals: the people who own the inputs and for whom the goods are made. Firms play a background role as the mechanism by which inputs are transformed into output; however, the *owners* of firms are important in our analysis because they are individuals in this economy.

An Exchange Economy

In an exchange economy, there is no production; goods are merely traded and consumed. Consider, for example, an island on which there are two goods and two consumers. An **Edgeworth box diagram** shows all the possible allocations for the inhabitants of the island. Given that each consumer has smooth and convex indifference curves and that both goods are essential, then any point at which the indifference curves are tangent to each other (that is, the marginal rate of substitution between the two goods is identical for both consumers) is a Pareto-optimal allocation. The set of such Pareto-optimal allocations forms the **contract curve**; if the allocation lies off the contract curve, consumers can agree to exchange goods in a mutually beneficial manner.

So far, we have not placed any structure on the mechanism by which resources are allocated; it may be prices as in a capitalist economy or it may be a centralized authority as in a planned economy. We have merely indicated what the final allocation must look like for the economy to be efficient. Because our focus so far has been the price system, it seems fitting to ask whether the allocation of resources under the price system will satisfy the efficiency criteria.

Given the initial allocation of goods between the two individuals and markets for both goods, these individuals will be willing to trade if their *MRS*s are not equal. For some prices announced by the Walrasian auctioneer, individuals respond by indicating their **net demand** (or **gross demand**) of and **net supply** (or **gross supply**) for the good. The level of consumption of each good is the solution to a constrained utility-maximization problem in which each individual sets $MRS = p_1/p_2$. When markets clear (that is, when demand (net or gross) equals supply (net or gross) in each market), the **competitive equilibrium allocation** is realized. **Walras' law** states that if at some p_1/p_2, demand equals supply in one market, then demand must equal supply in the second market; hence, p_1/p_2 is the competitive equilibrium price. Since all consumers face the same prices, all *MRS*s are equal; hence, there is no reallocation that would yield a Pareto improvement.

General Equilibrium with Production

Suppose that not only are there two individuals consuming two goods but also that each of these goods is produced by a fixed number of firms using two inputs and a *CRTS* technology. Given some simplifying assumptions, there are three necessary and sufficient conditions to achieve **efficiency** in the general equilibrium with production. Each condition is necessary in the sense that if *one* is not satisfied, efficiency is not achieved; they are sufficient in the sense that if *all* are satisfied, the equilibrium is a Pareto-optimal allocation.

The first condition, introduced in the exchange economy, is that there be **efficiency in consumption**. This requires that the *MRS* between the two goods must be identical for the two consumers, implying that the allocation of goods produced is Pareto-optimal for all. The second condition is **efficiency in production**; that is, the marginal rates of technical substitution between the two inputs must be identical for all firms. This condition implies not only that the bundle of goods being produced is in the **production possibility set**, but that it lies on the **production possibilities frontier**. Production and consumption are brought together in the third condition of **efficiency of product mix**; that is, the **marginal rate of transformation (*MRT*)** in the production of the two goods must equal the *MRS* in the consumption of the two goods.

Perfectly Competitive General Equilibrium with Production

Once again, let us ask whether the allocation of resources under the price system satisfies the efficiency criteria. The first condition of Pareto efficiency in consumption is satisfied in exactly the same manner as it is in an exchange economy. The competitive equilibrium is realized when all markets clear and consumers face the same prices, thus implying equality of their *MRS*s.

Next we consider production. In a perfectly competitive market, each firm minimizes its costs of production by equating its *MRTS* with the input price ratio w_1/w_2, where this price ratio clears the market. Because all firms are price-takers in a competitive market, the *MRTS*s are equal across firms; hence, the second condition of Pareto efficiency is satisfied.

Perfectly competitive firms maximize profits. This implies that firms selling products 1 and 2 set the value of the marginal product of an input equal to the price of the input. Then, for goods 1 and 2, $p_1/p_2 = MP_2/MP_1 = MRT$. Because consumers set $MRS = p_1/p_2$, this implies that $MRS = MRT$. Hence, the third condition of Pareto efficiency is satisfied: In a competitive equilibrium, the allocation of resources is Pareto-efficient.

Welfare Economics

The **first theorem of welfare economics** assures us that given the appropriate assumptions, a competitive equilibrium is efficient. That is, if all markets are competitive and there are no taxes, subsidies, or externalities, then the allocation of resources is efficient. But what happens if one (or more) of those requirements does not hold? For example, suppose that **market power** exists with a monopoly in one good and competition in the other. In this case, the third condition of Pareto efficiency ($MRS = MRT$) will not be satisfied in that consumers will want more of the monopoly good, but the monopolist won't produce it. A tax on a good will also violate the product-mix condition in that consumers will be willing to give up more of the untaxed good for the taxed good at the margin than is necessary in production.

When labour is one of the primary inputs in the model and leisure is one of the goods, the three efficiency conditions apply, and the competitive equilibrium is again efficient. However, as in the case of a sales tax or a monopoly in the goods market, an income tax or a monopsony in the labour market will create an inefficiency in the general equilibrium.

The **second theorem of welfare economics** states that for any given Pareto-optimal allocation of goods obtainable in the model, there exists a distribution of ownership of inputs such that the resulting competitive equilibrium is the Pareto-optimal allocation. Thus, to achieve equity, there must be some redistribution of the ownership of inputs. However, to achieve efficiency, all that is required is that competitive markets be used.

KEY WORDS

- Competitive equilibrium allocation
- Contract curve
- Edgeworth box diagram
- Efficiency in consumption
- Efficiency in production
- Efficiency of product mix
- First theorem of welfare economics
- General equilibrium
- Gross demand
- Gross supply
- Marginal rate of transformation
- Market power
- Natural identity of interests
- Net demand
- Net supply
- Production possibilities frontier
- Production possibilities set
- Second theorem of welfare economics
- Walras' law

CASE STUDY: THE NORTH AMERICAN FREE-TRADE AGREEMENT (NAFTA)

The United States, Canada, and Mexico are important trade partners. For example, approximately 80% of Canadian exports go to the United States, and 68% of Canadian imports come from the United States. In the past, this flow of goods and services across the border has been limited to some extent by the mutual imposition of tariffs and nontariff trade barriers. Many of these trade barriers between Canada, the United States and Mexico, have already been eliminated as a result of NAFTA, which came into effect on January 1, 1994. Proponents and opponents of the free-trade agreement are divided across industry lines; for example, the textiles and brewing industries in Canada oppose the free-trade agreement, arguing that they will not be able to compete with large American producers or cheap Mexican labour. In contrast, the minerals and lumber industries in Canada welcome the disappearance of trade barriers.

A Is the allocation of resources under trade barriers Pareto-efficient? If not, why do you think trade barriers were imposed in the first place?

B Is the allocation of resources under free trade Pareto-efficient? If so, why do you think there are so many groups against NAFTA?

EXERCISES

Multiple-Choice

Choose the correct answer to each question. There is only one correct answer to each question.

1 Firms A and B produce canoes and windsurfers. Firm A's *MRT* is one canoe for 10 windsurfers, and firm B's *MRT* is one canoe for 20 windsurfers. Which of the following is correct?
- **a** The allocation of resources is efficient.
- **b** Total output could be increased if A specialized in canoes and B in windsurfers.
- **c** Total output could be increased if A stopped producing altogether.
- **d** Firm B's actual production of windsurfers must be twice that of A.
- **e** None of the above.

2 Which of these conditions is *not* a necessary condition for Pareto efficiency in a general equilibrium?
- **a** The marginal rates of substitution between two goods must be the same for all individuals consuming those goods.
- **b** The marginal rate of transformation between two goods must be equal to the marginal rates of substitution for all individuals consuming those goods.
- **c** The marginal rates of technical substitution between inputs must be equal for all goods that use those inputs in production.
- **d** Production must take place on the production possibilities frontier.
- **e** All the above are conditions of Pareto efficiency.

3 Suppose that Yahong prefers apples to oranges considerably more than does Chin, and that Yahong and Chin face the same prices of apples and oranges. Define the *MRS* of apples for oranges as the amount of apples that an individual is willing to give up to get an additional orange. Then, at the utility-maximizing bundles of oranges and apples, which is true?
- **a** Yahong's *MRS* of apples for oranges exceeds Chin's *MRS* of apples for oranges.
- **b** Yahong will definitely consume more than her endowment of oranges.
- **c** Yahong's *MRS* of apples for oranges equals Chin's *MRS* of apples for oranges.
- **d** Both **b** and **c**.
- **e** None of the above.

Use Figure 13.1 to answer questions **4** and **5**.

4 Mary has an initial endowment of 2 apples and 8 oranges; Tom's initial endowment is 8 apples and 2 oranges. Which of the following is true?
- **a** Mary and Tom will not want to trade because they are each maximizing their utility.
- **b** If Mary traded some of her oranges for some of Tom's apples, both Mary and Tom could be better off.
- **c** If Mary traded some of her apples for some of Tom's oranges, both Mary and Tom could be better off.
- **d** Mary's *MRS* of apples for oranges equals Tom's *MRS* of apples for oranges at point *E*.
- **e** None of the above.

5 After trading takes place from the initial endowment *E*, the new allocation will be
- **a** Anywhere along curve *CC′*.
- **b** Along *SS′*.
- **c** Characterized by a lower *MRS* of apples for oranges for Mary than for Tom.

FIGURE 13.1

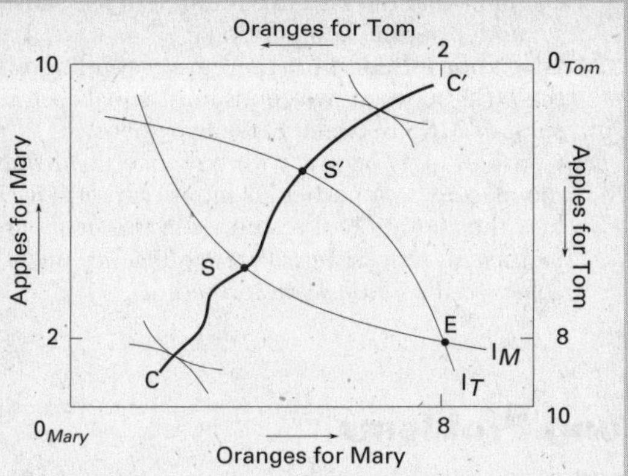

d All the above.
e Only **b** and **c**.

6 The *MRT* for goods A and B is
- **a** The ratio of the marginal products of the two inputs used in the production of *either* good A or B.
- **b** The ratio of the marginal products of an input used in the production of goods A and B.
- **c** The slope of the isoquants for goods A and B along the contract curve.
- **d** Both **b** and **c**.
- **e** None of the above.

To answer questions **7** and **8**, refer to Figure 13.2, which shows the production possibilities curve for food and clothing. The combination of the two goods being produced in the economy is given by point *E*. The distribution of food and clothing between the two individuals in the economy is described by point *C*.

7 The allocation of resources toward the production of 100 units of food and 200 units of clothing is
- **a** A Pareto-efficient mix of outputs if the slope of the production possibilities curve (*PPC*) at *E* equals the slope of the indifference curves at *C*.
- **b** Inefficient if the slope of the *PPC* exceeds the slope of the indifference curves (too much food is being produced).
- **c** Inefficient if the slope of the *PPC* is less than the slope of the indifference curves (too little food is being produced).
- **d** Pareto-efficient in production since the marginal rates of technical substitution between inputs are equal in the production of the two goods.
- **e** All the above.

8 If all markets are competitive, if there are no distortions, taxes, or subsidies in the system, and if point *E* is the mix of outputs produced in the general equilibrium, then which is correct?
- **a** The slope of *AB* is the ratio of the price of clothing to the price of food.
- **b** The ratio of the price of food to the price of clothing is given by the slope of the indifference curves at point *C*.
- **c** A change in the initial endowment of inputs to the two individuals will not change the competitive equilibrium.
- **d** The slope of the *PPC* equals the ratio of the input prices.
- **e** None of the above.

9 Goods 1 and 2 are produced in competitive markets. A tax on good 1 results in an inefficient allocation of resources because of which of the following?
- **a** The *MRS*s between good 1 and good 2 are not equal for all individuals.
- **b** The *MRTS*s between the inputs used in the production of good 1 and good 2 are not equal.
- **c** The *MRS*s between good 1 and good 2 are not equal to the ratio of the output prices.
- **d** The *MRS*s between good 1 and good 2 are not equal to the *MRT* between goods 1 and 2.
- **e** Both **c** and **d**.

10 Suppose that a perfectly competitive economy is operating on the production possibilities frontier with good 2 on the vertical axis and good 1 on the horizontal axis. If the marginal product of labour in the production of good 1 is 5 and the marginal product of labor in the production of good 2 is 1/2 in equilibrium, then which of the following is correct?
- **a** The *MRT* is 10 units of good 2 for one unit of good 1.
- **b** The *MP* of capital in the production of good 2 must be 1/10 the *MP* of capital in the production of good 1.
- **c** The marginal cost of good 1 is 10 times the marginal cost of good 2.

FIGURE 13.2

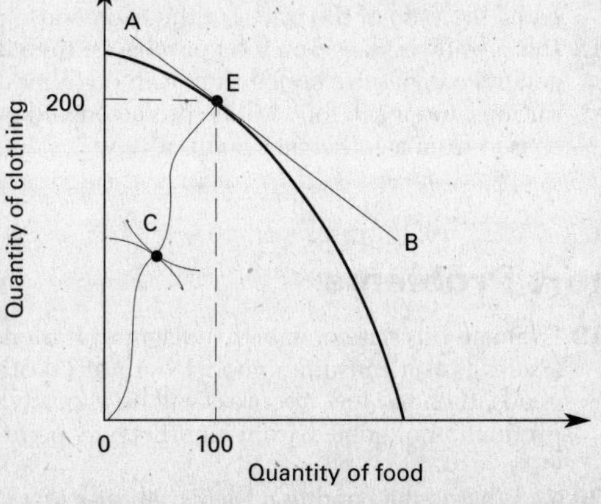

d The *MRT* cannot be determined without knowing the marginal product of capital in the production of good 1 and good 2.
e None of the above.

11 In a perfectly competitive economy, with utility-maximizing individuals and profit-maximizing firms, the equilibrium prices of goods 1 and 2 are \$5 and \$10, respectively. Then
a The *MP* of labour used in the production of good 2 must be two times the *MP* of labour used in the production of good 1.
b The *MRTS* between inputs in the production of good 1 must be 1/2.
c The production of good 1 must be twice that of good 2.
d The marginal cost of good 1 is one-half the marginal cost of good 2.
e None of the above.

True-False

12 If good Y is produced by polluting firms in a competitive industry, then the efficiency of the economy can be improved by imposing an excise tax on good Y, provided that no distortions exist elsewhere in the system.

13 The slope of the isoquants at 100 units of good 1 and 200 units of good 2 along a contract curve of production equals the slope of the production possibilities curves at output levels $x_1 = 100$ and $x_2 = 200$.

14 The *MRT* between goods 1 and 2 equals the ratio of the marginal products of an input used to produce those two goods.

15 The second theorem of welfare economics means that redistribution is Pareto efficient.

16 In a two-individual, two-good world, if Mary's net demand for bananas exceeds André's net supply, then the price ratio p_b/p_c has to be increased.

17 The condition for Pareto efficiency in consumption says that the *MRS* between two goods must equal the ratio of the prices of the two goods.

18 If a subsidy is placed on food purchases, then in a general competitive equilibrium with no other distortions, too much food will be produced and purchased from an efficiency point of view.

Short Problems

19 Evaluate this statement with a diagram: If there is a sales tax on consumer good 1 but not on other goods, then too few resources will be allocated to production of good 1 from an efficiency point of view.

20 a What is the condition for Pareto efficiency in exchange?
b Using a numerical example, give your intuition for the condition in **a**.
c Show that the Pareto condition in **a** is satisfied under perfect competition.

21 Give your intuition for the Pareto condition that the *MRT* between two goods must equal each consumer's *MRS* between those two goods.

22 Consider an economy with only one distortion: a monopsony in a particular input market. Discuss how the allocation of resources in this economy is inefficient. Discuss how Pareto efficiency might be achieved if a union were formed.

Long Problems

23 State the Pareto conditions for an economically efficient allocation of resources. Briefly describe the meaning of each condition. Then show whether *each* of the following market situations provides an economically efficient allocation of resources.
a Perfect competition
b A subsidy on each unit of food purchased
c A monopoly in the market for good 1; competition in the market for good 2

24 A million years ago, only two kinds of goods, wild boar and berries, were available. Two individuals, Ayla and Durc, lived in a particular forest and had no access to neighbouring tribes. Ayla has the usual negatively-sloped, convex indifference curves. Durc, however, likes only wild boar, but any berries he acquires can be costlessly fed to the snakes in the forest. There are 10 kilograms of wild boar and 10 bushels of berries in the forest. Each individual is endowed with 5 units of each commodity.
a Show the initial situation in an Edgeworth box diagram.
b Show the set of all Pareto-efficient outcomes of trade.
c If Durc and Ayla end up at a Pareto-efficient allocation after a trade, will Durc be left with some of the berries? Explain, using a diagram.

25 Consider an economy with no production. The economy is endowed with 50 bushels of alfalfa, *a*, and 50 bushels of barley, *b*. Two individuals, Mary and Larry, live in this economy and have the usual convex, negatively-sloped indifference curves. Larry has an initial endowment $(a, b) = (50, 0)$, and Mary has an initial endowment $(a, b) = (0, 50)$. This initial endowment is not on the contract curve. At the initial endowment, Larry's utility function is $U(b, a) = b + 2a$, and Mary's utility function is $U(b, a) = 2b + 10a$.
a If Mary offers a trade whereby she would give Larry three of her barley for one of his alfalfa, would Larry accept the trade? Why or why not? Illustrate your answer. Show, on the same diagram, the set of efficient trades these individuals would rationally make.

b Now introduce prices. One of the points on the set of efficient trades you illustrated in your diagram will be a competitive equilibrium. Show such a point and illustrate the equilibrium price ratio p_a/p_b.

26 Consider an economy with no production. The economy is endowed with 100 bushels of alfalfa a and 100 bushels of barley b. Two individuals, Tom and Harry, live in this economy. Tom has an initial endowment of $(a, b) = (80, 40)$ and Harry has an initial endowment of $(a, b) = (20, 60)$.

a Use a carefully labelled Edgeworth box diagram to illustrate the initial endowment. Label the initial endowment *A*. Assume that the initial endowment is not on the contract curve.

b Show, on the same diagram as in **a**, the set of efficient trades these individuals could rationally make. Next find a trade that makes them both better off and label this point *B*. State how much each person is giving up and receiving in the movement from *A* to *B*. What important condition of Pareto efficiency is satisfied at *B*?

***c** We know that one of the points in the set of efficient trades you found in **b** is a competitive equilibrium. Show this point on a diagram by deriving the "offer curves" for Tom and Harry. That is, at every price ratio, find the amounts of *A* and *B* that maximize each consumer's utility, given the price line. The point at which the two offer curves intersect identifies the competitive equilibrium price ratio.

27 Consider an individual who consumes both goods 1 and 2 and produces goods 1 and 2 with two factors of production: land and labour. She has a fixed endowment of both inputs.

a Show on a diagram her equilibrium when she cannot trade.

b Show on a diagram her equilibrium when she can trade at fixed prices p_1 and p_2 with an individual in another country who produces and consumes good 1 and good 2.

28 Review problem **26c** in this chapter. Now suppose that Tom acts like a monopolist in that he sets the relative price of alfalfa to barley. Show the relative price that Tom will set by drawing the relevant budget line through the initial endowment and indicating the final trade that will take place. How does this price ratio compare with the competitive equilibrium price ratio found in problem **26c**?

ANSWERS TO CHAPTER 13

Case Study

A No. Suppose that the market for lumber in the United States and Canada starts out as perfectly competitive. Now suppose that the United States places a tariff on every unit of lumber imported from Canada. The tariff will artificially increase the price of lumber in the United States. Consider a representative consumer in the United States and one in Canada. The U.S. consumer equates his *MRS* of other goods for lumber to the ratio of the tariff-inflated price of lumber and the price of other goods. The Canadian consumer will equate her *MRS* of other goods for lumber to a lower price ratio (because the price of lumber in Canada will simply equal the marginal cost of production). Hence, the *MRS*s will not be equal and, for a given product mix, too little lumber will be consumed in the United States. Moreover, the product mix is inefficient in that U.S. consumers are willing to give up more of other goods to get additional lumber than need be given up in production in Canada. Gains from trade could be realized if the trade barriers were removed.

Tariff barriers may be imposed for several reasons: (1) To protect infant industries — that is, industries that need protection from foreign competition to get started; (2) to affect the terms of trade when a country is large; (3) in response to strong lobbying pressure by a few groups when the benefits from trade barriers are concentrated among a few but the costs are dispersed over many. Recent research indicates that when markets are imperfectly competitive, there may be strategic benefits from unilateral trade restrictions.

B In an economy with no taxes, subsidies, or externalities, free trade will achieve an efficient allocation of resources. Although efficient, there may be resistance since the distributional effects in moving from a situation of trade barriers to one of free trade may be significant; that is, an allocation under free trade may be Pareto-efficient, but not Pareto-superior, to an allocation under trade barriers. Free trade may result in large employment shifts, workers will need to retrain for new jobs, and many companies will not survive the increased competition. Both efficiency and equity should be considered in a careful evaluation of government policies.

Multiple-Choice

1 b **2** e **3** c **4** b **5** b **6** b
7 e **8** b **9** d **10** b **11** d

True-False

12 T **13** F **14** T **15** F
16 T **17** F **18** T

Short Problems

19 If there is a tax on a good, a wedge between the price and the marginal cost of production will exist. Under a tax, $p_1 > w/MP_1$ (or MC_1); so $p_1/p_2 > MP_2/MP_1 = MRT$ (the tradeoff between good 1 and good 2 in production). Each individual will equate his *MRS* of good 2 for good 1 to the ratio of prices p_1/p_2; hence, $MRS > MRT$, implying that too little good 1 is produced, as shown in Figure A13.1. Note that the slope of the production possibilities frontier is less than the slope of the indifference curves in the final allocation.

20 a The *MRS*s between any two goods must be equal for all individuals consuming those two goods.

b Suppose that goods 1 and 2 are being consumed by individuals A and B. Individual A has an *MRS* of good 2 for good 1 equal to 5; individual B has an *MRS* of good 2 for good 1 equal to 1. That is, individual A is willing to trade up to five units of good 2 to get one more unit of good 1, whereas individual B is willing to give up one unit of good 1 for one unit of good 2. A possible trade, acceptable to both individuals, would be for individual 1 to give between one and five units of good 2 for a unit of good one. Trading will continue until the *MRS*s are equal.

c This condition is satisfied under perfect competition. At the utility-maximizing bundle of goods, each individual's *MRS* equals p_1/p_2. Since all individuals are price-takers, the ratio of prices is the same for all individuals; hence, the *MRS*s are equal.

21 The *MRS* of good 2 for good 1 represents the amount of good 2 that an individual is willing to give up to get another unit of good 1 and remain at the same level of utility. The *MRT* is the amount of good 2 that must be given up in production to release sufficient inputs to produce another unit of good 1. For example, if the *MRS* is greater than the *MRT*, the individual is willing to give up more good 2 than is necessary to get another good 1; hence, less good 2 and more good 1 should be produced and consumed. As this happens, the *MRS* falls and the *MRT* increases.

22 Assume that the monopsonist of an input Z is a competitor in the output market. The monopsonist will set the value of the marginal product equal to the *MFC* of Z, that is, $p[MP(z)] = MFC(z)$, where p equals the price of the good in the output market. This creates a wedge between the value of an additional unit of Z and the opportunity cost of using Z, as shown in Figure A13.2 by *AB*. An inefficient amount of other inputs will be used in lieu of Z. If a labour union can increase the wage rate to w^*, the supply curve of the input faced by the monopsonist will be perfectly elastic (up to the supply curve), and the value of the marginal product will be equal to the opportunity cost, as indicated by point *C* in the figure.

FIGURE A13.1

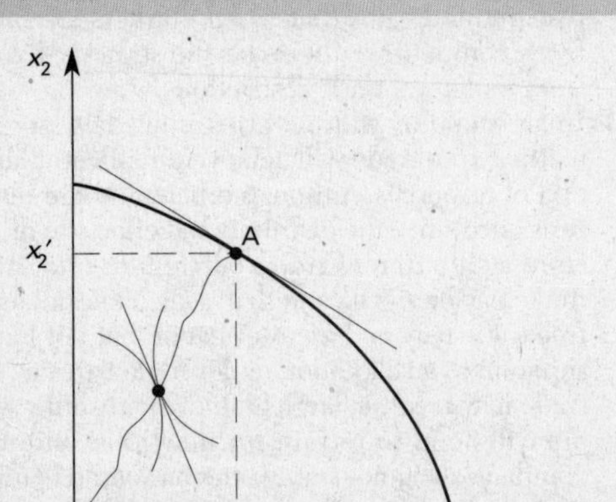

FIGURE A13.2

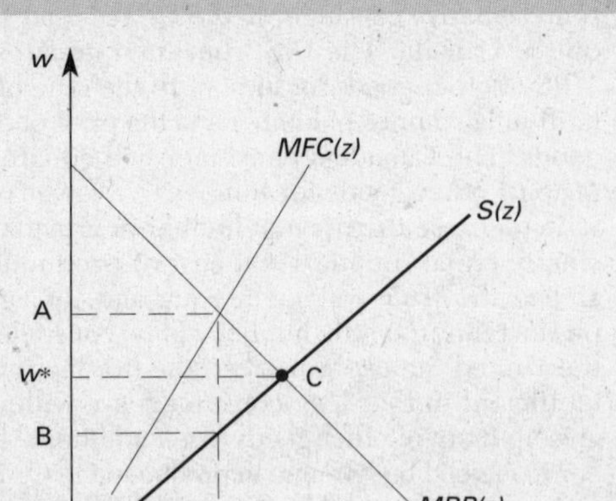

Long Problems

23 The efficiency conditions are

(1) $MRS_A = MRS_B$ for all goods 1 and 2 and all consumers A and B.

(2) $MRTS_1 = MRTS_2$ for all inputs 1 and 2 and all goods 1 and 2.

(3) $MRS = MRT$ for all goods 1 and 2 and all individuals.

a Consider each of the efficiency conditions. (1) Since every individual equates his *MRS* between every pair of goods to the ratio of prices of those two goods and since everyone faces the same prices, the *MRS* between those two goods must be the same for all individuals. (2) Since producers using two inputs, such as inputs 1 and 2, equate the *MRTS* between those inputs to the ratio of prices for those inputs, and all firms face the same input prices, the *MRTS* between those two inputs must be the same for all firms. (3) The *MRT* between two goods 1 and 2 is defined as the ratio of the marginal product of an input, such as input 1, in the production of good 2 divided by the marginal product for that input in the production of good 1. All producers of good 1 and good 2 satisfy $w_1 = p_1 MP_1^1$ and $w_1 = p_2 MP_1^2$ (where the subscript refers to the input and the superscript to the good), respectively, so $MP_1^2/MP_1^1 = MRT = p_1/p_2$. Since $MRS = p_1/p_2$, the *MRT* equals the *MRS* in a competitive economy.

b If a subsidy of s per unit is placed on food, then individuals are effectively facing a food price of $p_f - s$. They will set the *MRS* of other goods, good 2, for food equal to $(p_f - s)/p_2$. For profit-maximizing firms, $MRT = p_f/p_2$. Hence, $MRS < MRT$, and too much food is produced and consumed in the economy.

c A monopolist in the market for good 1 sets the marginal revenue product of an input, say input 1, equal to the price of the input. In a competitive market for good 2, firms set the value of the marginal product of the same input equal to the price of the input. Then, $p_1 MP_1^1 > w_1$ in the good 1 market and $p_2 MP_1^2 = w_1$ in the good 2 market. Taking the ratio of the two conditions gives $MRT = MP_1^2/MP_1^1 < p_1/p_2 = MRS$. Hence, the condition for efficiency in product mix is violated.

24 a The initial endowment is given by *E* in Figure A13.3, where Ayla's convex indifference curve intersects Durc's straight-line indifference curves. Since Durc does not like berries and can throw them away, increasing the bushels of berries does not increase his utility, for a given amount of wild boar.

b Given that Durc and Ayla start at *E*, they will trade within the shaded lens. The Pareto-efficient points that can be achieved are given by *CD* in Figure A13.3. Note that the indifference curves are not necessarily tangent at the corner solution. Nevertheless, along *CD*, Durc's indifference curve is the highest one that can be achieved given Ayla's indifference curves, and Ayla's is the highest indifference curve given Durc's indifference curves.

c Durc will not be left with any berries at a Pareto-efficient point. It is easy to see that Ayla can increase her utility by taking the berries that Durc wants to throw away.

25 Figure A13.4 illustrates the initial endowment *E*.

a First we have to establish the MRS for each individual. Both Mary and André consider barley and alfalfa to be perfect substitutes. We can see

FIGURE A13.3

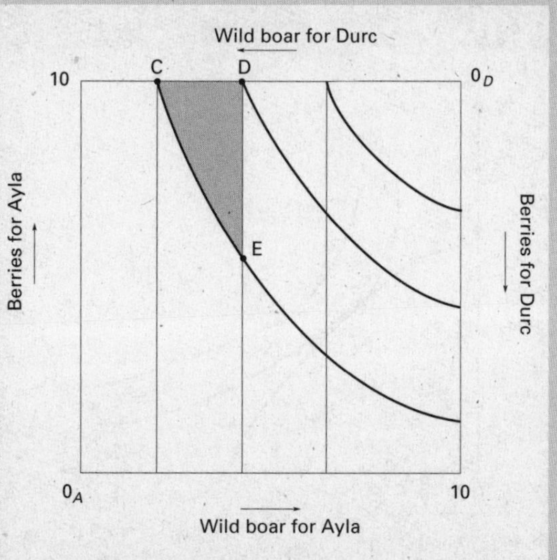

FIGURE 13.4

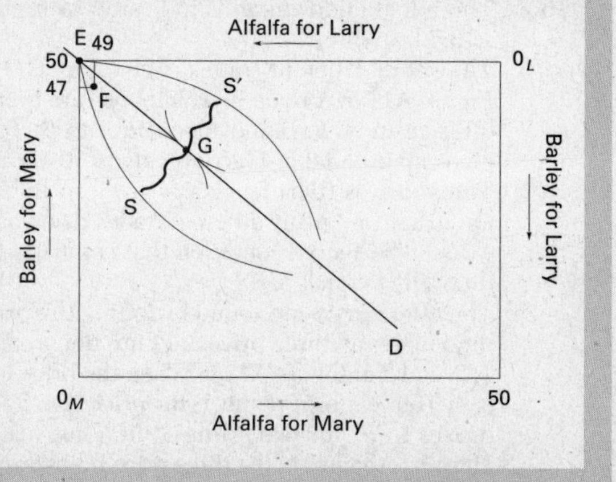

FIGURE A13.5

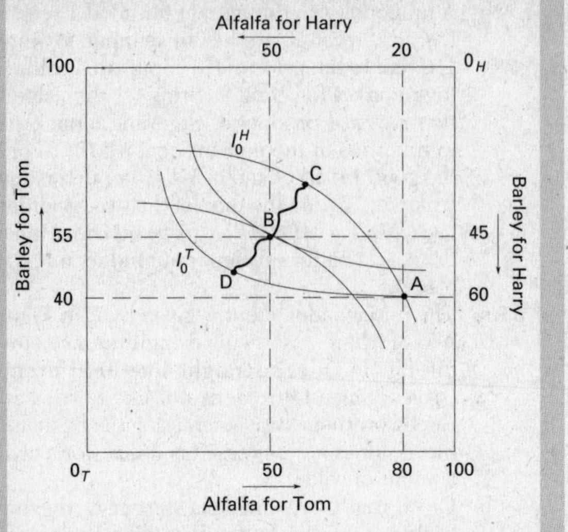

FIGURE A13.6

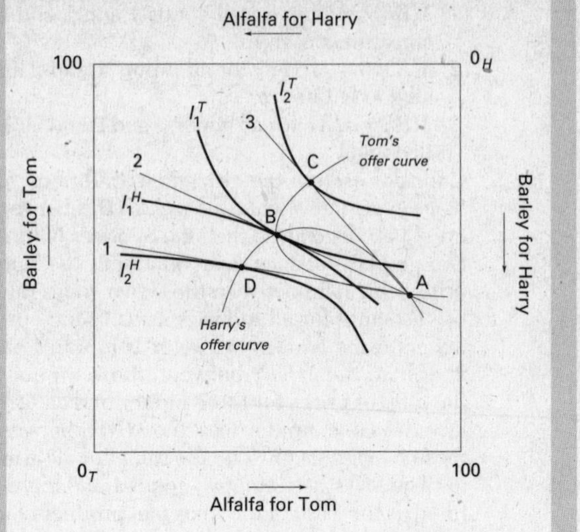

this by calculating the MRS, obtained by the ratio of the marginal utility of alfalfa to the marginal utility of barley. Mary's MRS for barley and alfalfa is 5 while Larry's is 2. Since Mary is willing to trade at most five barley for one alfalfa and Larry needs only two barley for one alfalfa to keep him at the same utility level, the trade could take place. This trade might be a point such as *F*. An efficient set of trades will lie on the curves *SS′*, along which $MRS_M = MRS_L$, where MRS_M and MRS_L are Mary's and Larry's marginal rates of substitution of barley for alfalfa, respectively.

b Suppose that line *ED* is the budget constraint that reflects the price ratio p_a/p_b. The budget constraint passes through the initial endowment. The competitive equilibrium is point *G* on *SS′*, where $MRS_M = p_a/p_b = MRS_L$.

26 a The initial endowment is indicated in Figure A13.5 by point *A*.

b The set of efficient trades is given by *CD* in Figure A13.5. A trade in which both are better off is given by *B*. In moving from *A* to *B*, Tom gives up 30 alfalfa; Harry receives 30 alfalfa. Tom receives 15 barley; Harry gives up 15 barley. (There are many different trades that would work.) The Pareto condition that is satisfied is that MRS_T equals MRS_H.

***c** The offer curves are found by letting the price ratio increase; three price lines are denoted by *1*, *2*, and *3* in Figure A13.6. When the price line is *1*, Tom chooses point *A*; for price line *2*, he moves to *B*; for price line *3*, he chooses *C*. Harry's responses to the three price ratios are *D*, *B*, and *A*, respectively; hence, Tom's offer curve is given by *ABC*, and Harry's offer curve is given by *ABD*. The competitive equilibrium price ratio is given by price line 2 through the intersection of the two offer curves, point *B* in the figure. At *B*, $MRS_T = MRS_H = p_a/p_b$.

27 a When an individual cannot trade, she will maximize her utility subject to the production possibilities frontier at point *A* in Figure A13.7.

b The individual who can trade at fixed prices p_1 and p_2 faces a budget constraint given by the line *BDC*, where the slope of $BDC = p_1/p_2$. The

FIGURE A13.7

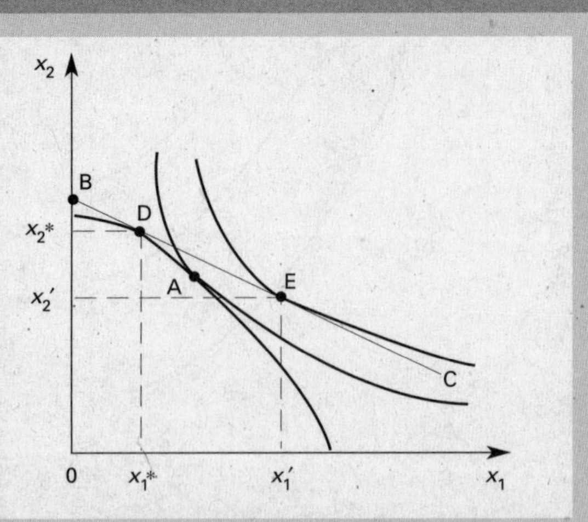

individual will produce those amounts of good 1 and good 2 given by point *D*, where the *MRT* equals the ratio of prices, but now can maximize her utility subject to the budget constraint and reach a higher utility level at *E*. That is, she can import $x_1' - x_1^*$ from the other country and export $x_2^* - x_2'$.

28 If Tom is a monopolist, he will want to set the price p_a/p_b that maximizes his utility. The initial endowment *A* and Harry's offer curve are illustrated in Figure A13.8. Harry's offer curve *ABD* represents Harry's reaction to announced prices and, hence, is a constraint on Tom's maximization problem. Tom will choose the bundle on his highest indifference curve, tangent to *ABD*; this bundle is denoted by point *F*. The ratio of monopoly prices is given by the slope of the price line *MA*. This price ratio is higher than the competitive ratio of prices (the slope of *AC*); that is, as a price setter, Tom will set a price for alfalfa, the good that he wants to sell, that is higher than the competitive price.

FIGURE A13.8

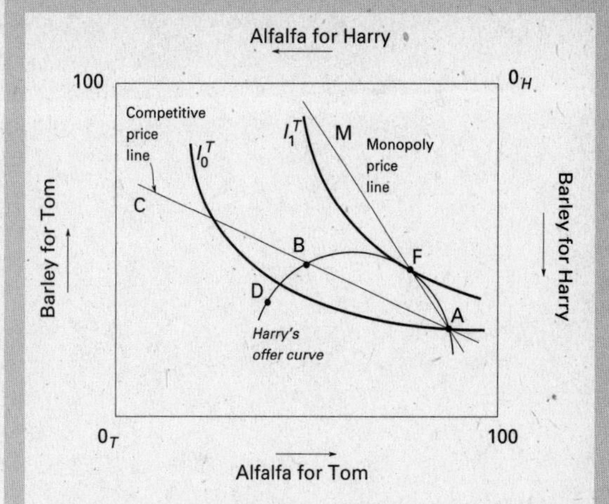

CHAPTER 14

Price Discrimination and Monopoly Practices

Chapter Summary

In the monopoly equilibrium studied in Chapter 10, we found that the monopolist sets its price where $MR = MC$ resulting in a deadweight loss to society. This deadweight loss can be thought of as unrealized profit; this chapter looks at how the monopolist can obtain some of this profit.

Price Discrimination, Market Segmentation and Extracting Consumer Surplus

Price discrimination tries to segment the market into smaller components, charging each component a different price. The ideal **market segmentation** would have the monopolist charging each consumer his or her reservation price — known as first-degree or **perfect price discrimination**. In this case, the monopolist would extract the entire surplus from the market; the last unit sold would be where price equals marginal costs, leading to the most efficient output from the point of view of society. A second type is second-degree or **ordinary price discrimination** in which the monopolist identifies different groups of customers and charges them different prices. The monopolist chooses output where the aggregate marginal revenue curve (the horizontal summation of the group marginal revenue curves) equals marginal cost. Each group is allocated output in a way that equalizes marginal revenue across all market segments. The third type of price discrimination is sometimes referred to as third-degree price discrimination, but is usually known as **multipart pricing** or **block pricing**. In this case, different prices are charged for different quantities of the good; a **price schedule** associates different prices with different quantity blocks. **All-or-nothing pricing** is a special case of multipart pricing. The **all-or-nothing demand** curve indicates the average amount that a person would be willing to pay for a given quantity rather than have nothing at all. This sort of demand may be pertinent for choices within personal relationships.

Perfect price discrimination rarely, if ever, happens. It may be approximated by, say, your accountant who has plenty of information about your ability to pay. Don't forget, however, that a great deal of monopoly power is required to get away with price discrimination. Ordinary price discrimination is more common, and requires two basic conditions: each market segment must have a different elasticity of demand at any given price; and no **arbitrage** can be possible across these markets to eliminate the possibility that the low-price group will resell to the high-price group. The market can be segmented in two ways: **direct identification** requires an individual to identify his or herself in order to qualify for the lower price (e.g., senior and student discounts); **self-selection** induces individuals to reveal their category voluntarily. For instance, business long-distance telephone calls usually take place during the day at a higher price than calls made outside of business hours when people elect to make pleasure calls. Although price discrimination contravenes the Canadian *Competition Act*, many examples of price discrimination can actually be justified on the basis of costs, rendering it complicated to prosecute firms for this type of behaviour. Monopsonists may also practice **ordinary monopsonistic price discrimination**, like when a single buyer of labour input pays a different wage to members of different groups. To qualify as discrimination, this differential should not reflect any productivity differences between the groups.

A two-part tariff, in which the customer is charged a price equal to marginal cost plus a fixed "entry fee", is one way for the monopolist to extract surplus from its consumers. A **tie-in sale** is another way. In this latter case, the firm ties the sale of a good for which it has monopoly power to the sale of another good which is available in a competitive market.

KEY WORDS

All-or-nothing demand

All-or-nothing pricing

Arbitrage

Block pricing

Direct identification

Market segmentation

Multipart pricing

Ordinary monopsonistic price discrimination

Ordinary price discrimination

Perfect price discrimination

Price discrimination

Price schedule

Self-selection

Tie-in sale

CASE STUDY: SORTING OUT THE DIFFERENCES BETWEEN CONSTRUCTION WORKERS AND DENTISTS

Several years ago, a chemical company sold plastic molding powder (methyl methacrylate) to two types of customers: construction companies and dentists. The plastic powders sold to the construction companies and dentists were identical except for two things: It was rumoured that an arsenic compound was put into the plastic powder sold to the construction companies, and the price of the plastic powder sold to the dentists was 25 times higher.

A What economic principle does this case involve?

B What would the chemical company be trying to achieve if it had put arsenic in the molding powder sold to the construction firms?

C Do dentists and construction firms have the same demand curve for molding powder? What might make their demand curves differ?

D Are the two necessary conditions for ordinary price discrimination satisfied in this case? Explain.

E This chemical company has some sort of market power that allows it to price discriminate. Suggest some possible sources of its market power.

EXERCISES

Multiple-Choice

1 Which of the following is the clearest example of ordinary price discrimination?
- **a** A barber charges women with short hair more than men with hair of a similar length.
- **b** Business travel costs more than pleasure travel.
- **c** At the end of the season, clothes are sold at a discount.
- **d** Both **a** and **b**.
- **e** All of the above.

2 Suppose that the inverse market demand curve is $p = 10 - q$; monopoly costs are constant at $2. What is the gain to society to perfect price discrimination?
- **a** $16
- **b** $8
- **c** $64
- **d** $32
- **e** None of the above.

3 In equilibrium, we know that the price of a good in market 1 is $2 whereas it is sold for $3 in market 2. From this we can conclude that:
- **a** The elasticity of demand in market 1 is 2/3 times the elasticity of demand in market 2.
- **b** Consumers in market 1 are more price elastic than are consumers in market 2.
- **c** Consumers in market 1 are less price elastic than are consumers in market 2.
- **d** Both **a** and **b**.
- **e** Both **a** and **c**.

4 Suppose that the inverse demand is $p = 6 - q$, and the monopoly faces a constant marginal cost of $2. If the monopoly can impose a two-part tariff, what will be the optimal entry fee to charge?
- **a** $16
- **b** $8
- **c** $24
- **d** $36
- **e** $12

To answer questions **5** and **6**, refer to Figure 14.1.

5 Suppose that a monopolist producing in the market in Figure 14.1 is not allowed to practice any form of price discrimination. At y_1, the monopolist
- **a** Would be maximizing profit.
- **b** Would set price equal to p_1.
- **c** Would earn a profit of CD.
- **d** Would do all the above.
- **e** Would do only **a** and **b**.

6 Now suppose that the monopolist in Figure 14.1 can perfectly price discriminate and produces y_2 units of output. The monopolist
- **a** Would be maximizing profits.
- **b** Would set the same price for all units.
- **c** Would make a profit equal to AB times y_2.
- **d** Would be making zero profit.
- **e** Would do both **a** and **c**.

To answer questions **7** and **8**, consider the following information. The demand facing a monopolist is $y = 100 - (p/2)$. Marginal costs are constant at 40.

7 If the monopolist is not able to practice price discrimination, the profit-maximizing price for the monopolist is
- **a** 120
- **b** 60

FIGURE 14.1

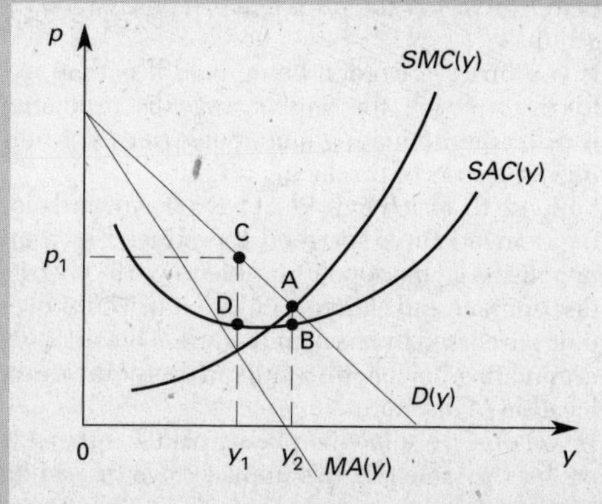

c 80
d 40
e None of the above.

8 If the monopolist is able to perfectly price discriminate, then the price set for the *marginal* unit of output will be
a 120
b 60
c 80
d 40
e None of the above.

9 A travel agent, with market power in a particular town, offers ski holiday packages. Two different prices are set for students and nonstudents. The travel agent knows that the price elasticities of demand (in absolute value) for ski holidays by students and nonstudents are 2 and 6, respectively. Then, the price for nonstudents set by the price-discriminating travel agent will be
a Three times the price of a student ticket.
b One-third the price of a student ticket.
c Five-thirds the price of a student's ticket.
d Three-fifths times the price of a student's ticket.
e None of the above.

10 The price elasticity (in absolute value) at y_0 in Figure 14.2 is
a 5
b 0
c 3
d 2
e None of the above.

True-False

11 The efficiency loss under perfect price discrimination is larger than under either pure monopoly or ordinary price discrimination.

12 Monopoly is always inefficient because it generates a deadweight loss to society.

13 In a segmented market, the higher the price elasticity, the higher the price that can be charged that group.

14 If you observe women being paid less than men for the same job, this implies wage discrimination.

15 A price-discriminating monopolist does not minimize the costs of producing output.

16 Suppose that each individual has a downward-sloping demand curve for good Y produced by a monopolist. The monopolist is able to perfectly price discriminate and charge a different price for every unit purchased by every individual. This price-discriminating behaviour results in an inefficient allocation of resources.

17 If you observe some men being paid less than others for the same job, this implies wage discrimination.

FIGURE 14.2

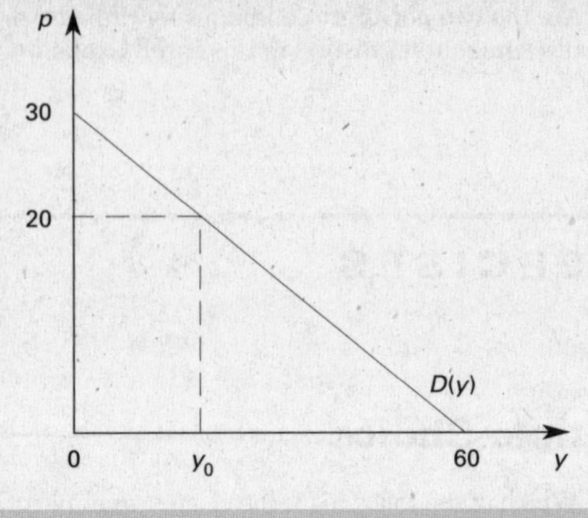

18 A profit-maximizing monopolist would always prefer to block price than offer a single price.

19 The higher the price elasticity of demand (in absolute value) for a product by a particular group of individuals, the lower will be the price set by a profit-maximizing, price-discriminating monopolist.

Short Problems

20 In a well-known women's clothing store that caters to women who wear classic clothing, twice a year a sale is held at which time the normally well-dressed sales representatives don aprons and the hitherto beautifully arranged clothing is piled on tables. Discuss what is going on here.

***21** Suppose that a monopolist faces the demand curve $q = 50 - 0.5p$, and has a total cost curve of $3q^2 + 100$.
a What are the profit-maximizing price, output and level of profits of this firm?
b Suppose that the monopolist can perfectly price discriminate, calculate its profit-maximizing price, output and level of profit (no single price!!).
c Suppose, now, that perfect price discrimination is not possible, but the monopolist can segregate the market into two groups, each with a demand $q = 25 - 0.25p$. How will this affect your answer to part **a**?

***22** An ordinary price discriminating monopolist has identified two markets. The first has a demand represented by: $q = 50 - p$, and the second has a demand $q = 25 - p$. Its cost function is $C = 10 + q^2$.
a What is the profit-maximizing price and output strategy for this firm? Discuss what is happening in this situation.

b Suppose that the monopolists costs fall to $C = 10 + 0.5q^2$. How will this affect your answer to **a**?

23 Automobile insurers in many jurisdictions charge young males considerable more than young females. Is this a classic case of sex discrimination?

24 What two conditions are necessary for a monopolist to be able to successfully practice ordinary price discrimination?

25 Manufacturers often offer coupons in newspapers or rebates to consumers that return the bill of sale. Why would coupons or rebates be offered rather than simply reducing the price?

26 A doctor in a small town faces the following demand curve for her services and the long-run cost conditions illustrated in Figure 14.3.

a If the doctor is a monopolist in the town but is unable to price discriminate, will she be willing to practice in this town? Why or why not?

b What are the price and quantity of services that maximize the consumers' plus producer's surplus? Using the information provided in Figure 14.3, would the town, *as a whole*, be better off with the presence of the doctor? Why or why not? Algebraically determine the net surplus from the doctor's services. How might the town convince the doctor to stay so that everyone is made better off?

27 The only racquetball club in town faces a set of potential members, each of whom has a demand function

$$p = 5 - 0.1y$$

where y is the number of court bookings demanded per month and p is the price per booking (in dollars). The marginal costs of providing a unit of court booking are constant and equal to \$2. The club charges a fixed membership fee, which each buyer must pay to make bookings, and also charges for each booking. Assuming no income effects on the demand for the commodity, determine the membership fee that will be set.

FIGURE 14.3

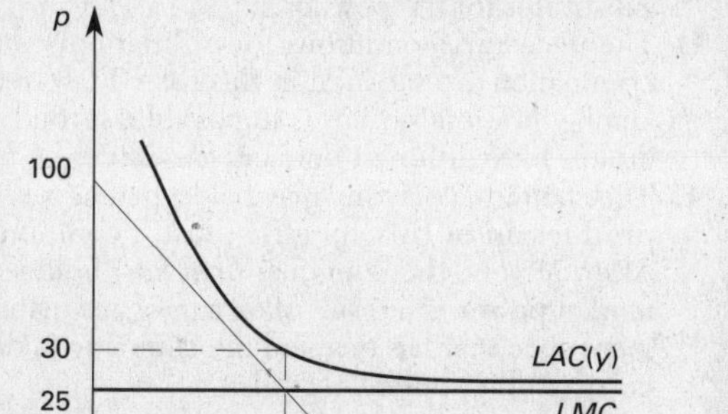

28 In the 1960s, IBM practiced a policy of leasing its computers to customers only if the customers purchased all their computer cards from IBM. The price of the cards was set at a level exceeding the marginal cost of production. This practice of forcing consumers to purchase a second item for the privilege of buying some other good is called **tying**. In the 1970s, the U.S. Justice Department charged IBM with tying to lessen competition.

a Why do you think this tying arrangement was profitable for IBM?

b In some cases, the optimal pricing strategy for a monopolist selling two complementary goods, one being a durable good and the other a variable input (e.g., computers and cards, or cameras and film), is to set the price of the variable good equal to its marginal cost of production and to charge a price for the durable good equal to consumer surplus. Why didn't IBM follow this pricing strategy?

Long Problems

29 Provide an explanation for the following observations: **i)** bananas are sold for \$1.50 a kilogram or \$5.00 for 8 kilograms; **ii)** Cartier watches can only be sold in specially outfitted boutiques; **iii)** the designer label on clothing is marked with indelible ink when sold in a discount store; **iv)** GST is charged on individual muffins, but not on six or more muffins.

30 In remote communities like Iqaluit, Rankin Inlet and Inuvic in Canada's far north, consumer goods are much more expensive than they are elsewhere. Groceries in particular are extremely expensive; even at a high price, fresh fruit and vegetables, when available, are typically of poor quality. One enterprising grocer near Edmonton has discovered that he can sell groceries in these communities at a price cheaper than is charged by local stores. Northern residents fax their grocery lists to this grocer, who proceeds to put together the order, package it in boxes, and then they are sent via air to the relevant communities. Residents of Iqaluit and elsewhere find that they can get fresher, higher-quality products at a lower price once account is taken of transportation costs, than they can at their local grocery.

a Discuss the economics of this situation.

b What would economic theory predict about the long-run consequences of the actions of this Edmonton entrepreneur?

31 Commodity X is produced by a profit-maximizing firm that has a monopoly both in its domestic market and in a foreign market. This firm charges different prices for its domestic market (p_d) and its foreign market (p_f), where $p_d > p_f$. The firm's marginal cost curve is positively sloped for all output.

a Illustrate the monopolist's optimum price.

b Suppose that the government introduces a consumer subsidy of \$1 per unit that is paid only on units of X sold in the domestic market and not on foreign units. Analyze the effects of this subsidy on the domestic and foreign prices, total revenue from sales abroad and at home, total production costs, and total profits. Explain.

32 Bell Canada (BC) is a supplier of telephone services. In the long run, the marginal cost of providing telephone services is zero, but there is a fixed installation cost of \$30 per individual. Suppose that BC offers "blocks" with the pricing schedule shown in the table.

Number of Message Units	Average Cost to Consumer (\$)
0	0
20	0.80
40	0.60
60	0.40

Why would BC follow such a pricing schedule? Would increasing the number of blocks (beyond 60 units) increase profits? Explain carefully.

33 A theatre has a monopoly on the rights to show movies in the town of Swift Current. For its feature film of the week, it faces the following demands:

Adults: $p_a = 16 - y_a$

Children: $p_c = 10 - \frac{y_c}{2}$

where p_a is the price per adult ticket, p_c is the price per child ticket, y_a is the quantity of adult tickets purchased and sold, and y_c is the quantity of child tickets purchased and sold. The marginal costs of printing and selling the tickets are

$$MC(y) = \frac{y}{3}$$

and

$$TC(y) = \frac{y^2}{6}$$

where $y = y_a + y_c$.

a The monopolist can practice ordinary price discrimination. Determine the equilibrium prices and quantities for adults and children.

b Now suppose that the monopolist is banned from practicing price discrimination. Determine the equilibrium price and quantity in this case.

c Has there been an increase in the economic efficiency (or social welfare) due to the law against price discrimination in **b**? Why or why not?

ANSWERS TO CHAPTER 14

Case Study

A Ordinary price discrimination.

B The chemical company would be trying to separate its market by preventing arbitrage, or resale, between the two groups of customers. If the powder sold to construction firms did not contain arsenic, then dentists could purchase the powder from construction workers at a lower price than that charged by the manufacturer.

C No, dentists have a more inelastic demand, which allows the chemical manufacturer to charge them a higher price. Dentists require a much smaller amount of the powder than construction companies, and the cost of the plastic powder is therefore only a small part of the dentist's total costs. As a result, it is not worthwhile for dentists to find substitutes for the powder.

D The necessary conditions for ordinary price discrimination are satisfied in this case. First, resale among different groups is impossible; second, the groups have different demand elasticities.

E The chemical company may hold a patent over the production of this specific plastic compound. Alternatively, the chemical firm may hold some market power as a result of an aggressive management style that has enabled the company to deter entry of other potential rivals.

Multiple-Choice 14

1 a 2 b 3 b 4 b 5 e
6a 7 a 8 d 9 c 10 d

True-False

11 F 12 F 13 F 14 T 15 F
16 F 17 F 18 T 19 T

Short Problems

20 This store is practicing ordinary price discrimination where it is inducing individuals to self-select into two groups: those who want to purchase clothes in a nice environment, with attentive sales people, and who can do so at their own pace; and those who are willing to give up service for a better monetary price. In addition, this first group might value wearing the latest fashions (although this is less likely because this particular store tends to sell more timeless pieces). The second group is happy to rummage through piles of sweaters looking for their size and generally serve themselves in order to save some money. Typically, it takes longer to find the appropriate item under sale conditions. Once the clothes leave the store, nothing distinguishes the sale clothes from the full-price ones.

***21 a** The monopolist will maximize profits (note that the demand function needs to be inverted and expressed as $p = 100 - 2q$), given by $\pi(q) = 100q - 2q^2 - 3q^2 - 100$. The first-order condition for a maximum is that $\pi'(q) = 0$ (which results in the condition that $MR = MC$ to maximize profits). Thus, $10q = 100 \Rightarrow q = 10 \Rightarrow p = 80 \Rightarrow \pi =$ \$400. (Because the second derivative of the profit function is negative, we know that $q=10$ is indeed a maximum.)

b Under perfect price discrimination, the monopolist charges each individual his or her reservation price, so there is no single market price. The last unit sold will be where $p = MC \Rightarrow p = 6q \Rightarrow 100 - 2q = 6q \Rightarrow q = 12.5 \Rightarrow p = 75$. The monopolist will acquire all of the surplus, profits are thus $100*(12.5) - 5*(12.5)^2 - 100$ plus $25*(12.5)*0.5$ (i.e., the triangle above $p = 75$ and below demand), which equal \$368.75 + \$156.25 = \$525.

c If you maximize $\pi(q_1, q_2)$ you will discover that $q_1 = q_2 = 5$ and hence $p = 80$, i.e., there is no gain from pricing differently in the two markets. This result should have been obvious because the elasticity of demand of these two demand curves is identical at every point.

***22 a** The monopolist will choose q_1 and q_2 to maximize total revenue (TR) given by: $(50 - q_1)*q_1 + (25 - q_2)*q_2 - 10 - (q_1 + q_2)^2$. $\partial TR/\partial q_1 \Rightarrow q_1 = (25 - q_2)/2$, and $\partial TR/\partial q_2 \Rightarrow q_2 = (25 - 2q_1)/4$. Solving these two expressions simultaneously gives us $q_1 = 12.5$ and $q_2 = 0$. To see what is happening here, look at Figure A14.1. The monopolist will produce where the horizontal sum of the marginal revenues equals its marginal cost. In Figure A14.1 this occurs at point A. It is thus only profitable to produce for the first market.

b By contrast, when costs fall, the monopolist will undergo the same exercise but this time $q_1 = 15.625$ and $q_2 = 3.125$, which corresponds to point B on Figure A14.1. Notice that the MC has now fallen which makes it worthwhile to sell to the market with the smaller demand.

23 From a statistical perspective, young males tend to get into more accidents than young females. Part of this result may stem from the fact that young males tend to drive more than their female counterparts. It is difficult for an insurance company to measure kilometres driven by young males in order to vary their rates with this factor. As a result, young males are charged a higher price. Some argue that rates should start off the same across new drivers and then rise significantly with accidents. Insurance companies appear to be moving towards such a policy. The differences between male and female new driver rates does not appear to be as high now in comparison to earlier years.

24 For a firm to successfully practice price discrimination, it must be able to segment the market in such a way that there can be no resale of the goods among groups and that the groups have different price elasticities of demand.

25 Since relatively more price-elastic customers are likely to take advantage of the coupons or rebates, this is a price-discriminating strategy.

FIGURE A14.1

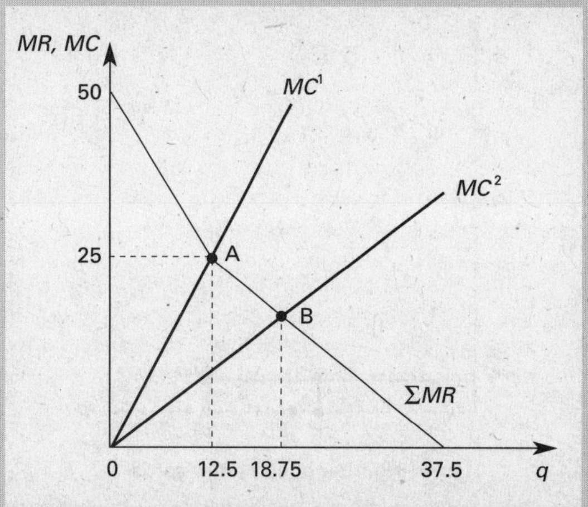

26 a No, she cannot cover her costs at *any* output level.

b The combination of $p = \$25$ and $y = 40$ maximizes consumers' plus producer's surplus. The town would be better off with the doctor because total surplus, equal to 1 500 (the area under the demand and above the $LMC(y)$), would exceed total costs, equal to 1 200. The doctor would stay in the town if she were allowed to perfectly price discriminate.

27 The monopolist will set a price per booking equal to the marginal cost, that is, \$2; 30 bookings will be made. The fee equals consumer surplus at this price and quantity: $(5 - 2)30/2 = 45$.

28 a This was a way for IBM to price discriminate without having to identify the more inelastic users. If larger users have more inelastic demands, then by forcing customers to buy cards at the monopoly price, IBM effectively charged a higher price for the "package" to customers with more inelastic demands.

b The pricing strategy described is profit-maximizing given identical customers. If customers have different demands for the joint product and IBM is unable to price discriminate explicitly on the computer (that is, charge different prices for the computer, based on individuals' consumer surplus), then the "indirect" price discrimination strategy followed by IBM may be profit-maximizing. To see this, consider Figure A14.2, in which a high and a low demand of two representative consumers are illustrated. If the price of cards is set equal to the marginal cost (assumed to be zero) and the computer price is set equal to the consumer surplus under the *low* demand, then total profits are $2 \times AOB$. Alternatively, if price p^* is charged for the cards and Ap^*D for the computer, then low-demand customers will pay $AOED$ for the package, which is less than AOB, whereas high-demand customers will pay $AOFGD$ for the package, which is greater than AOB. This strategy leaves the monopolist with larger profits.

FIGURE A14.2

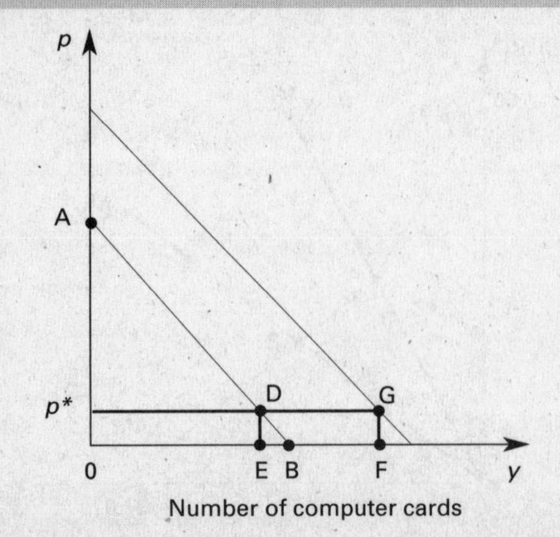

Long Problems

29 i) An example of ordinary price discrimination. Only those shopping for a large number of individuals would buy the 8 kilograms of bananas even though it is a great deal. Bananas are not storable, so individuals or small families would not find it in their best interest to buy such a large quantity. One exception would be if individuals banded together, purchased bundled commodities, and then divided them up among themselves. The problem is that this strategy is time consuming to put into operation (finding people, deciding who should shop, and so on), so it is probably not worthwhile to undertake for something like bananas. People thus self-select into the appropriate category.

ii) Cartier dealers are trying to ensure that no bargain stores sell their product in order to preserve the mystique or status associated with owning such a watch. Here is a case where market segmentation may not be worthwhile because part of the demand for such a high-end product comes from the fact that it is not available elsewhere.

iii) This is a classic case of segmenting the market and having people self-select themselves into the high-priced boutique group or the low-priced discount store group. To prevent arbitrage (buying at the low-priced discount store and re-selling at a higher price), manufacturers often require the discount store to either remove or indelibly mark their labels. The brand name is often quite discernible after being partially removed or marked in some way, but these actions destroy part of the rent attributable to the label itself. (Some manufacturers refuse to allow their products to be sold in discount stores or "factory outlet" malls because they are afraid that this would reduce the value to their clients of their goods. Cartier watches would be an example of this).

iv) Without detailing the vagaries of the Canadian tax system, one interpretation of this phenomenon where individual items are taxed and bundled items are not is that it discriminates against single individuals in favour of families or groups.

30 a This is an interesting situation. It would appear that the grocery stores in Iqaluit and other northern communities consider themselves to have enough market power to monopoly price. They obviously did not consider competition from a location as geographically removed as Edmonton as a likely possibility. An interesting question to ask is why other firms have not entered into this market if prices are so high? One answer is that what we are observing is a short-run phenomenon and entry will indeed occur.

b In the long run, we would fully expect the actions of the Edmonton entrepreneur to result in the local grocers lowering their prices. We might also observe grocers from other locations starting to perform the same long-distance shopping service for northern clients. Either way, grocery prices should fall.

31 a Figure A14.3a shows the domestic market, A14.3b the foreign market, and A14.2c the horizontal summation of the two marginal revenue curves *AB* and *CG* (or the aggregate marginal revenue curve *DEF*) and the marginal cost curve. Equate the marginal cost with the aggregate marginal revenue curve. Let MC^* be the intersection of the two curves. Then set MC^* equal to the marginal revenues from the two markets. Since the domestic demand is more inelastic, the price in the domestic market, p_d^*, will be higher than in the foreign market, p_f^*.

b Domestic demand and the corresponding marginal revenue curve will increase by $1 at every quantity (marginal revenue is *A′B′* in Figure A14.4a). This results in a shift in the aggregate marginal revenue curve to *D′E′F′* as shown in Figure A14.4c. As indicated in Figure A14.4b, this reduces output and increases price in the foreign sector to y_f' and p_f', and increases both quantity and price in the domestic sector to y_d' and p_d' as shown in the figure. Total revenue from sales abroad will fall because the price has increased along the elastic part of the demand curve; however, the increase in profits from the domestic sector more than compensates for this decline, resulting in larger total profits.

32 BC is practicing block price discrimination. BC would increase blocks beyond $y = 60$ only if the marginal cost of doing so (zero in this case) were less than the additional revenue. To find the additional revenue, the marginal revenue must be determined. The marginal revenue is found by calculating the change in total revenue with the change in output (total revenue = average revenue × output).

Total Revenue	y	Marginal Revenue
0	0	
16	20	16/20 = 0.8
24	40	8/20 = 0.4
24	60	0/20 = 0

Note that marginal revenue equals marginal cost at $y = 60$. No more blocks will be offered.

33 a To determine the solution under ordinary price discrimination, one must horizontally add the marginal revenue curves from the two markets. The marginal revenue curves are

$$MR_a = 16 - 2y_a \quad \text{and} \quad MR_c = 10 - y_c$$

Rewrite the marginal revenue curves with quantity on the right-hand side:

$$y_a = 8 - \frac{1}{2}MR_a \quad \text{and} \quad y_c = 10 - MR_c$$

Adding the two curves and setting $y_a + y_c = y$ gives the aggregate marginal revenue curve

$$MR(y) = 12 - \frac{2}{3}y$$

FIGURE A14.3

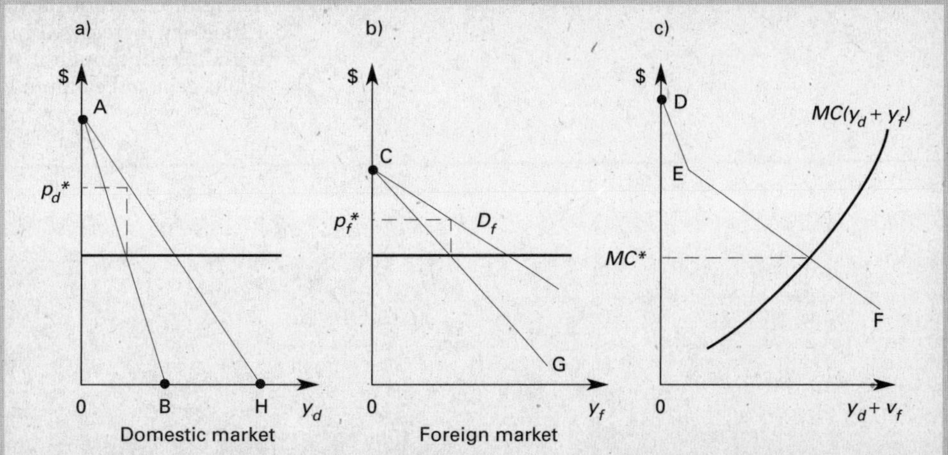

FIGURE A14.4

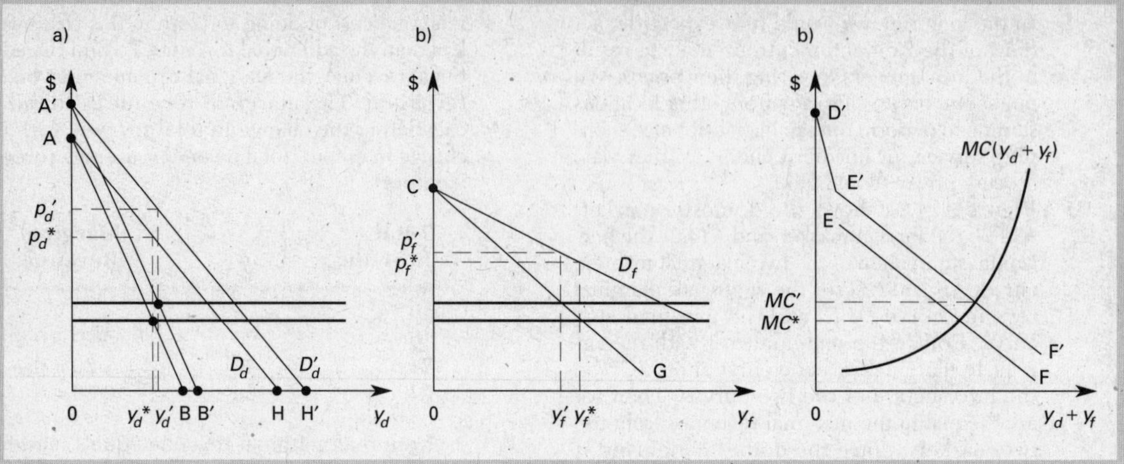

Setting $MR(y) = MC(y)$ gives $y = 12$. At this quantity, $MC = 4$. Marginal cost is set equal to the marginal revenues in each of the markets to determine the sales in each market: $y_a = 6$ and $y_c = 6$. Prices in each market are determined by substituting the quantities into the respective demand curves: $p_a = \$10$ and $p_c = \$7$.

b The nondiscriminating monopolist will set $MR(y)$ (the aggregate marginal revenue curve) with marginal cost. As in **a**, $y = 12$. The price is determined by substituting y into the aggregate demand curve (the horizontal summation of the two demand curves) $p = 12 - y/3$; hence, $p = \$8$. So, $y_a = 8$ and $y_c = 4$. (Note that this price is between the two prices under price discrimination.)

c *Under discrimination:*

$$\text{consumer surplus (adults)} = \left(\frac{1}{2}\right)(6)(6) = 18$$

$$\text{consumer surplus (children)} = \left(\frac{1}{2}\right)(3)(6) = 9$$

$$\text{profits to firm} = \text{revenues} - \text{costs}$$

$$= [(10)(6) + (7)(6)] - \frac{(12)(12)}{6}$$

$$= 102 - 24 = 78$$

Therefore, total surplus = 18 + 9 + 78 = 105.

Without discrimination:

$$\text{consumer surplus (adults)} = \left(\frac{1}{2}\right)(8)(8) = 32$$

$$\text{consumer surplus (children)} = \left(\frac{1}{2}\right)(2)(4) = 4$$

$$\text{profits} = (8)(12) - \frac{(12)(12)}{6} = 72$$

Therefore, total surplus = 32 + 4 + 72 = 108. Efficiency increases if price discrimination is not allowed, though it should be noted that adults gain and children lose as a result of the ban.

CHAPTER 15

Game Theory and Oligopoly

Chapter Summary

Distinguishing Features of Oligopoly

The "theory" of **oligopoly** does not have quite the elegant simplicity of the theories of monopoly and perfect competition. When one considers the definition of oligopoly — competition among the few — the reason for the relative complexity of oligopoly models becomes evident. In monopoly, only one firm, unthreatened by entry, produces in the market; in competition, many small firms produce, and no one firm perceives itself as capable of affecting market conditions. An oligopoly involves more than one firm, but not so many that a firm's actions can go unnoticed by its rivals. It is this interdependence among rivals' actions that distinguishes oligopoly from the other two market structures.

How should we model that interdependence? How do firms think in the real world? Does a firm believe that its rival will not react to its pricing strategy? At the other extreme, does it think that its rival will follow its every action? Does that behaviour change if one firm is established in the market and the other firm is a new entrant in the market? And what exactly do firms choose: price, quantity, advertising, or something else? To answer these questions, we will use the important tools of **game theory** and will focus on firms that produce homogeneous goods.

Game Theory

A game is a situation in which two or more **players** interact. Each player chooses their **strategies** (for example, price or output) so as to maximize his or her **payoff**, given the strategies of the other players. The mapping from strategies of rival players to the strategy that maximizes a player's payoff is called a **best response function**. The **equilibrium strategy combination** is a **Nash equilibrium**, or **Cournot-Nash equilibrium**, if each strategy in the combination maximizes each of the player's payoff, given the other players' strategies in the combination.

The Oligopoly Problem

We begin with a famous game of conflict (the **prisoner's dilemma**) between two firms (a **duopoly**) to introduce the problems that can arise. In this game each firm can produce a large or small quantity. A **dominant strategy**, that is, each firm's best response to *any* strategy of its rival, is to produce a large output. The "dilemma" is that in equilibrium, both firms produce large quantities when, in fact, they would be better off if they could agree to restrict outputs. The "prisoner" part of the name of this game refers to the original application of this game to two prisoners accused of committing a crime, who face a decision of whether to reveal their "inside information" or keep quiet.

The prisoners' dilemma game illustrates the basic oligopoly problem: The pursuit of self-interest leads to an equilibrium in which both firms are worse off. So, oligopolists have an incentive to collude. However, if this cooperative agreement is not a Nash equilibrium, then it is not a **self-enforcing agreement** and so oligopolists will have an incentive to cheat on the agreement. We explore this oligopoly problem further with the two famous models of Cournot and Bertrand oligopoly.

Cournot and Bertrand Oligopoly Models

The questions posed earlier suggest some of the many aspects, absent from monopoly and competition, that one must consider when modeling an oligopolistic market. Two short-run models of noncooperative behaviour — the **Cournot model** and **Bertrand model** — differ in the choice variable of the firms. Cournot firms choose quantity; Bertrand firms choose price. In both cases, a Nash equilibrium is found in which each firm's strategy is profit-maximizing given the other firm's strategy; that is, firms are individually rational. With **isoprofit curves** (or indifference curves for the firm) we can show that this equilibrium does not maximize the joint profits of the firms. Alternatively, the strategy combinations are said to be self-enforcing. As the number of firms increases in the Cournot model, the competitive solution is reached; however, in the Bertrand model, the equilibrium characterized by price equals marginal cost, is invariant to the number of firms.

If firms were to behave cooperatively and collude on their choice of quantity and price, the best they could achieve would be the monopoly solution. If the profits were equally divided, all firms in the market would be better off than in either the Cournot or Bertrand noncooperative solution (assuming identical cost conditions for the firms). This **collusive model** is collectively rational; that is, it maximizes joint profits, but it is not individually rational because each firm has the incentive to cheat by producing more output than allotted under collusion or by shaving its price.

The Cournot and Bertrand models are simply prisoners' dilemma games. If the games played by noncooperative agents were repeated, and the agents were to devise **credible punishments** providing sufficient disincentives to cheat, then the collusive solution could be both individually and collectively rational. Note that if a game is repeated infinitely it is known as a **supergame**.

Endogenous Market Structure

When market structure becomes endogenous — that is, when the number of firms is no longer fixed — the models of oligopoly become more complicated and fascinating. Under the assumptions of Cournot behaviour and knowledge of the "rules of the game" by all existing and potential firms in the industry, market structure is easily endogenized in this model through the introduction of **setup costs**, costs required to enter the market. From the perspective of an established firm in the market, setup costs are **sunk** and have no effect on the firm's profit-making decisions. However, from the point of view of the potential entrant, the setup costs are avoidable by not entering and hence are important to the firm's entry decision. Moreover, if entry occurs, the nature of the oligopoly behaviour affects the decision to enter: The more cooperative the oligopoly is after entry, the more attractive entry will be. For example, in the case of Bertrand behaviour, a "second" firm will never find entry profitable for positive setup costs; hence, monopoly is always predicted to arise.

Strategic Behaviour

The established firm can be more aggressive and can behave strategically in such a way that a potential rival will not find entry profitable. Sylos-Labini suggests one way: In the **limit-output model** (known also as the **limit-price model**) an established firm can set a **limit output** (or **limit price**), such that there is no profitable output level that the entrant can produce, which is the **no-entry condition**. The limit output, though possibly exceeding the monopoly output, may be profitable for the established firm to produce if it is entry-deterring. Although the Sylos postulate is instructive in strategic behaviour by established firms, it is based on the unattractive assumption that the **potential entrants** take as given the current output of the established firm as an indication of the future output that will be produced by the established firm. This threat is not necessarily credible; that is, if the entrant *actually* enters despite the established firm's threat, the established firm may find a different output choice more profitable.

This brings us to recent developments in the economics literature. If an established firm makes a **gross profit**, i.e., its revenues exceed variable costs, then these serve as an **inducement to entry**. It follows that some **barriers to entry** must be in place protecting these profits. The established firm may deliberately establish these barriers by incurring setup costs (advertising, research and development outlays) with the intention of discouraging entry. Other barriers may naturally arise from the technology in place, for example, due to production economies of scale. Spence distinguishes between two types of actions: **positioning** and **reacting**. First, a firm may want to position itself prior to the entry of a rival in a way that will make its threats credible. For example, to indicate that it will produce more output if entry occurs, the firm may purchase additional equipment or carry excess inventories; or to show that it will fight a price war, the firm may incur some expenditures on advertising specifically about a price war before the war is actually fought. Second, firms can also react to rivals after entry occurs.

KEY WORDS

Barrier to entry
Bertrand model
Best response function
Collusive model
Cournot model
Cournot-Nash equilibrium
Credible punishments
Dominant strategy
Duopoly
Equilibrium strategy combination
Game theory
Gross profit
Inducement to entry
Isoprofit curves
Limit output
Limit-output model

Limit price
Limit-price model
Nash equilibrium
No-entry condition
Noncooperative behaviour
Oligopoly
Players
Payoff
Positioning
Potential entrant
Prisoners' dilemma
Profit matrix
Punishment strategies
Reacting
Self-enforcing agreement
Setup costs
Strategies
Sunk costs
Supergame

CASE STUDY: TACIT COLLUSION OR GIVING CONSUMERS A GOOD DEAL?

Several practices of firms look harmless or even beneficial to consumers, but may actually be strategies for facilitating collusion. These strategies are called "facilitating practices."

One such practice is the *Most-Favoured Customer Clause* (MFC): A guarantee to pay current customers the difference between the price they paid and the lowest price offered during some prescribed period. The MFC reduces each firm's incentives to shave price since any firm decreasing its price must give a rebate to all previous customers. Since no firm has the incentive to lower price under an MFC clause, the actual price will be higher than in the absence of this policy.

The practice of offering MFC guarantees is not uncommon; for example, you may have encountered it in your purchases. NutraSweet, a monopoly producer of aspartame, wrote MFC into its contracts with Coke and Pepsi just prior to the expiration of its patent in Canada.

A Is the MFC clause self-enforcing (individually rational) or collectively rational (maximizes joint profits)?

B The MFC clause above is presented as an "anti-competitive" practice, that is, one that is used to raise prices. What might be a more innocuous rationale for offering MFC clauses? For example, can you think of a reason why Coke and Pepsi may want NutraSweet to offer them an MFC guarantee?

C Can you think of another "facilitating practice"?

EXERCISES

Multiple-Choice

Choose the correct answer to each question. There is only one correct answer to each question.

1 The payoff matrix in Figure 15.1 gives the profits from spending either $1 000 or $2 000 on advertising to firms A and B, net of costs. The first number in each cell is the payoff to firm A, and the second number is the payoff to firm B, in thousands of dollars. The Nash equilibrium to this game is

a Firm A will spend $1 000 and firm B will spend $2 000 on advertising.
b Both firms will spend $2 000 on advertising.
c Both firms will spend $1 000 on advertising.
d Neither firm will advertise at all.
e None of the above.

2 Two firms behave as Cournot duopolists in the market for soft drinks. The firms face identical con-

FIGURE 15.1

Firm A		Firm B: $1000	Firm B: $2000
	$1000	10,10	1,15
	$2000	15,1	3,3

stant marginal costs of c and a market demand $p = a - by$. In equilibrium,

a The two firms will produce identical quantities equal to $a/3b$.
b The market price in this case will exceed the market price if the two firms colluded.
c The industry output will equal two-thirds the market demand at $p = c$.
d The market price will be $a/3$.
e None of the above.

3 As the number of firms in a Cournot oligopoly gets large,
a Output produced by each firm increases.
b Industry output increases, and price falls to the competitive level.
c The market price approaches the collusive price.
d The oligopolists behave in a more collectively rational manner.

FIGURE 15.2

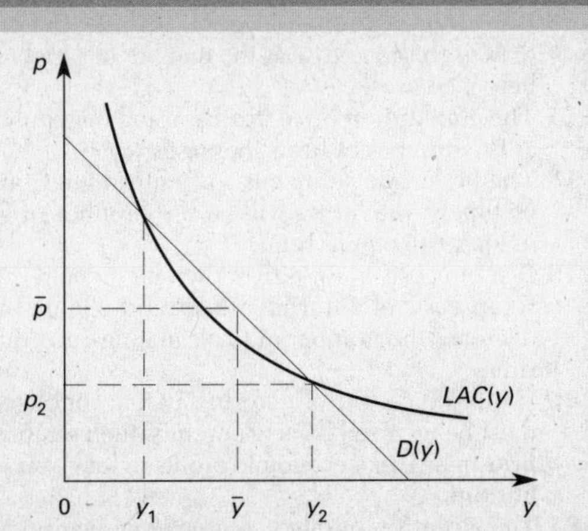

e None of the above.

4 In the limit-output model,
a An entrant can be deterred from entering the market even if it has the same technology as the established firm.
b The limit output will be greater than or equal to the monopoly output in the absence of a threat.
c An entrant responds to the residual demand, which is the market demand remaining after subtracting the established firm's output.
d All the above.
e Only **b** and **c**.

5 For a Bertrand oligopoly,
a The equilibrium price is equal to the monopoly price.
b The equilibrium price exceeds the price set by Cournot duopolists, assuming identical market conditions.
c The equilibrium concept is based on joint profit maximization.
d The equilibrium price equals the competitive price.
e None of the above.

6 Figure 15.2 shows an entrant firm's long-run average cost curve and the market demand. Under the Sylos postulate, if the established firm sets an output level equal to $\bar{y}$,
a The potential entrant will enter the market between output levels y_1 and y_2.
b The potential entrant will not enter the market because the long-run average cost exceeds the residual demand at every quantity.
c The potential entrant will enter the market because the entrant does not believe the established firm will continue to produce $\bar{y}$.
d The potential entrant will enter the market and price will fall to p_2.
e None of the above.

To answer questions **7–8**, consider Figure 15.3, which shows the reaction functions of two Cournot firms. Each firm has marginal costs equal to zero; market demand is $p = 1 - y$.

7 In Figure 15.3,
a Firm 1's reaction function is CD; firm 2's reaction function is BE.
b Firm 1's reaction function is BE; firm 2's reaction function is CD.
c Distances OB and OD equal the monopoly output, $y = 1/2$.
d Both **a** and **c**.
e Both **b** and **c**.

8 Suppose that only firm 2's marginal costs increase to 1/4. Then which of the following will occur?
a Firm 2's reaction curve will shift downward.
b Firm 1's reaction curve will shift upward.
c The new equilibrium set of outputs (y_1^*, y_2^*) will lie along CD, with $y_2^* < y_1^*$.
d Both **a** and **c**.
e Both **b** and **c**.

FIGURE 15.3

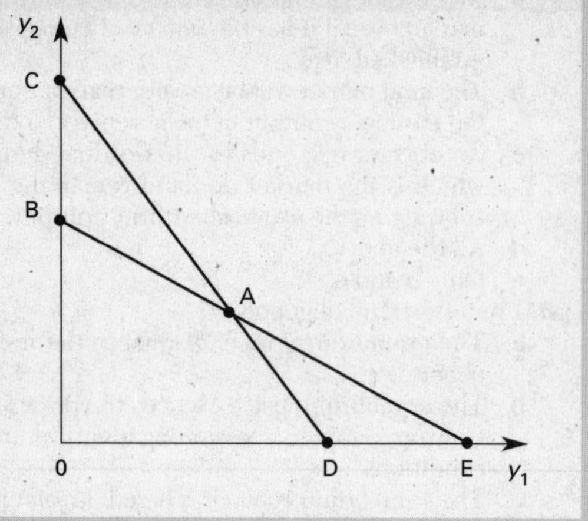

FIGURE 15.4

Mary \ John	Mud wrestling	Stay home
Mud wrestling	4, 2	1, 1
Stay home	0, 0	2, 4

9 Suppose firms sequentially enter a market. The firms face the same constant marginal costs of production and positive setup costs. The demand for the product is linear. Let n_C, n_B, and n_M be the long-run numbers of firms under Cournot, Bertrand and collusive behaviour. Then

- **a** $n_C > n_B > n_M$
- **b** $n_B > n_M > n_C$
- **c** $n_M > n_C > n_B$
- **d** $n_C > n_M > n_B$
- **e** None of the above.

To answer questions **10-11**, consider the game illustrated in Figure 15.4, in which John and Mary choose where to go one evening: Mud Wrestling or Stay Home. The payoffs are given in the table below. The first number in each cell refers to Mary's payoff; the second number to John's payoff.

10 In the above game,

- **a** Stay Home is a dominant strategy for John.
- **b** Mud Wrestling is a dominant strategy for Mary.
- **c** Mud Wrestling is a dominant strategy for both John and Mary.
- **d** Stay Home is a dominant strategy for both John and Mary.
- **e** Neither John nor Mary has a dominant strategy.

11 In the above game,

- **a** There is a unique Nash equilibrium in which both John and Mary choose Mud Wrestling.
- **b** There is a unique Nash equilibrium in which both John and Mary choose Stay Home.
- **c** There are two Nash equilibria in which both John and Mary choose the same place (either Mud Wrestling or Stay Home)
- **d** There are two Nash equilibria in which John and Mary choose different places (one goes to Mud Wrestling and the other Stays Home).
- **e** There is no Nash equilibrium.

12 For a Cournot oligopoly with n firms facing constant marginal costs c and market demand $p = 1 - y$, the equilibrium price will be

- **a** $(1 + cn)/(n + 1)$
- **b** $(1 - c)n/(n + 1)$
- **c** c
- **d** $a/2$
- **e** None of the above.

True-False

13 Industry output in a duopoly model of Cournot behaviour exceeds the industry output under collusive behaviour.

14 The larger the setup costs faced by the entrant, the larger will be the limit output chosen by the established firm in the Sylos model.

15 The more firms that produce in a Cournot oligopoly, the larger is the industry output.

16 If firms in a Cournot oligopoly collude, the incentives to cheat increase as the number of cartel members increases.

17 The equilibrium price in a Bertrand oligopoly falls as the number of firms increases.

18 The larger the setup costs of entering a Cournot oligopoly, the larger will be the number of firms in long-run equilibrium.

19 If setup costs are positive, then an increase in the setup costs of entering a Bertrand oligopoly will decrease the number of firms in long-run equilibrium.

20 If the setup costs of entering a Cournot oligopoly must be incurred by new entrants, then established firms may make economic profits in long-run equilibrium.

21 The incentive to collude is greater among Bertrand oligopolists than among Cournot oligopolists, everything else held constant.

22 Bertrand pricing behaviour and positive setup costs are sufficient to deter potential entrants from a market in which one firm is producing as a monopolist.

23 The Nash equilibrium concept is based on joint profit maximization.

24 Suppose $p = 1 - y$ is the inverse demand and $c_1 = 0.6$ and $c_2 = 0.2$ are constant marginal costs of firms 1 and 2, respectively. Then, in a Bertrand-Nash equilibrium, only firm 2 will produce at a market price equal to 0.2.

25 Suppose the industry is characterized by the inverse demand function $p = 20 - y$, where p = market price and y = market quantity. Marginal costs of production are constant and equal to 5, and each firm must pay a fixed entry fee of F to enter the industry. Firms in the industry behave as Cournot oligopolists. Then, if four firms enter the industry in the long run, F must be greater than or equal to 9.

FIGURE 15.5

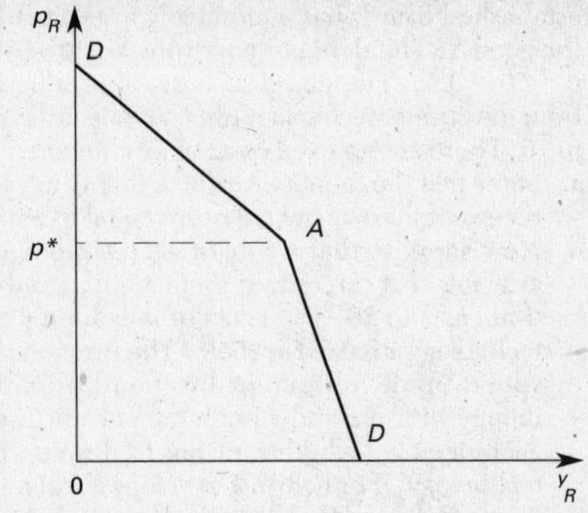

Short Problems

26 In a famous Canadian case, three sugar refineries (Atlantic, Redpath and St. Lawrence) were accused in 1975 of conspiring to fix prices (they were ultimately acquitted). These companies would charge identical delivered prices bases on prices posted daily by Redpath. Such a scheme is called *base-point pricing*. Essentially, all refiners would quote the same price to any given customer regardless of actual transportation costs. The quoted price would equal the base price plus transportation costs from *one* location regardless of that refiner's actual location. Why would firms be willing to adopt such a price practice?

27 Suppose that a ban on advertising is imposed in the cigarette industry, which we assume to consist of two firms. Show, using a simple game-theoretical model, how this policy may result in higher equilibrium profits for the two firms.

28 Suppose that two firms in the same market tacitly agree to share the market. Show that this agreement results in the collusive outcome when the firms' cost curves are identical.

29 Suppose that a firm in an oligopolistic industry faces the kinked demand curve for its product shown in Figure 15.5, where p^* is the current equilibrium price in the industry.

a Why might the firm believe that its demand curve has this shape?

b Explain why the price of the commodity may stay constant even if input prices, and therefore costs, change.

30 The International Air Transport Association (IATA), a trade association consisting of most of the world's international airlines, sets the rates for international routes. Two basic fare levels are set by IATA for its members to follow: regular and excursion fares. IATA designates the fares that must be set on specific routes. Because IATA members cannot compete with each other in prices on these routes, many IATA member airlines offer tourist travel packages including the airline flight, hotel accommodation, vehicle rental, and sightseeing tours, in order to attract customers.

a Why is it in the interest of the airlines *as a group* to charge an identical price?

b Why do the IATA members offer the travel packages?

c Explain why IATA might want to check each package offered and have the right to veto any offerings.

31 In some industries, collusive agreements among firms in the industry are stable; that is, they last for a long time. OPEC, for example, was formed in the early 1960s, dominated the oil market in the 1970s, and has persisted as a reasonably strong force in the petroleum market ever since. Other collusive arrangements — for example, in the copper market — have had histories of instability. What factors contribute to the stability (or instability) of a cartel?

*32 Consider the following symmetric Cournot triopoly in which three firms are producing a homogeneous product for which the inverse demand function is $p = 1 - (y_1 + y_2 + y_3)$, where y_i is the output of firm i. Costs of production are zero. Suppose that if two firms merge, then the marginal firm will compete symmetrically with the remaining unmerged firm. That is, after a merger there will be two Cournot firms with zero costs. Show that no two firms will have the incentive to merge. Explain this result.

Long Problems

*33 Consider the following game. A firm, call it the established firm I, has a monopoly in the market for good Y. The demand curve for Y is given by $p = 50 - 0.5y$. The marginal costs of production from the current technology are constant and equal to 10. There are no fixed costs of production.

a Show that the monopoly profits that firm I will receive if there is not entry are equal to $800.

b Now suppose that a substitute technology is available that can reduce the marginal production costs to $0. The costs of developing the technology are fixed at $550. (The firms cannot speed up development by spending more money.) Firm I and a potential entrant E are each deciding whether or not to develop the technology. If only firm I develops it, then the firm will discard the old technology and simply produce as a monopolist with the new technology. If only firm E develops it, then the firms will produce as Cournot duopolists, in which case, firm I will have marginal costs $MC_I = 10$ and firm E will have marginal costs $MC_E = 0$. If both develop the technology, they will produce as Cournot duopolists, where both firms I and E will have marginal costs equal to zero. If no one develops it, the status quo discussed in **a** will occur. Show the following:

(1) The monopoly profits to firm I, if *only* firm I develops the new technology, are $700.

(2) The Cournot profits to firms I and E, if *only* E develops the technology, are $\pi_I = \$200$ and $\pi_E = \$250$.

(3) The Cournot profits to firms I and E, if *both* firms develop the technology, are $\pi_I = \pi_E = \$5.56$.

c Given the profits in **a** and **b**, construct a payoff matrix for firms I and E with strategies "develop" (D) and "do not develop" (N). Show that if both firms move simultaneously in this game, there is only one Nash equilibrium, in which only firm E develops the technology. Give an intuitive explanation for that result.

d Would your answer in **c** change if firm I could move first in the research game? Explain. Would your answer change if firm E could move first? Explain.

*34 Two firms produce products that are perfect substitutes for each other, but the costs of production are different for the two firms. The demand and cost conditions are described by

$$p = 100 - \frac{(y_1 + y_2)}{2}$$

and

$$MC_1 = 19 \qquad MC_2 = y_2$$

where p is the market price, y_1 is the quantity produced by firm 1, y_2 is the quantity produced by firm 2, MC_1 is the marginal cost of production by firm 1, and MC_2 is the marginal cost of production by firm 2.

a Derive the quantity reaction function for each firm on the assumption of Cournot behaviour (that is, each firm maximizes its profits with respect to quantity, given its rival's output). Determine the equilibrium quantities for each firm and the market price.

b What will happen to industry output and price if the two firms maximize joint profits rather than behave as Cournot duopolists? Determine the equilibrium price and quantity in the collusive case.

c Illustrate your results in **a** and **b** with a diagram that includes the firms' reaction functions and isoprofit curves.

*35 There are two Cournot firms in the widget industry. The graph in Figure 15.6 shows their Cournot reaction functions. The inverse demand is $p = 1 - (1/2)y$, where p = market price and y = market output. The firms face constant average production costs.

a Given the information in Figure 15.6:

(1) Show that the constant average costs for firms 1 and 2 respectively are $c_1 = 0.3$ and $c_2 = 0.2$.

(2) Determine the quantities at A and B on Figure 15.6.

(3) Derive the Cournot–Nash equilibrium price and firm quantities.

b Suppose the firms decide to collude and maximize joint profits rather than compete as Cournot duopolists. If sidepayments are possible, what will be the market price and quantity and firm quantities that maximize joint profits? Show that firm 1 will have the incentive to deviate from the cooperative solution. Explain the intuition behind this behaviour.

FIGURE 15.6

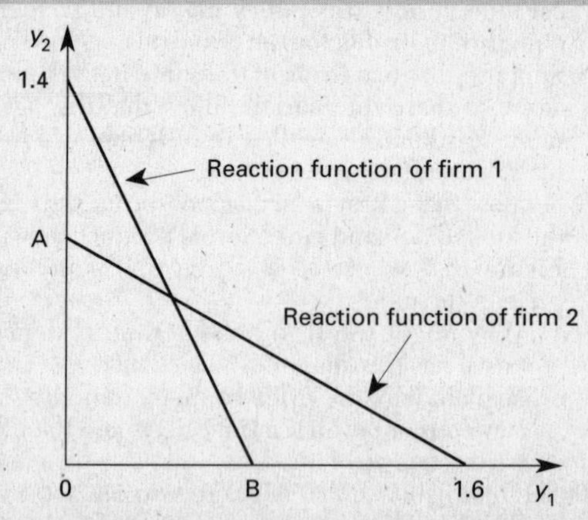

***36** Suppose that an industry is characterized by the inverse demand function

$$p = 1 - y$$

and zero variable costs. Firms in the industry reach a Cournot–Nash equilibrium in quantities.

a Find the equilibrium price, profits per firm, if there are
(1) Two firms
(2) Three firms
(3) N firms

b Suppose that variable costs are still zero, but each firm incurs a setup cost of 0.05. Repeat (1), (2), and (3) from **a**. If there is free entry into the market, what will be the long-run equilibrium number of firms?

c Suppose each firm believes that if it produces in this market, it will sell $1/N$ of total output. Under this assumption, what will be the long-run equilibrium number of firms? Compare this answer with the one in **b**.

***37** An established firm in the market for widgets faces the following demand and cost conditions:

$$p = 100 - \frac{y}{2}$$

$$MC_1 = 40$$

where p is the price and y is the quantity demanded. A second firm is considering entering this market. If this firm enters, it can produce only with a production technology that has constant marginal costs,

$$MC_2 = 40$$

If both firms produce in the market, they will behave as Cournot duopolists.

a Find the Sylos limit output when setup costs of entry equal $450.

b Will the incumbent have the incentive to set the limit output to deter entry?

38 The oil cartel OPEC sells oil in the world market along with many smaller firms and oil-producing countries. A reasonable approximation of actual behavior by the smaller and fringe firms in this market is that they take the price set by OPEC and do not believe that their production of oil can have a large effect on the price. Figure 15.7 shows the cost and demand conditions for this oil market: MC_f is the horizontal summation of the fringe firms' supply curves, MC_c is the marginal cost curve of the cartel, and $D(y)$ is the market demand.

a Under the assumption that OPEC is a profit-maximizing cartel, indicate the price that OPEC will set and the resulting output shares by the cartel and the fringe firms. (*Hint*: OPEC will want to take the fringe's reactions to its price announcements into account in choosing price. To do this, OPEC will subtract the output that the fringe firms will be willing to produce at every price and then will set its price using the "residual" demand that remains.)

b Given your solution in **a**, what might have been the reason for OPEC's surprise in 1976 when it discovered that the demand for oil was not as price-inelastic as had been thought?

c If the cost curves in the figure are short-run curves, what would you expect to happen in the long run if OPEC continued to set price at the short-run profit-maximizing level you found in **a**.

***39** Mac N. Ro, Inc., has a monopoly in the production of tennis shoes. The marginal cost of producing shoes is $18. Mac Ltd., however, does not have the facilities for selling the shoes to consumers, so it sells them wholesale to a firm that, in turn, sells the shoes to consumers in a monopoly retail market. The retail firm faces marginal costs equal to the wholesale price of the shoes, p_w, plus marginal retail costs of $10. The consumer demand for tennis shoes is given by $p = 100 - y$.

a Determine the wholesale and retail prices and the market output.

b Show that Mac Ltd. could increase profits by vertically integrating forward into the retail business. That is, it would produce *and* sell the shoes, incurring a total marginal cost of $28.

c Can you think of an alternative to vertical integration that would yield the same profits?

FIGURE 15.7

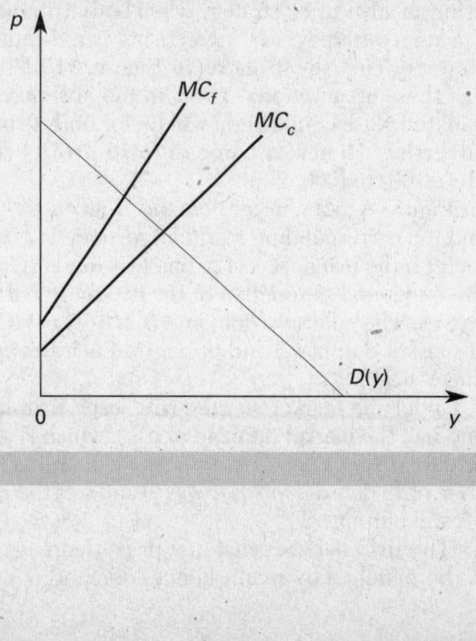

ANSWERS TO CHAPTER 15

Case Study

A The MFC guarantee is unusual in that it is both self-enforcing and collectively rational. That is, given that the firms have committed to offer an MFC to consumers, then it is not in the firms' individual interest to lower price. It is also collectively rational in that this strategy moves the firms closer to joint profit-maximization.

B Customers may be willing to pay for an MFC guarantee for insurance reasons. That is, if customers are firms that purchase inputs that require large capital outlays, it may want insurance from the supplier of those inputs that it will receive any price reduction offered to its competitors.

C *Meeting Competition Clause* is another example of a facilitating practice. Under this strategy, a firm promises to match a lower price of a competitor. This serves as an information exchange device in that customers must inform a seller of a lower price set by a competitor in order to get a discount. That is, customers provide information on cheating cartel members.

Multiple-Choice

1 b 2 c 3 b 4 d 5 d 6 b
7 d 8 d 9 c 10 e 11 c 12 a

True-False

13 T 14 F 15 T 16 T 17 F 18 F
19 F 20 T 21 T 22 T 23 F 24 F 25 F

Short Problems

26 This practice is a collusive agreement by firms. Without this agreement, firms would compete in prices. Joint profits are higher under this agreement. This strategy may not be individually rational, however, because firms will have an incentive to lower the price below the collusive price for nearby customers.

27 Assume two things: (1) Profits to both firms using the strategy of no advertising are higher than those using an advertising strategy when both firms adopt the same strategy; (2) Advertising is a dominant strategy. The payoff matrix in Figure A15.1 satisfies these assumptions. Thus, in the absence of a ban, the Nash equilibrium will be for both firms to advertise. Hence, a ban can raise profits from (100, 100) to (200, 200).

28 In Figure A15.2 market demand is given by $D(y)$ and the corresponding marginal revenue is $MR(y)$; $mc(y)$ is the marginal cost of one firm, and $MC(y)$ is the horizontal summation of the two marginal cost curves. The collusive outcome is $MR(y) = MC(y)$, at market output y^* and price p^*. Each firm produces $1/2y^*$.

Under the market-sharing rule, each firm faces one-half the market demand or $d(y)$, which is identical to $MR(y)$. Each firm equates the marginal revenue of its demand $mr(y)$ to $mc(y)$ and sets the price p^* and output $1/2y^*$.

29 a The firm believes that any price decrease will be matched by rivals; hence, demand is more inelastic for low prices. Furthermore, any price increases will not be matched; hence, demand is more elastic at high prices.

b Because of the kink in the demand, the marginal revenue is discontinuous. Hence, $MC(y)$ can increase over a large range and $MR(y)$ equals $MC(y)$ at the same output level y^* and price p^*, as shown in Figure A15.3.

FIGURE A15.1

Firm 1 \ Firm 2	Advertise	Do not advertise
Advertise	100, 100	300, 50
Do not advertise	50, 300	200, 200

FIGURE A15.2

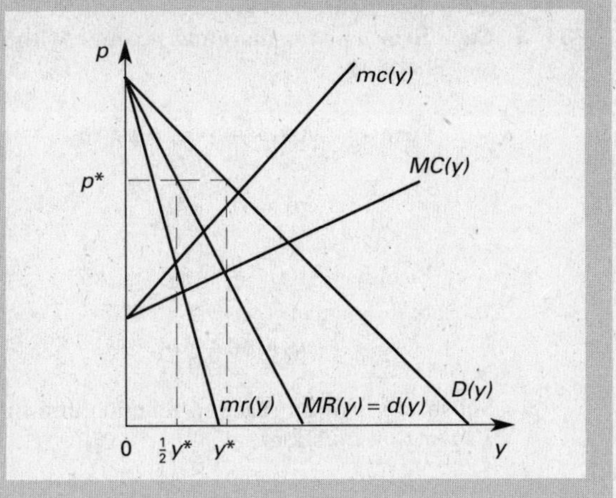

FIGURE A15.3

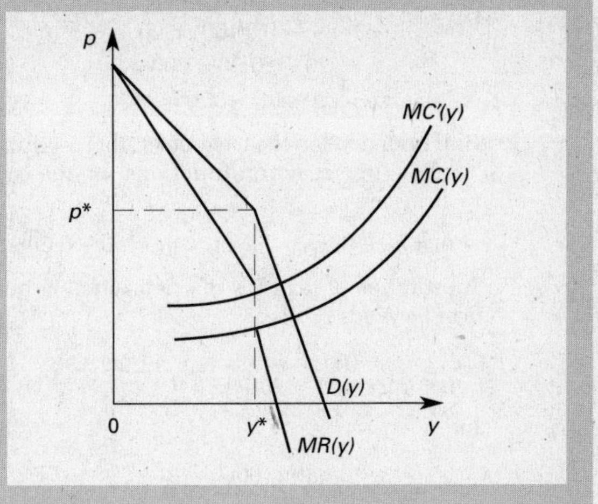

30 a Collusion results in larger profits for the group as a whole.

b The travel packages may be a way of disguising price cuts, or they may represent non-price competition.

c Since the travel packages may be a way of cheating on the collusive agreement, IATA's right of veto is a way to police the agreement.

31 A cartel will be more stable the fewer the firms in the cartel because cheaters can be more easily detected. Stability of the cartel is also more likely if entry barriers into the market are high. If supply from firms outside the cartel can respond quickly to increases in the cartel price, the cartel will be unstable. For example, if there are fixed supplies of resources, fewer entrants will be able to enter the market and put downward pressure on price. The more there is to lose by cheating on the cartel, the less likely there will be cheating. The fewer substitutes that exist for the good and the less elastic is the demand for the good, the more stable the cartel becomes.

***32** The profits of each firm in a Cournot oligopoly are $1/(N+1)^2$, where N is the number of firms in the market. Since $N = 3$, firm profits are 1/16. If two firms merge, then there will be $N = 2$ firms in the market, so firm profits are 1/9. In order for two firms to have the incentive to merge, it must be that both firms are made better off under the merger. However, under the merger, the two merging parties earn a total of 1/9, whereas by not merging each firm earns 1/16, or a total of 1/8. Hence, no two firms will have the incentive to merge in this case. The intuition for this result is that the merging firms cut back on output, but because Cournot reaction functions slope downward, the nonmerging party will respond to this cutback with an increase in its quantity, thus eliminating any benefits from merging.

Long Problems

***33 a** Monopoly price and quantity are found by equating MR_I and MC_I.

$$MR_I = 50 - y = 10 = MC_I \quad \text{so } y = 40$$
$$p = 50 - (0.5)(40) = 30$$
$$\pi = (30 - 10)40 = \$800$$

b (1) If only firm I develops the technology,

$$MR_I = 50 - y = 0$$
$$y = 50$$
$$p = 50 - (0.5)(50) = 25$$
$$\pi = (50)(25) - 550 = 700$$

(2) Reaction functions are found for $MC_I = 10$ and $MC_E = 0$:

$$MR_I = 50 - 0.5y_E - y_I = 10$$

which implies that $y_I = 40 - 0.5y_E$ and

$$MR_E = 50 - 0.5y_I - y_E = 0$$

so

$$y_E = 50 - 0.5y_I$$

Substitute the second equation into the first:

$$y_I = 40 - 0.5(50 - 0.5y_I)$$

so

$$y_I = 20 \qquad y_E = 40$$
$$p = 50 - (0.5)(60) = 20$$
$$\pi_I = (20 - 10)20 = 200$$
$$\pi_E = (20)(40) - 550 = 250$$

(3) If both develop the technology, then — from (2) — the reaction functions for the two firms are

$$y_I = 50 - 0.5y_E \quad \text{and} \quad y_E = 50 - 0.5y_I$$

Substitution of firm E's reaction function into firm I's yields

$$y_I = y_E = \frac{100}{3} \quad \text{and } p = 50 - \frac{200}{6} = \frac{50}{3}$$

and

$$\pi_I = \pi_E = \left(\frac{50}{3}\right)\left(\frac{100}{3}\right) - 550 = 5.56$$

c The Nash equilibrium set of strategies is "develop" (D) for the entrant and "do not develop" (N) for the incumbent. As indicated in Figure A15.4, N is a dominant strategy for firm I: Whether firm E chooses D or N, firm I can do better by choosing N rather than D. For the entrant, D is a dominant strategy.

d If firm I could move first or firm E could move first, the answer in **c** would not change. Let firm I move first. It knows that whatever it does, firm E will choose D. Hence, firm I chooses the strategy with the larger payoff, N, and firm E follows with D. If firm E moves first, it knows that whatever it does, firm I will react by choosing N. Hence, firm E chooses the strategy with the largest payoff, D, and firm I follows with N. This result follows from the fact that each firm has a dominant strategy.

FIGURE A15.4

Incumbent \ Entrant	D	N	
D	5.56, 5.56	700, 0	5.56
N	200, 250	800, 0	200
	250	0	

*34 **a** Each firm equates marginal revenue with its marginal cost.

Firm 1: $100 - \frac{y_2}{2} - y_1 = 19$, so

$$y_1 = 81 - \frac{1}{2}y_2$$

Firm 2: $100 - \frac{y_1}{2} - y_2 = y_2$, so

$$y_2 = 50 - \frac{1}{4}y_1$$

Substitute firm 2's reaction function into firm 1's reaction function:

$$y_1 = 81 - \left(\frac{1}{2}\right)\left(50 - \frac{1}{4}y_1\right)$$
$$= 56 + \frac{1}{8}y_1$$

Solving for y_1 gives

$$y_1 = 64$$

Substitute $y_1 = 64$ into firm 2's reaction function:

$$y_2 = 50 - \frac{64}{4} = 34$$

Then, total output is $y = y_1 + y_2 = 98$, and market price is $p = 51$.

b If the two firms collude and maximize joint profits, they will allocate output to each firm so as to minimize total production costs. The horizontal summation of the marginal costs is shown in Figure A15.5. This problem is similar to a multiplant monopolist. That is, the two firms will choose output in each "plant" where $MC_1 = MC_2$ or

$$y_2 = 19$$

FIGURE A15.5

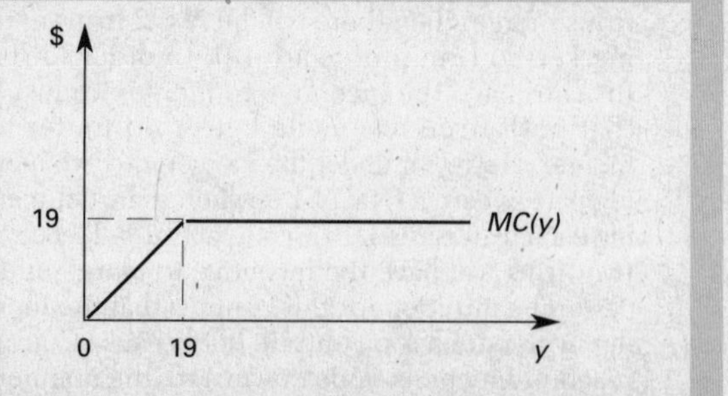

Total output is found by equating marginal revenue to the marginal cost of each firm. Since $MC_1 = MC_2 = 19$, total output is given by

$$100 - y = 19$$
$$y = 81$$

Equations (1) and (2) imply that $y_1 = 62$, $y_2 = 19$, and $p = 59.5$.

c In Figure A15.6, firm 1's reaction function, $y_1 = 81 - (1/2)y_2$, is given by *AB* and firm 2's reaction function, $y_2 = 50 - (1/4)y_1$, is *CD*. The Cournot–Nash equilibrium is given by *E* at quantities (64, 34). The isoprofit curves through point *E* reveal an area (shaded in the diagram) in which both firms could be better off; that is, profits of both firms could increase if they produced an output combination within the shaded area.

°35 a (1) In Figure 15.6 are firm 1's and firm 2's reaction functions. The point $(y_1, y_2) = (0, 1.4)$ on firm 1's reaction function implies that firm 1's "best response" to firm 2's output of $y_2 = 1.4$ is to set $y_1 = 0$. This means that at this output level of firm 2, firm 1 could not make positive profits for any positive output level; that is, market demand must equal firm 1's average cost. Algebraically, this implies: $1 - (1/2)(1.4) = c_1$, or $c_1 = 0.3$. Similarly, $y_2 = 0$ is firm 2's best response to firm 1's output $y_1 = 1.6$. Therefore, at this output, demand equals firm 2's average cost: $1 - (1/2)(1.6) = c_2$, or $c_2 = 0.2$.

(2) On firm 1's reaction function, point *B* is the monopoly output of firm 1 (that is, the output that firm 1 would choose if firm 2 produced zero output) and point *B* is the monopoly output of firm 2 (that is, the output that firm 2 would choose if firm 1 produced 0 output). Then A is given by

$$1 - y_2 = 0.2 \quad \text{so} \quad y_2 = 0.8$$

And B is given by

$$1 - y_1 = 0.3 \quad \text{so} \quad y_1 = 0.7$$

(3) Using the information above, we can find the reaction functions for firms 1 and 2. Reaction function for firm 1 is derived below:

$$1 - (1/2)y_2 - y_1 = 0.3 \quad \text{so} \quad y_1 = 0.7 - (1/2)y_2$$

Similarly, firm 2's reaction function is

$$1 - (1/2)y_1 - y_2 = 0.2 \quad \text{so} \quad y_2 = 0.8 - (1/2)y_1$$

Substitute firm 2's reaction function into firm 1's reaction function gives

$$y_1 = 0.7 - (1/2)(0.8 - (1/2)y_1)$$

which implies

$$y_1 = 0.4$$

Substitute this value of y_1 into firm 2's reaction function to get

$$y_2 = 0.8 - (1/2)(0.4) = 0.6$$

Finally, the market price is given by

$$p = 1 - (1/2)(0.4 + 0.6) = 0.5$$

b If the firms collude and sidepayments are possible, then only firm 2, the lower-cost firm, will produce. Firm 2 will produce at the monopoly output, $y_2 = 0.8$ and market price will be $p = 1 - (1/2)(0.8) = 0.6$. Firm 1 will produce 0, but will be paid profits by firm 2 so that it will agree to collude. However, this solution is not individually rational. That is, firm 1 will have the incentive to cheat by producing positive output. This can be seen by determining firm 1's individually rational "best response" to $y_2 = 0.8$. From firm 1's reaction function: $y_1 = 0.7 - (1/2)(0.8) = 0.3 > 0$. That is, firm 1 will have the incentive to produce positive output under the cooperative solution.

°36 a (1) For two firms, the profit function for each firm (for example, firm 1) is $(1 - y_1 - y_2)y_1$. Firm 1's reaction function is given by

$$1 - y_2 - 2y_1 = 0 \quad \text{so} \quad y_1 = \frac{1}{2} - \frac{y_2}{2}$$

Similarly, firm 2's reaction function is

$$y_2 = \frac{1}{2} - \frac{y_1}{2}$$

Solving the two equations simultaneously for

FIGURE A15.6

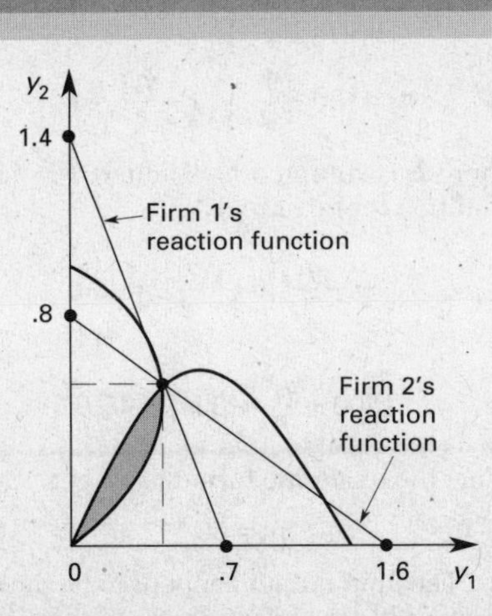

y_1 and y_2 gives

$$y_1 = y_2 = \frac{1}{3}$$

$$p = 1 - \frac{2}{3} = \frac{1}{3}$$

$$\pi = \pi_2 = \frac{1}{9}$$

(2) For three firms, the reaction function of firm 1 is given by the condition

$$1 - y_2 - y_3 - 2y_1 = 0$$

Then the equations that are solved simultaneously for y_1, y_2, and y_3 are

$$y_1 = \frac{1}{2} - \frac{y_2}{2} - \frac{y_3}{2}$$

$$y_2 = \frac{1}{2} - \frac{y_1}{2} - \frac{y_3}{2}$$

$$y_3 = \frac{1}{2} - \frac{y_1}{2} - \frac{y_2}{2}$$

Solving the three equations gives

$$y_1 = y_2 = y_3 = \frac{1}{4}$$

$$p = 1 - \frac{3}{4} = \frac{1}{4}$$

$$\pi_i = \frac{1}{16}, \quad i = 1, 2, 3$$

(3) For N firms, the reaction function for each firm (consider firm 1 again) is given by

$$1 - y_2 - y_3 - \cdots - y_N - 2y_1 = 0$$

But since the firms have identical costs, $y_1 = y_2 = \cdots = y_N$ in equilibrium, the profit-maximization condition can be written as

$$1 - (N + 1)y_i = 0$$

which implies that $y_i = 1/(N + 1)$, $i = 1, \ldots, N$, and

$$p = 1 - \frac{N}{N+1} = \frac{1}{N+1}$$

$$\pi = \left(\frac{1}{N+1}\right)^2, \quad i = 1, \ldots, N$$

b With setup costs, the price and quantities will be the same. However, profits will be smaller by 0.05. In the long run, the number of firms will be such that

$$\left(\frac{1}{N+1}\right)^2 - 0.05 = 0 \quad \text{so} \quad N = 3.47$$

Assuming that the number of firms must be an integer, $N = 3$.

c If each firm believes that it will sell $(1/N)$ of total output, then it will maximize

$$\pi = (1 - Ny)y - 0.05$$

where y is the output of a representative firm. Profit-maximization gives

$$1 - 2Ny = 0 \qquad p = 1 - \frac{1}{2} = \frac{1}{2}$$

$$y = \frac{1}{2N}$$

Note that the collusive output and price are reached. The reason is that each firm thinks its rivals will do exactly the same thing, so they are able to collude tacitly and set the monopoly output. In the long run, firms will enter until

$$\pi = \frac{1}{4N} - 0.05 = 0 \quad \text{so} \quad N = 5$$

Note that more firms are attracted into the industry because monopoly profits rather than oligopoly profits are shared.

***37 a** If the incumbent has y_1 units of output, then the reaction function for the entrant is

$$MR_2 = 100 - \frac{y_1}{2} - y_2 = 40$$

so

$$y_2 = 60 - \frac{y_1}{2}$$

If the second firm entered, total output in the industry would be

$$y = y_1 + y_2 = y_1 + 60 - \frac{y_1}{2} = 60 + \frac{y_1}{2}$$

Price can be written in terms of y_1 as

$$p = 100 - 0.5\left(60 + \frac{y_1}{2}\right) = 70 - \frac{y_1}{4}$$

and the profits to the entrant would be

$$\pi_2 = \left(30 - \frac{y_1}{4}\right)\left(60 - \frac{y_1}{2}\right) - F$$

where F is setup costs. Then, if $F = 450$, the condition for no entry is

$$\left(30 - \frac{y_1}{4}\right)\left(60 - \frac{y_1}{2}\right) = 450$$

so

$$1800 + \frac{y_1^2}{8} - 30y_1 = 450$$

Using the quadratic formula, we get

$$y_1 = 60$$

b Yes. The limit output happens to be the output that would be chosen by a monopolist, unthreatened by entry. In this case, entry is said to be blockaded.

*38 a Figure A15.7 shows the market demand curve $D(y)$ and the marginal costs curves of the fringe MC_f, and of the cartel MC_c. At p_1, MC_f equals the market demand, and the fringe will supply the entire market; the cartel supplies zero. At p_2, the fringe supplies zero, so the cartel will satisfy the entire market. The residual demand for the cartel is dd′. The marginal revenue of the residual demand is set equal to the marginal costs of the cartel, MC_c. The profit-maximizing quantity of the cartel is y_c^*, and the price is set from the residual demand at p^*. The fringe equates p^* with MC_f and produces y_f^* output.

b OPEC may have calculated the elasticity from the market demand rather than the residual demand.

c If the fringe firms were making a profit at p^*, more firms would try to enter, through increased production, exploration of new reserves, or development of substitutes for oil. If this entry is successful, MC_f will shift to the right, and the residual demand of the cartel will shift inward, pushing the price down.

*39 a Given that the monopolist sets a wholesale price p_w, the retailer maximizes

$$\pi = (100 - y)y - (p_w + 10)y$$

Profits are maximized where

$$100 - 2y = p_w + 10$$
$$p_w = 90 - 2y$$

This relationship gives the demand by the retailers for the shoes. Mac N. Ro, Inc., now maximizes

$$\pi = p_w y - 18y$$
$$= (90 - 2y)y - 18y$$

Profit-maximizing output and prices are

$$y = 18 \quad p_w = 90 - 36 = \$54$$
$$p = 100 - 18 = \$82$$

Note that there are two markups: The manufacturer sets a price \$36 higher than the marginal costs of \$18, and the retailer sets a price \$18 over its marginal costs of \$54 + \$10. The markup by the retailer lowers the manufacturer's profit. Manufacturer's profits are $\$36 \times 18 = \$648$.

FIGURE A15.7

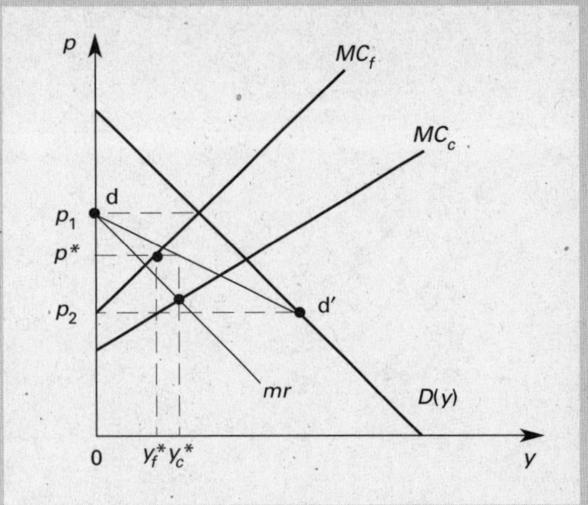

b Mac N. Ro could do better integrating into the retail market. In this case, marginal costs would be \$28. Then profits would be

$$\pi = (100 - y)y - 28y$$

Profit-maximization would occur where $MR(y) = MC(y)$ or

$$100 - 2y = 28 \quad \text{so} \quad y = 36, p = \$64$$

Profits would equal \$1 296.

c Alternatively, Mac could impose a ceiling of \$64 on the retail price, that is, he could require the retailer to set a price no greater than \$64. By setting a wholesale price of \$54 (the vertical integration price minus the retailer's average cost), Mac could earn the same profits as under vertical integration, whereas the retailer would only be able to cover costs.

CHAPTER 16

Product Differentiation

Chapter Summary

Differentiated Products

In the marketplace of the real world, consumers can choose among a variety of **differentiated products**. Buying a CD player can be a time-consuming activity, given the range of available components. The variety of personal computers that flood the market turns a purchase decision into a complex course on the semiconductor chip. Even choosing among ice cream flavours can be a complicated decision.

Why does product differentiation exist? The variety of products offered in the marketplace is a response to differences in consumer preferences. However, we do not observe every individual consuming exactly his or her favourite variety of a product. Product differentiation is limited by the producer setup costs required to develop a new product type. Which products will an entrepreneur choose to produce and how many products will be available? To answer these questions, we need to extend our previous models to allow for the endogenous choice of the number of goods and their characteristics. Two types of models have been developed in the economic literature for analyzing markets with differentiated products: the Chamberlin model and the address model of monopolistic competition.

Chamberlin Model of Generalized Competition

In the generalized competition model, or the **Chamberlin model of monopolistic competition** for a large number of firms, product differentiation of a particular sort is introduced: symmetric product differentiation. That is, although each firm in a monopolistically competitive market offers a different product, the demands for the differentiated products are symmetric. At identical prices, all firms service the same number of customers. This **symmetry assumption** can be illustrated by an example in which consumer preferences are uniformly distributed over all the products: For 24 consumers and four products A, B, C, and D, six consumers would choose A as their first choice; of the remaining consumers (who chose B,C, and D as their first choice), six would choose product A as their second choice; and so on. This distribution would apply to each product, A, B, C, and D. In equilibrium, the *degree* of product differentiation is characterized by the number of firms in the market.

How is the equilibrium determined in a monopolistically competitive industry? To answer this question, it is useful to identify the demand curve faced by the firms. Given the symmetry restriction, each firm actually faces two demands: The symmetric demand curve of the firm when all rival firms' prices are held constant (the *dd* curve) and the firm demand when all firms' prices change simultaneously (the *DD* curve). The *dd* curve is *more elastic* than the *DD* curve. Moreover, the introduction of an additional product into the market shifts both the *dd* and *DD* curves downward because the new product attracts $(1/n)$th of the customers.

The Nash price equilibrium of the monopolistically competitive model occurs when each firm's price choice maximizes profits, given the prices of rival firms. In the short run, the equilibrium prices for all firms will be identical and will satisfy the condition that the marginal revenue of the *dd* curve must equal the marginal cost at the price at which the *DD* and *dd* curves intersect. In the long run, another condition is added: Firms must make zero profits. Since a new entrant into the market captures $n/(n + 1)$ of the quantity produced by an established firm in the market, it receives almost the same profit as firms currently in the market. Hence, for the **large-number case**, profits for all firms must be zero in equilibrium — known also as the **no-entry condition**. As in the Cournot and Bertrand models, the solution is individually rational but not collectively rational. Collusion would lead to a higher price. In the **small-numbers case**, Chamberlin argued that firms will engage in tacit collusion.

In the Chamberlin model, the equilibrium price is **inefficient** because it exceeds marginal cost. Another potential inefficiency may arise in the number of products that are offered. When all products that generate additional surplus greater than the development costs are offered, then product diversity is **cost-benefit efficient**.

Address Model of Spatial Competition

Often competition between products is localized; that is, each product competes only with the neighbouring products. A neighbouring product can have a literal interpretation (two movie theatres next door to each other compete) or a figurative one (Sugar Pops cereal competes with Marshmallow Krispies but not with Natural Granola cereal). The Chamberlin model of product differentiation would not be appropriate for analyzing such products because an entrant's demand function is not symmetric to the demand curves of the existing firms. A model of spatial product differentiation, also called an **address model**, is needed.

In the address model, assumptions very similar to those of the Hotelling model are adopted: Consumers are evenly distributed along a geographical space, traveling to a store is costly, and costs increase with distance traveled. A consumer is willing to patronize the product (or store) with the lowest price plus travel costs from his location: price plus travel costs result in a **delivered-price schedule**. Each firm will choose a location and/or price that maximize(s) profits, given its rivals' choices. In the short run, the number of firms is fixed, so positive profits can be made in equilibrium. There exists a **market boundary** between each of the firms which separates the market into those consumers who would buy from the firm to the left from those who would patronize the firm to the right.

In the long run, firms enter the market. Given that the entering firm must incur setup costs of development, we can determine the entry condition for long-run equilibrium. This condition indicates how far apart the firms can locate without having further entry take place. Because of the nonsymmetric product differentiation, firms can earn profits in this equilibrium, unlike in the Chamberlin model. Since supranormal profits are possible in the address model, established firms may practice a strategy of **product proliferation** in which they preempt potential entrants by locating their outlets in several places.

As in the Chamberlin model, the equilibrium price in the address model is inefficient. Moreover, the efficiency of product diversity can be assessed. The efficient number of outlets *minimizes* the total cost of supplying the products. The Nash equilibrium may be characterized by too much product diversity compared with the efficient solution.

KEY WORDS

Address model	Large-numbers case
Chamberlin model monopolistic competition	Market boundary
Cost-benefit efficient	No-entry condition
Delivered-price schedule	Product proliferation
Differentiated product	Small-numbers case
Inefficient	Symmetry assumption

CASE STUDY: THE CEREAL CASE

In 1972, the U.S. Federal Trade Commission (FTC) charged (but failed to convict) the four largest cereal producers — Kelloggs, General Foods, General Mills, and Quaker Oats — with a "shared monopoly" in which they allegedly colluded in product proliferation with a large number of different types of cereals and engaged in intensive advertising. In an interesting paper, Schmalensee (1978)[1] discusses the facts of the case and analyzes the economics of the government complaint. Some of the facts are that the top four companies had 85% of the market; between 1950 and 1970, the number of brands on the market increased from 25 to 80; before 1970 there was no significant entry from firms outside the market; after 1970 several outsiders successfully introduced natural cereals, and only one entrant (Pet) was still in the market by the late 1970s.

A Why would the FTC be concerned with product proliferation of the cereal producers? How might a strategy of product proliferation be profitable?

B Might this behaviour be consistent with a noncollusive oligopoly selling differentiated products?

[1] R. Schmalensee (1978). "Entry Deterrence in the Ready-to-Eat Breakfast Cereal Industry," *Bell Journal of Economics*, Autumn: 305–327.

EXERCISES

Multiple-Choice

Choose the correct answer to each question. There is only one correct answer to each question.

1 Good X is produced in an industry characterized by the Chamberlin model of monopolistic competition. Then, which of the following is true?
- **a** Since the firms face downward-sloping demands, they can make economic profits in the long run.
- **b** There are significant barriers to entry in the market for X.
- **c** Firms operate at excess capacity in the long run.
- **d** Only **b** and **c**.
- **e** None of the above.

2 In the Chamberlin model of monopolistic competition with large numbers, each firm believes that
- **a** If it lowers its price, all the rivals will lower their prices.
- **b** If it raises its price, all the rivals will raise their prices.
- **c** If it changes its price, none of the rivals will react by changing their prices.
- **d** Only **a** and **b**.
- **e** None of the above.

3 In the long-run equilibrium in the Chamberlin model with large numbers,
- **a** Economic profits are zero.
- **b** Price exceeds marginal cost.
- **c** The *DD* curve intersects the *dd* curve.
- **d** All the above.
- **e** Only **a** and **c**.

FIGURE 16.1

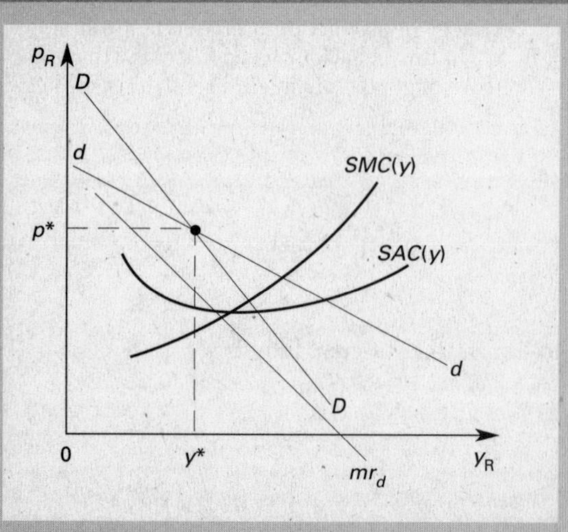

4 Figure 16.1 shows the *dd* and *DD* curves for a Chamberlin monopolistically competitive firm. The current price set by the firm is p^*. Which of the following is correct?
- **a** Some firms will want to leave the industry.
- **b** The firm will want to set marginal revenue of the *dd* curve equal to its marginal cost and lower its price.
- **c** Price p^* is the short-run equilibrium price but not the long-run equilibrium price because the firm is making economic profits.
- **d** Price p^* is neither a short-run equilibrium price nor a long-run equilibrium price.
- **e** Both **b** and **d**.

5 If the demands for three goods X, Y, and Z are symmetric, then
- **a** The number of people who prefer X to Y equals the number of people who prefer Y to Z.
- **b** Among the individuals for whom X is the first choice, the number of people who prefer Y to Z equals the number of people who prefer Z to Y.
- **c** The number of people for whom X is the first choice equals the sum of the number of people for whom Y is the first choice and the number of people for whom Z is the first choice.
- **d** All the above.
- **e** Only **a** and **b**.

To answer questions **6** and **7**, refer to Figure 16.2. Make the following assumptions: Firms A, B, and C are located at −1, 0, and 1, respectively. Individuals are distributed evenly along a circle (of which only a segment is shown in the figure). Each customer demands only one unit of the good. The total price to the consumer is the price charged by the firm, p, plus the travel costs, assumed to be 1 per unit of distance.

6 What is true about the three firms in the market?
- **a** If the prices charged by firms A and B are the same, then the market boundary between firms A and B is one-half the distance between the two firms, regardless of the price charged by C.
- **b** The market area of firm B increases as its price

FIGURE 16.2

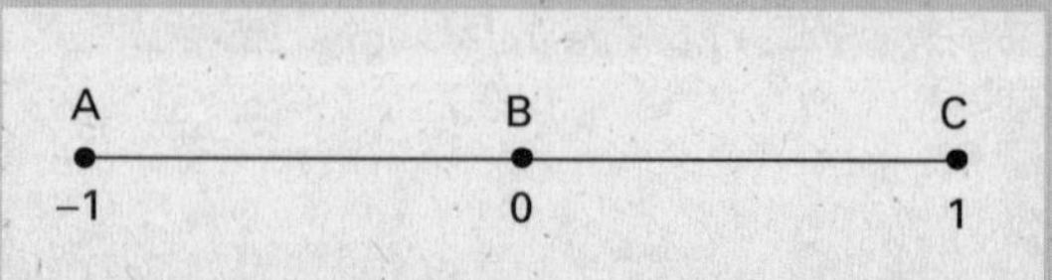

relative to its rival's price increases.

c The price set by firm B will be lower than the prices set by firms A and C in equilibrium.

d The firms will not make short-run profits.

e None of the above.

7 In the long run, an entrant that takes the location and prices of the established firms as fixed will

a Face a demand curve symmetric to those of the established firms.

b Underestimate the size of its potential profit by taking prices as given.

c Want to locate halfway between firms A and B or between firms B and C, given that identical prices are set by firms A, B, and C.

d Set a price for its product equal to marginal cost.

e None of the above.

8 Two firms are located at opposite ends of a line of unit length. Firm 1 is located at 0 and firm 2 at 1, as shown in Figure 16.3. Consumers are distributed evenly along the line and each customer demands one unit of the good. The total price to the consumer is the price charged by the firm, p_i plus the travel costs, assumed to be t per distance. Costs of production are zero. Let x denote the market boundary between the two firms. Then

a The prices charged by firms 1 and 2 satisfy: $p_1 + tx = p_2 + t(1 - x)$.

b The demand curve facing each firm is given by $x_1 = 1/2 - (p_1 - p_2)/2t$ and $x_2 = 1/2 - (p_2 - p_1)/2t$, respectively.

c The equilibrium prices set by both firms equal t and each firm gets one-half of the market (that is, $x = 1/2$).

d All of the above.

e None of the above.

True-False

9 In the long run, firms in a Chamberlin model of monopolistic competition do not make monopoly profits. Therefore, this type of market structure is just as efficient as perfect competition.

10 Since all brands of cornflakes are made of essentially the same ingredients, they cannot be classified as differentiated products.

FIGURE 16.3

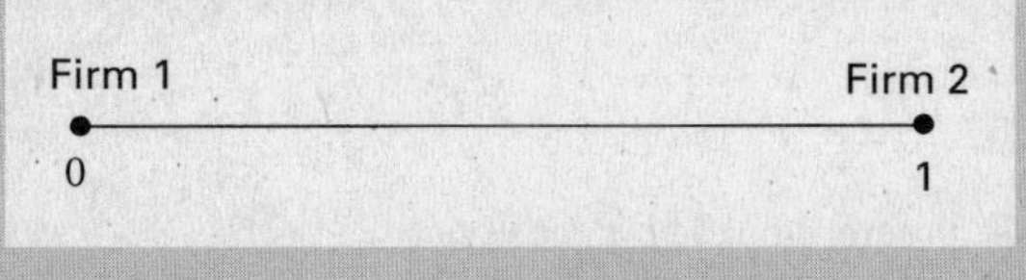

11 The symmetry assumption made in the Chamberlin model of monopolistic competition implies that if it pays one firm to decrease its price, then it pays all rival firms with identical costs to decrease their prices.

12 If a new product is introduced in a market characterized by $n - 1$ Chamberlin firms, then that product will attract $(1/n)$th of all customers in that market.

13 The *dd* curve faced by firms in a Chamberlin model of monopolistic competition is more inelastic at every price than is the *DD* curve along which all prices of all products change simultaneously.

14 The equilibrium price in the Chamberlin model of monopolistic competition is collectively rational but not individually rational.

15 In the address models of spatial competition, an entrant into the market faces a demand that is symmetric to the demand curves of the firms already in the market.

16 In a model of spatial competition in which firms are evenly distributed around the circumference of a circle, the short-run profits to each firm increase as the distance between firms increases, everything else held constant.

17 In a model of spatial competition, firms can make positive long-run economic profits because demands are not symmetric.

18 In both the Chamberlin model of monopolistic competition and the address models of spatial competition, the amount of product diversity is always efficient.

Short Problems

19 A study of the U.S. banking industry found that long-run average costs at current output levels as a percentage of efficient average costs were different for banks of different sizes. In particular, the smaller the size, the larger were long-run average costs relative to efficient average costs. These results show that banks of many different sizes can persist in the industry and that many operate at an average cost higher than the minimum of average costs. Do these facts imply that barriers to entry must be significant?

20 Give an intuitive explanation of why supranormal profits are not earned in the Chamberlin model of monopolistic competition, whereas in a model of spatially differentiated products, established firms can earn supranormal profits in the long run.

21 In a paper in *The Bell Journal of Economics* (Spring 1981), West tests the following hypothesis, established by Eaton and Lipsey: Under certain conditions, "It will always pay an existing firm to blockade entry by locating new plants in an expanding mar-

ket at a time before it will pay a new firm to enter."[2] West collected 1978 data on supermarket locations from the Greater Vancouver Regional District of British Columbia. Safeway, Ltd., and Kelly Douglas & Company, Ltd., were two large companies in his data set, and all other firms were considered members of the competitive fringe. Through a statistical method, West showed that the process by which firms locate was consistent with the process theoretically predicted by Eaton and Lipsey's locational model. Why would a large supermarket adopt a preemptive strategy in which it locates its stores sufficiently close to each other to make entry unprofitable? Does the established firm have to cluster its outlets until its profits, as well as those of the potential entrant, fall to zero? What implications does this behaviour have for mom-and-pop grocery stores?

22 In the early 1980s, the Bertrand Report[3] on the major oil companies in Canada, subsidiaries of the United States and British oil companies, contended that the major oil companies had cost Canadians $6 million over the previous five years. One accusation was directed at the companies' marketing sector: Too many of their gasoline stations existed in particular locations, resulting in inefficiencies and, more importantly, acted as a deterrence to independent gasoline stations entering the market. Evaluate.

23 A common practice of manufacturers of brand-name products selling through retailers is to establish exclusive territories. Under this practice, the manufacturer gives each retailer a local monopoly that precludes competition from other retailers in her territory. Why would manufacturers want to give market power to its retailers?

Long Problems

24 Assume that firms in a Chamberlin model face constant marginal production costs of c plus a fixed entry cost.

a Show the long-run equilibrium of a firm in this market on a diagram. Assume that the equilibrium price is $4.

b The manufacturer of the product sold by the retail firms now stipulates that the product must not be sold at any price below $5, and is able to enforce this policy of resale price maintenance. With the help of your diagram, analyze the possible long-run effects of this price restriction.

c Why would a manufacturer want to establish resale price maintenance?

25 Good Y is produced in an industry characterized by Chamberlin monopolistically competitive firms with identical costs and identical demands. In the long run, each firm faces constant marginal costs of production and a license fee per year that equals F, regardless of the output level produced. The license fee is a payment to produce in the industry. Suppose that the license fee doubles. Show on a diagram the new long-run equilibrium for a representative firm.

26 Commodity Y is produced by Chamberlin firms in a constant-cost industry. Initially, in long-run equilibrium, each firm produces 20 units of output per week. In this equilibrium, the Y-producing firms are spending $5 per unit of output on antipollution chemicals to satisfy government standards.

Dr. E. Mission has invented a device that would make the antipollution chemicals unnecessary. If she offers to supply the device to Y-producing firms at $100 per week per firm regardless of their level of output, will they accept her offer in the long run? Explain, using diagrams. (You do not need to show the new long-run equilibrium.)

***27** Three Italian pizza parlors, A, B, and C, are equally spaced along a circular street of 90 equally spaced houses. (For example, firm A is at 0, firm B is at 30, and firm C is at 60.) One person lives in each house. The restaurants use the same pizza recipe and face the same production costs of $10 per pizza; only the locations are different. Customers patronize the restaurant with the lowest total price of a pizza: the price per pizza plus the transportation costs to the restaurant (equal to $1 per house that must be passed on the way to the restaurant). Each customer buys only one pizza per week, regardless of the price.

a Determine the demand curve facing firm B, given identical prices set by the competitors.

b Determine the equilibrium pizza price and quantity sold by each restaurant in the short run. For each firm, calculate the short-run profits earned and illustrate the market boundaries.

c Pizza parlors are a lucrative business on this street. Luigi, a chef at one of the pizza parlors, is thinking of quitting his job and opening up his own pizza parlor on the street. What is Luigi's demand function, given that the prices and locations of the established firms are fixed? Are these assumptions reasonable? Why or why not?

d If the setup costs of entering this market are $600, will Luigi enter, given your answer in **c**? Why or why not? What will be the profits of the established firms, given Luigi's decision?

---

[2] B.C. Eaton and R.G. Lipsey (1979). "The Theory of Market Preemption: The Persistence of Excess Capacity and Monopoly in Growing Spatial Markets." *Economica*, **46**(May): 149–158.

[3] R.J. Bertrand (1981). *Canada's Oil Monopoly*, Toronto: James Lorimer.

ANSWERS TO CHAPTER 12

Case Study

A Brand proliferation in "cereal characteristic space" might be profitable if it deters entrants from the market. By crowding the product space with a large number of sufficiently similar brands, new entrants would be unable to introduce profitably a new cereal. Hence, cereal producers would be able to preserve their monopoly power. For this reason, the FTC was concerned with the possibility of this strategic behaviour. Moreover, this practice could be welfare decreasing if too many brands were introduced, that is, if the social benefits from an additional brand were less than the additional cost of providing it.

B Substitution of nonprice competition (introduction of new brands, advertising, etc.) for price competition is not unusual in concentrated, differentiated oligopolies. However, whether more brands were introduced or more advertising took place than would have been profit-maximizing in the absence of collusion is difficult to determine.

Multiple-Choice

1 c **2** c **3** d **4** e
5 e **6** e **7** c **8** d

True-False

9 F **10** F **11** T **12** T **13** F
14 F **15** F **16** T **17** T **18** F

Short Problems

19 If the industry is monopolistically competitive, then there are no barriers to entry. The empirical evidence suggests that the industry may be monopolistically competitive because the small and medium firms are operating with excess capacity.

20 In the Chamberlin model of monopolistic competition, firms' demands are symmetric. Hence, an entrant into the market can expect to take away some customers from every rival. In particular, it expects to sell $n/(n + 1)$ of the output sold by the previous entrant. For a large number of firms, the quantity is nearly identical to that sold by the previous entrant; hence, if profits are being earned in the industry, entry will occur. In spatial competition, an entrant can expect to take business away from only the two closest neighbours. Therefore, if a firm enters at the same price as its closest neighbours, it can expect to sell only one-half of an established firm's output. Entry may not be profitable, even if the established firms are currently earning profits.

21 By preventing entry, the large supermarket could preserve its monopoly power. The established firm has to cluster its outlets close enough that if entry occurs, the entrant will make negative profits. This does not imply that the established firm must be making zero profits. Insofar as mom-and-pop grocery stores serve the same customer group, it is possible for large supermarket chains to prevent entry by mom-and-pop stores.

22 As in problem **21**, the major oil companies may find strategic clustering of their gasoline stations profitable in certain areas if they can successfully deter entry by the independent gasoline stations.

23 A manufacturer might establish exclusive territories (ET) to guarantee monopoly profits. Then, the manufacturer could extract those profits from the retailers through a fixed fee. If retailers were perfectly competitive, the manufacturer could achieve this outcome by setting a high wholesale price to retailers. An efficiency explanation for establishing ET is that ET encourages retailers to invest in consumer services and advertising that will increase the demand for the product. Without ET, retailers would free-ride on each other's sales efforts, thus eliminating any incentives to invest in such activities.

Long Problems

24 a The long-run equilibrium price and output for a representative firm are \$4 and y_R^*, shown in Figure A16.1a.

b Suppose that a minimum price of \$5 is set, as in Figure A16.1b. Then, because *all* firms must raise their prices to \$5, each firm will move up its *DD* curve to point G and produce y_R' units of output. Hence, profits are made, so some firms will enter the industry. This will cause the

FIGURE A16.1

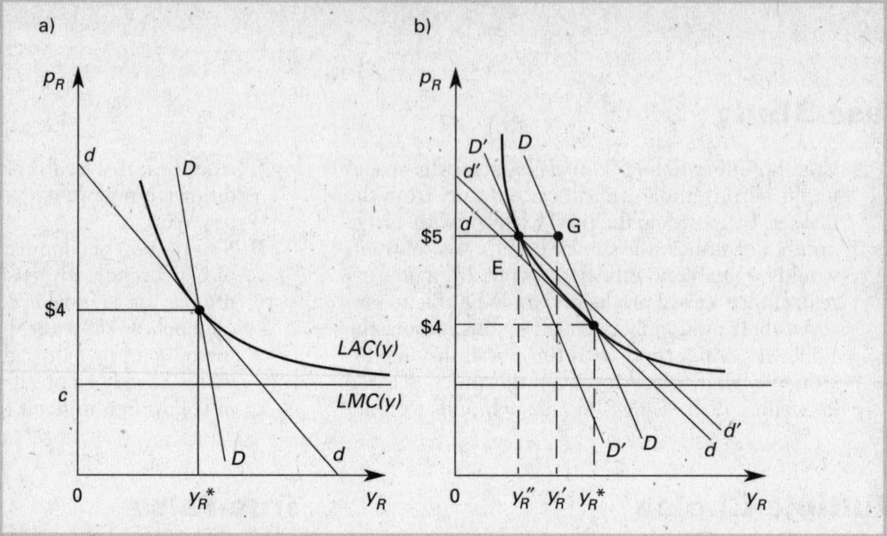

DD curve to shift down until it intersects with the $LAC(y)$ curve at a price of \$5 (point E). That is, at the new long-run equilibrium, shown by point E, each firm produces y_R'' and makes zero profits. Note that because price is artificially constrained to \$5, the $LAC(y)$ curve is not tangent to the $d'd'$ curve at the new equilibrium.

c As in problem **23**, resale price maintenance may be used to encourage retailers to invest in consumer services and advertising. Under this pricing practice, a retailer making such investments and then charging a price to reflect this additional cost, knows that it will not be undercut by a rival retailer.

FIGURE A16.2

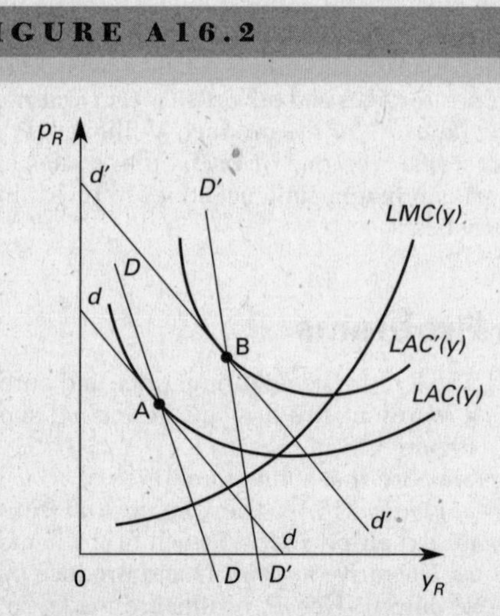

25 The initial equilibrium is at point *A* in Figure A16.2. If the license fee doubles, then the $LAC(y)$ curve will slide up the $LMC(y)$ curve to $LAC'(y)$. Firms are making a loss and will want to exit from the industry. As they exit, the *DD* demand curve and the *dd* demand curve will shift to the right ($D'D'$ and $d'd'$, respectively) until $LAC'(y)$ is tangent to the $d'd'$ curve at the intersection of the two new demand curves: for example, at point *B* in the figure.

26 The long-run equilibrium of a firm at 20 units of output and a price p_R* is shown by point *A* in Figure A16.3. Under the \$5 charge for antipollution chemicals, all the cost curves shift upward by \$5 to $LAC'(y)$ and $LMC'(y)$. With Dr. E. Mission's invention, the original $LAC(y)$ curve will slide up the original $LMC(y)$ curve to $LAC''(y)$ while the $LMC(y)$ curve remains the same because \$5 per unit no longer has to be paid. At 20 units of output, the average charge for Dr. E. Mission's invention is \$5. Hence, the $LAC''(y)$ curve intersects $LAC'(y)$ at 20 units of output and reaches its minimum when it intersects the $LMC(y)$ curve. Since the demand in the absence of Dr. E. Mission's invention, *dd*, lies above $LAC''(y)$ for some interval of output, the invention is profitable and firms will accept it.

***27 a** Let the price of pizza charged by firm B be p_b. Then the cost to an individual x' distance away from B is $p_b + x'$. If the individual buys from firm C instead, the cost of the pizza is $p' + 30 - x'$, where p' is the price charged by C. Then, the market boundary x' must satisfy

FIGURE A16.3

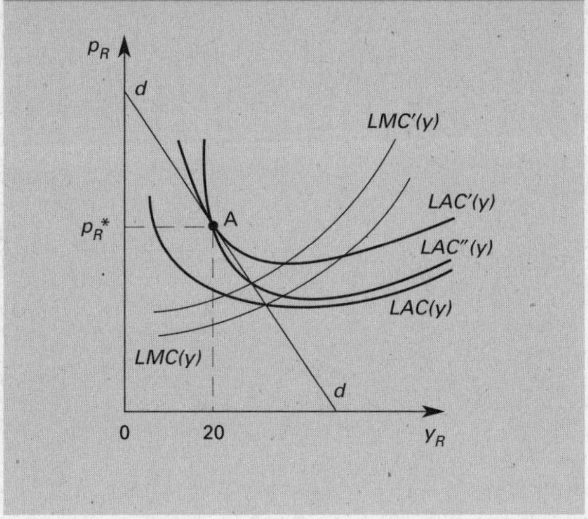

$$p_b + x' = p' + 30 - x'$$
$$x' = \frac{30 + p' - p_b}{2}$$

If pizza parlor A also charges p', then the market for firm B is $2x'$; hence, the quantity produced by B is $2x'$, or the demand curve for B is

$$y = 2x' = (30 + p' - p_b)$$

or

$$p_b = p' + 30 - y$$

b In the short-run, firm B will set marginal revenue equal to marginal cost (= 10) to get the profit-maximizing quantity and price:

$$p' + 30 - 2y = 10$$

or

$$y^* = \frac{p' + 20}{2}$$

The profit-maximizing y^* is substituted into the demand curve in **a** to determine the price set by firm B:

$$p_b = p' + 30 - \frac{p'}{2} - 10 = \frac{p' + 40}{2}$$

But since all firms are identical, the equilibrium price is

$$p^* = \frac{p^* + 40}{2} \qquad \text{so } p^* = 40$$

and

$$y^* = 30$$

Short-run profits of the established firms are given by

$$\pi_E = (p^* - 10)y^* = (30)^2 = 900$$

The market boundaries for each firm are illustrated in Figure A16.4.

c Suppose that Luigi decides to locate between firms A and B. If both A and B are charging p^* for their pizzas, and x is the market boundary between Luigi and the two firms, then

$$p_L + x = p^* + 15 - x$$

so

$$x = \frac{p^* + 15 - p_L}{2}$$

where p_L is Luigi's price. Since Luigi's market is $2x$, his demand curve is

$$y_L = 2x = p^* + 15 - p_L$$

In **b**, we found that $p^* = 40$. Substituting this into Luigi's demand curve and rearranging it gives

$$y_L = 40 + 15 - p_L \quad \text{so} \quad p_L = 55 - y_L$$

Luigi's competitors are likely to respond to his entry into the market by changing their prices and/or locations. Hence, Luigi is overestimating his demand by holding prices and locations of his rivals constant.

d Luigi maximizes his postentry profits by equating marginal revenue of the demand to marginal cost. That is,

$$55 - 2y_L = 10 \quad \text{or} \quad y_L = 22.5$$

Profit-maximizing price is

$$p_L = 55 - 22.5 = 32.5$$

FIGURE 16.4

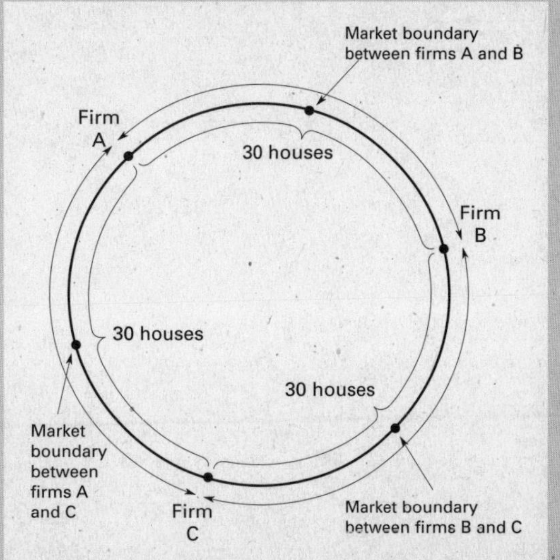

Profits to Luigi are

$$\pi_L = (22.5)(22.5) - K = 506.25 - K$$

where K is the entry cost. Since K is larger than 506.25, Luigi's profits would be less than zero, and so he will not enter the market. In this case, the established firms will earn profits of $\pi_E = 900 - K = 300$.

CHAPTER 17

Choice Making Under Uncertainty

Chapter Summary

Decisions with Risky Outcomes

In this chapter, we allow the consumer to enter the interesting and unpredictable world of **incomplete information**. In this world, an individual with imperfect information faces decisions that embody **risks**; that is, several outcomes from the decision are possible, each occurring with some probability.

An example of such a decision is a lottery. An individual, Martha, is a sweepstakes winner. Her prize is a choice between *A* dollars for certain and a gamble that pays $1 million with probability of 1/2 and pays nothing otherwise. *A* is the opportunity cost of the gamble and the **expected monetary value** of the lottery is $500 000. If *A* were less than $500 000, it would be perfectly reasonable for Martha *not* to take the gamble. In general, the **expected monetary value hypothesis** may be stated as follows: individuals will choose the option with the largest expected monetary value. It turns out that this hypothesis only holds for certain types of individuals (risk neutral ones) who are not typical of the general population.

Expected-Utility Hypothesis

This example suggests that the decision to undertake risk depends on something more than simply a comparison between the certain outcome (the opportunity cost of the gamble) and the expected monetary payoff of the **prospect** (gamble or set of probabilities with associated outcomes). Bernoulli argued that the reservation price of a risky choice is equal to the **expected utility** of that choice rather than to the expected monetary payoffs, where the expected utility is a weighted average of the utilities associated with the payoffs. The weights are probabilities of outcomes, where the probabilities are either objectively known or are **subjective probabilities.**

The **expected utility hypothesis** has been theoretically justified, proving that an expected-utility function exists for a set of reasonable assumptions on preferences over risky prospects. Central to the theory of expected utility is the **continuity**

assumption that guarantees that individuals are willing to make some trade-offs between risky and riskless prospects. Along with two other assumptions of substitution and ordering, continuity implies the **expected utility theorem**: If an individual prefers one prospect to another, then the preferred prospect has greater expected utility; if an individual is indifferent between prospects, then their expected utilities must be the same. The **von Neumann-Morgenstern utility function** satisfies these requirements. Although the expected utility hypothesis can be used to analyze a variety of economic problems with risky prospects, it is not appropriate when preferences depend on the state of the world.

Attitudes Towards Risk

Under the expected-utility hypothesis, a taxonomy can be defined over an individual's attitudes towards risk. Define a riskless prospect as one that offers the expected payoff from some lottery, *A*, with probability 1. Then, an individual is said to be **risk-neutral** if his utility from that riskless prospect equals the expected utility from the risky prospect *A*. Such individuals have a constant **marginal utility of wealth**. If the utility of the riskless prospect exceeds the expected utility from the risky prospect *A*, then the individual is **risk-averse** and has a diminishing marginal utility of wealth. In this case, the additional utility that is possible from undertaking the risky prospect is not large enough to offset the loss in utility that is possible from that prospect. Finally, an individual who is **risk-inclined** will receive more utility from the risky prospect than from the riskless option. We generally expect most individuals to be risk-averse.

The optimal amount of risk for any individual may be determined with the use of an **expected value line** which, in a two-state world, joins all points of equal expected value. If we superimpose on the same graph an individual's indifference curve map, where each curve represents the same expected utility level, we can determine the optimal risk combination for individuals with different kinds of preferences for risk.

Risk Pooling and Insurance

Risk-averse individuals attempt to shed risk. When two individuals face independent risks, they may agree to enter into a **risk-pooling** arrangement, in which they share in any losses that either or both individuals incur. This risk-pooling arrangement is a type of insurance. To find out when an individual would fully insure herself against some risk (that is, pay for insurance that would fully compensate her in the event of a disaster), we need to determine the **certainty equivalent** of the prospect (that is, the amount of money that would leave the individual with a utility level equal to the expected utility of the risky asset). An individual will fully insure herself against risk if the cost of the insurance is less than the individual's **reservation demand price** for the insurance, which equals the difference between the initial wealth and the certainty equivalent. The supply decision will depend on the firm's **reservation supply price,** defined as the price that will at least cover the costs associated with providing any given level of insurance. If risk-neutral insurance firms are willing to supply the insurance, an individual can be left with a level of wealth equal to the expected wealth in the absence of insurance but without risk! Notice, however, that in the presence of **asymmetric information** firms may not be willing to fully insure individuals whose riskiness is unknown to the insurer. A second mechanism by which risk is shed is **risk spreading**. In this case, an indivisible and risky asset is owned by several individuals or firms. Risk-averse individuals may prefer to own part of a risky asset rather than the entire amount.

KEY WORDS

Asymmetric information

Certainty equivalent

Continuity assumption

Expected utility

Expected utility hypothesis

Expected utility theorem

Expected monetary value

Expected monetary value hypothesis

Expected value line

Incomplete information

Marginal utility of wealth

Prospects

Reservation demand price

Reservation supply price

Risk

Risk-averse

Risk-inclined

Risk-neutral

Risk pooling

Risk spreading

Subjective probabilities

von Neumann-Morgenstern utility function

CASE STUDY: RISK PREFERENCES FOR PROVINCIAL LOTTERIES

David, like most people, insures his house and is relatively averse to risk, but at the same time enjoys a weekly gamble in the provincial lottery. David appears to have inconsistent preferences since on one hand he is willing to pay a premium to reduce any risks he faces, while simultaneously he engages in a gamble. Maybe he doesn't know that the odds of getting hit by lightning are better than winning the lotto jackpot in his province. Or maybe he is just not your average guy!

On the contrary, this behaviour is not unusual. For example, the total sales of lottery tickets in millions of dollars and the total prizes given away in percent of total sales in the year 1997 for various regions are as follows:[1]

	Total Sales	Prizes
Atlantic Region	$452.24	54%
Quebec	$597.01	59%
Ontario	$2066.7	50%
British Columbia	$867.45	53%

As can be seen, for every dollar bet, the amount paid out in prizes ranges from 50 cents in Ontario to 59 cents in Quebec. This means that the expected monetary payoffs of the lottery are negative since the prize money is less than the ticket sales in each province. Thus, ordinary economic theory would surmise that only risk-loving people would engage in such an activity, but this does not appear to be the case.

A Why does the lottery business continue to prosper and thrive in a society that is mostly averse to risk? Although there may be psychological reasons for buying lottery tickets, give an economic explanation why individuals engage in this risky activity.

B Draw and label a graph to illustrate the reasoning behind people buying insurance (a risk-averse behaviour) while, at the same time, playing the lottery (risk-loving behaviour).

C Give other possible reasons for this phenomenon.

[1] See lottery corporations' *Annual Reports,* for Ontario, Quebec, Atlantic Region and British Columbia 1996/97.

EXERCISES

Multiple-Choice

Choose the correct answer to each question. There is only one correct answer to each question.

1 A person who places a smaller utility on gaining \$1 000 than on losing an equal amount
- a Has an increasing marginal utility of money associated with larger amounts of money.
- b Would pay \$1 000 for a lottery ticket that paid either \$2 000 with probability 1/2 or \$0 with probability 1/2.
- c Has a declining marginal utility of money associated with larger amounts of money.
- d Is correctly described by both **b** and **c.**
- e None of the above.

Questions **2** and **3** pertain to a consumer with a utility function given by

$$U = \left(\frac{w}{500}\right)^{1/2}$$

where U is utility and w is wealth. Ordinarily, the consumer expects his income to be \$40 500. However, he faces the possibility that his house will burn down, reducing his income to \$4 500. This unfortunate event occurs with probability 1/3.

2 The consumer's expected utility, if uninsured, is
- a 57
- b 14
- c 114 000
- d 7
- e None of the above.

3 The most the consumer would be willing to pay for full insurance is
- a \$32
- b \$98 000
- c \$24 500
- d \$16 000
- e None of the above.

4 A lottery with a 1/2 chance of winning \$100 000 and 1/2 chance of losing \$80 000
- a May well be accepted by a risk averter.
- b Will never be accepted by a risk averter.
- c Will never be accepted by a risk-neutral person.
- d Will always be accepted by a risk-averse individual.
- e None of the above.

5 When the price of a lottery ticket is \$10, Barb is observed buying two per week, when the price increases to \$15, Barb only buys one. From this we may conclude that:
- a Barb is risk averse.
- b Barb is risk inclined.
- c Barb is risk neutral.
- d Lotteries are a normal good for Barb.
- e None of the above.

6 Suppose that the probability of winning one million dollars is 0.00001, and the price of the lottery ticket is \$10, then
- a A risk-neutral individual would take the gamble.
- b A risk-inclined individual would take the gamble.
- c A risk-averse individual would take the gamble.
- d Both **a** and **c**
- e All of the above.

7 The expected value of the prospect (0.02, 0.48, 0.50; 10 000, 10, 0) is:
- a \$204.80
- b \$5 004.80
- c \$4 800.00
- d \$4.80
- e Cannot determine without additional information.

8 If $U(0.5w_1 + 0.5w_2)$ exceeds $0.5U(w_1) + 0.5U(w_2)$ then this individual is:
- a Risk neutral.
- b Risk inclined.
- c Risk averse.
- d Irrational.
- e None of the above.

9 Suppose that the utility of wealth is given by $U(w) = w^{1/2}$. If there are two states of the world, each occurring with probability 1/2, and a prospeet pays \$100 in state 1 and \$36 in state 2, then the certainty equivalent of the prospect
- a Is \$68.
- b Is \$8.
- c Is \$64.
- d Cannot be calculated without more information.
- e None of the above.

10 For two prospects with the same expected value,
- a A risk-neutral individual will be indifferent between the two prospects.
- b A risk-averse individual will prefer the prospect with the larger spread in the outcomes.
- c A risk-inclined individual will prefer the prospect with the smaller spread in the outcomes.
- d A risk-averse individual will be indifferent between the two prospects.
- e None of the above.

11 An individual is risk-averse if

a The certainty equivalent of a prospect is greater than the expected monetary value of the prospect.

b The expected utility of the prospect is larger than the utility of the expected value of the prospect.

c The utility of the certainty equivalent is greater than the utility of the expected value of the prospect.

d He is not willing to take a gamble at a price equal to the expected monetary value of the gamble.

e None of the above.

True-False

12 A risk-averse individual would never be willing to pay more than the expected loss from a risky project for full insurance.

13 An individual with a constant marginal utility of wealth is risk neutral.

14 If the insurance company charges a premium equal to an individual's certainty equivalent, then only a risk neutral individual would buy the insurance.

15 A risk-averse individual prefers all certain prospects over a particular risky prospect.

16 Given two prospects with the same expected value, a risk-averse individual prefers the prospect with the smaller spread in the outcomes.

17 The certainty equivalent of a prospect for a risk-averse individual is less than the expected value of the prospect.

18 Given two prospects, (0.5, 0.5: 100,0) and (0.7, 0.3: 30, 70), the risk-averse individual will definitely prefer the second prospect because the spread in the outcomes is smaller.

19 An expected utility maximizer with a utility function $U(w) = w^{1/2} + 0.1w$ would prefer to keep his initial wealth of \$1 000 rather than enter into a lottery (0.4, 0.6: \$2500, 0). (The outcomes stated in the lottery include the initial wealth and the price of the lottery ticket.)

20 A risk-averse individual will never buy a risky asset.

21 If the marginal utility of income is diminishing, then the expected utility of a prospect exceeds the utility of the expected value of the prospect.

22 If a risk-averse individual with \$500 income assigns a utility of 100 to \$450 and a utility of 120 to \$500, and if he is willing to pay \$50 at maximum for a lottery ticket that pays \$250 with probability 1/2 and \$0 with probability 1/2, then the utility of \$700 is 140.

Short Problems

23 Jill has a utility function of the form $U(w) = w^{1/2}$ where w is wealth. She obeys the expected utility hypothesis. Her initial wealth is \$4. She also has a lottery ticket that will be worth \$12 with probability 1/3, \$5 with probability 1/3, and \$0 with probability 1/3. What is the lowest price, p, at which she will sell her ticket?

24 Suppose that, in the absence of medical insurance, individuals who break an arm pay, on average, \$500 for medical services. Assume the probability that an individual breaks her arm is 0.01 per year and the costs of providing insurance are zero. Will a competitive insurance industry provide insurance against the medical costs of broken arms at \$5 for risk-neutral individuals, greater than \$5 for risk-averse individuals, and less than \$5 for risk-inclined individuals? Why or why not?

25 Explain, using a diagram, why a risk-averse individual, choosing between two prospects with the same expected value, prefers the prospect with the smaller spread in the outcomes.

26 To purchase eight tickets for the subway, an individual must pay \$5 and then deposit one of the tickets in the ticket box. Why doesn't the subway clerk simply give seven tickets for the \$5 and allow the customer entry into the station?

27 Winfred Whiz is playing on a game show. He must choose between two offers. The first offer is a payment of \$2 000, which he can take for simply being on the show, or he can enter a gamble. In the gamble, he chooses one of two curtains that conceal two items. He makes a draw for curtain 1 or 2 from a hat and then receives the gift behind the curtain picked. He knows that behind one curtain is an automobile valued at \$4 000 and behind the other curtain is a set of encyclopedias valued at \$500. If his initial wealth is \$1 000 and his utility function can be described by $U(w) = 1 - 1000/w$, then what must be the probability of drawing the car for Winfred to be indifferent between the two choices?

28 Explain the relationship between the certainty equivalent of some gamble and the maximum price of insurance that a risk-averse individual would be willing to pay.

29 A risk-neutral individual's preference ordering over prospects can be based entirely on the expected values of the prospects. Explain why this is true.

30 Let A, B, C, and D represent four gambles available to an individual, where

$$A = (0.8, 0.2\colon 4000, 0)$$
$$B = (1, 0\colon 3000, 0)$$
$$C = (0.2, 0.8\colon 4000, 0)$$
$$D = (0.25, 0.75\colon 3000, 0)$$

If the individual chooses B over A and C over D, is his behaviour consistent with the axioms of expected utility theory? Explain.

31 Ms. Gamble currently has an income of \$25 000. Assign the utility number 100 to this income level and the utility number 85 to the income level \$20 000. It is known that Ms. Gamble would be willing to pay a maximum of \$5 000 for a lottery ticket that yields \$10 000 with a probability of 3/5 (and yields zero otherwise). What is the utility number appropriate to the income level of \$30 000? Explain.

32 In a recent Kodak case, Kodak was charged with requiring purchasers of Kodak copy machines to also purchase a service contract with Kodak rather than have their machines serviced by independent firms. Why doesn't Kodak simply allow customers to service the product in a separate maintenance market?

33 In Chapter 9 we talked about the expected costs of criminal activity in terms of the expected value of penalties. We looked at the two ways of increasing this expected cost: by increasing the probability of getting caught (p) and by increasing the fine (F). Using expected utility analysis, discuss the pros and cons associated with increasing p versus increasing F to stop people from illegal parking in downtown Victoria.

34 "When evaluating the accident propensity of a population, it is better to have fewer individuals as it cuts down on the amount of information that is needed." Discuss this statement.

Long Problems

35 Betty Bat loves the Toronto Blue Jays. She has followed their exploits since she was five years old. In two consecutive years (1992 and 1993) they won the World Series, and Betty thinks they can do it again. Betty has just thought up a clever plan. She has \$1 000 of savings that she has hidden under her bed. She could spend \$600 of the \$1 000 in making Blue Jays championship paraphernalia: buttons, cups, pens, and so on. Then, if the Blue Jays win, she estimates that she would earn \$1 500. If the Blue Jays lose, she won't be able to sell any of her stock. Betty figures that the Blue Jays have a 0.6 chance of winning the World Series. Betty's utility function is given by $U(w) = w^{1/2}$.

a If Betty is an expected utility maximizer, will she make the \$600 investment into Blue Jays championship gadgets?

b Calculate the certainty equivalent of Betty's clever prospect.

c Suppose that a friend offers her insurance. He says to Betty, "If you pay me F dollars whether or not the Blue Jays win, then, in the event that the Blue Jays lose, I will pay you \$1 500, the amount that you would have earned had the Blue Jays won the World Series. If the Blue Jays win, I will pay you nothing." What is the maximum value of F that Betty is willing to pay for the insurance policy? If Betty's friend is risk-neutral, will he gain by this venture? Explain.

d If Betty purchases the insurance on the \$600 investment, might a moral hazard problem arise in which Betty shirks on her efforts to sell the Blue Jay merchandise? Why or why not?

36 An individual is about to place a bet on her favourite racehorse, Lightning Speed. She can make one of two bets. Each bet costs \$100. In the first option, she bets that Lightning Speed will win the next race. If Lightning Speed wins, the individual will receive \$1 000 (not including the ticket price); otherwise, she receives \$0. There is a 1/5 chance that the favorite horse will win. For the second option, she places a bet on Lightning Speed in the second and third races. If Lightning Speed wins in the second race, she receives a chance to play in the third race. There is a 1/4 chance that the favourite horse will win in the second race. If Lightning Speed wins in the third race, the individual receives \$1 000; if Lightning Speed loses in either the second or third race, she receives \$0.

a Assuming that the individual satisfies the assumptions of expected-utility theory, what must be the probability of Lightning Speed winning the third race for the individual to be indifferent between the two bets?

b Which assumption of expected-utility theory has to be satisfied to answer **a**?

37 Suppose $w_1 > w_2 > w_3 > w_4$, and $U(w_1) + U(w_4) = U(w_2) + U(w_3)$, where w is wealth. Show that any individual (regardless of preferences toward risk) would prefer $(p, 1-p: w_1, w_4)$ over $(p, 1-p: w_2, w_3)$ if $p > 1-p$. Give the intuition behind this answer.

***38** Suppose you know the utility functions of four individuals: 1) $U(w) = 2w^{2/3} + 10$; 2) $U(w) = 100w^2$; 3) $U(w) = 50w$; 4) $U(w) = 0.5w^{1/2}$.

a Use calculus to determine the individuals' attitude towards risk.

b Suppose that each individual has an income of \$1 000 and is an expected utility maximizer; the following lottery is offered: (0.2, 0.8: 100 000, 0). If the price of a ticket is \$100, who will participate in the lottery?

ANSWERS TO CHAPTER 17

Case Study

A One economic explanation for this phenomenon is offered by Milton Friedman and L.J. Savage.[2] They suggest that an individual's utility curves may be convex for low and high incomes, but concave for a small range of income in the middle. With this sort of function, risk-taking behaviour varies with income. The two convex sections of the utility function may correspond to different socioeconomic levels and the concave one may be the transition from one to the other. This means that an increase in income that does not raise the person to another status level will exhibit diminishing marginal utility even if there is an increase in the relative position of the consumer within his own "class." However, an increase in income that shifts the person into a higher class will yield increasing marginal utility. Thus, people may be willing to pay a premium to receive a chance at elevating their social standing.

B Figure A17.1 illustrates a utility function, consistent with the willingness of people to purchase insurance and lottery tickets. A person with an initial income of I^* has a concave utility curve to the left and convex utility curve to the right. Because his utility curve is concave to the left of I^*, he will be willing to insure himself against risks that would leave him at I_1 (e.g., fire, theft, illness). To see this, note that a line drawn from the two points on the utility curve at I^* and I_1 is everywhere below the utility curve; hence, an expected utility-maximizing individual will want to insure himself. On the other hand, he may be willing to participate in a lottery that pays a large sum of money, $I_2 - I^*$, with some probability at the cost of lottery ticket (e.g., $I^* - I_1$), even if the probability of winning is small.

FIGURE A17.1

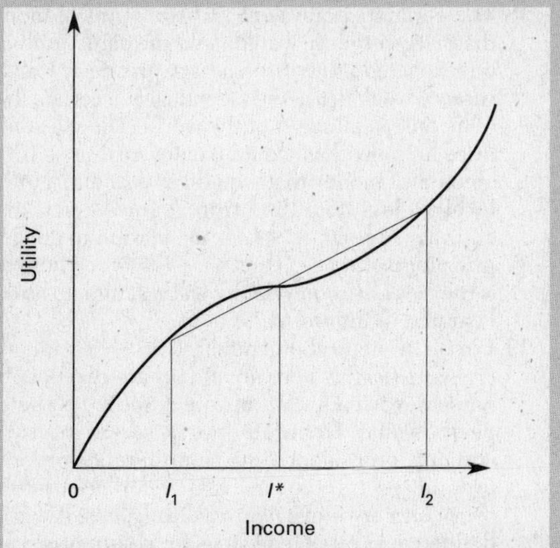

C One criticism of the explanation for the insurance-lottery decisions is its implications that only a certain group of people, particularly with middle-range incomes, are most likely to gamble and to take out insurance. A more conventional explanation for why people simultaneously gamble and insure is that people engage in gambling as a form of entertainment and recreation rather than only regarding it as an income-determining activity. That is, gambling is a consumption good rather than an investment good.

Alternatively, there could be asymmetric information between the players and the lotto company. Players typically have incomplete information about the actual and different probabilities of the games and suffer from the usual limitations of assessing and evaluating information in a rational and consistent manner.

[2] M. Friedman and L. Savage (1948) "The Utility Analysis of Choice Involving Risks." *Journal of Political Economy*, **56** (August): 279–304.

Multiple-Choice

1 c 2 d 3 d 4 a 5 e 6 a
7 a 8 c 9 c 10 a 11 d

True-False

12 F 13 T 14 F 15 F 16 T 17 T
18 F 19 T 20 F 21 F 22 T

FIGURE A17.2

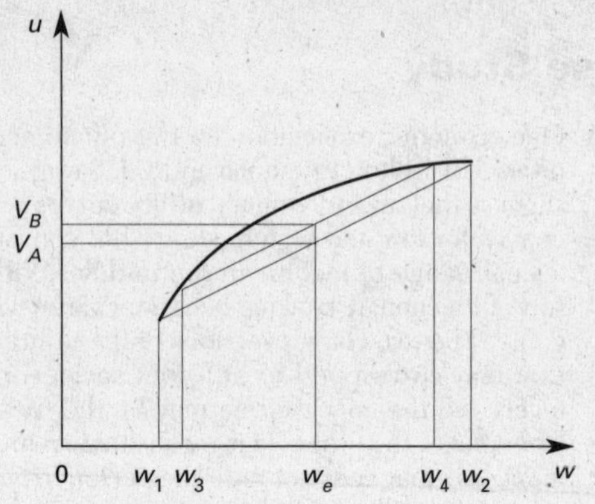

Short Problems

23 The lowest price, p, satisfies

$$u(4+p) = (1/3)[u(4+12) + u(4+5) + u(4+0)].$$

Substituting in the utility function,

$$(4+p)^{1/2} = (1/3)[16^{1/2} + 9^{1/2} + 4^{1/2}]$$

Solving for p yields $p = 5$.

24 No. If the insurance company is risk-neutral, it will provide insurance at a price equal to the expected cost from an accident. The expected costs are $500(0.01) = 5$ for all individuals, regardless of their preferences toward risk.

25 Figure A17.2 shows an individual's utility function and two prospects $A = (^1/2, ^1/2\text{: } w_1, w_2)$ and $B = (^1/2, ^1/2\text{: } w_3, w_4)$. The expected values of the two prospects are equal: $(w_1 + w_2)/2 = (w_3 + w_4)/2 = w_e$. The expected utility of A, the prospect with the larger spread, is less than the expected utility of B. Since a risk-averse individual has diminishing marginal utility of income, the individual prefers a prospect that has a smaller down-side risk (that is, the one with the chance of *losing* a smaller amount of money) than the one that has a chance of winning more money.

26 This is a monitoring device to ensure that the clerk does not attempt to pocket any of the revenues from ticket sales.

27 For Winfred to be indifferent between the two choices, the probability of drawing the car must satisfy

$$\begin{aligned} &U(2\,000 + 1\,000) \\ &= p[U(4\,000 + 1\,000)] + (1-p)[u(500 + 1\,000)] \\ &= U(1\,500) + p[U(5\,000) - U(1\,500)] \end{aligned}$$

Substituting the utility values into this expression gives

$$1 - \frac{1\,000}{3\,000} = 1 - \frac{1\,000}{1\,500} + p\left(\frac{1\,000}{1\,500} - \frac{1\,000}{5\,000}\right)$$

or

$$p = \frac{5}{7}$$

28 The certainty equivalent is the amount of money that with certainty would yield the same utility as the expected utility from a risky prospect. Full insurance would leave the individual at a certain level of income in all states of the world. The maximum price an individual would pay for insurance is the amount of money that would leave him at a utility level no less than the utility from the certainty equivalent wealth. Let I_r be the maximum demand price for insurance. Then $w_0 - I_r = w_{ce}$, where w_{ce} is the certainty equivalent wealth. I_r and w_{ce} are illustrated in Figure A17.3.

29 For a risk-neutral individual, $U(w_e) = p[U(w_1)] + (1-p)[U(w_2)]$, where w_1 and w_2 are two possible outcomes from a risky prospect and w_e is the expected value. Hence, $w_e = w_{ce}$, where w_{ce} is the certainty equivalent. Since a preference ordering over prospects is the same as a preference ordering over certainty equivalent wealth values, it can be defined over expected values for risk-neutral individuals.

30 If B **P** A, then

$$U(3\,000) > 0.8[U(4\,000)] + 0.2[U(0)] \qquad (1)$$

If C **P** D, then

FIGURE A17.3

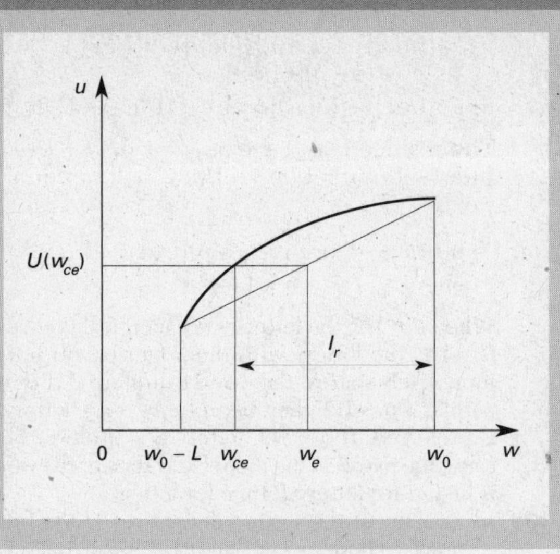

$$0.2[U(4\ 000)] + 0.8[U(0)] >$$
$$0.25[U(3\ 000)] + 0.75[U(0)] \quad (2)$$

Both sides of equation (2) are multiplied by 4 and the equation is then rearranged to give

$$U(3\ 000) < 0.8[U(4\ 000)] + 0.2[U(0)] \quad (3)$$

Since inequalities (1) and (3) cannot occur simultaneously, the behaviour is not consistent with expected-utility theory.

31 Ms. Gamble has the option of taking the assured prospect of $25 000 if she chooses not to buy a lottery ticket. Alternatively, she can purchase a ticket and face the risky prospect: (3/5, 2/5: w_1, w_2), where w_1 and w_2 are given by

$$w_1 = 25\ 000 + 10\ 000 - 5\ 000 = 30\ 000$$
$$w_2 = 25\ 000 + 0 - 5\ 000 = 20\ 000$$

Since $5000 is Ms. Gamble's reservation price for the lottery ticket, then it must be the case that

$$U(25\ 000) = 3/5[U(30\ 000)] + 2/5[U(20\ 000)]$$

Substituting $U(25\ 000) = 100$ and $U(20\ 000) = 85$ implies that $U(30\ 000) = 110$.

32 An efficiency explanation may be the following: If customers cannot identify when a fault in a product is attributable to the product being defective or to poor maintenance, then independent service companies may not have the incentive to repair the product properly; that is, there may be a moral hazard problem. The manufacturer has the incentive to repair the product carefully since its reputation would otherwise suffer.

33 By increasing the probability of getting caught, and reducing the fine, the "gamble" of whether or not to park illegally becomes more interesting for those individuals who dislike risk. Of course, if the probability of a parking ticket becomes very small and the fine becomes very high, then the variance in income between the two states of the world is increased. Only risk inclined individuals would likely illegally park in this case.

34 When evaluating the accident propensity of a population of individuals insurance companies rely on the law of large numbers to set premiums. In a large population, the distribution of accidents among individuals of different characteristics is likely to approximate the actual riskiness of individuals. Thus, for instance, in a large population of young male drivers it is typically found that their accident propensity is higher than in a large population of young female drivers. Hence, young males are often charged a higher premium. In a small population, it is difficult to make accurate predications about the likely riskiness of any one individual.

Long Problems

35 a If the Blue Jays win (state 1), Betty will earn $1 500 in revenues less the $600 from the investment, or net revenues of $900. Given her initial income of $1 000, $w_1 = \$1\ 900$. If the Blue Jays lose, she will lose the $600 and have a total wealth of $w_2 = \$400$. Betty will undertake the investment if the expected utility from the prospect exceeds the utility from keeping the $1 000 under her bed. That is,

$$U(1\ 000) < 0.6[U(1\ 900)] + 0.4[U(400)]$$

Substituting in the expression for the utility function gives

$$(1\ 000)^{1/2} < 0.6(1\ 900)^{1/2} + 0.4(400)^{1/2}$$
$$31.6 < 26.15 + 8 = 34.15$$

Yes, Betty will invest the $600 in the risky prospect.

b The certainty equivalent is that level of wealth, w_{ce}, that yields the same utility as the prospect; that is,

$$w_{ce}^{1/2} = 34.15 \quad \text{and} \quad w_{ce} = \$1\ 166.22$$

c Betty receives $1 500 if the Blue Jays win or lose (or a net revenue of $900 in addition to the initial income) under the insurance plan. At maximum, she is willing to pay the amount of money from her total certain income of $1 900 that will leave her at the same level of utility as with the certainty equivalent. That is,

$$(1\ 900 - F)^{1/2} = 34.15$$

and so

$$F = \$733.78$$

Betty's reservation price for the "insurance policy" is \$733.78. The friend will offer the insurance policy because the expected cost of the policy, 0.4(1 500) = \$600, is less than F.

d The insurance company pays only if the Blue Jays lose, an event that is beyond Betty's control. Moreover, it is assumed that the profits in this case are zero, regardless of her efforts. Hence, there is no moral hazard problem on effort. However, if the payment by the insurance company depended on the profits she earned in the "bad" state, then there could be a moral hazard problem if Betty shirked on her efforts to sell the merchandise.

36 a The two prospects can be written as

$$A = (1/5, 4/5: w_0 + 900, w_0 - 100)$$
$$B = [1/4, 3/4: (p, 1 - p; w_0 + 900, w_0 - 100); w_0 - 100]$$

The expected utility from each prospect is

$$V_A = (1/5)[U(w_0 + 900)] + (4/5)[U(w_0 - 100)]$$
$$\begin{aligned} V_B &= (1/4)(p[U(w_0 + 900)] + (1 - p)[U(w_0 - 100)]) + (3/4)[U(w_0 - 100)] \\ &= (1/4)p[U(w_0 + 900)] + (1 - 1/4p)[U(w_0 - 100)] \\ &= \hat{p}[U(w_0 + 900)] + (1 - \hat{p})[U(w_0 - 100)] \end{aligned}$$

Then, $V_A = V_B$ if $\hat{p} = (1/4)p = 1/5$, which implies $p = 4/5$.

b To answer part **a**, the substitution assumption of compound prospects must be satisfied; that is, the simple prospect (1/5, 4/5: w_0 + 900, w_0 – 100) must be equivalent to the compound prospect B.

37 An individual prefers $A = (p, 1 - p: w_1, w_4)$ over $B = (p, 1 - p: w_2, w_3)$ if

$$p[U(w_1)] + (1 - p)[U(w_4)] > p[U(w_2)] + (1 - p)[U(w_3)]$$
$$p[U(w_1) - U(w_2)] > (1 - p)[U(w_3) - U(w_4)]$$

Then, since $U(w_1) + U(w_4) = U(w_2) + U(w_3)$, $U(w_1) - U(w_2) = U(w_3) - U(w_4)$, and substitution yields

$$p[U(w_1) - U(w_2)] > (1 - p)[U(w_1) - U(w_2)]$$

or

$$p > 1 - p$$

When $p = 1/2$, the lotteries are identical; hence, if $p \neq 1/2$, the lottery with the larger payoff in the more likely state of the world is preferred. For example, if $p > 1/2$, then because $w_1 > w_2$, lottery A is preferred. If $p < 1/2$, lottery B is preferred because the payoff in the more likely state of the world is higher for lottery B than for lottery A.

***38 a** Looking at the second derivatives of the functions we find for 1) $U'' > 0$, 2) $U'' < 0$, 3) $U'' = 0$, and 4) $U'' < 0$. Thus, individuals 1 and 4 are risk averse, 2 is risk inclined and 3 is risk neutral.

b In this case everyone will participate in the lottery. Notice, first, that the expected value of the lottery is \$20 000, much higher than the price of the ticket, hence all risk-neutral and risk-inclined individuals would buy a ticket. If you look at the utility of the risk-averse individuals without the lottery (e.g., for individual 1 this is 200.46 and for individual 4 it is 15.81) and compare their expected utility after the lottery (1 053.45 and 43.76 respectively), then it is clear that this gamble will be undertaken by everyone.

CHAPTER 18

Asymmetric Information, the Rules of the Game, and Externalities

Chapter Summary

Although powerful, the neoclassical model presented thus far leaves several phenomena unexplained. Because we have ignored questions about *how* economic activity is organized, we have ignored questions dealing with the **distribution of property rights**. For instance, we have focused primarily on goods which are produced by private, profit-maximizing firms. Many goods, however, are provided by **nonprofit firms** in which no individual is allowed to keep any resulting profits. Government also provides certain goods and services, as do family units. In this chapter we examine how asymmetric information and property rights affect economic exchange.

Externalities, the Coase Theorem, Transaction Costs and Property Rights

An **externality** occurs when the behaviour of one agent affects the utility or profit of another agent without compensation. It may have a positive effect — like when neighbours benefit from my beautiful front garden — or the externality may be negative — like when a lead smelter emits toxic pollutants into the air. In a world of symmetric information and zero **transaction costs**, the **Coase theorem** states the final allocation of resources is independent of the initial allocation of property rights. For instance, suppose we have two neighbours, Paul who enjoys listening to the Smashing Pumpkins played very loudly in his backyard, and Claude who enjoys peace and serenity in his back yard. According to the Coase theorem, irrespective of who has the initial property right (i.e., either Paul has the right to loud music or Claude has the right to peace and quiet) the final outcome will be the same. The reason for this result is that the two parties can bargain over the outcome — with the person who values the final outcome the most being able to obtain it. The Coase theorem, however, relies on the fact that transactions costs are zero or very low. In our simple example, costs are likely to be low as it involves only two people. Imagine the problems associated with transacting when a whole community is affected by the loud noise. Transaction costs refer to the costs associated with establishing and maintaining property rights.

Asymmetric Information, Transaction Costs and the Coase Theorem

Transaction costs occur because information is costly to obtain. However, it is the asymmetry of information between parties that lies at the heart of transaction costs. One solution is to try to eliminate these asymmetries, but this is impossible or impractical in a number of instances. Don't forget that there are enormous gains to specialization — it would simply be impossible for all of us to know enough about, say, automobiles to be able to determine if our mechanic is telling the truth or not!

Responses to Externalities

One way to get around the problem of transaction costs is to have the government (or court) assign the correct (i.e., socially desirable) distribution of property rights initially. Another solution arises through the **internalization** of the external costs (benefits) imposed on a third party. For instance, a firm that produces high-quality headsets (with long cords) may be able to solve our loud music problem in the absence of a negotiated settlement. A key aspect of transaction costs concerns **free riders** — those who benefit from a situation without paying any costs. A neighbour to the other side of Paul who also enjoys peace and quiet may be able to free-ride on the settlement reached between Paul and Claude (assuming, of course, that the settlement resulted in the reduction of noise).

Governments may also impose **public regulation** to solve problems that arise when transaction costs are high. Prohibiting certain activities (like the production of chlorofluorocarbons, or smoking in certain buildings), taxing activities (like cigarette and alcohol consumption), and setting regulatory standards (like on automobile emissions) are all examples of public regulations. Having identified the externality problem, policy makers must then determine the goal (or target) to be achieved and which of the array of possible **regulatory mechanisms** to use to achieve it. Governments may also respond by a policy of **nonintervention**, doing nothing because it is not cost effective to intervene.

Public Goods

Public goods have positive externalities for the entire community. In comparison to a **rivalrous good** like an apple, public goods are **nonrivalrous goods**; that is, my consumption of the good does not preclude someone else from consuming it and vice versa. If, in addition to being nonrivalrous, public goods are **nonexcludable goods** (that is, no one can be denied access to it), like Halley's comet, then they are **pure public goods**.

The problem with public goods, especially pure public goods, is that they will not be produced in sufficient quantities by a profit-seeking firm. If no one can be denied access, no entrepreneur — no matter how clever — could convince individuals to pay for the good; hence, it must be provided by a public authority. Certainly, this is the case for pure public goods such as defense and advertising-free TV stations. (An interesting exception to this rule for pure public good is commercial TV broadcasting, supplied by private firms. In this case, the good is redefined as the *excludable* and *rivalrous* service of time to advertise to a captive audience, and so the presence of private firms in this market becomes evident.)

How much of the good will public agencies provide? As for any other externality, the government must undertake a **cost-benefit analysis**. The **marginal social**

value is the sum of marginal values of the public good by all of its users of the public good, that is, the vertical summation of individual demand curves for the public good which results in the **demand function for public goods**. There is one catch. If the tax to pay for the public good is proportional to consumer's revealed value, then self-interested consumers will attempt to free-ride by underestimating their true value of the project — known as the **revealed-preference problem**. If the tax bill is independent of the project and the project is undertaken as long as the sum of announced valuations exceeds the project's costs, then each individual with positive valuation will announce a sufficiently large valuation to ensure that the project will be undertaken, regardless of the announcements by the other consumers. Similarly, if individuals split equally the cost of the project, then publicly announced valuations will not be truthful.

KEY WORDS

Coase theorem

Cost-benefit analysis

Demand function for public goods

Distribution of property rights

Externality

Free-riders

Government intervention

Internalization

Marginal social value

Nonexcludable goods

Nonintervention

Nonprofit firms

Nonrivalrous goods

Property right

Public goods

Public regulation

Pure public goods

Regulatory mechanism

Revealed-preference problem

Rivalrous goods

Transaction costs

CASE STUDY: SHOULD INFORMATION BE GIVEN AWAY?

Information is a public good. Your knowledge of a mathematical formula does not prevent another individual from being able to "consume" that mathematical formula. Similarly for an invention: A computer whiz who discovers a supercomputer can try to keep that information secret, but the inventor's "consumption" of the information on that invention does not destroy the information. If the cost of transmitting the information were zero, the *social* marginal cost of sharing the information would be zero. Hence, as long as someone benefits from acquiring that information, an efficient allocation of the information involves free access to the information. Even if that information were costly to acquire at the time of the discovery, those costs are "sunk" and are therefore not relevant to the information transfer decision.

A What effect would the imposition of the socially optimal rule for information transfer have on the rate of technological progress? Explain.

B One way of encouraging research is through the mechanism of patents. A patent gives private property rights to an inventor for 17 years. Even if this legal protection solves the research problem, will the *use* of the information be efficient? Why or why not?

C Can you think of a scheme that would encourage the socially optimal level of research and use of the innovation? Discuss possible problems with your scheme.

EXERCISES

Multiple-Choice

Choose the correct answer to each question. There is only one correct answer to each question.

1 Consumers of public goods are likely to

a Overstate their true preferences if they expect to be taxed in accordance with their marginal private benefit.

b Understate their true preferences if the tax is independent of the project and if the project is undertaken when the total announced valuations exceed the project costs.

c Understate their true preferences if they expect to be taxed in accordance with their marginal private benefits.

d Act in accordance with **a** and **b**.

e None of the above.

2 Alison lives above a posh restaurant. Every night before retiring, she practices her trumpet. Suppose that it would cost $100 per night to find an acceptable alternative venue for Alison's practice sessions; and the restaurant loses $500 per night whenever she practices overhead. The socially acceptable solution is

a For the restaurant to rent the alternative place for Alison's sessions.

b For Alison to pay for an alternative place in which to practice.

c For the restaurant to suffer the noise.

d For Alison to play elsewhere. Who pays for it depends upon the initial allocation of property rights.

e Cannot say without knowledge of their respective utility functions.

Use Figure 18.1 for problems **3** and **4**. The marginal value curves of national defense for two representative consumers, Jean and Aline, are given by *MN* and *MQ*. The marginal cost of national defense is given by $MC(y)$.

3 The marginal social value of $\hat{y}$ units of public defense for these two individuals is

a *OB*, the marginal value to the individual with the higher value.

b *OA*, the marginal value to the individual with the lower value.

c OP^*

d $OB + OA$

e None of the above.

4 The optimal amount of the public good to provide, given the two individuals' marginal value curves, is

a The amount of national defense given by the intersection of the vertical summation of *MN* and *MQ* with $MC(y)$.

b Oy^*

c $O\hat{y}$

d The amount of national defense given by the intersection of the horizontal summation of *MN* and *MQ* with $MC(y)$.

e None of the above.

Refer to Figure 18.2 for problems **5** and **6**. Snowmobiles are noisy and impose unpleasant costs on cross-country skiers who like to get away from all the noise and the fast pace of city life. Figure 18.2 shows the total cost *TC* and total benefits *TB* of snowmobiles as a function of the number of snowmobiles purchased.

5 If the current number of snowmobiles is $\hat{y}$, then

a The optimal number of snowmobiles is being purchased.

b The *TB* of snowmobiles exceeds the *TC* of snowmobiles.

FIGURE 18.1

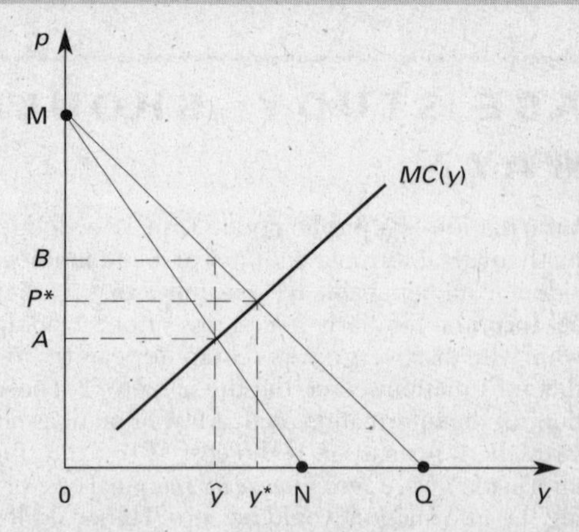

FIGURE 18.2

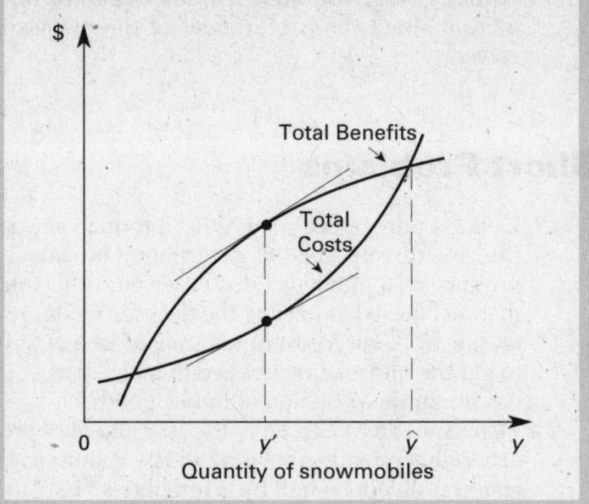

c The marginal benefit of an additional snowmobile is less than the marginal cost of an additional snowmobile.
d The *TB* of snowmobiles is less than the *TC* of snowmobiles.
e None of the above.

6 At y' snowmobiles,
a The government may want to impose a tax on snowmobiles to decrease their number.
b The government will want to give property rights to the cross-country skiers and allow the two parties to reach an agreement.
c The government may want to ban snowmobiles from certain areas.
d The government will not want to do anything (more than it already may be doing) because y' is the optimal number of snowmobiles.
e The government may want to adopt either **a**, **b**, or **c**.

Use Figure 18.3 to answer questions **7** and **8**. Alex and George are roommates. Alexander likes to listen to hard-rock music; George prefers classical music. The more hard-rock CDs that Alex buys, the more hours George has to listen to this "noise." Figure 18.3 shows Alex's and George's preferences of hard-rock music and the composite commodity relative to the initial situation, *H*, in which Alex buys zero hard-rock CDs. The utility levels for Alex and George at H are u_A and u_G, respectively. Both individuals have incomes of $150; each hard-rock CD costs $10.

7 According to the diagram,
a If George has property rights on the amount of noise in the room, then he would be willing to pay Alex $5 not to purchase two CDs.
b If Alex has property rights on noise in the room, he would be willing to pay George $20 for the right to play two CDs.
c Alex is willing to pay $75 for the right to purchase four CDs.
d Alex is willing to pay $45 for the right to purchase six CDs.
e None of the above.

8 According to the diagram,
a Alex is willing to pay increasing amounts of money for the right to buy additional CDs.
b George is willing to pay decreasing amounts of money for the right not to listen to the CDs.
c Using cost-benefit analysis, the number of CDs that maximizes net social benefit is less than four.
d Using cost-benefit analysis, the number of CDs that maximizes net social benefit is greater than six.
e None of the above.

FIGURE 18.3

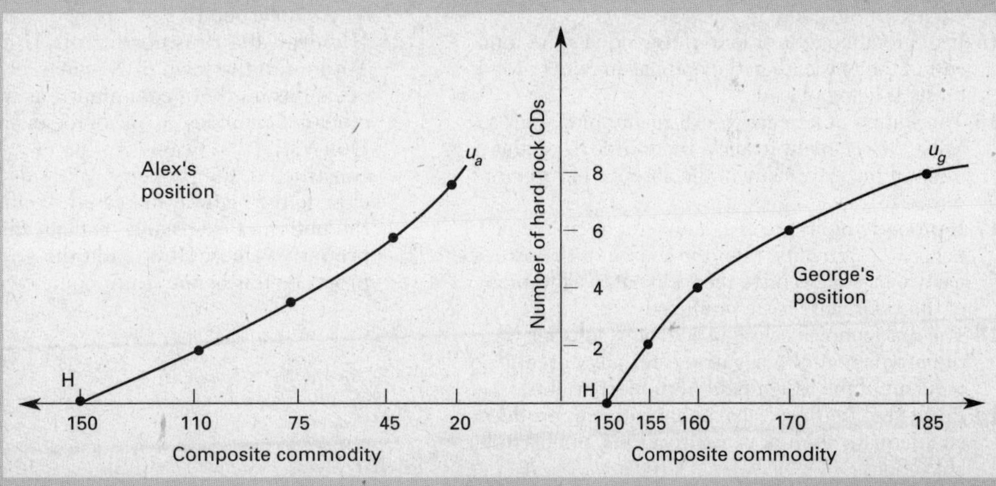

9 In the absence of regulation and well-defined property rights,
- a The quantity of a negative externality will be less than the optimal quantity.
- b The quantity of a positive externality will be greater than the optimal quantity.
- c The recipient of a negative externality may want to bribe the source to reduce the amount of the externality.
- d The source of the positive externality may want to bribe the recipient to accept more of the externality.
- e None of the above.

10 The government considers untertaking a project that would benefit two individuals, A and B, at a cost of K. The project will be carried out if the sum of the announced valuations of A and B, x_a and x_b, respectively, exceed K. Then the announced valuations will be the true valuations of the project if
- a Each individual A pays $K/2$, and individual B pays $K/2$.
- b Individuals A and B pay x_a and x_b, respectively.
- c Individuals A and B pay an amount that is independent of their announced valuations.
- d Individuals A and B each pay an amount equal to $(x_a + x_b)/2$.
- e None of the above.

True-False

11 If individual A provides a positive externality to individual B, then too little of the externality will be produced in the absence of a bribe.

12 A nonrivalrous good is one for which my consumption of the good does not preclude the possibility of anyone else benefiting from it.

13 A competitive market will produce too little of a pure public good.

14 The marginal social value curve for a public good is the horizontal summation of individual demand curves for the good.

15 If the total benefit of loud music equals the total cost of the music, then the optimal amount of loud music is being played.

16 The source of a negative externality may want to bribe the recipient to allow the source to produce more of the externality in the absence of property rights.

17 If property rights are assigned to the recipient of a negative externality, then the source of the externality may want to bribe the recipient to allow more of the externality to be produced.

18 The distributional consequences of negotiating over the production of a negative externality are independent of the assignment of property rights.

19 Profit-seeking firms have no incentive to produce an adequate amount of nonrivalrous, nonexcludable goods.

20 Solving the problem of externalities through assignment of property rights is inefficient since it requires the government to gather detailed information about the preferences of the parties involved.

Short Problems

21 Define a pure public good. What information would the government need to determine how much to produce of a public good? How would this information be used in making the decision? Comment on the problems a government might face in trying to get the information needed to make correct decisions on the provision of public goods.

22 Define an externality. Does the assignment of property rights provide a solution to the resource allocation problems posed by externalities? Explain.

23 Show graphically how overall economic efficiency can be increased by the presence of a strong union that achieves a wage rate above the equilibrium wage in its negotiations with a perfectly competitive industry that is creating negative externalities.

24 Discuss forms of government intervention that might be useful in combating a negative externality.

25 What is the rationale for requiring motorists to have drivers' licenses? Automobile insurance? Fastened seat belts?

26 Refer back to multiple-choice questions 7 and 8 and Figure 18.3. Construct the benefits to Alex and the cost to George from listening to hard-rock CDs. Show that the net social benefits are maximized at six CDs.

27 Show whether each of the following market situations provides an economically efficient allocation of resources.
- a A polluting monopolist in the market for good 1 and nonpolluting competition in the market for good 2
- b A public good

28 Highway 404 runs north from Highway 401 in Toronto to the town of Newmarket. It thus connects this northern community, as well as several other communities, to one of the main arteries (the Don Valley Parkway) into the city. When it was constructed, the property values of those houses close to the highway increased significantly. Using the notion of externality, explain this increase in property values. How could the government expropriate this benefit from home owners?

Long Problems

*29 Suppose that paved sidewalks are public goods. There are two people in the country, Mr. A and Ms. C. The marginal cost curve for paved sidewalks is given by $MC = 10 + 2y$.

a Describe the free-rider problem regarding the provision of nonrivalrous goods.

b Suppose that the true marginal value curve for A for paved sidewalks is given by

$$y_a = 50 - \frac{p}{2}$$

and the true marginal value curve of B for paved sidewalks is given by

$$y_b = 25 - p$$

Find the efficient quantity of paved sidewalks.

30 Analyze an optimal tax system for firms in a polluting industry when the pollution damage takes the following forms:

a Pollution damage D (in dollars) increases in the firm's output y in the following way: $D = cy$, where c is a constant; the firm is in a purely competitive industry.

b Same as **a** but the firm is a monopolist.

*31 A city wants to clean up its pollution and so collects the following facts: Automobile traffic emits 20 tonnes annually, and industrial pollution is 15 tonnes. Evidence is that cleanup of automobile emissions (a) and industrial pollution (i) could be accomplished at the following costs:

$$C_a = \frac{y_a^2}{2} + 7$$

and

$$C_i = y_i^2 + 35$$

where y_a and y_i are automobile and industrial pollution reductions, respectively. Hence, $MC_a = y_a$ and $MC_i = 2y_i$.

Moreover, the benefits of pollutant reduction are:

$$B = 0.25y^2 + 2y + 49$$

where $y = y_a + y_i$.

a Mayor Clean argues that *all* pollutants should be banned. Under what conditions would his proposal be economically efficient?

b The mayor's advisor suggests an "equitable" solution. If automobile emissions are reduced by 16 units and factory emissions by 10 units, then the cleanup costs in each sector will be equal to 135. Total cleanup costs will be 270. Criticize this analysis.

c What is the economically optimal level of cleanup from each source?

d Suggest a public policy mechanism for achieving this optimal level.

32 Recently, mushroom farmers in the British Columbian lower mainland have been found responsible for any adverse effects stemming from the odours associated with this activity. Let's suppose that a swanky resort abuts a mushroom farm. Suppose too that the profit maximizing quantity of mushrooms each month is 500 kilograms, which yield a profit to the farmer, Harold, of $5 000 (these are very special mushrooms!). The following table shows the monthly profit associated with decreasing quantities of mushrooms and the intensity of odour emanating from the operation (10 is very strong, 0 is very weak).

Quantity Mushrooms (kgs)	Profit ($)	Odour Intensity
500	5 000	10
400	4 000	8
300	3 000	5
200	1 000	2
100	– 500	0

Helga owns the swanky resort which caters to discerning customers who want to sit on a veranda enjoying the fresh air and soak in the outdoor hottub. For this, each customer would pay $1 000 for the weekend. However, whenever the odours from the mushroom farm exceed "5," Helga has to cater to her clients indoors, for which they are only willing to pay $750 for the weekend. Helga can accommodate ten clients each weekend. It costs Helga $500 per client irrespective of whether they go outside or stay inside.

a What is the socially desirable outcome?

b Discuss how the ruling regarding the smells affects Harold and Helga? How is the resulting equilibrium affected?

c Instead of one mushroom farmer, suppose that there were 100 mushroom farms in the vicinity, each of which contributed 1% to the odour affecting Helga's resort. Will this affect your answers to **a** and **b**?

ANSWERS TO CHAPTER 18

Case Study

A Without property rights on intellectual property, the rate of technological progress would be low. Inventors would be unwilling to invest in research activities if they could not collect the reward from their achievements.

B No. The inventor will have a monopoly over the invention and will produce a suboptimal level of output from the invention.

C Designing an efficient scheme for encouraging innovation is very difficult. Through a contest, the government could allow firms to compete for certain projects. The winner (the one able to develop the project most cost effectively) could receive a lump-sum reward, and the invention would be available to all firms. However, this scheme has its problems. Most importantly, it requires considerable knowledge by the government to identify socially desirable projects and to ensure that the winning firm engages in the socially desirable amount of research and development.

Multiple-Choice

1 c **2** d **3** d **4** a **5** c
6 d **7** d **8** e **9** c **10** e

True-False

11 T **12** T **13** T **14** F **15** F
16 F **17** T **18** F **19** T **20** F

Short Problems

21 A pure public good is nonrivalrous in that my consumption does not preclude another person from consuming the good, and is nonexcludable in that no one can be denied access to it. To determine how much of the public good to produce, the government would need to know the marginal valuation curves of all persons and the marginal cost of producing the public good. The optimal production of the public good would be that amount for which the marginal cost equals the vertical summation of the marginal valuations. Individuals would not reveal their true marginal valuation of a public good if they thought they could have access to it regardless of the valuation announced.

22 An externality is a benefit that is received from, or a cost that is imposed by an individual who acts in self-interest. The assignment of property rights is important in solving the externality problem. To see this, consider the example of a steel mill producing pollution, a negative externality to a downstream farming community. If the farming community were given property rights to clean air, then the steel mill would have to pay for the right to pollute the air; if the steel mill were given property rights, the farming community would have to bribe the steel mill not to pollute.

23 Suppose that a competitive industry produces pollution. The marginal social cost of production is given by $MSC(y)$ in Figure A18.1. However, the private firms worry only about the private costs, $MPC(y)$. In a competitive market, demand equals supply at y', p'. The efficient allocation of resources is where demand equals the $MSC(y)$; that is, at y^*, p^*. If a union can raise the wage such that the marginal private costs increase to $MPC'(y)$, then the competitive market will produce the efficient output y^*.

24 The government could give property rights to the recipients so that the recipients could charge the source of the externality. This would force the

FIGURE A18.1

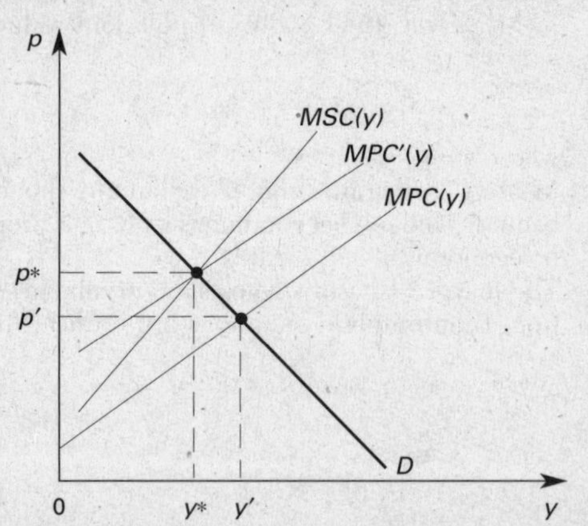

source to bear the negative costs of the externality. Alternatively, the government could tax the source of the externality, but then the government would need detailed information about the costs of the externality. Finally, the government might bribe the source to get rid of the externality with a cleanup subsidy.

25 Individuals without drivers' licenses are a negative externality on other individuals. By requiring drivers' licenses, the government can control the amount of this externality. Similarly, automobile insurance and seat belts are intended, in part, to protect individuals from poor driving by other individuals.

26 The benefits to Alex and the costs to George from the hard-rock music are illustrated in Figure A18.2. The benefit curve was derived from Alex's indifference curve in the left-hand panel of Figure 18.3. For example, the benefit from two CDs is given by his income ($150) minus the cost of the two CDs ($20), minus consumption of the composite commodity associated with two CDs ($110). So, Alex's willingness to pay for the right to purchase two CDs is $150 – $20 – $110 = $20. That is, the benefits from two CDs are measured by the expenditures on Alex's composite commodity that he is willing to give up, less the costs of the hard-rock CDs. The costs to George are measured by the increase in expenditures on his composite commodity that keeps him indifferent between no hard-rock music and two CDs of the music. From Figure 18.3, this amount is equal to $5 ($155 – $150).

Note that Alex's benefits increase at a decreasing rate, whereas George's costs increase at an increasing rate. Net benefits are maximized where the marginal benefit equals the marginal cost of an additional CD. This occurs at (approximately) six CDs, where the marginal benefit and marginal cost equal 10.

27 a A polluting monopolist sets $MR_1 = MC_1$. Competitive firms set $p_2 = MC_2$. Then in the market allocation, $MR_1/p_2 = MC_1/MC_2$. If the market allocation were efficient, then it would satisfy $p_1/p_2 = MSC_1/MC_2$, where MSC_1 is the marginal social cost of producing good 1. Since $p_1 > MR_1$ but $MSC_1 > MC_1$, it is possible that the polluting monopolist is producing the efficient level of good 1, or less than or greater than the efficient level.

b Every individual consuming the public good sets her *MRS* of good 2 (other goods) for the public good, good 1, equal to the ratio of prices; hence, the market sets $MRS = p_1/p_2 = MRT$. However, for a Pareto-efficient allocation of resources, the *summation* of *MRS* across all individuals ΣMRS, must equal the *MRT*. Since *MRT* in a competitive equilibrium is less than ΣMRS, too little of the public good is produced.

28 The value of properties is affected by their proximity to other land uses, like dumps (which cause property values to fall) and highways that usually cause property values to increase. Note that in the case of highways, properties too close to the road may decrease in value while those farther away will increase. This change in property values is because of the externality emanating from the highway. Too close means that a noise externality will impose a cost on residents; those slightly farther away will benefit from the decrease in travel time into Toronto (for the 404 case) but will not be burdened by the noise. The increase in property values may be expropriated by the government through property taxes. As the value of a property increases, property taxes typically do likewise. It is possible for the entire positive externality to be internalized through property taxes.

FIGURE A18.2

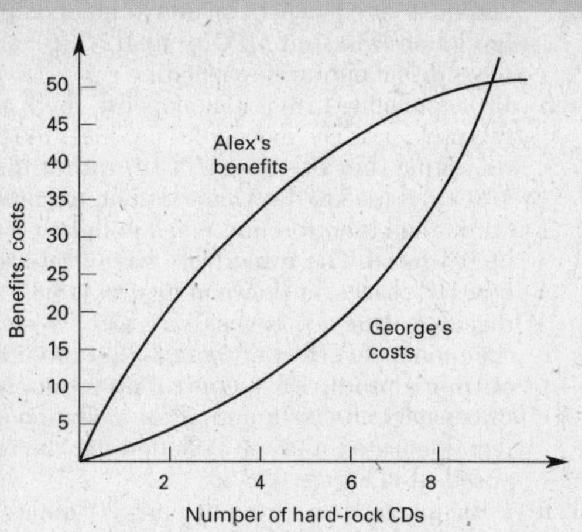

Long Problems

***29 a** If the individuals think that someone else will pay for the paved sidewalks, then no one will pay for them because everyone will believe that they can have them for nothing.

b The efficient quantity of paved sidewalks is found by equating the vertical summation of the marginal benefit curves with the marginal cost curve. To find the vertical summation of the marginal value curves, rewrite the functions as

$$p_a = 100 - 2y_a \quad \text{and} \quad p_b = 25 - y_b$$

Then the vertical summation is $MB = 125 - 3y$. Equating with $MC = 10 + 2y$ gives $125 - 3y = 10 + 2y$, so $115 = 5y$ and $y = 23$.

30 a The private market equilibrium with pollution is shown by the intersection of demand and the marginal private cost curve, $MPC(y)$, in Figure A18.3a. $MSC(y)$ is higher than $MPC(y)$ at every output. A tax equal to t^* on every unit of output (pollution) will shift $MPC(y)$ to $MPC'(y)$, and the efficient output is reached.

b If the polluting firm is a monopolist, there are two problems: The monopolist produces too little output; but because $MPC(y)$ rather than $MSC(y)$ is used to determine output, too much output and therefore too much pollution may be produced. The two effects may offset each other by chance, as shown in Figure A18.3b. In this case, no action is necessary. Otherwise, if the monopoly effect dominates and too little output is produced, a control on monopoly prices might be instituted; if the pollution effect dominates, a tax on pollution may be imposed, as in Figure A18.3a.

***31 a** If the marginal cost from banning 20 tonnes of auto emissions equals the marginal cost from banning 15 tonnes of industrial pollution, which in turn equals the marginal benefit from eliminating 35 units of pollutants, then total cleanup would be efficient.

b The mayor's advisor wants to equate *total* costs of automobile and industrial emissions rather than marginal costs of these two sources of pollution. Moreover, total costs equal total benefits under his plan, whereas marginal costs should be equated with marginal benefits.

c To find the optimal level of cleanup equate the marginal benefits with the horizontal summation of marginal costs; the latter is found by rewriting MC_a and MC_i as $y_a = MC_a$ and $y_i = MC_i/2$. Then, $y = y_a + y_i = 3MC/2$, so $MC = 2y/3$. Equate marginal costs with marginal benefits:

$$\text{MB} = \frac{y}{2} + 2 = \frac{2y}{3} = MC \quad \text{so} \quad y = 12$$

To find the allocation of the 12 units between automobile pollutants and industrial pollutants, set $MC = MC_a = MC_i$. At $y = 12$, $MC = 2 \times 12/3 = 8$. Then, $MC_a = 8$, so $y_a = 8$. $MC_i = 8$, so $y_i = 4$.

d To achieve the optimal level of pollution, a tax on emissions can be imposed.

32 a If Harold produces his profit maximizing quantity of mushrooms, Helga loses $2500*4 per month or $10 000. She would be willing to offer Harold $10 000 per month for him to reduce production to 300 kilograms. Harold would lose $2 000 from such a reduction, hence would be willing to accept any compensation of at least $2 000. The marginal value of mushroom farming 500 kilograms a month is less than the marginal value to Helga's resort. From society's perspective, it is better to have Harold produce only 300 kilograms per month and allow Helga to cater to her clients outdoors.

b Prior to the finding that mushroom farmers were responsible for any damages from their odours, those affected (like Helga) would have to "buy" the right for odour-free air from the farmers. After the finding, Helga would not have to buy the right. As long as transaction costs are low, it should not matter who has the initial right from the point of view of the final equilibrium. Note, however, that who has the initial right affects the *distribution* of income. Before the finding, Helga had to pay Harold, afterwards she does not.

FIGURE A18.3

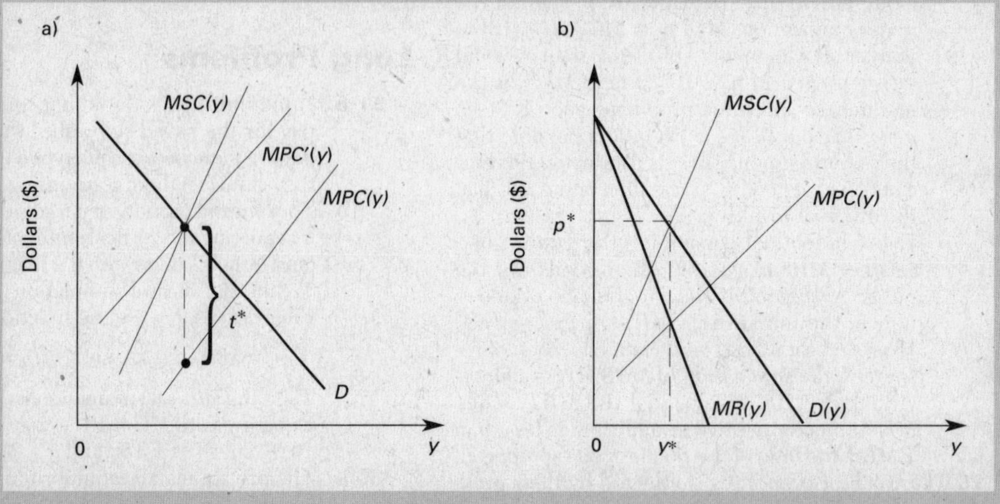

c If there were many mushroom farmers then the assumption of zero (low) transaction costs would be violated. Helga, to obtain clean air before the finding would have to bargain with each farmer. Because of hold-out problems, where some farmers may refuse to accept an offer in the hope of receiving a higher one, or monitoring problems, a deal may simply not be struck. In this case, the socially desirable situation, i.e., odour-free air, may not be obtainable in the absence of government intervention.

CHAPTER 19

The Theory of the Firm

Chapter Summary

What Is the Firm?

We begin our analysis of the **firm**. For the most part, the textbook view of the firm is that of a "black box," an entity that takes inputs and turns them into outputs for sale. Modern theory of the firm has given economists insights into the existence and internal organization of the firm. In this chapter we ask why firms are organized as they are, why they exist, and what determines their sizes.

Organization of the Firm

Firms vary in size and organizational structure. One important dimension of the organizational structure of the firm is the degree of separation between ownership and control. In an **owner-operated firm**, one person owns the firm and makes all the decisions. In a **partnership**, both the ownership and the decision-making responsibilities rest with two or more individuals. In the predominant organizational structure of the publicly held corporation, management and control are mostly entirely separate. Whatever the organizational structure, the resulting **residual claimancy** plays an important role in affecting the incentives facing the owners of the firm.

The first big puzzle at the heart of the theory of the firm is the following: A firm is a cooperative venture, requiring all individuals to work toward the objectives of the firm, whatever they may be. Why would individual workers who are motivated by self-interest behave in such a way as to promote the interests of this cooperative venture? The simple answer is that the firm adopts an institutional structure that best achieves its objectives, given the self-interests of individuals. For example, if maintaining a high quality of the output is important to the firm, then individuals should not be paid according to their production volume alone.

Optimal Institutional Arrangement

If the self-interested behaviour of individuals is intrinsically in conflict with the firm's interest, why are firms made up of more than one individual? Corporations with hundreds or thousands of employees are the norm rather than the exception. To answer this question, we compare two simple organizations: a one-person firm and a two-person partnership. If there is no technological advantage in having **team production**, as in a partnership, then, indeed, a one-person firm is the optimal institutional arrangement. In this case, the individual is the sole resident claimant and is rewarded the entire profits earned from his effort. Under an equal partnership, the individuals receive only one-half the earnings from their efforts; hence, each partner earns less income and has lower utility compared with the single-person firm. In this case, the Pareto-optimal organizational form is the single-person firm, because no other organizational form will leave all parties at least as well off and at least one party better off.

Team Effort and Partnerships

If we recognize that the team effort of two individuals can raise the output of the firm compared with the sum of the outputs from two individuals struggling on their own, then a partnership may be desirable. However, if costs of monitoring individuals are zero, then an alternative, owner-managed structure to the partnership is Pareto-preferred. Under this alternative, one teammate is contractually obligated to put forth the optimal effort; she receives zero for any level of shirking. The other teammate, who adopts the role of the owner and manager, is also motivated to put forth the optimal effort because she is the exclusive residual claimant; hence, this owner-managed arrangement is Pareto-preferred to a partnership and to a single-person firm.

When is a partnership Pareto-optimal? Note that the owner-managed firm has an advantage over the partnership in that a single individual captures all the profits from her efforts but has the disadvantage that the other partner is paid a fixed salary, independent of the profits that could be earned from any additional effort. Therefore, the second individual must be monitored. Because the payment to both individuals in a partnership is tied partly to the profits produced by their efforts, the incentive to shirk is limited; hence, if **monitoring costs** are very high, a partnership will be the preferred institutional arrangement. The Pareto-preferred organizational form selected depends on the possible productivity gains and monitoring costs associated with any given set of circumstances.

Specialization and Division of Labour

Adam Smith provided another reason for observing multiperson firms: **specialization** and **division of labour**. When tasks can be sequentially divided and workers can specialize in one or a few of them, output is expected to rise as a result of practice and repetition, reduction in setup time, and technical progress. Other reasons for observing multiperson firms are risk sharing and risk pooling.

Why are firms the sizes that they are? Why do they transact in the market to obtain inputs rather than produce inputs within the firm? Coase suggests an answer to these questions: When the organizational costs of operating within a firm exceed the transaction costs of coordinating activities through the market, the firm will stop its expansion.

Firms may not have a choice between producing inputs or transacting in the market. If firms use **specific inputs** (as opposed to **generic inputs**) that are used solely by a particular firm, then that firm will have a difficult time convincing someone else to provide them. Both parties will require contractual protection, guaranteeing that the input will be produced and purchased at some specified price. Whether or not the market is used will depend on the trade-off between coordination difficulties within a firm and contracting costs in the market.

KEY WORDS

- Division of labour
- Firm
- Generic inputs
- Monitoring costs
- Owner-operated firm
- Partnership
- Residual claimancy
- Specialization
- Specific inputs
- Team production

CASE STUDY I: SELF-IMPOSED PUNISHMENTS

An American was taking a boat ride up the Yangtze River when she observed a disturbing sight. A group of strong but exhausted men, rowing the boat, were being whipped and shouted at by an overseer. She complained of this brutality to the captain, demanding that he immediately stop this abuse. He reluctantly informed her that there was nothing that he or anyone else could do because the men were the ones who hired the overseer to punish them in this way.[1]

A Explain why the rowers of the boat were willing to pay for such treatment.

B How might the overseer be encouraged to put forth the optimal level of effort?

CASE STUDY II: BELL CANADA: THE FIRM VERSUS THE MARKET

Bell Canada was the monopoly provider of local and long-distance telephone services in Ontario and Quebec until the deregulation of the long-distance market in 1992. One reason why this market was opened up for competition was that the costs associated with providing long-distance telephone service were reduced considerably with the advent of new technologies. It is clear that Bell Canada's monopoly hold on local telephone calls is eroding as well. No longer is it necessary to lay cables to connect each household to the telephone service; various wireless technologies are rendering the costs associated with entering the telephone market much more affordable. With this backdrop, Bell Canada has been changing the structure of its firm. Before, it used to deal with all aspects of telephone delivery, maintenance and service. Now, if there is a problem with phone service, the customer has to contract with one of many private service technicians, and this service is no longer provided free of charge. Recently, Bell Canada hit the news again with the announcement that it was divesting itself of the telephone operator service. The idea is that it will contract with another company to provide telephone operator service, rather than provide the service in house. Given the changing nature of telephone service provision, provide an economic reason why Bell Canada would divest itself of various services as a result of competition. What does this imply about contracting costs?

[1]Anecdote by S. Cheung in J.C. McManus (1975), "The Cost of Alternative Economic Organization," *Canadian Journal of Economics*, **8** (August): 334–350.

EXERCISES

Multiple-Choice

Choose the correct answer to each question. There is only one correct answer to each question.

1 Multiperson firms can arise under which of the following conditions?
  a When the production from more than one individual working together exceeds the sum of output from individual efforts.
  b When the risks from capital investments required for production are large.
  c When the costs of monitoring are small.
  d All the above.
  e Only **a** and **c**.

2 A piece rate paid to workers has which of the following effects?
  a Induces workers to produce a high-quality product.
  b Always results in a divergence between the interest of the individual worker and the interests of the firm.
  c Induces the workers to produce a large volume of product.
  d Does not reward the worker for any of the added product from his effort.
  e None of the above.

To answer questions **3** and **4**, refer to Figure 19.1, which shows the income–effort line for individual 1 under a single-person firm OB, given by $y_1 = Ae_1$ and the indifference curves for the individual. Lines *CD* and *EF* are income–effort lines under a partnership.

FIGURE 19.1

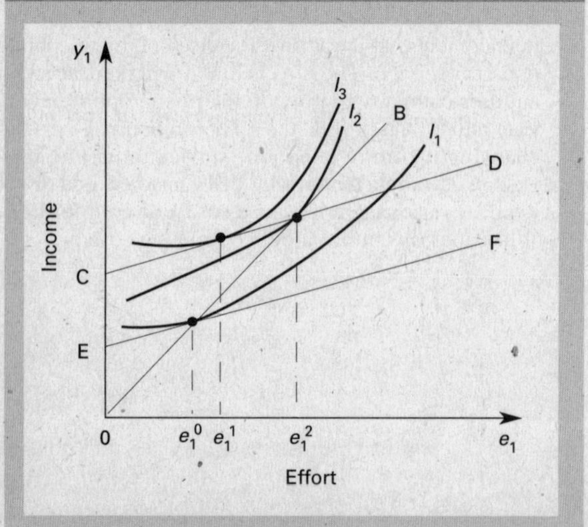

3 Suppose that an individual enters into a partnership in which all profits are split equally between the two individuals, and both individuals have identical preferences and technologies. Then the effort that each individual will put forth in equilibrium
  a Is e_1^0.
  b Is e_1^1.
  c Is e_1^2.
  d Cannot be shown because the diagram illustrates only *one* individual's indifference curves and income-effort line.
  e None of the above.

4 Suppose that the partnership results in a higher level of output than the sum of outputs from individual efforts; that is, $y = B(e_1 + e_2)$, where $B > A$. Then, which of the following is true?
  a The partnership can never be a Pareto improvement over the single-person firm.
  b The partnership may be a Pareto improvement over the single-person firm if *B* is sufficiently large.
  c The partnership will always be a Pareto improvement over the single-person firm if monitoring costs are sufficiently low.
  d The partnership will always be a Pareto improvement over the single-person firm if the individuals are risk-neutral.
  e None of the above.

5 Suppose that the output of a team exceeds the sum of the outputs from individual production; then which of the following is true?
  a A partnership is always a Pareto improvement over a single-person firm.
  b An owner-managed organization always dominates a partnership.
  c An owner-managed organization dominates a partnership if monitoring costs are sufficiently low.
  d A partnership always dominates an owner-managed organization because it does not require monitoring.
  e None of the above.

6 In which of the following ways is team production different from specialization?
  a Individuals' effort levels can be assessed under team production but not under specialization.
  b Team effort is more productive than isolated production, whereas specialization is less productive than isolated production.
  c Specialization occurs in stages; team production does not.

d There are setup costs for every job in specialized production, but there are no setup costs for jobs produced by a team.
e None of the above.

7 A residual claimant of a firm
a Is paid a fixed wage.
b Receives the profits of the firm after all wages and costs are paid.
c Has the incentive to put forth less effort than under a fixed-wage contract.
d Is always the manager of the firm.
e None of the above.

8 Production activities are likely to be organized within a firm rather than through the market when
a Market transaction costs are small.
b Benefits from increased output from team production are less than the costs of monitoring the team.
c Specialization and division of labour increase production.
d The production process requires generic assets.
e All the above.

9 Specific capital required by a firm's production process
a Has no (or very few) alternative uses.
b Will be produced in the firm requiring it if contracting costs are large.
c Can result in bargaining problems when it is produced by a firm other than the one requiring it.
d All the above.
e Only **b** and **c**.

True-False

10 When monitoring costs are high, a partnership may be a Pareto improvement over the owner-managed team.

11 If there are no benefits from team production, then the one-person firm dominates the partnership organization of the firm.

12 When team production is more productive than individual production, a partnership is always more efficient than an owner-managed organization because in the owner-managed case only one person is a residual claimant.

13 When team production is more productive than individual production, an owner-managed organization is preferred to a single-person firm if monitoring costs are zero.

14 Fixed-wage contracts encourage more shirking than contracts that tie the wage to output, holding everything else constant.

15 Team production and specialization in production are identical in that the effort of each worker is impossible to assess.

16 In the absence of a contract or good will, a firm requiring a specific input is more likely to produce the input within the firm rather than purchase the input in the marketplace.

17 Firms are more likely to emerge when transaction costs of writing and enforcing contracts are large.

18 Specialized production and team production are the same in that both are sequences of separate, specialized activities.

19 Because competitive markets pay workers the value of their marginal product, thus inducing the efficient level of effort, there is no need for firms ever to integrate into input production (that is, pay workers to produce some good within the firm).

Short Problems

20 Explain why firms integrate into input production (that is, pay workers to produce some goods within the firm) rather than use the market for these transactions.

21 List some factors that determine the size of a firm.

22 Using the theory developed in this chapter, explain the poor teaching performance by some professors at your university.

23 Although there are many owner-managed firms in existence today, the majority of commerce is carried out in the modern corporation. Unlike the owner-managed firm, the owners (shareholders) delegate many of the decision-making duties of the corporation to a manager, who is not necessarily an owner of the firm. Briefly discuss the reasons for this separation of ownership and control, the types of problems which might result from this arrangement, and ways to mitigate these problems.

24 In small towns, McDonald's hamburger franchisees pay a fixed initial fee for the franchise and a percentage of the profits earned to the franchisor. Why are both the franchisee and the owners residual claimants?

25 Senior managers are paid bonuses on ex post profits and their contracts also provide them with "golden parachutes," which are guarantees of generous severance payments in the event that they are fired. Explain this contract.

26 After World War I, British coal miners were paid a piece rate — that is, a payment per ton of coal — to encourage them to work at an efficient level of effort. Nevertheless, many of the coal mines in Britain were shut down before all the economically extractable coal was mined. A sub-optimal *amount* of effort by the coal miners cannot be blamed for the inefficient production of coal. Can you suggest a reason why the economically extractable coal was not mined? (*Hint*: Because the coal miners' wages were tied to the output, monitoring was, perhaps wrongly, presumed to be unnecessary.)

Long Problems

27 Two individuals are deciding whether to form a partnership or to continue operating as single-person firms. For the case of team production (two workers), the output–effort relationship is $y = B(e_1 + e_2)$, where y is total income and e_i is the effort of the ith worker, $i = 1, 2$; for a single-person firm, $y_i = Ae_i$, where y_i is the ith individual's income, and $A < B$. All workers have identical preferences over effort and income: Utility increases in y_i and decreases in e_i. Workers choose the utility-maximizing level of effort, given the income–effort relationship.

  a If monitoring costs are zero, which institutional arrangement — a single-person firm, an equal partnership, or an owner-managed firm — will be Pareto-dominant? Explain, using a diagram.

  b Suppose that monitoring costs are equal to M and are equally split between the two individuals. On a diagram, show a situation in which the individuals are indifferent among all three forms of organization.

28 Small raspberry farms in the Fraser Valley in British Columbia hire pickers every summer to harvest the crop. There are two aspects to the performance of a berry-picker: A good picker picks a lot of berries each day and picks the rows *clean* (that is, does not leave the small berries or the hard-to-get-at berries on the bushes). The contract established between the farm owners and the pickers specifies that the pickers be paid a rate per pound or volume for the amount picked (usually about one-third of the wholesale value). In addition, the rows that a picker has finished are checked randomly for cleanliness. If the rows are not clean, then the picker does not receive the payment.

  a Identify the potential problems associated with berry picking under a piece-rate contract (that is, the incentives to shirk). Analyze the efficiency of the particular organizational arrangement described in solving these problems.

  b Describe some alternative contracts that could be established for berry picking and compare them with the observed contract.

*29 Sarah and Sean are furniture movers. They are interested in adopting the efficient organizational form for a moving business. Working alone, each has a production function of $y_i = 3e_i$, where y_i is income in dollars and e_i is effort in hours. Working together as a team, because of the advantages of team production in moving, they are able to achieve the production function $y = 4(e_1 + e_2)$, where y is now total income. Both have a utility functions given by

$$U_i = \frac{y_i}{(e_i + 2)^2}$$

so that

$$MRS_i = \frac{2y_i}{(e_i + 2)}$$

  a If both individuals set up *independently* as owner-managers, find the level of effort expended by each, the income received, and the utility level attained. (*Hint*: Draw a diagram and decide what you need to calculate before doing anything else.)

  b If Sarah and Sean form a *partnership*, sharing their total income equally, what will the effort levels, income, and utilities be?

  c Explain the two factors at work that lead your answer in **b** to be different from that in **a**.

  d What are the Pareto-optimal levels of effort, income, and utility under team production by Sean and Sarah?

  e What organizational form might Sean and Sarah adopt to achieve **d**? What condition is required for this to be possible?

ANSWERS TO CHAPTER 19

Case Study I

A The rowers realized that every member of the team has an incentive to shirk. In the absence of shirking, output from the team exceeds the sum of output from individual efforts. Hence, the rowers hired a monitor to prevent the team members from shirking.

B Make him a residual claimant.

Case Study II

When Bell Canada had the monopoly on telephone service, it may have made sense to have their own maintenance people because they specialized in the technology. BC could train these people to deal with their specific apparatus and specifications (i.e., maintenance was a specific input). Furthermore, as a regulated monopolist, BC may not have been subject to the same pressures to operate in a cost efficient manner. With competition, the pressures in that respect would be greater. Also, with many different types of telephones in use, BC may have found it difficult to distinguish between problems that arose because of its lines versus problems associated with another company's apparatus. So, from a contracting perspective, when BC had the monopoly and was providing the service "free of charge" then they had more incentive to provide the service internally. Now, with all sorts of other firms on the market, and the pressure to keep costs and prices low, the incentive to provide this service internally is lower (the service has become more "generic"). The telephone operator situation is an interesting one. Again, when BC had the monopoly, it would make sense to own ancillary services to the extent that they could keep better control over the quality of service provided (or, perhaps to the extent that costs were not an overriding concern). Now, with competition, BC is under pressure to keep costs low so that it can compete over price. Contracting out this service may be cheaper to the extent that wage costs elsewhere may be lower. Also, with changing technology, the operators need not be close to the BC offices; again providing incentive to contract out rather than provide the service internally.

Multiple-Choice

1 d 2 c 3 a 4 b 5 c
6 c 7 b 8 c 9 d

True-False

10 T 11 T 12 F 13 T 14 T
15 F 16 T 17 T 18 F 19 F

Short Problems

20 When transaction costs of writing separate contracts for every market transaction are large, input supplies are uncertain, the benefits from team production exceed the costs of monitoring the team, or specialization and division of labour increase production, firms will integrate into input production.

21 When the cost of carrying out a transaction within the firm exceeds the cost of that transaction in the marketplace, a firm will stop growing. Increasing monitoring costs and diseconomies of scale will affect the size of the firm.

22 The output of a university — knowledge acquired by the students — is a product of a team effort by all professors. However, there is little monitoring of professors' efforts (except for end-of-year evaluations), and because wages are not tied to effort (except through merit increases), the professor has an incentive to shirk.

23 When there are many shareholders, it may be more efficient to delegate the decision-making duties of the corporation to a manager. However, the manager of a corporation may have objectives that are different from the profit-maximization goals of the shareholders. To minimize the problems that might arise, the manager might be paid shares of the firm or be given an incentive contract that aligns the manager's interest with those of the shareholders. Moreover, if the manager strays too far from profit-maximization, the manager risks the possibility of a takeover of the firm that would replace him with superior management.

24 When monitoring costs are high, franchisees are made residual claimants to ensure that they maintain the quality and reputation of McDonald's. Since the owners of McDonald's are also residual claimants, they have the incentive to continue to develop new products and to advertise.

25 Senior managers are paid bonuses on ex post profits to discourage the manager from shirking. The severance payments protect managers from opportunism on the part of owners after the managers have sunk specific capital into the job.

26 Because the coal miners' wages were tied to their effort, the miners attempted to produce large volumes of coal. This meant mining the coal in the large seams that was the easiest to extract. Since the miners were not monitored, they passed over coal in the narrow seams, which was more difficult to reach. The large setup costs of returning the capital equipment to the unmined coal exceeded the return from this coal, which would have been economical to extract in the first shift.

Long Problems

27 a The owner-managed arrangement dominates the other two relationships. The income-effort lines for individual 1 under the owner-managed firm, partnership, and single-person firms are given by OC, DB, and OA, respectively, in Figure A19.1. In a single-person firm, the individual maximizes utility at E; under a partnership, the individual moves to point F; and in the owner-managed arrangement, the individual chooses point G. In this example, the partnership and single-person arrangements are shown to yield the same level of utility.

b Monitoring costs will shift line OC down by $M/2$ to $O'C'$. In Figure A19.2, the individual is shown to be indifferent between the owner-managed situation at point G and the partnership (where

FIGURE A19.1

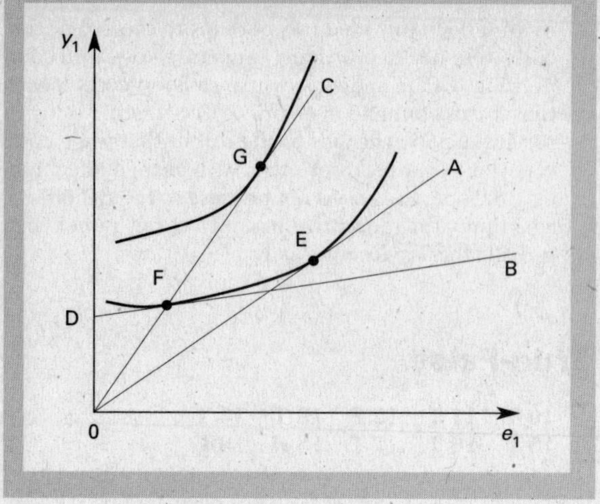

FIGURE A19.2

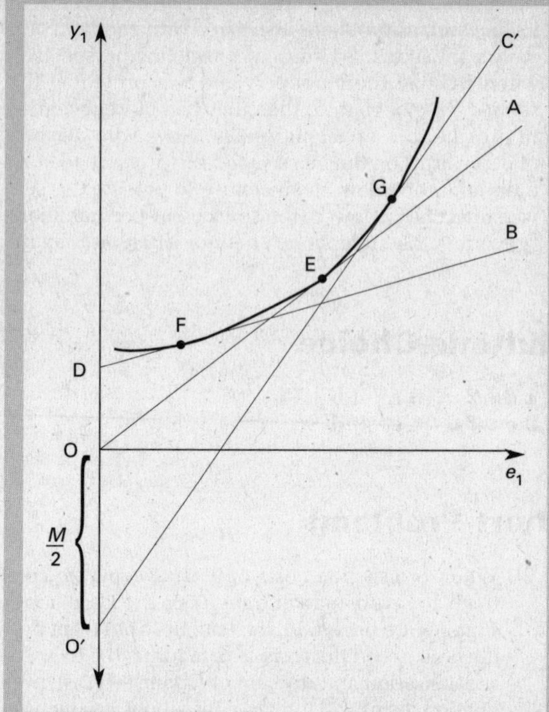

monitoring is not necessary) at point F. As in part **a**, the optimal levels of effort and income under a single-person firm at point E yield the same utility as the partnership.

28 a The shirking problem in berry picking under a piece-rate contract is in the cleanliness of the picking. Under this contract and at a given effort level, the picker is interested in maximizing the quantity of berries picked per hour. In balancing the "intensive margin" of more berries picked in a section against the "extensive margin" of moving faster down the sections, the picker will tend to move very quickly, reaching for the large berries on the outside branches and leaving both the small berries and the berries in the middle of the bushes that are hard to reach. The farmer, however, wants to maximize the *stock* of output from a field, where the stock equals the intensity (pounds of berries per section) times the number of sections. Under various contracts, a conflict could arise between the intensity desired by the farmer and that supplied by the pickers. The actual contract, which includes a piece rate and a random check for cleanliness, eliminates this potential conflict.

b The observed contract is a sharing contract. Two other contracts could be offered: a wage contract and rental contract. Under a wage contract, the worker would receive a fixed amount and, therefore, must be monitored. If his effort were monitored directly but could not be monitored perfectly, then the potential shirking problem would be reversed compared with the piece-rate contract; the worker would have no incentive to choose the wrong intensity but would be inclined to shirk on effort to the extent that he could get away with it. As in the first contract, the worker must be monitored.

A rental contract has the picker buying the rights to a given plot of land for the season, then selling the berries herself after picking them. All incentive problems in picking are *internalized*. However, this arrangement leads to buyers spending money to determine the quality of the plots that they are considering purchasing. This expenditure on information may be costly.

°29 a Set *MRS* equal to marginal product of effort:

$$\frac{2y_i}{e_i + 2} = 3$$

Substitution of the production function $y_i = 3e_i$ yields $6e_i/(e_i + 2) = 3$, which implies that $e^* = 2$, $y^* = 6$, and $U^* = 3/8$. The solution is illustrated in Figure A19.3 for $i = 1$.

b Now *MRS* equals marginal product of effort, where the marginal product is one-half of the *total* marginal product; that is,

$$\frac{2y_i}{e_i + 2} = 2$$

implies that $y_i = e_i + 2$. Substitution of the individual's production function $y_i = 4(e_i + e_j)$ into this equation gives $2(e_i + e_j) = e_i + 2$. By symmetry, $e_i = e_j = e'$ in equilibrium, and $e' = 2/3$, $y' = 2 \times 4/3 = 8/3$; $U' = 3/8$. The solution is illustrated in Figure A19.4 for $i = 1$.

FIGURE A19.3

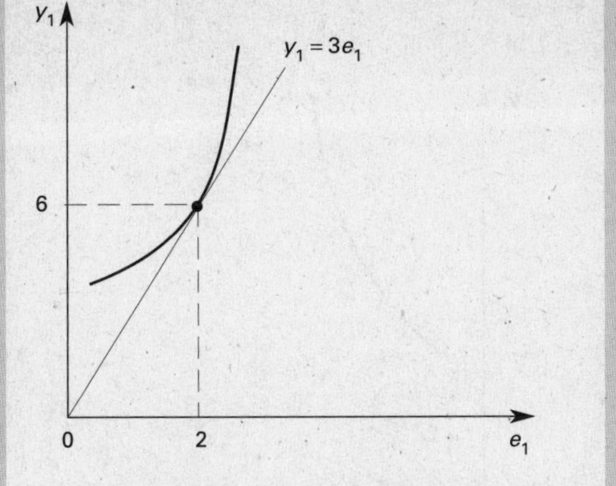

FIGURE A19.4

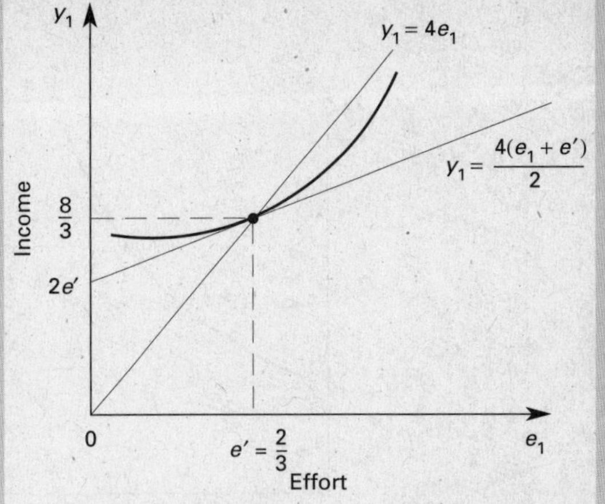

c The partnership is more productive because of team production, but the partnership involves an efficiency loss because each worker receives only one-half of the marginal product of increased effort; hence, effort is reduced in equilibrium. In this example, these two effects cancel, leaving utility unchanged.

d Under the Pareto-optimal organization, each individual is paid the full marginal product for her effort. That is, set *MRS* equal to total marginal product:

$$\frac{2y_i}{e_i + 2} = 4$$

Substitute production function $y_i = 4e_i$ to yield $e'' = 2$; $y'' = 4 \times 2 = 8$; $U'' = 1/2$.

e Either worker — say, Sarah — could set up as owner-manager and hire the other worker on the following contract: Put forth e'' effort and earn y'' income or get zero for any effort level less than e''. Given this contract, e'' will be the optimal level of effort for Sean, as shown in Figure A19.5a. Given that Sarah is now the residual claimant, she gets the full marginal product of any increase in her own effort; hence, she will put forth the Pareto-efficient amount e'' and get y''. Sarah's solution is shown in Figure A19.5b. (Sarah's effort and income are subscripted by 1, Sean's by 2.) The condition required for this solution is costless monitoring of Sean's effort.

FIGURE A19.5

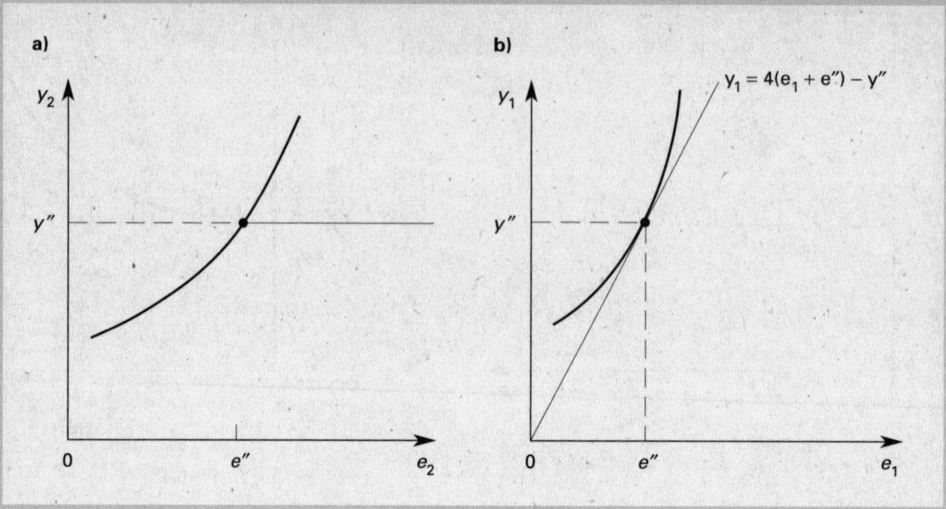

CHAPTER 20

Asymmetric Information and Market Behaviour

Chapter Summary

This final chapter introduces the very important topic of asymmetric information in the market. What happens when buyers and sellers have different information sets? As you can well imagine, this situation occurs rather often in the real world.

Reputations

When your car breaks down on the highway, given a choice you will ask for it to be towed to a brand name garage. Why? Because you are sure to obtain some basic standard of work which is covered by a national warranty. At home, you might choose a different garage. You are likely to have "your" mechanic, someone who, perhaps, owns his or her own garage and who you trust to provide high-quality service. This trust stems from repeated dealings with the mechanic which results in a long-term, mutually beneficial, relationship. The problem here is one of asymmetric information and the importance of reputation in solving this problem.

Reputation, or good will, requires the investment of sunk costs — costs which are irreversible However, sunk costs, while helping to solve one problem, may contribute to the **hold up** problem whereby after the firm has made the irreversible investment, its customers have the incentive to try to renegotiate the price of the product. Because sunk costs are irrecoverable, the firm has the incentive to accept a renegotiated price that does not cover these costs. Knowing this problem leads to two possible solutions: integration and long-term contracts. **Vertical integration** occurs when two firms at different vertical stages of production merge. The downstream firm will not then hold the upstream firm hostage in the presence of sunk costs. **Horizontal integration** is the merging together of two firms involved in the same activity. **Long-term contracts** may alleviate the hold up problem by binding two parties to a long-run relationship in which there are mutual benefits.

Adverse Selection, Signaling and Moral Hazard

Each individual has certain **hidden characteristics** which are not easily revealed to others, that can result in **adverse selection**. The insurance market is particularly prone to this problem. An insurance rate for a particular category of, say, driver is based on supplying insurance for all individuals in that category. Suppose we have two groups of drivers: high risk and low risk. A **full-information equilibrium** would have each driver paying a price that reflected their own riskiness. However, because low-risk drivers cannot communicate convincingly that they are low risk, the insurance company can only offer one contract at an average rate (a **pooling contract**). At that rate, only high-risk drivers will buy the insurance (adverse selection) and low-risk drivers will be forced out of the market resulting in a **market failure**. Akerlof referred to this situation in the used-car market as the "lemons principle."

One solution to the lemons problem is through **signaling**. If the low-risk drivers could acquire a signal of their quality, say by taking and passing a well-recognized driving school examination, then insurance firms could use this signal as a **screening** device to separate the two types of drivers.

Another asymmetric information problem arises not from hidden characteristics but rather from **hidden actions**. **Moral hazard problems** occur when individuals, through their actions, can affect the likelihood of a particular outcome arising. Again, the insurance industry provides many examples. The probability of an accident arises whenever an individually is fully insured. Why? Because, the individual has less incentive to take care when fully insured. Deductibles, in which the insured individual pays a part of his or her own damages, help to improve the moral hazard problem.

KEY WORDS

- Adverse selection
- Full-information equilibrium
- Hidden actions
- Hidden characteristics
- Hold up
- Horizontal integration
- Long-term contracts
- Market failure
- Moral hazard problems
- Pooling contract
- Screening
- Signaling
- Vertical integration

CASE STUDY: THE NO-FAULT VERSUS LIABILITY AUTOMOBILE INSURANCE DEBATE[1]

In many jurisdictions, if you are involved in an automobile accident and it is your fault, the victim can sue you for damages. Hence, individuals purchase liability or third-party automobile insurance which will cover these losses. If a claim is made against your insurance policy, your insurance rates will typically increase. Critics of this system point to the long delays in compensating victims of accidents, with court cases that often take years to settle, arguing that lawyers are the principal winners in such a system. Rather than relying on the liability system, some have argued that automobile insurance should be provided on a first-party basis, i.e., the insurance should cover the insured person's losses, and the legal regime should be a no-liability (or no-fault) one. In such a regime, irrespective of who caused the accident, each person would be covered by his or her own insurance package. In a pure no-fault regime, suits for damages are not permitted. Proponents of this sort of regime argue that it results in victims being compensated in a timely, equitable manner. The major argument against no-fault automobile insurance is that it may result in individuals driving less carefully, leading to an increase in accidents.

Presently in Canada, five Canadian provinces (Quebec, Ontario, Manitoba, Saskatchewan and British Columbia) have some form of no-fault automobile insurance systems in place. The strongest no-fault system is in operation in the province of Quebec where, since 1978, all bodily injury accidents are covered by first-party insurance in a purely no-fault regime in which it is impossible to sue for additional compensation. The amount of coverage available is set out in a chart which essentially dictates how much one can expect under various circumstances.

A What is the role of the liability system in inducing safe driving? How is this role affected by the presence of liability insurance? How will your driving record affect insurance prices?

B Explain the moral hazard associated with no-fault insurance. Can you think of ways to reduce this moral hazard?

C Automobile insurance coverage is compulsory in all Canadian provinces. Can you explain this fact with reference to adverse selection?

EXERCISES

Multiple-Choice

1 Suppose that a camera manufacturer provides an unlimited one-year warranty with its product. This
- **a** Helps to alleviate the adverse selection problem in the market for cameras.
- **b** May result in a moral hazard problem on the part of consumers.
- **c** May signal to consumers that this camera is of low quality.
- **d** Both **a** and **b**.
- **e** All of the above.

2 Suppose that there are two kinds of used cars on the market — high and low quality — and two colours of cars, red and blue. The high quality cars have a value of $1 000 and the low quality cars are worth $500. 60% of the high quality cars are blue while only 30% of the low quality cars are blue. How much would a risk neutral individual be willing to pay for a blue car?
- **a** $750
- **b** $833
- **c** $682
- **d** $318
- **e** None of the above.

3 Suppose that health insurance is privately provided and not compulsory. A company offers a pooling contract to anyone who wants insurance at a price which reflects the various risks in the population at large. Economic theory would predict that:

[1] Readers interested in insurance economics are urged to read *Contributions to Insurance Economics*, G. Dionne (ed.), Kluwer Academic Publishers, Boston, 1992. Details regarding the no-fault-liability debate in Quebec are contained in R. A. Devlin "Liability Versus No-Fault Automobile Insurance Regimes: An Analysis of the Experience in Quebec," in pp.499–520 of this book.

a Smokers would be more likely to buy insurance than would non-smokers.
b Older people would be more likely to buy insurance than would younger people.
c Risk-averse individuals would be more likely to buy insurance in comparison to risk-neutral individuals.
d Both **a** and **b**.
e All of the above.

4 Which of the following policies would help to solve the adverse selection problem in health insurance markets.
a Coinsurance in which the insured person has to pay 10 per cent of all costs.
b Compulsory insurance for all individuals.
c Government provided insurance rather than private insurance.
d Both **a** and **c**
e All of the above.

To answer questions **5** to **7**, refer to Figure 20.1, which illustrates the utility function of two risk-averse individuals. Both individuals have initial wealth w_0. Each individual faces the uncertain outcome that her house will be robbed, in which case she will incur a loss of L. The probability of this event is p_1 for individual 1 and p_2 for individual 2. The proportion of low-risk individuals is 1/2.

5 If the market for insurance is competitive and if insurance companies cannot distinguish between high-risk and low-risk individuals, then
a Only individual 1 will purchase insurance.
b Only individual 2 will purchase insurance.
c Both individuals 1 and 2 will purchase insurance.
d Neither individual will purchase insurance.
e No firm will be willing to supply an insurance policy.

FIGURE 20.1

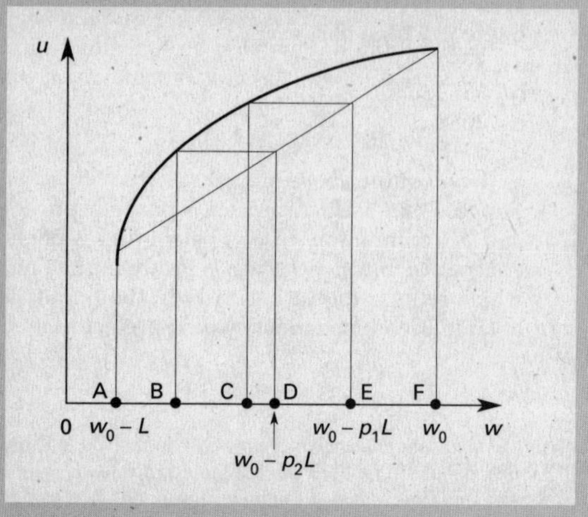

6 If the insurance company cannot distinguish between high-risk and low-risk individuals, then
a The maximum premium that individual 1 is willing to pay for the insurance is CE.
b The maximum premium that individual 2 is willing to pay for the insurance is BF.
c If both low- and high-risk individuals purchase insurance, the minimum price that the insurance company will be willing to accept for the insurance policy exceeds DF.
d Since only low-risk individuals will purchase the insurance, the price of the insurance will be CF.
e None of the above.

7 If low-risk and high-risk individuals can be identified and the market is competitive, then
a Insurance will be sold at two prices, BD for the high-risk individuals and CE for the low-risk individuals.
b Insurance will be sold at two prices, DF for the high-risk individuals and EF for the low-risk individuals.
c Only the high-risk individuals will buy insurance at a price of DF.
d Insurance will be sold at one price, less than DF and greater than EF.
e None of the above.

Answer questions **8** to **11** with reference to the following information. Let's suppose that the automobile market consists of 30% high risk drivers and 70% low risk drivers, the insurance company cannot distinguish between them. The probability of an accident for a high-risk driver is 0.20 and for a low-risk driver 0.05. It costs $10 000 for each accident, regardless of who caused it. Insurance is not compulsory and individuals are risk neutral.

8 If the insurance market were perfectly competitive, the equilibrium price of insurance would be:
a $950
b $2 500
c $600
d $2 000
e None of the above.

9 If the insurance market were publicly run (i.e., monopoly with zero profits), the equilibrium price would be:
a $950
b $2 500
c $600
d $2 000
e None of the above.

10 If insurance became compulsory and the market was competitive, the equilibrium price of insurance would be:
a $950
b $2 500
c $600
d $2 000
e None of the above.

11 Suppose that the probability of an accident increased for low risk drivers to 0.1, how would the price of insurance change relative to your answer in question **8**?
a Increase.
b Decrease.
c Remain the same.
d Cannot say without further information.
e None of the above.

True-False

12 Adverse selection is a market failure that occurs when individuals have information about themselves that they cannot communicate to the market.
13 A moral hazard problem exists in the insurance market when high-risk individuals pretend to be low-risk individuals.
14 Cooperative degree programs at universities help improve adverse selection in the labour market.
15 The private life insurance market will never insure a cancer victim.
16 By making it costly to fire a worker, unions help improve the problems associated with adverse selection in the labour market.
17 If consumers cannot tell the different between high and low quality jeans, then both types of jeans will have the same, average-quality price.
18 The essential difference between fixed costs and sunk costs is that the former is usually smaller in magnitude than the latter.
19 If insurance companies had complete information, then adverse selection would not be a problem but moral hazard would remain one.

Short Problems

20 Categorize the following practices as trying to alleviate moral hazard (M), adverse selection (A), alleviate both (B) or neither problem (N): **i)** life insurance bonus for non smokers, **ii)** age discount for movie theatre, **iii)** automobile insurance surcharge on young males, **iv)** higher salary for young, blond, females, **v)** wage premium for university graduate, **vi)** compulsory health insurance, **vii)** compulsory military service for all individuals between the ages of 20 and 25, **viii)** $500 deductible for automobile fire and theft.
21 In a recent article, Day and Devlin[2] showed that people who volunteer typically do better on the paid labour market than their non-volunteering counterparts. In other words, *ceteris paribus*, volunteers earn higher incomes than non-volunteers. Explain this phenomenon with reference to informational asymmetries in the labour market.
22 In the province of Quebec, driving school is compulsory in order to obtain a driving licence. These schools are private and charge a fee of around $250 per course. Discuss the impact of this policy on **i)** the number of young people who obtain licences, **ii)** the usefulness of a driving school certificate as a signal of good quality for insurance purposes.
23 When one buys a major appliance (e.g., a fridge or stove) in a large department store, one is offered the option of buying an extended warranty, i.e., a warranty that extends the initial guarantee by some period of time. This extended warranty is usually quite costly — often priced at some 30 per cent of the original price of the appliance. Who is likely to buy these warrantees? Can you think of an informational asymmetry that these warrantees are designed to overcome?
24 "The fact that good and bad used cars can be found on the market today suggests that Akerlof's lemon principle does not hold true." Comment on this statement.

Long Problems

25 a Consider the following model provided by Spence in his 1973 paper.[3] Suppose that there are two types of people: high- and low-productivity workers. If a worker is known to be highly productive, then she would receive a wage of 2; if she is known to have low productivity, then she would receive a wage of 1. Assume that education does not increase an individual's productivity but simply awards the individual with a certificate. Assume that high-productivity individuals incur education costs $C^H = x/2$, where x = units of education, and that low-productivity individuals incur education costs $C^L = x$. Using this model of job market signaling, describe how education can have a value to certain individuals even if it does not increase their productivity.

[2] K. M. Day and R. A. Devlin, (1998) "The payoff to work without pay: volunteer work as an investment in human capital," *Canadian Journal of Economics*, **31**(5): 1179–1191.

[3] Spence, M. (1973) "Job Market Signalling," *Quarterly Journal of Economics*. **87:** 355–374.

b Are some signaling equilibria Pareto-improving over others? That is, would an increase or a decrease in the critical level of the signal, set by the employer to separate the good from the poor workers, make some employees better off without making others worse off? Explain.

26 This question is another application of Spence's model from question **25**. In this case, let's suppose there are equal amounts of two types of workers: high- and low-productivity. The high-productivity workers are worth \$2 000 per week for a firm, while the low-productivity workers are worth \$1 000 per week. It is impossible for the firm to distinguish between these workers prior to hiring and observing them.

a Suppose that, once hired, the firm cannot fire an employee. What will determine the salary paid to new employees?

Suppose, now, that risk-neutral individuals can signal their quality, albeit imperfectly, by taking and passing a course given at the local college. The probability that a high-productivity worker will pass the course is 0.8 while the probability that a low-productivity worker will pass is only 0.2. It costs \$20 000 to register for this course.

b Assume that the firm hires everyone who takes the course at \$2 000 per week and everyone else at \$1 000 per week. Individuals are hired on a one-year contract. Who will take the course and under what circumstances?

c Discuss the role of the tuition fee, employment regulations (like minimum length of contract, ability to fire) on this labour market.

27 The main street running through an established neighbourhood in downtown Ottawa is filled with a variety of boutiques, cafes and restaurants serving the surrounding neighbourhood and, if you don't mind fighting for a parking spot, people from farther afield. One of these boutiques specializes in young children's clothing. These clothes are of high quality but are extremely expensive. If you go into this store, however, you will find that it operates under an unusual policy. It allows a prospective buyer to take several items home to see which piece is suitable — on the strength of a name and telephone number. You are allowed to keep the items for 24 hours, after which time you are expected to return the pieces you do not want and pay for the pieces, if any, you do want.

a Analyze this policy given the tools described in this chapter.

b Would you expect this policy to work in a suburban mall? Why or why not?

c Why does the store owner not ask people to pay for the items and then receive a refund after they are returned?

28 Until recently, there was very little difference in tuition fees within any given province in Canada. Indeed, the differential across all Canadian universities was relatively small. The trend now is towards charging differential fees across programs and differential fees across universities. Some argue that this will lead to the sort of two-tiered system currently in operation in the United States, where, with notable exceptions, there are high-quality private institutions which charge very high tuition fees, and lower-quality public institutions. Suppose that Canada is indeed moving in this direction. Discuss the implications of this move on the ability of a university education to provide a signal to the labour market regarding the productivity of an individual.

29 Many spokepersons of the women's movement have argued that women must be twice as good as men to be hired for many management positions. Explain how this argument could be valid, using the model of job market signaling in question **25**.

30 Let's suppose an insurance market with high- and low-risk drivers: 10% of the market has high-risk individuals whose probability of an accident is 0.115 per year; low-risk individuals have an accident probability of 0.05. Suppose each accident costs \$20 000, insurance is not compulsory, and all individuals are risk neutral.

a Determine the full-information insurance package offered by a competitive insurance industry and compare it to the incomplete information package.

b Suppose insurance becomes compulsory, how does this affect your answer in part **a**?

c Suppose that insurance companies know that the low-risk individuals are risk averse and that their utility function may be expressed as $U(w) = w^{1/2}$. Insurance is not compulsory. Will this change your answer to part **a**?

ANSWERS TO CHAPTER 20

Case Study

A In a liability system, individuals are responsible for paying the damages arising from accidents for which they were responsible, thus encouraging individuals to drive with appropriate care. Liability insurance will cover these damages, but the insurance premium will increase after an 'at fault' accident. Individuals are thus motivated to drive with appropriate care as otherwise their premiums will rise. Furthermore, under a liability insurance system, the driver who caused the accident will not receive any compensation for his or her losses, which provides individuals with additional incentives to drive with care.

B Individuals who are insured for losses irrespective of whether they caused the accident (i.e., those with no-fault insurance coverage) will drive less carefully compared to those who are not insured if they caused the accident. Some of this moral hazard may be reduced by adjusting the insurance premiums for careless drivers in the no-fault regime, also by a careful monitoring of driving behaviour (e.g., increased fines for speeding, running red lights, and so on).

C If automobile coverage were not compulsory, we would expect to find that proportionately more high-risk drivers buy automobile insurance than do low-risk drivers. Insurance companies who set their prices based on average riskiness would find themselves making losses as the average riskiness of the driving population would be higher than expected. Like Akerlof's 'lemon principle', it is possible that if insurance companies cannot distinguish between high- and low-risk drivers, that the market for low-risk driver insurance could disappear altogether. Compulsory insurance solves this adverse selection problem by forcing all drivers to purchase insurance. Insurance companies can then use their information on the average riskiness of the population) to set their premiums.

Multiple-Choice

1 b **2** b **3** e **4** b **5** c
6 b **7** b **8** d **9** d **10** a **11**b

True-False

12 T **13** F **14** T **15** F **16** F
17 F **18** F **19** F

Short Problems

20 **i)** A, **ii)** N, **iii)** A, **iv)** N, **v)** A, **vi)** A, **vii)** A, **viii)** M.

21 Because potential employers cannot fully observe the "quality" of a job candidate, certain activities like volunteering may provide him or her with more information. If the candidate actually volunteered for this company, then, of course, lots of information can be gained. Normally, we observe people volunteering for other organizations and then using this experience to help them gain employment. This may work through contacts, the acquisition of skills, or by the signal that volunteering provides regarding the dedication (or whatever) of the job candidate.

22 Costly driving schools may have the effect of reducing the number of very young drivers on the road (the $250 is like the fixed cost of admission to the activity). On the one hand, this may have the effect of reducing accidents to the extent that there are fewer new drivers on the road. On the other hand, because driving schools are compulsory insurance companies have lost the signal associated with a driving school diploma. Thus, insurance premiums may increase for newer drivers.

23 Extended warrantees are usually purchased by individuals who know that they are going to be using the appliance a lot, e.g., families with many children. The presence of the extended warrantee is thus a means to separate the market into high- and low-use consumers. The information asymmetry has to do with the intensity of use, and hence the probability that a defect may arise during the warrantee period.

24 In the current used car market, there are several ways in which the seller can signal the quality of the vehicle. For instance, warrantees can be provided. Also, mechanical inspections can be done by independent mechanics.

[4]M. Friedman and L. Savage (1948, August). "The Utility Analysis of Choice Involving Risks," *Journal of Political Economy*, **56:** 279–304.

Long Problems

25 a If the employer does not know the productivity of workers, she can separate the high- and low-productivity workers through an education requirement. For example, she can set an education level x^* to separate the high- from the low-productivity workers. If $x \geq x^*$, she will pay 2; if $x < x^*$, she will pay 1.

As indicated in Figure A20.1, high-productivity workers earn more from getting x^* units of education because $2 - x^*/2 > 1$. Low-productivity workers earn more from not getting educated because $1 > 2 - x^*$, hence, there is a signaling equilibrium.

b If the level of the signal were raised above x^*, the low-productivity workers would be no worse off because they would continue not to get educated; however, for larger x^*, high-productivity workers would have to expend wasteful resources to acquire the additional units of the signal.

26 a The expected value of productivity: 0.5(2000) + 0.5(1000) = \$1500 provides the upper bound on the salary. (The assumption that the individual cannot be fired is important, otherwise, after one month presumably the firm would fire all low-productivity workers and only keep the high-productivity ones.)

b Both types of workers stand to gain \$500 per week or \$26 000 a year if they pass the course. The expected value of the course for the high-productivity worker is 0.8*(26 000) = \$20 800 while its expected value for the low-productivity worker is \$5200. As long as the expected gain from the course exceeds \$26 000, the course will be taken.

c As the tuition fee increases, the chances of only having high-productivity people take the course increases (notice that there is an upper bound to the fee), and vice versa. The longer the contract, the higher the chance that low-productivity people will take the course. As firing someone becomes easier, the less important is the course because the firm can simply fire or adjust the salary of a low-productivity individual.

27 a Because of the location of this store, we expect that mostly "high-end" shoppers from the neighbourhood will enter into it to browse. Thus, presence on the street may be considered as a signal of ability to pay.

b No. In a suburban mall you have both high- and low-end shoppers. The group is heterogeneous and comes from all over the city. The chances of a customer not returning the items is too great.

c If she simply had people pay for the items and then return them for a refund, she would be like all the other stores. This policy differentiates her store. It also means that the customer does not have to go through any hassle paying for items he or she does not want; the store bears all the risk.

28 With differential fees, what might occur is that the university becomes a signal of household wealth rather than ability (unless, of course, the universities have policies of funding less-wealthy, but bright, students). In schools that charge high fees what often happens is that all students pass; in other words, there is a danger that the only screening which occurs is upon entering the university and not on exiting. With same fees, the screening is more likely to be done on abilities and not wealth and hence the signal from a university degree (or courses) may be stronger.

29 Use problem **25** to answer this question. Suppose that men and women face the same costs $C = x/2$ for acquiring x units of education. However, because employers have less information on women's abilities, they require the cutoff education level between high- and low-productivity women to be higher than the cutoff for men. For example, if women have education $x \geq x_w^*$, then they will be paid 2; if men have education $x \geq x_m^*$, where $x_w^* > x_m^*$, they will be paid 2. Figure A20.2 shows the cost curves and the signaling cutoff level for men and women. Note that $2 - x_m^*/2 > 1$, so men will get x_m^* units of education. However, $2 - x_w^*/2 < 1$, so women do not get the required amount of the signal to get the higher wage (even though they are equally productive). For women to receive the same wage as men in this model, they must have lower costs of getting educated (that is, they must be more productive).

30 a The full-information equilibrium would set premiums according to the expected losses for each risk group. High risk drivers would be charged \$2300 each year and the low risk drivers charged \$1000. If the insurance company does not know the riskiness of each driver, it must charge only one price. Which price? If it charges a price

FIGURE A20.1

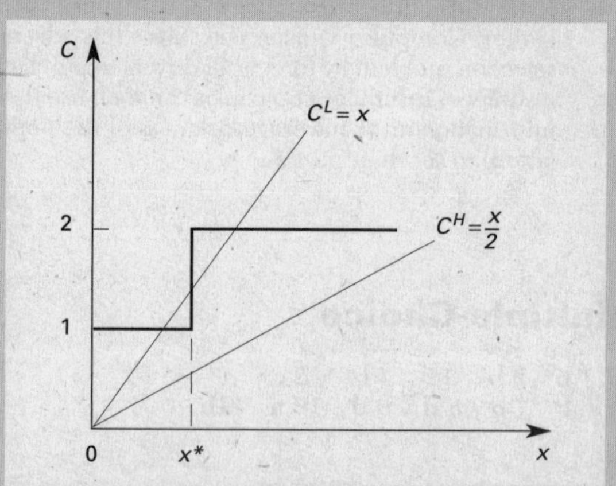

based on its expected payout given both groups are in the market then it would charge 0.1*2300 + 0.9*1000 = $1130. But, the low risk drivers would not pay this price. Thus, only high risk drivers would buy the insurance (adverse selection). Knowing this, the insurance company will offer only one contract at $2300. So, with incomplete information, only the high-risk drivers will be able to buy insurance (one market is missing).

b If insurance becomes compulsory, then adverse selection is avoided. All drivers will buy insurance hence the insurance company can charge a pooled price of $1130. High-risk drivers are better off and low-risk ones are no worse off, thus it is a socially preferable (Pareto improving) situation.

c If the insurance company knows that the low-risk drivers are risk averse it can calculate how much these individuals would be willing to pay to avoid all risk. Without insurance, the low-risk driver's utility would be $0.95*(40\ 000)^{1/2} + 0.05*(20\ 000)^{1/2} = 197.07$. We can then determine the maximum amount that this individual would be willing to pay for insurance, given by $(40\ 000 - p)^{1/2} = 197.07$, thus $p = \$1163$. Knowing this, the company can charge the pooled price of $1130 since both groups will buy it. Thus, having some information about the risk preferences of individuals can greatly improve the situation. Now, even without compulsory insurance the pooled-insurance price can be charged.

FIGURE A20.2

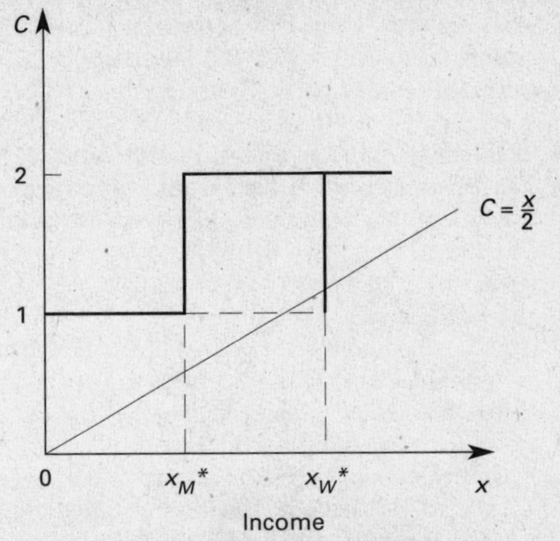